THE PREEXISTENT SON

THE PREEXISTENT SON

Recovering the Christologies of
Matthew, Mark, and Luke

Simon J. Gathercole

WILLIAM B. EERDMANS PUBLISHING COMPANY
GRAND RAPIDS, MICHIGAN / CAMBRIDGE, U.K.

Published 2006 by

Wm. B. Eerdmans Publishing Co.

2140 Oak Industrial Drive N.E., Grand Rapids, Michigan 49505 /

P.O. Box 163, Cambridge CB3 9PU U.K.

Printed in the United States of America

11 10 09 08 07 06   7 6 5 4 3 2 1

Library of Congress Cataloging-in-Publication Data

Gathercole, Simon J.

    The preexistent Son: recovering the christologies of Matthew, Mark, and Luke /
    Simon J. Gathercole.

       p.   cm.

    Includes indexes.

    ISBN-10: 0-8028-2901-5 / ISBN-13: 978-0-8028-2901-6 (pbk.: alk. paper)

    1. Jesus Christ — History of doctrines — Early church, ca. 30-600

    2. Bible. N.T. Gospels — Criticism, interpretation, etc.   I. Title.

BT198.G35   2006

232′.809015 — dc22

                                       2006015825

www.eerdmans.com

Contents

Preface

Writing a second book is in some ways more daunting than doing a Ph.D. In the case of the doctoral thesis, one has an eagle-eyed and more experienced scholar reading the thing and warning you off areas of clear and present danger. After that, no one quite gives your work the same attention again. But since it continues to be a very risky business writing something without trying it out on other people first, there are a number of people I must thank for their patience and advice.

First of all, I should thank my New Testament colleagues in Aberdeen — Francis Watson, Andrew Clarke, Pete Williams, and Howard Marshall. Francis Watson first provoked me to think more deeply about preexistence and alerted me to the work of Robert Jenson, which was the main stimulus for writing this book. In addition, most of the chapters here have been inflicted on our long-suffering weekly New Testament Seminar. I am also grateful to the similar seminars in St. Andrews and Cambridge — the former for its encouragement in the project, the latter for giving me a good going over. Much of Part II was given as the Gheens Lectures at Southern Seminary and the annual Biblical Studies Lectures at Beeson Divinity School. I am grateful for these invitations and for the probing questions and encouragement from staff and students, especially Tom Schreiner.

Most of the research on chapter 5 was carried out in the Institut für antikes Judentum und hellenistische Religionsgeschichte at the University of Tübingen; my thanks to Hermann Lichtenberger for again hosting me there as a *Gastwissenschaftler*. Peter Stuhlmacher, Martin Hengel, and subsequently Otfried Hofius also gave generously of their time. The Royal Society of Edinburgh gave generously of its coffers in much appreciated support of the trip. Since then, the UK Arts and Humanities Research Board funded me for a year's study leave to complete the project, for which I am extremely thankful.

Other individuals whose support of the project deserves note include Richard Bauckham, Larry Hurtado, and William Horbury, for their time and very helpful suggestions. Jimmy Dunn continued to give fantastic help with grant applications even when we disagreed on some exegetical matters: however, let the record show that the trigger for writing this book was much more the work of Jenson and Karl-Josef Kuschel than *Christology in the Making!* Thanks so much for your continued support, Jimmy. Crispin Fletcher-Louis read parts of chapters 10 and 12 and has been a loyal friend and continual encouragement. My Aberdeen colleague Francesca Murphy read a draft of chapter 14. My students Joseph Dodson, Ben Reynolds, and Preston Sprinkle read the whole manuscript and offered a number of very helpful criticisms, and Chris Asprey checked my translations from German. Closer to home, my wife Rosie and daughter Martha have been delightful company through the process. But I dedicate this book to my parents, Brian and Lynne Gathercole, for their unwavering support over the years. This book is at least a small token of my appreciation for a debt I can never repay. They have always looked after me and set me an example to look up to.

Finally, thanks to the team at Eerdmans again for their helpfulness and efficiency. Again, I'm delighted that the contract has made the generous provision that I'm entitled to fifty percent of any motion picture rights deriving from this book. Mr. Weinstein, if you are reading this and Miramax is interested, please don't hesitate to get in touch.

Soli Deo Gloria

SIMON J. GATHERCOLE

Abbreviations

ABD	Anchor Bible Dictionary
AnBib	Analecta Biblica
AsSeign	*Assemblées du Seigneur*
ATANT	Abhandlungen zur Theologie des Alten und Neuen Testaments
b.	Babylonian Talmud
BAR	*Biblical Archaeology Review*
BECNT	Baker Exegetical Commentary on the New Testament
BETL	Bibliotheca Ephemeridum Theologicarum Lovaniensium
Bib	*Biblica*
BJRL	*Bulletin of the John Rylands Library*
BThSt	Biblisch-theologisch Studien
BWANT	Beiträge zur Wissenschaft vom Alten und Neuen Testament
BZ	*Biblische Zeitschrift*
BZNW	Beihefte zur Zeitschrift für die neutestamentliche Wissenschaft
CBQ	*Catholic Biblical Quarterly*
CEJL	Commentaries on Early Jewish Literature
CGTC	Cambridge Greek Testament Commentary
EDNT	*Exegetical Dictionary of the New Testament,* ed. H. Balz and G. Schneider. Grand Rapids: Eerdmans, 1990-93.
EKK	Evangelisch-katholischer Kommentar zum Neuen Testament
ET	English translation
ETL	*Ephemerides theologicae Lovanienses*
ExpT	*Expository Times*

FRLANT	Forschungen zur Religion und Literatur des Alten und Neuen Testaments
FS	Festschrift
HNT	Handbuch zum Neuen Testament
HSM	Harvard Semitic Monographs
HTK	Herders theologischer Kommentar zum Neuen Testament
HTR	*Harvard Theological Review*
ICC	International Critical Commentary
IJST	*International Journal of Systematic Theology*
j.	Jerusalem Talmud
JAAR	*Journal of the American Academy of Religion*
JBL	*Journal of Biblical Literature*
JBT	*Jahrbuch für biblische Theologie*
JETS	*Journal of the Evangelical Theological Society*
JSJ	*Journal for the Study of Judaism*
JSNT	*Journal for the Study of the New Testament*
JSNTSS	Journal for the Study of the New Testament Supplement Series
JSOTSup	Journal for the Study of the Old Testament Supplement Series
JSPSupS	Journal for the Study of the Pseudepigrapha Supplement Series
JTS	*Journal of Theological Studies*
KEK	Kritisch-exegetischer Kommentar über das Neue Testament
m.	Mishnah
NHC	Nag Hammadi Codices
NIBC	New International Biblical Commentary
NICNT	New International Commentary on the New Testament
NIGTC	New International Greek Testament Commentary
NovT	*Novum Testamentum*
NovTSuppS	Novum Testamentum Supplement Series
NTD	Das Neue Testament Deutsch
NTOA	Novum Testamentum et Orbis Antiquus
NTS	*New Testament Studies*
PG	Patrologia graeca
PTSDSSP	Princeton Theological Seminary Dead Sea Scrolls Project
PVTG	Pseudepigrapha Veteris Testamenti Graece
RCataT	*Revista Catalana de Teologia*
RevB	*Revue Biblique*
*RGG*³	*Religion in Geschichte und Gegenwart*, ed. K. Galling. Tübingen: Mohr, 1957-65
RHPR	*Revue d'histoire et de philosophie religieuses*

RSR	*Recherches de science religieuse*
SacPag	Sacra Pagina
SANT	Studien zum Alten und Neuen Testaments
SBLDS	Society of Biblical Literature Dissertation Series
SBLSP	*Society of Biblical Literature Seminar Papers*
SBT	Studies in Biblical Theology
SJT	*Scottish Journal of Theology*
SNTSMS	Society for New Testament Studies Monograph Series
SNTSU	Studien zum Neuen Testament und seiner Umwelt
ST	Studia Theologica
SUNT	Studien zur Umwelt des Neuen Testaments
SVTP	Studia in Veteris Testamenti pseudepigrapha
TDNT	*Theological Dictionary of the New Testament,* ed. G. Kittel and G. Friedrich. Grand Rapids: Eerdmans, 1964-76.
THKNT	Theologischer Handkommentar zum Neuen Testament
TrinJ	*Trinity Journal*
TS	*Theological Studies*
TSAJ	Texte und Studien zum antiken Judentum
TSK	*Theologische Studien und Kritiken*
TWNT	*Theologisches Wörterbuch zum Neuen Testament,* ed. G. Kittel and G. Friedrich. Stuttgart: Kohlhammer
TZ	*Theologische Zeitschrift*
VC	*Vigiliae Christianae*
VD	*Verbum Domini*
WBC	Word Biblical Commentary
WMANT	Wissenschaftliche Monographien zum Alten und Neuen Testament
WUNT	Wissenschaftliche Untersuchungen zum Neuen Testament
ZAW	*Zeitschrift für die alttestamentliche Wissenschaft*
ZKG	*Zeitschrift für Kirchengeschichte*
ZNW	*Zeitschrift für die neutestamentliche Wissenschaft*
ZTK	*Zeitschrift für Theologie und Kirche*

Introduction

I. Theme: The Preexistence of Christ in Matthew, Mark, and Luke

> It is not by chance that when dealt with in a monograph, a [New Testament] writer's conceptions are often not really made historically intelligible or are even wrongly understood. . . . Most dangerous of all is a monograph on simply a single concept. . . .[1]

So wrote William Wrede, in part of his attack "against separating doctrinal concepts" in early Christian religion. Indeed, anyone attempting to study preexistence would perhaps be especially liable to incur posthumous disapproval from Herr Wrede, since the pre-incarnate life of the Son is scarcely ever, if at all, dealt with at length as a theme in the NT. Nevertheless, the preexistence of Christ is the focus of attention in this monograph. For the time being, we can use as a minimal working definition of preexistence "the life of the Son prior to his birth"; beyond that, we will not presuppose any particular "nature" of preexistence. Rather, in the course of the following chapters, the concept will be filled out by features which will become evident in the exegesis.

The really controversial point to be made in this book is that *the preexistence of Christ can be found in the Synoptic Gospels.* This goes against the general consensus, of which the following comments are representative:

1. W. Wrede, "The Task and Methods of 'New Testament Theology,'" in R. Morgan, ed., *The Nature of New Testament Theology: The Contribution of William Wrede and Adolf Schlatter* (SBT; London: SCM, 1973), 68-116 (91).

1

Did Matthew's readers perceive the "Son of God" appellation to carry the connotation of a cosmic being, descended from the heavens, one with the Father, and returning to his former glory? An obvious difficulty with such a supposition is Matthew's complete lack of interest in the pre-existence of Jesus, a motif so prominent in, for example, John's Gospel.[2]

The Greek translation of Ps. 110.3 implies that the king, or the messiah, is pre-existent and angel-like. The Gospel of Mark, however, does not imply pre-existence. . . . The Similitudes [*1 Enoch* 37–71] and *4 Ezra*, however, imply that the Son of Man is a pre-existent heavenly being. Mark does not seem to attribute pre-existence to Jesus.[3]

In Lucan christology, there are four phases of Christ's existence. The first begins with the virginal conception. . . . In Lucan christology there is no question of Jesus' pre-existence or incarnation. Many NT interpreters rightly reckon with the pre-existent sonship of Jesus in Pauline theology and with the incarnation of Jesus in Johannine theology; but neither of these aspects of his existence emerge in the Lucan portrait of him.[4]

Clearly, then, for these scholars, a preexistent Messiah is a feature of early Jewish texts such as *1 Enoch* and *4 Ezra* and of some early Christian writers like Paul and John, but is certainly not an idea held by the Synoptic Evangelists. As some readers will already be aware, these scholars illustrate a strong consensus on this point, as will become clearer in the surveys of scholarly views throughout the present study.

II. Previous Research

This consensus has clearly not always been in place. In the opinion of premodern, pre-critical interpreters of the Gospels, it was widely held that preexistence could be found in all four Gospels. Similar conclusions to those found in traditional exegesis have been reached by conservative critical scholars such as Schlatter and Hofius.[5] Again, in French scholarship, conservative

---

2. D. Verseput, "The Role and Meaning of the 'Son of God' Title in Matthew's Gospel," *NTS* 33 (1987), 532-56 (539).

3. A. Yarbro Collins, "Mark and His Readers: The Son of God among Jews," *HTR* 92 (1999), 393-408 (395, 407).

4. J. A. Fitzmyer, *The Gospel according to Luke: Introduction, Translation and Notes* (Anchor; New York: Doubleday, 1981), 1:196, 197.

5. For example, A. Schlatter, *Das Evangelium nach Lukas aus seinen Quellen erklärt* (Stuttgart: Calwer, 1931). See also the various studies by O. Hofius which touch on the Gospels,

Roman Catholics have held a similar position. M. Lagrange's commentaries in the first half of the twentieth century are a good example of this. In the second half, A. Feuillet argued strongly for preexistence on the basis of a Wisdom-christology throughout the Gospels;[6] P. Benoit advanced the case on more traditional divine-christological grounds.[7]

On the other hand, the history-of-religions school in the late-nineteenth and early-twentieth century reached some similar conclusions about preexistence, but by entirely different means. Scholars like Richard Reitzenstein and Wilhelm Bousset argued strongly for the view that the titles in the Gospels such as "Son of Man" and "Lord" had their origins in Iranian thought and in Hellenistic mystery religions and represented primeval, divine figures, and so these images were carried over into the Synoptic Gospels.[8] One of the most influential advocates of this school of thought was Martin Dibelius, who argued that Jesus' earthly ministry was a temporary appearance of the heavenly son in human form;[9] Rudolf Bultmann perhaps held a similar view, though this has been debated.[10] In any case, a number of those influenced by Dibelius and Bultmann have argued that preexistence was to be found in the Synoptics. Johannes Schreiber, for example, has been strongly influenced by Bultmann's Gnostic redeemer-myth paradigm and has consistently made the case that Christ's preexistence undergirds Mark's Gospel.[11]

It is largely in reaction either to traditional-conservative exegesis or to the excesses of the history-of-religions school that the current consensus — that there is no preexistence christology in the Synoptic Gospels — has emerged. Another factor here has been an increasing recognition of the differ-

---

including "Ist Jesus der Messias? Thesen," *JBT* 8 (1993), 103-29; "Die Allmacht des Sohnes Gottes und das Gebet des Glaubens," *ZTK* 101 (2004), 117-37.

6. A. Feuillet, "Jésus et la Sagesse Divine d'après les Évangiles Synoptiques. Le 'logion johannique' et l'Ancien Testament," *RevB* 62 (1955), 161-96.

7. P. Benoit, "Préexistence et Incarnation," in idem, *Exégèse et Théologie* (Paris: Cerf, 1982), 4:11-61.

8. See, e.g., R. Reitzenstein, *Das mandäische Buch des Herrn der Grösse und die Evangelienüberlieferung* (Sitzungsberichte der Heidelberger Akademie der Wissenschaften; Heidelberg: Winter, 1919).

9. M. Dibelius, *From Tradition to Gospel* (New York: Scribner, 1935).

10. R. Bultmann, *The History of the Synoptic Tradition* (Oxford: Blackwell, 1968). At one point, he seems to have allowed that Mark did have an understanding of Christ's preexistence as it was probable that he "as a Hellenistic Christian of the Pauline circle, already looked on Jesus as the pre-existent Son of God" (*History of the Synoptic Tradition*, 253). However, he also comments that: "The only essential element of the Christ myth not yet adopted by Mark is the preexistence of Jesus. This dogmatic idea clearly does not lend itself so easily to a presentation of the life of Jesus; John was the first who was able to use it in this way" (349).

11. See the discussion of Schreiber later in this Introduction.

ences between the Synoptic Gospels and John. A further reason is that — with the conservatives, against the *religionsgeschichtliche Schule* — there has been a growing acknowledgement of the historical character of much of the Synoptic material, especially in Mark and "Q." On the other hand, what is a constant in much critical scholarship — in agreement with Bultmann, *et al.,* and against traditional exegesis — is that Jesus could not have regarded himself as preexistent. Again, then, the combination of these has meant that a fairly firm scepticism about preexistence in the Synoptic Gospels has become the norm.

The strength of the consensus is evident from the fact that it is held across party lines. Of the quotations cited near the beginning of this chapter, for example, the comment on Luke comes from a moderate Catholic, and that on Matthew from a conservative evangelical; furthermore, one can find an almost identical statement to Verseput's on Matthew in Maurice Casey's *Cadbury Lectures.*[12] Similarly, both Anglo-American and German scholars alike have emphasized the contrast between the "earthly" Messiah of the Synoptic Gospels and the "heavenly" Son in John.[13]

Representatives of the Consensus

This can be seen further in some of the major studies which have been focused on our theme.

F. B. Craddock (1968)

One of the first major monographs to deal specifically with preexistence in recent times was that of Craddock.[14] Craddock's work has a strongly theolog-

12. See P. M. Casey, *From Jewish Prophet to Gentile God: The Origins and Development of New Testament Christology* (Louisville: Westminster/John Knox, 1991), 151, on Matt. 11.27: "He is just the slightest step away from the pre-existence which he was not interested enough to state."

13. This contrast is evident in, e.g., A. Harnack, "'Ich bin gekommen.' Die ausdrücklichen Selbstzeugnisse Jesu über den Zweck seiner Sendung und seines Kommens," *ZTK* 22 (1912), 1-30. Gnilka talks of how Markan christology has not yet reached the stage of a Johannine preexistence christology: J. Gnilka, *Das Evangelium nach Markus.* Volume 1: *Mk 1–8,26* (Einsiedeln: Benziger, 1978), 89: "Die Formulierung klingt johanneisch, hat sich aber noch nicht zur Höhe des Präexistenzgedankens entwickelt" (on Mark 1.38). D. L. Bock, *Jesus According to Scripture: Restoring the Portrait from the Gospels* (Grand Rapids: Baker/Leicester: Apollos, 2002), frequently talks of the first three Evangelists viewing Jesus "from the earth up," while John works "from heaven down" (e.g., 24).

14. F. B. Craddock, *The Pre-existence of Christ in the New Testament* (Nashville: Abingdon, 1968).

ical orientation; the lengthy third chapter ("Meanings Past and Present") cautiously argues that preexistence should not be understood in traditional terms, but is rather expressive of Jesus as "revelatory of the Transcendent" (p. 184). The book begins with a discussion in chapter 1 of Jewish conceptions (pp. 29-80), and the second major part (pp. 81-150) deals with Paul, John, Hebrews, and Revelation. The focus is on Paul, which dominates more than half of the NT chapter, and Craddock's thesis is that for Paul "the pre-existence of Christ is presented in relation to creation, to incarnation, and to history" (p. 86). On the other hand, there is not a single discussion of a text from the Synoptic Gospels. In this respect, Craddock is typical of much NT scholarship: many commentators and exegetes do not even raise the possibility of seeing preexistence in the Gospels of Matthew, Mark, and Luke.

J. D. G. Dunn (1980)

A much more substantial treatment of the theme came in J. D. G. Dunn's controversial *Christology in the Making*,[15] a work which has had considerable influence on both exegetes and theologians alike.[16] Dunn's book had its origins both in the exegetical struggles of works contemporaneous with it and in theological controversy in the late 1970s (the Myth of God Incarnate debate). What provoked most discussion was his attribution of a doctrine of preexistence only to John in the NT. The other NT authors (including Paul) may have thought of Jesus as the embodiment of divine Wisdom, but of a divine Wisdom who was a personification of God rather than having actual prior existence.[17] Preexistence is thus one of the last attributes of Christ to develop in the NT, at the end of the first century.

Within this framework, then, Dunn does not find preexistence in the Synoptic Gospels. For example, after discussing a number of Markan references to the title "Son of God," Dunn comments, "It is fairly clear there is no thought of pre-existence in all this."[18] The closest one gets to such an idea in the Synoptics is Matthew's representation of Christ as the incarnation of Wisdom, but again, this is not the incarnation of a preexistent Wisdom who ex-

15. J. D. G. Dunn, *Christology in the Making: An Inquiry into the Origins of the Doctrine of the Incarnation* (London: SCM, 1980).

16. To take one example on the theological side, see J. Macquarrie, *Jesus Christ in Modern Thought* (London: SCM, 1990), 57 and *passim*.

17. This position has been nuanced, but by no means retracted, by Dunn in his *The Theology of Paul the Apostle* (Grand Rapids: Eerdmans/Edinburgh: Clark, 1998), 274-75. See the further discussion of Dunn in chapter 1 below.

18. Dunn, *Christology in the Making*, 47.

isted as a person.[19] "There is no real indication that Matthew had attained a concept of incarnation, had come to think of Christ as a pre-existent being who became incarnate in Mary's womb or in Christ's ministry (as incarnate Wisdom). . . . [T]he thought of Christ's pre-existence or a doctrine of incarnation had not yet occurred to him."[20]

As far as Matthew, Mark, and Luke are concerned, Dunn's exegesis has generally been found to be convincing. Where his conclusions have not been widely accepted is on Paul. It is generally reckoned that there are simply too many references to a situation in which Christ existed before the incarnation (Phil. 2.6-8; 2 Cor. 8.9, etc.), which even extends to his action in creation (1 Cor. 8.6; Col. 1.16). If this critique of Dunn is right, as will be argued in Chapter 1, this has implications not only for Dunn's exegesis of Paul, but for his entire reconstruction of early Christian thinking about preexistence. In particular, the problem highlighted is that if we know that Paul wrote often about preexistence in the 50s and 60s, then can it still be the case for Matthew that "the thought of Christ's pre-existence or a doctrine of incarnation had not yet occurred to him"? It seems likely that Paul was too influential for his christology not to have had a very wide distribution. This is not by any means to say that Paul's christology would necessarily have *influenced* the likes of Matthew, but it does make it difficult to argue that preexistence christology would have "not yet occurred" to the Synoptic Evangelists.

G. Schimanowski (1985)

In German scholarship, the first major treatment in recent years came from G. Schimanowski.[21] As the subtitle (The Jewish Presuppositions of Early Christian Pre-existence Christology) perhaps suggests, the book is more concerned with the OT and Jewish background than with exegesis of the NT. The latter occupies only a brief section at the end (pp. 309-44).

The book covers an impressive range of material from the OT through to the Rabbinic literature. In the first part, which is concerned with Wisdom, Schimanowski considers the reflection on Wisdom in the OT and beyond extremely important for Jewish thought, and that the great majority of the statements in early Judaism describe Wisdom as a being clearly distinct from

---

19. J. D. G. Dunn, "Incarnation," in idem, *The Christ and the Spirit*. Volume 1: *Christology* (Grand Rapids: Eerdmans/Edinburgh: Clark, 1998), 30-47 (44-45). (Reprinted from *ABD* 3:397-404.)

20. Dunn, *Christology in the Making*, 257.

21. G. Schimanowski, *Weisheit und Messias. Die jüdischen Voraussetzungen der urchristlichen Präexistenzchristologie* (Tübingen: Mohr, 1985).

God (p. 105). Schimanowski is more cautious about the idea of a preexistent Messiah figure in the Septuagint: he discusses LXX Mic. 5.1; Ps. 109.3; and Psalm 72, concluding that it is difficult to argue for the idea of preexistence in these passages, although they were later open to a preexistence interpretation (pp. 112-53). He is much more positive about the Son of Man figure in the Similitudes of *1 Enoch*, who has been associated with Wisdom in Proverbs 8 (pp. 192, 204). Similarly, the Messiah in *4 Ezra 7* is preexistent, though not quite in the same manner as the figure in *1 Enoch*.[22]

Unfortunately for our purposes, the treatment of the material in the Synoptic Gospels is extremely brief, since the preexistence of Christ is really dealt with only in Paul. Two passages from Luke are discussed, the first being Luke 11.49-51, where Schimanowski is concerned merely with the preexistence of Wisdom. Schimanowski then implies that a further step is taken in Luke 13.34-35 in that there is some kind of association of the coming of the Messiah with Wisdom forsaking the Temple, even if not yet an actual "Wisdom christology" (pp. 313-14).

J. Habermann (1990)

A more substantial treatment of preexistence in the NT itself (645 pages!) comes from J. Habermann.[23] One very useful part of the book is the long history of research at the beginning (pp. 21-89). This takes in almost all of the major studies of preexistence from the nineteenth and twentieth centuries, focusing in particular on views of the origin and nature of preexistence in the NT in general, but also with attention to the interpretation of certain passages.

The focus of Habermann's work, however, is the exegesis of Phil. 2.6-11; 1 Cor. 8.6; 10.1-13; Col. 1.15-20; Heb. 1.1-4 and the Johannine Prologue, on which there is extremely detailed attention to every word and phrase. Habermann emphasizes that preexistence is always presumed in these passages rather than developed — hence it is clear that belief in the preexistence of Christ was not confined only to the authors of the NT documents, but would also have been held by the intended audiences of, say, Paul's epistles.[24] Furthermore, it is to be noted that preexistence often emerges at particularly important points in the

---

22. He considers the figure in *4 Ezra* simply to exist in a certain form prior to his revelation on the earth, rather than to exist from the beginning, as in the Similitudes. Schimanowski, *Weisheit und Messias,* 197.

23. J. Habermann, *Präexistenzaussagen im Neuen Testament* (Europäische Hochschulschriften; Frankfurt-am-Main: Lang, 1990).

24. We shall return to this point in chapter 1.

NT books: Col. 1.15-20 and the introductory statements in Hebrews and John, for example (p. 415). Some of Habermann's points correspond to observations frequently made in German scholarship in particular: that preexistence is not the object of theological speculation (p. 416), that it confirms the truth that salvation comes from *outside* the world (p. 429), and that it is inseparably tied to soteriology (p. 417). Particularly important is the observation (implicitly *contra* Dunn) that it is *personal* preexistence which is in view in the NT: it is always the person of Jesus Christ who is talked of as preexistent and who is the "decisive criterion of personal pre-existence" (p. 421).

Again, however, as far as our interest in the Synoptic Gospels is concerned, Habermann's conclusions are entirely negative. In his conclusion, he discusses very briefly the passages in Matthew often associated with Wisdom and concludes that Matthew regards Jesus as "the personified Wisdom of God" (p. 427).[25] Habermann does not consider this to indicate preexistence, however, and forcefully repeats the point — following his *Doktorvater* F. Hahn — that the origin of preexistence christology is the ascension of Jesus, not any sayings of Jesus (p. 428).

K.-J. Kuschel (1990 [ET: 1992])

Even more negative as far as Matthew, Mark, and Luke are concerned is Karl-Josef Kuschel's extremely significant study of preexistence.[26] Kuschel follows Dunn's exegesis of 1 Cor. 8.6 and 2 Cor. 8.9, and ends up with a similarly minimalist view of preexistence in Paul (pp. 291, 296-97). Kuschel does allow a hint of preexistence in the pre-Pauline hymn in Phil. 2.6-11, but not enough for it to constitute a "christology of pre-existence" (pp. 262-63). And in any case, Kuschel argues, "the hymn stands 'in isolation' in the whole of Pauline theology" and cannot be regarded as Pauline in a proper sense (p. 298). As such, "there is no sign of any unambiguous and explicit statement about preexistence in the christology outlined by Paul himself" (p. 303).

Needless to say, with such scepticism about the Pauline texts, Kuschel is even more unequivocal when it comes to the Synoptic Gospels, as can be seen from the title of his section on Matthew, Mark, and Luke: "Why It was Impossible to Narrate the Pre-Existence of Christ" (p. 308). In his discussion of Mark, Kuschel focuses on the "Son" title, arguing that it is used in neither an

---

25. This conclusion relates specifically to Matt. 23.34-36.

26. K.-J. Kuschel, *Born before All Time? The Dispute over Christ's Origin* (London: SCM, 1992 [1990]). We restrict the discussion here to a brief outline of Kuschel's exegesis of the NT. This will be developed further in the final chapter.

adoptionist nor a heavenly sense (pp. 311-13). In fact, it is even the case that in Mark "we evidently have a deliberate disregard of, a decision against, any Christological statement about pre-existence" (p. 316). Matthew and Luke similarly "exclude" the notion of preexistence in their incorporation of the virginal conception, which, Kuschel hints, is in the final analysis incompatible with preexistence.[27]

Despite Kuschel's frequent claims to represent mainstream positions in NT exegesis, most exegetes both in Anglo-American and German-language scholarship would probably not follow his interpretation of Paul. When it comes to the Synoptic Gospels, however, his views — similar as they are to those of Dunn, Schimanowski, and Habermann — certainly would represent the majority.[28]

Laufen, et al. (1997)

The most recent substantial contribution to the German discussion is a book of essays edited by Rudolf Laufen.[29] This inter-disciplinary collection contains, in addition to biblical material, treatments of the idea of preexistence in Indian perspective, in Islamic thought, as well as in trinitarian theologies ancient and modern. Some of the NT contributions are from figures we have already examined — Schimanowski, Habermann, and Kuschel. However, the biblical chapters cover the Jewish background, John, Paul, and Hebrews, with nothing on the Synoptic Gospels. This is clearly no accidental oversight, as Laufen's initial contribution divides the NT into a chart in two halves: those books and sections with preexistence christologies, and those without. He places the Gospels of Matthew, Mark, and Luke clearly among the latter.[30]

---

27. Kuschel, *Born before All Time,* 318, where he notes Brown's reference to the "fundamental difference" between the two ideas, since in a preexistence christology the conception cannot be a real "begetting." Hence for Kuschel it is no coincidence that there is no preexistence christology in Matthew and Luke; the fact is virtually determined by the presence of the virginal conception.

28. In this respect, Schenke is rather over-optimistic in his comment that while formerly exegetes answered the question of whether there is preexistence in Mark in the negative, the situation is now changing: "Erst in neuerer Zeit mehren sich wieder die bejahenden Stimmen." L. Schenke, "Gibt es im Markusevangelium eine Präexistenzchristologie?" *ZNW* 91 (2000), 45-71 (50 n. 11). Schenke cites some examples, but in reality they are still very much *(me miserum!)* in the minority.

29. R. Laufen, ed. *Gottes ewiger Sohn. Die Präexistenz Christi* (Paderborn: Schöningh, 1997). The volume is in part a response to the work of Kuschel.

30. R. Laufen, "Der anfanglose Sohn: Eine christologische Problemanzeige," in idem, ed., *Gottes ewiger Sohn,* 9-29 (12): "Christologien ohne Präexistenz."

The Optimists

Despite the strong consensus illustrated above, there have nevertheless been some vocal opponents of it in recent times. Some of the attempts have been revivals of older lines of interpretation, such as the Gnostic scheme of Bultmann and his allies or the enthusiasm for Wisdom christology in the history-of-religions school in the early twentieth century.[31]

M. J. Suggs (1970)

The early 1970s were certainly a second heyday for Wisdom christology: three monographs appeared on the subject in the space of only three years.[32] The first of these was by M. Jack Suggs.[33] Suggs focused on the way in which Matthew adapted material from "Q" and began by arguing that the background against which to read Q is not Gnosticism, but a kind of early Jewish wisdom speculation which tends in a Gnostic direction (p. 13). When it comes to the Evangelist's theological redaction of Q, Suggs argues that Matthew edits his source *"in order to identify Jesus with Wisdom,"* and as a result, "it would not greatly overstate the case to say that *for Matthew* Wisdom has 'become flesh and dwelled among us'" (p. 57).[34] Suggs sees this theological device, then, as the way in which Matthew develops a preexistence christology in a much stronger sense than is allowed for by Dunn: "speculation about the pre-existent Sophia constituted an important element in Matthew's understanding of Christ" (p. 97).

Felix Christ (1973)

Following the work of Suggs, a book appeared shortly after in German, by Felix Christ.[35] After a survey of the various characteristics and functions of

31. See, e.g., H. Windisch, "Die göttliche Weisheit der Juden und die paulinische Christologie," in A. Deissmann, ed., *Neutestamentliche Studien. Georg Heinrici zu seinem 70. Geburtstag* (Leipzig: Hinrichs, 1914), 220-34.

32. Suggs and, to a lesser extent, Christ received fairly heavy criticism from M. D. Johnson, "Reflections on a Wisdom Approach to Matthew's Christology," *CBQ* 36 (1974), 44-64. There have, nevertheless, been more studies since, although they have been somewhat more restrained. See, e.g., C. Deutsch, *Hidden Wisdom and the Easy Yoke: Wisdom, Torah and Discipleship in Matthew 11:25-30* (JSNTSS; Sheffield: JSOT, 1987); F. T. Gench, *Wisdom in the Christology of Matthew* (Lanham: University Press of America, 1997).

33. M. J. Suggs, *Wisdom, Christology and Law in Matthew's Gospel* (Cambridge: Harvard University Press, 1970).

34. Italics original.

35. F. Christ, *Jesus Sophia. Die Sophia-Christologie bei den Synoptikern* (ATANT 57; Zürich: Zwingli, 1970).

Lady Wisdom in Jewish literature, he asks the question: "Is Jesus, if he is more than Solomon, perhaps Wisdom itself?" (p. 62). The aim of the second half of the book, on the Synoptic tradition, is to answer "yes" to this question. He identifies the key passages in the debate as Matt. 11.19, 25-30 and 23.34-39 (with their respective Lukan parallels) and in each case examines activities which are shared in common by Wisdom and Jesus. So, for example, Wisdom comes, converts the elect, and summons Israel to obey the Law, but is rejected by the majority (p. 80). In addition, Wisdom's quality of preexistence is thereby also attributed to Jesus (e.g., p. 130). This is not just the case in Matthew's Gospel; in fact, this christology goes all the way back to Q, perhaps even to Jesus himself (pp. 129-30, 154).[36]

R. Hamerton-Kelly (1973)

The third was Hamerton-Kelly's *Pre-existence, Wisdom and the Son of Man.*[37] It is particularly notable for our purposes in that it is one of the few treatments to have substantial discussion of the Synoptic Gospels (pp. 22-102). There is a tension running through Hamerton-Kelly's book, however, that has generally led to a negative assessment by other scholars. On the one hand, Hamerton-Kelly is a maximalist. To take one example, he identifies preexistence as an attribute of the Son of Man partly because of the identification of that figure with Wisdom. Thereafter, whenever there is a reference to the suffering and resurrection of the Son of Man, and especially to the Son of Man's authority in rising from the dead, this is taken to flag up the whole story: from preexistence to incarnation to suffering and resurrection, then his "return to eternity" and final coming (pp. 58-60).[38]

However, it is vital to realize when reading Hamerton-Kelly on the Synoptics that when he talks of preexistence, he is making a sharp distinction between *real* and *ideal* preexistence. If real preexistence means an actual existence in heaven before the figure's earthly manifestation, ideal preexistence, on the other hand, means simply preexistence *in the mind of God,* and Hamerton-Kelly argues strongly for the latter rather than the former: so, for example, he can talk of Matthew's genealogy as evidence for this kind of preexistence (p. 78). This has misled some scholars and left Hamerton-Kelly open to more criticism than he perhaps deserves. His use of preexistence language in con-

---

36. This is in contrast to Suggs and following Christ's Doktorvater, Oscar Cullmann.

37. R. G. Hamerton-Kelly, *Pre-existence, Wisdom, and the Son of Man: A Study of the Idea of Pre-existence in the New Testament* (SNTSMS; Cambridge: Cambridge University Press, 1973).

38. Hamerton-Kelly makes this point in reference to Mark 8.31; 9.9, 31; 10.33.

nection with Mark 1.38 leads Arens to criticize him for seeing preexistence in the passage. For Hamerton-Kelly, "Jesus confirms his divine origin" in this statement, which "implies pre-existence" (pp. 48, 64).[39] Similarly, Dunn takes him to task for offering the transfiguration as evidence for preexistence, but again Hamerton-Kelly was talking only of *ideal* preexistence (pp. 53-56).[40]

On the other hand, one cannot help but feel that Hamerton-Kelly is partly to blame for the misunderstandings. The category of ideal preexistence is not only confusing (especially when referred to simply as "pre-existence") but also rather redundant. Already in 1974, Wayne Meeks noted in his review of Hamerton-Kelly that the concept of ideal preexistence is rather vacuous because a concept of divine omniscience would mean that *everything* is ideally preexistent in the mind of God.[41] More recently, McCready has made the same point: "The problem with ideal pre-existence is not that it is untrue, but that it is trivial. Ideal pre-existence is merely another name for divine foreknowledge."[42] As a result of the problems with Hamerton-Kelly's categories, hardly any have followed his exegetical conclusions.

J. Schreiber (1993)

Johannes Schreiber is the author of an often-quoted article from 1961 which takes as its starting point for the investigation of Mark the research of Wrede on the messianic secret and Bultmann on the nature of the Hellenistic kerygma.[43] Similarly, in his more recent *magnum opus* Schreiber's understanding of the intellectual environment of Mark's christology is clear from his reliance on Bultmann and from his explicit statements about Mark's use of "the Gnostic myth."[44] He further notes, for example, that "sending" in the

39. For the criticism, see E. Arens, *The ΗΛΘΟΝ-Sayings in the Synoptic Tradition: A Historico-Critical Investigation* (Orbis Biblicus et Orientalis 10; Freiburg: Universitätsverlag Freiburg/Göttingen: Vandenhoeck und Ruprecht, 1976), 207.

40. The criticism comes in Dunn, *Christology in the Making*, 89 and the accompanying n. 121.

41. W. A. Meeks, Review of Hamerton-Kelly, *Pre-existence, Wisdom, and the Son of Man*, in *JBL* 93 (1974), 617-19.

42. D. McCready, "'He Came from Heaven': The Pre-existence of Christ Revisited," *JETS* 40 (1997), 419-32 (424). "Redundant" is probably a better term than "trivial," if one regards divine foreknowledge as an important doctrine!

43. J. Schreiber, "Die Christologie des Markusevangeliums," *ZTK* 58 (1961), 154-83. Schreiber describes these elements (among others) as the "Ausgangspunkt" for his own work, which proceeds "aus diesen Ergebnissen bisheriger Forschung" (155, 156).

44. J. Schreiber, *Die Markuspassion. Eine redaktionsgeschichtliche Untersuchung* (BZNW 68; Berlin: de Gruyter, 1993), 375.

Gospel should be interpreted along the lines of the heavenly Son's descent from the Father in Gnosis and in John's Gospel (p. 374).

Against this background, Schreiber treats the individual passages in Mark's Gospel. First, he argues that the Spirit is the driving force in Jesus' mission, and even the determinative factor for his identity (p. 219).[45] This Spirit is of course preexistent, and so in this respect — because Jesus' person is so bound up with the Spirit — Jesus is also preexistent, especially as "Son of God" (pp. 229-30). Of course, then, so are all the prophets who were also Spirit-bearers (p. 227).[46] Schreiber also considers the Son of Man a kind of "divine man," who exercises the power in his ministry that was expected only at the end of time; hence, his coming is a coming "to earth" (pp. 222, 223). In the discussion of "the pre-existent Lord," the "heavenly scenes" of Mark 1.2-3 and 12.35-37 feature heavily. The former, narrated by Isaiah, reports God addressing his Son, the Lord, before the incarnation and promising to prepare his way; the latter has David looking, by the Spirit, into the heavenly throne room, where he sees *the* Lord saying to *his* Lord, "Sit at my right hand" (Ps. 110.1), and at the same time, David actually also addresses Jesus (pp. 238-40). These are some of the main lines of Schreiber's argument, although the relation between Jesus' preexistence and the passion is also a central concern.[47]

L. Schenke (2000)

The Catholic scholar Ludger Schenke's support for preexistence in Mark has been clear for some time, at least since his commentary on the Gospel.[48] In a recent article, Schenke addresses at length the question: "Is there a preexistence christology in the Gospel of Mark?" — which he answers with a resounding *Ja!*[49] Schenke begins by making some preliminary methodological points about the compatibility of christological ideas which scholars too easily divorce from one another (pp. 53-54) and about christology being the *presupposition*, rather than the *theme*, of Mark's Gospel (p. 48). He then explains how a number of passages in Mark apparently presuppose a background of

---

45. In the original, "die entscheidende, Jesus bestimmende und treibende Kraft."

46. The same applies in particular to John the Baptist, who is also Elijah *redivivus* (225-26).

47. See especially the section "Die Kenosis des Präexistenten" (*Markuspassion*, 240-50), and indeed the title of the book.

48. L. Schenke, *Das Markusevangelium* (Urban-Taschenbücher; Stuttgart: Kohlhammer, 1988), 114.

49. Schenke, "Gibt es im Markusevangelium eine Präexistenzchristologie?" *ZNW* 91 (2000), 45-71.

preexistence christology. As in his commentary, one focus is the territory familiar from Schreiber above: the heavenly scenes in Mark 1.2-3 and 12.35-37 in which Jesus is addressed as "Lord." Indeed, Schenke concludes that the argument of 12.35-37 only works on the presupposition of the idea of preexistence (p. 66). The transfiguration is also important for Schenke: understood against the background of Hellenistic Judaism, it can be seen that Jesus appears for a moment as he really is (p. 62). Similarly, the sea miracles are epiphanies of Jesus as a heavenly, divine being (pp. 58-59). Most interesting for our purposes is Schenke's use of the "I have come" sayings, which will be discussed at length later. He argues that these also imply preexistence, and should not be reduced simply to referring to Jesus' purpose in his ministry (p. 64).

There is a great strength in Schenke's approach over against the other "optimists" discussed here. Specifically, the others to a greater or lesser extent construct a template from early Judaism (Lady Wisdom) or Gnosis (the redeemed redeemer) and map it onto the Gospels. On the other hand, Schenke follows a more inductive approach. He is, nevertheless, certainly a maximalist when it comes to finding preexistence in Mark; the present monograph — while an optimistic one — will be more circumspect.

The "New History of Religion School"[50]

Finally, we come to a growing movement in scholarship which cannot be classified among either the cautious pessimists or the dissenting optimists. Specifically, these scholars reject an evolutionary or conventionally developmental approach to christology[51] and tend toward the view of George Caird that "the highest christology of the NT is also its earliest."[52] A number of important works in the last two decades have further contributed to a shaking of the foundations in this respect. We will focus here on two scholars who have been particularly influential.

---

50. A phrase coined by M. Hengel in his jacket blurb for the second edition of L. W. Hurtado, *One God, One Lord: Early Christian Devotion and Ancient Jewish Monotheism* (Edinburgh: Clark, [2]1998). It is an open secret that this new *Schule* is known, rather more informally, as the "Early High Christology Club."

51. For the distinction, see J. D. G. Dunn, "The Making of Christology: Evolution or Unfolding?" in idem, *The Christ and the Spirit*, 1:388-404.

52. G. B. Caird, *New Testament Theology*, completed and edited by L. D. Hurst (Oxford: Clarendon, 1994), 343; cf. the similar comments in R. J. Bauckham, *God Crucified: Monotheism and Christology in the New Testament* (Carlisle: Paternoster, 1998).

R. J. Bauckham

Several particularly important studies have come from Richard Bauckham, and a two-volume *magnum opus* on the subject is still to appear from him.[53] Bauckham's principal emphasis has been on the inclusion of Jesus within the divine identity and on the worship of Jesus. Bauckham identifies God, the one who alone is to be worshiped, as the creator and ruler of all things; this is a description which cannot be applied to any mediator-figures in early Judaism, no matter how exalted. He argues, furthermore, that: "The concern of early Christology, from its root in the exegesis of Psalm 110:1 and related texts, was to understand the identification of Jesus with God."[54] Such exegesis of Psalm 110.1 is of course clearly found in the Synoptic Gospels (Mark 12.35-37; 14.62 and their parallels). Furthermore, Bauckham considers that Matt. 11.27 par. Luke 10.22, with its statement that "all things have been committed to me by my Father," locates Jesus at God's side on the one heavenly throne: "By including Jesus in the full cosmic scope of God's sovereignty, NT terminology places Jesus clearly on the divine side of the distinction between God and 'all things.'"[55] He considers Matthew's Gospel as portraying Jesus as worshiped even before Easter.[56]

L. W. Hurtado

Following the lead of an early essay by Bauckham, early Christian devotion to Jesus has been the emphasis in much of the work of Larry Hurtado.[57] Most important as far as the Synoptic Gospels are concerned is his essay "Pre–70 CE Jewish Opposition to Christ-Devotion," which contains a discussion of Paul, as well as sections on "Blasphemy in the Synoptics" (pp. 36-37), and "Christ-Devotion and Jewish Opposition" in Matthew (pp. 38-42), in Luke-Acts (pp. 42-44), and in Mark (pp. 44-49).[58] Hurtado emphasizes the way in which the Synoptic Gospels reflect the worship practices of the milieux in which they

53. Provisionally entitled *Jesus and the Identity of God: Jewish Monotheism and New Testament Christology.* Bauckham has published a much abbreviated version in *God Crucified.*

54. R. J. Bauckham, "The Throne of God and the Worship of Jesus," in C. C. Newman, J. Davila, G. Lewis, eds., *The Jewish Roots of Christological Monotheism: Papers from the St Andrews Conference on the Historical Origins of the Worship of Jesus* (Leiden: Brill, 1999), 43-69 (64).

55. Bauckham, "The Throne of God and the Worship of Jesus," 64.

56. Bauckham, "The Throne of God and the Worship of Jesus," 67.

57. Hurtado expresses particular indebtedness to R. J. Bauckham, "The Worship of Jesus in Apocalyptic Christianity," *NTS* 27 (1981), 322-41.

58. L. W. Hurtado, "Pre–70 CE Jewish Opposition to Christ-Devotion," *JTS* 50 (1999), 35-58.

originated[59] and "manifest a full pattern of exalted christological claims and accompanying devotional practices that amount to something considerably more than merely claiming royal-messianic status for Jesus" (p. 38). This is particularly true of Matthew's Gospel: "In Matthew, not only is Jesus the ultimately authoritative spokesman for God, whose teachings supervene any other relative authority, he is also the Son of God who combines full messianic significance and transcendent divine-like status as well" (p. 40).

Together, Bauckham, Hurtado, and other scholars have opened the way for a greater appreciation of the fact that the Synoptic Gospels do not simply offer a "primitive" christology wherein Jesus is presented as a fundamentally prophetic figure, or as a merely human Messiah. Rather, he is, in some sense, "divine" and "transcendent." (These terms will occupy us further in Chapter 2.) An increasing number of scholars are in fact coming to conclusions similar to those of Bauckham and Hurtado and arguing for a considerably exalted christology in the Synoptic Gospels.[60]

However, where these scholars have not yet really ventured is into the discussion of preexistence in the Synoptic Gospels. Bauckham mentions the issue in passing, but in a very early article in 1978.[61] Hurtado has recently commented — again, very briefly — that although he does not think that the first three Evangelists mention preexistence, that is not to say that they are ignorant of it.[62] It is at the very least unclear how such an exalted picture of a *divine* Jesus would be conceivable in an early Jewish-Christian context *without* preexistence.[63] The aim of the current study, then, is to push this line of research further by arguing that the portrait of Jesus in the Synoptic Gospels

---

59. Cf. also Horbury, who considers the "Lord, Lord" saying in Matt. 7.21 to have been shaped by the Christ cult. W. Horbury, *Jewish Messianism and the Cult of Christ* (London: SCM, 1998), 114.

60. See for example P. G. Davis, "Mark's Christological Paradox," *JSNT* 35 (1989), 3-18; J. Marcus, *The Way of the Lord: Christological Exegesis of the Old Testament in the Gospel of Mark* (Louisville: Westminster/John Knox, 1992); C. Williams, *I Am He: The Interpretation of 'Anî Hû' in Jewish and Early Christian Literature* (Tübingen: Mohr, 1999), 214-54.

61. R. J. Bauckham, "The Sonship of the Historical Jesus in Christology," *SJT* 31 (1978), 245-60 (257): "Apart from the pre-existence and full divinity of the Son in the Fourth Gospel, most aspects of Jesus' sonship according to John can be paralleled from the Synoptic tradition."

62. L. W. Hurtado, *Lord Jesus Christ: Devotion to Jesus in Earliest Christianity* (Grand Rapids: Eerdmans, 2003), 323.

63. However, since the current book is in part a response to the claims of theologians such as Robert Jenson that a trinitarian theology does not necessarily require preexistence in the classical sense, I will resist the temptation to argue *from* divine identity *to* preexistence. See R. W. Jenson, *Systematic Theology. Volume 1: The Triune God* (Oxford: Oxford University Press, 1997), 138-44.

is of a figure who in some way preexisted in heaven prior to his earthly ministry. None of this is to say that the present research *assumes* the conclusions of this "new history of religion school," however.

Conclusion

The account of these three groups of scholars above, then, has illustrated the strong consensus in NT scholarship that there is no preexistence christology in the Synoptic Gospels. This should, however, be tempered by two considerations. First, there are still a minority who are much less sceptical. Second, there is also a growing school of thought which is acknowledging that the portrayal of Christ in the Gospels in fact shows strong signs of including heavenly and divine contours to Christ's identity. This tendency in current scholarship may indicate — despite the majority report — that the time is ripe for a reconsideration of preexistence in Matthew, Mark, and Luke.

III. Approach

This book is a study of the Synoptic Gospels in the sense that it is an analysis of the Gospels as they stand. It pays little attention to questions of tradition history, sources, and the relationship between the canonical Gospels and *Thomas* or the elusive "Q." We are in addition not particularly concerned to trace the origins and development of the doctrine of preexistence in early Christianity. Similarly, it is not a study of the historical Jesus: we are interested almost exclusively in the interpretation of the *Greek* texts of the Gospels as they would have been understood by their earliest readers, and questions of Aramaic originals have little place here.

In general, it is not the contention of the present study that there has been a profound failure of *method* on the part of previous studies. Rather, there are perhaps two problems which this book attempts to remedy. First, we are attempting to set the statements — in particular the "I have come" sayings — in their Jewish context. This is, of course, a cliché in NT studies at present, and the task has of course been attempted before. However, the study of the relevant statements under the microscope in this book has been hampered by a lack of appreciation of which Jewish traditions constitute the proper matrix of interpretation for the Synoptic Gospels at the relevant points. One can of course argue anything by means of cross-references, and approaches hitherto have, I would contend, been marred by misuse of both Jewish and early Christian parallels.

Second, the attempt here is to steer a course between the Scylla of maximalism and the Charybdis of minimalism. As was said above, one of the reasons for the current scepticism about preexistence christology in the Synoptics is the abandonment of the Gnosis paradigm, which tended to see heavenly redeemers at every possible opportunity. On the other hand, the consensus — it will be argued throughout this study — is based on an over-cautious and atomistic approach to the sources, again, especially as far as the "I have come" sayings are concerned.

The Stages of the Argument

The approach taken by the present book consists of four stages, corresponding to the four parts of the book. Part I consists of prolegomena which do not contribute to the argument *per se* but attempt to make it more plausible, since it is acknowledged that, despite the advances of the "new history of religion school," NT scholarship is still some way away from recognizing the portrait of Jesus put forward in the present book. The first chapter aims to make the (rather uncontroversial) case that preexistence christology was widespread in the Mediterranean prior to AD 70, primarily as a result of the influence of Paul. If this is right, then it is more likely that the Synoptic Evangelists were at least aware of the idea of Christ's preexistence. The second chapter comes to the Synoptic Gospels themselves, not (yet) in order to conclude that Christ is presented as preexistent, but to argue that he is portrayed in numerous other ways as transcending normal human limitations, particularly as transcending the heaven-earth divide and the God-creation divide. In Matthew's Gospel, Jesus even transcends space in his promise to be present with the disciples wherever they gather in his name (and this even *prior* to the resurrection: Matt. 18.16-20).

Part II represents the most important argument in the book, the argument which is pushed most strongly and on which Parts III and IV to some extent depend. Here, it is argued that *the "I have come" sayings are the clearest indications in the Synoptic Gospels of a preexistence christology.* The formula "I have come to . . ." is most characteristic elsewhere of angelic figures, who make such statements in order to summarize the purpose of their visits to the human realm. There is, in the first place, a *prima facie* case for seeing a coming *from* somewhere in the "I have come to . . ." sayings. It is then argued (in chapter 4) that the standard explanations of the "I have come" sayings arguing for a prophetic, messianic, or other similar account of his ministry simply do not work; the angelic parallels (discussed in chapter 5) are both qualitatively closer and quantitatively far greater in number than those adduced for a prophetic or messianic status of Jesus. The exegesis of the "I have come" sayings of Jesus further points in this direction (chapter 6). Derivatively, if the "I have come" sayings indicate preexistence, then the "I have been sent" sayings point in the same direction as well (as argued in chapter 7), although on their own they could easily have indicated a merely prophetic christology.

Part III examines the way in which the advocates of Wisdom christology (such as those noted above) interpret particular passages in the Synoptic Gospels, particularly Matthew. As we have seen, it is in this corner of NT scholarship that the attempts to argue for preexistence christology in the Synoptics have usually taken place. In fact, however, it will be argued that this is a blind alley as far as the idea of the preexistence of Christ is concerned; none of the passages in fact makes the point (as most scholars recognize). However, one of the key statements often supposed to witness to a Wisdom christology is important for our purposes: Jesus' statement "Jerusalem, Jerusalem, who kills the prophets and stones those sent to her, how often have I longed to gather your children, as a bird gathers her nestlings under her wings. But you have not been willing" (Matt. 23.37; cf. Luke 13.34). Here Jesus does speak as a person who transcends the time of his earthly ministry in his reference to his longing throughout the entirety of Israel's history to call the nation to God.

Part IV investigates the possibility of reference to preexistence in the *designations* of Jesus used by the Synoptic Gospels: "Messiah," "Lord," "Son of Man," and "Son of God" (chapters 10-13). First, the title "Messiah" is not particularly significant for our purposes, although the divine origin of the Christ is evident from Mark 12.35-37 par. Where messiahship in the Gospels does carry with it a sense of preexistence, however, is in the *Benedictus,* in which Luke refers to Jesus using the messianic image of the ἀνατολή. In Luke 1.78, this ἀνατολή, already a heavenly figure in some early Jewish depictions, is said further to "visit from on high." On the other hand, the title "Lord" (chapter 11), while having a divine sense in the Gospels, does not clearly have connotations of heavenly preexistence; possible exceptions to this are Mark 1.2-3 and 12.35-37, which as we have already seen are taken by some scholars as depicting heavenly scenes in which the preexistent Jesus is addressed by God and David. In chapter 12, the "Son of Man" designation is examined, and preexistence is most clearly seen in the references to the "coming of the Son of Man," as will have been argued in Part II. The Son of Man offers little evidence of preexistence independent of the "coming" motif, although there is a possibility that (a) the preexistence of the kingdom in the Gospels carries with it a sense of a preexistent Son of Man, and (b) that Matt. 13.35 is evidence of speech by this preexistent Son of Man. Both of these points are extremely tentatively advanced, however. Finally, the title "Son of God" (discussed in chapter 13) is important because of its heavenly connotations, and the motif of preexistence is touched on in Mark 12.6 par., as is argued in chapter 7.

Like many treatments of the theme of preexistence, the present study was born out of an interest in the theological issues at stake rather than in the first instance out of current debates in NT scholarship. The final chapter will discuss some recent attempts to reconceptualize the classical doctrine of Christ's preexistence, some aspects of which I have discussed elsewhere.[64] These last two chapters (13 and 14) focus in different ways on the paradoxical fact that the preexistent, heavenly Son (seen in his radiant glory in the transfiguration) is the very person who is sent by the Father into the world to be crucified by humankind and to give his life as a ransom for many.

---

64. S. J. Gathercole, "Pre-existence and the Freedom of the Son in Creation and Redemption: An Exposition in Dialogue with Robert Jenson," *IJST* 7 (2005), 36-49.

PART ONE

Prolegomena

CHAPTER 1

Preexistence in Earliest Christianity

The first two chapters here do not contribute *directly* to the argument for preexistence in the Synoptic Gospels, but function rather as prolegomena. (Since Julius Wellhausen wrote a 568-page *Prolegomena*, two chapters is really not so bad.) These two chapters aim to establish that the case for preexistence is highly plausible, or even that one would actually *expect* to find such a christology in Matthew, Mark, and Luke. Chapter 2 aims to accomplish this by arguing that the heavenly and divine contours of Jesus' identity might encourage the reader to think in terms of a heavenly preexistence of Christ as well. The function of this first chapter is to provide a broader context in earliest Christianity for the interpretation of the Synoptic Gospels. The argument here is simple: *that preexistence christology is already widespread among various individuals and in various different communities around the Mediterranean well before AD 70.* If this is right, then the case for the Synoptic Evangelists having a knowledge of the idea becomes more and more plausible. To this end, we will explore certain key passages from Paul, Hebrews, and finally Jude, as well as their wider implications for the history of earliest Christianity. The evidence from Paul is the most significant; that of Hebrews and Jude is not so certain.

I. Paul

Dating the Pauline correspondence before AD 70 is unproblematic, at least as far as the undisputed Paulines are concerned. We will focus here on a selection of passages which provide the clearest evidence for preexistence. A summary analysis of these will suffice here, since there is general agreement on their interpretation, at least as far as preexistence is concerned.[1] The exegesis of Murphy-O'Connor[2] and Dunn[3] will be noted, however, since they are the two major critics of the majority view.

Active, Personal Preexistence: Philippians 2.6-8 and 2 Corinthians 8.9

For many scholars, Philippians 2 constitutes the highest point of christological reflection in the NT. Certainly for a number the so-called "Philippians hymn" is the clearest statement of preexistence:[4]

> Who, *being in the form of God,*
> > did not reckon equality with God as something to be exploited,
> > but *emptied himself,*
> *Taking the form of a servant,*
> *Coming in human likeness.*
> And being found in appearance as a man,
> > he humbled himself, becoming obedient to death —
> > even death on a cross.

Two key points are relevant to the preexistence discussion. First, as is often noted, the Philippians hymn talks of Christ at the outset "being in the form of

1. For recent statements, see B. Byrne, "Christ's Pre-existence in Pauline Soteriology," *TS* 58 (1997), 308-30; M. Hengel, "Präexistenz bei Paulus?" in C. Landmesser, H.-J. Eckstein, and H. Lichtenberger, eds., *Jesus Christus als die Mitte der Schrift: Studien zur Hermeneutik des Evangeliums* (BZNW 86; Berlin/New York: de Gruyter, 1997), 479-518; T. Söding, "Gottes Sohn von Anfang an. Zur Präexistenzchristologie bei Paulus und den Deuteropaulinen," in R. Laufen, ed., *Gottes ewiger Sohn. Die Präexistenz Christi* (Paderborn: Schöningh, 1997), 53-93; more recently and briefly, L. W. Hurtado, *Lord Jesus Christ: Devotion to Jesus in Earliest Christianity* (Grand Rapids: Eerdmans, 2003), 118-26.

2. The key articles by J. Murphy-O'Connor are "Christological Anthropology in Phil. 2.6-11," *RevB* 83 (1976), 25-50; and "1 Cor. 8.6: Cosmology or Soteriology?" *RevB* 85 (1978), 253-67.

3. In addition to numerous articles, J. D. G. Dunn's earlier statement can be found in his *Christology in the Making: An Inquiry into the Origins of the Doctrine of the Incarnation* (London: SCM, 1980), *passim;* the most recent summary can be found in the section "The Preexistent One" in his *The Theology of Paul the Apostle* (Grand Rapids: Eerdmans/Edinburgh: Clark, 1998), 266-93.

4. G. B. Caird (L. D. Hurst, ed.), *New Testament Theology* (Oxford: Clarendon, 1994), 343; K.-J. Kuschel, *Born before All Time? The Dispute over Christ's Origin* (London: SCM, 1992 [1990]), 243-66.

God" and then "taking the form of a servant."[5] Thus there is a dramatic sequence in these two parallel statements that implies a prior state, or preexistence, "in the form of God," and then a subsequent "form of a servant."

Second, enclosed within these parallel statements is the way in which this movement to "form of a servant" takes place. Crucial here is the description of the incarnation as a *voluntary act.* If Christ "emptied himself," then he is not merely the passive envoy of the Father; the Son, too, is a willing subject of the mission and himself undertakes to assume the form of a servant. His act of emptying himself in the incarnation is paralleled with his act of humbling himself to the point of death. Again, then, there is a strong implication of preexistence, this time from the fact that Christ himself *acted* in the event of the incarnation.

Murphy-O'Connor and Dunn have raised the most well-known objections to seeing preexistence in Philippians 2. According to the former, "A surprise . . . awaits anyone who dispassionately looks for the evidence."[6] On the next page, still near the beginning of Murphy-O'Connor's article, he concludes: "It now appears that the notion of preexistence is only part of the *Vorverständnis* with which exegetes approach the hymn."[7] Murphy-O'Connor's rather cavalier dismissal here rests on questioning the standard view of the "form of God" (μορφὴ θεοῦ), which he thinks is the sole ground for preexistence. There is no discussion of the fact that the incarnation is described in Phil. 2.6-8 as a free act of Christ. Dunn is more cautious than Murphy-O'Connor, but still refuses to see any preexistence of Christ independent of Adamic imagery: "It is the prehistorical existence of Adam as a template on which a vivid Adam christology begins to be drawn."[8] Despite his protests against "either-or exegesis,"[9] Dunn does not give due weight to "emptied himself" (ἑαυτὸν ἐκένωσεν), and so preexistence loses out to Adam christology.

The point still stands, then, that we have in Philippians 2 active, personal preexistence. As Wright puts it, "No mere personification, then, but a person, a conscious individual entity, is envisaged."[10] And in his excellent summary of Phil. 2.6-8: "The pre-existent son regarded equality with God not

---

5. As is frequently noted, "form" (μορφή) refers not to form *in contrast to* reality, but form as *reflection of* reality.

6. Murphy-O'Connor, "Christological Anthropology," 30.

7. Murphy-O'Connor, "Christological Anthropology," 31.

8. Dunn, *Theology of Paul the Apostle,* 292.

9. Dunn, *Theology of Paul the Apostle,* 284, 286-87.

10. N. T. Wright, *The Climax of the Covenant: Christ and the Law in Pauline Theology* (Edinburgh: Clark, 1991), 97.

as excusing him from the task of (redemptive) suffering and death, but actually as uniquely qualifying him for that vocation."[11]

2 Cor. 8.9 does not emphasize the point quite so strongly; the reflexive pronoun in the phrase "he emptied *himself*" in Philippians 2 is distinctive. But the statement ". . . though he was rich, he became poor, so that you through his poverty might become rich" is still clear evidence of preexistence. That "he was rich" supplies a prior state of the Son. This perhaps picks up on Jewish apocalyptic language in which heaven is seen as built of gold and other precious metals and jewels. Alternatively, there may well be a reference to the glorious union of the Father and the Son in eternity, as in John 17.5, where Jesus talks of "the glory that I had with you before the world existed." In 2 Cor. 8.9, as is common in Paul, the incarnation and cross are telescoped into a single action[12] reinforcing the point (often made in German scholarship) that Paul sometimes employs preexistence in order to emphasize the gracious character of the work of Christ on the cross. Phil. 2.7-8 and 2 Cor. 8.9 are both particularly good examples of this.

Descent from Heaven:
1 Corinthians 15.47 and Romans 10.6

Despite attempts to argue to the contrary, there seems to be a fairly clear reference in 1 Cor. 15.47 to Jesus, the second Adam, having come from heaven: "the second man is from heaven." The contrast here is not simply between human beings in their Adamic state and those who belong to Christ: the depiction of Christ as "from heaven" is not simply another way of saying "heavenly" in the sense that his people are also "heavenly" in 1 Cor. 15.48. In Paul's argument here, a person's identity is determined by one's relation either to Adam or to Christ and by the respective origins of these two individuals. Just as Adam literally (in Paul's mind) came from the dust of the earth (Gen. 2.7), so it is perfectly natural for Paul to speak of Christ as having come down from heaven.

This is perhaps seen again in Romans 10.6-7:

> The righteousness that is by faith speaks thus: "Do not say in your heart, 'Who will ascend into heaven?' (that is, to bring Christ down), or 'Who will descend to the abyss?' (that is, to bring Christ up). . . ."

11. Wright, *Climax of the Covenant*, 83-84.

12. Compare Rom. 8.3. On this point in general, see F. B. Watson, "Is There a Story in These Texts?" in B. W. Longenecker, ed., *Narrative Dynamics in Paul: A Critical Assessment* (Louisville: Westminster/John Knox, 2002), 233.

Here, however, it is possible that Paul is focusing primarily on the first element (in v. 6): believers have no need of Christ's physical presence in their midst because they have "internalized" the Gospel (vv. 8-10). In this case, the reference would be to bringing Christ down from heaven where he is *now*. It then would be possible (though still rather strange) that the second element ("bringing Christ up" in v. 7) is simply determined by the other elements of Deuteronomy 30. It is probably more likely, however, that the *sequence* of Christ coming down then going up refers to the sequence of incarnation and ascension, and thus to preexistence. But this is much less clear than the statement in 1 Corinthians 15.

The Lord as Creator: 1 Corinthians 8.6; Colossians 1.16

Paul's interpretation of the *Shema* in 1 Cor. 8.6 is the first place in which he identifies Christ as co-creator with God, talking of "one Lord, Jesus Christ, through whom all things came, and through whom we live." This is a concept he shares with the Johannine Prologue, and (as we shall see) the Epistle to the Hebrews.

What is striking here is that Paul does not identify Jesus purely as an eschatological figure, but also as a protological figure, involved in the very act of creation, with God the Father. This places him at the beginning in Genesis 1, indeed, before the beginning. The roles of God and Christ in creation are not identical: creation is *through* Christ, and *from* the Father. What this means precisely is difficult to determine, but it does not detract from the essential point of Christ's preexistence and involvement in creation.[13]

Murphy-O'Connor's attempt to remove preexistence from Paul's statement here rests on a number of false assumptions. First, he argues that the prepositions point to a movement "from," "through," and "to." This movement, he contends, must have a single direction and can only refer *either* to cosmology *or* to soteriology. "It cannot be both."[14] This seems surprising,

---

13. See, for example, R. J. Bauckham, *God Crucified: Monotheism and Christology in the New Testament* (Carlisle: Paternoster, 1998), 36-40; O. Hofius, "Christus als Schöpfungsmittler und Erlösungsmittler. Das Bekenntnis 1 Kor 8,6 im Kontext der paulinischen Theologie," in idem, *Paulusstudien II* (WUNT; Tübingen: Mohr, 2002), 181-201 (especially 189-91).

14. Murphy-O'Connor, "1 Cor. 8.6," 264. The same either-or is found in Kuschel's argumentation: "1 Kor 8,6 ist also nicht kosmologisch-protologisch, sondern eschatologisch-präsentisch. . . ." K.-J. Kuschel, "Exegese und Dogmatik — Harmonie oder Konflikt? Die Frage nach einer Präexistenzchristologie bei Paulus als Testfall," in Laufen, ed., *Gottes ewiger Sohn*, 143-61 (154).

since creation seems to be rather prominent in the verse. The focus in the verse is not on movement but on beginnings. Secondly, Murphy-O'Connor offers other contributing points, such as the fact that acclamations such as that in 1 Cor. 8.6 are "essentially related to power as experienced" and point to a context in Christian gatherings where "the saving power of Christ was experienced most intensely." Cosmology would be an "abstract and theoretical element" in such a context; the focus is rather "the salvific action of God in Christ."[15] This all seems rather vague, however, and continually gets away from what Paul is actually saying.

Dunn's exegesis reaches the same result via a different route. He argues that in the Jewish background to Paul's thinking here it is Wisdom "through whom all things were made" and that Paul identifies Christ as the embodiment of that personified Wisdom. There is preexistence here, "but it is the preexistence of divine Wisdom. That is, the preexistence of God."[16] Hurtado's comment on Dunn's exegesis here recalls the situation with Murphy-O'Connor: "The problem with this is that it is not what the Pauline passage actually says."[17]

Christ's action as Lord in the work of creation is seen again in Col. 1.16:

> . . . because in him all things were created,
>> in heaven and on earth, things seen and unseen,
>>> whether thrones or dominions, whether principalities or powers;
>>> all things were created through him and for him.

Here the phenomenal scope of Christ's creative power is highlighted, and the prepositions "in" (in the first line above) and "through" (in the last) show the precise role which Christ plays in a creation which is also "for" him. Again, then, we have a considerably strong argument for preexistence from this passage, as well as from 1 Cor. 8.6.

The Sending of the Son: Galatians 4.4 and Romans 8.3

It is commonly (and correctly) observed that "sending" is not in itself a term which presupposes the preexistence of the envoy; as we shall see in more detail later, prophets are also "sent."

However, in Rom. 8.3 we have a reference to sending which points

15. Murphy-O'Connor, "1 Cor. 8.6," 258.
16. Dunn, Theology of Paul the Apostle, 274-75.
17. Hurtado, Lord Jesus Christ, 126, in response to Dunn, Theology of Paul, 274.

strongly in the direction of preexistence:[18] "God sent his own Son, in the likeness of sinful flesh. . . ." Here the key point is the specification of the Son's mission as "in the likeness of sinful flesh," which strongly suggests that in the action of the Father's sending, the Son takes on a condition (the flesh) which he had not previously possessed.[19]

The other important statement of this kind is in Gal. 4.4: "God sent forth his Son, born of a woman, born under the Law. . . ." Four factors are important here. First, there is the similarity between this formula here and that in Rom. 8.3, where the sense of incarnation is much clearer. Moreover, the statement here in Gal. 4.4 stands in parallel to the sending of the Spirit (v. 6). Particularly important, however, is the verb used here. It is not simply ἀποστέλλειν ("send"), but ἐξαποστέλλειν, "send *forth*." This gives a much stronger impression of a mission from God or from the heavenly council. Finally, there is Pannenberg's observation that in this verse "sending is related to the birth, to earthly existence, and to entering into earthly circumstances and relations."[20] Commentators who detect preexistence in this statement, then, are almost certainly correct. And if Galatians is to be dated around AD 48-49, as I would reckon, this is all the more striking.

Christ and Israel: 1 Corinthians 10.4, 9

Much discussed has been the question of what Paul meant when he wrote that in Israel's experience in the wilderness, they drank water from a rock, "and that rock was Christ" (1 Cor. 10.4). Various options have been consid-

---

18. See on this the helpful comments of Douglas Campbell, "The Story of Jesus in Romans and Galatians," in Longenecker, ed., *Narrative Dynamics in Paul*, 119. Campbell makes the helpful categorical distinction between the sending of a *preexistent* person and an "immanent" sending, which is equivalent to a commission or command.

19. Later in the same chapter (Rom. 8.32), Paul talks of God as "the one who did not spare his own Son but gave him up for us all." Again, this is a very compressed statement, probably encompassing both incarnation and cross together, but what is highlighted here is the *love* of God seen in the work of Christ. Byrne emphasizes this point, highlighting that what is at stake with preexistence in Paul is "nothing less than the Pauline view of God who in Jesus Christ has reached out to the world in a costly vulnerability of love" ("Christ's Preexistence," 311). Byrne goes on to amplify this in connection with Rom. 5.15, where he sees the grace of Christ as depicting "Christ's act as an exercise of self-emptying love sufficient to overcome the mass of selfishness involved in human sinfulness of all time" ("Christ's Preexistence," 328).

20. W. Pannenberg, *Systematic Theology* (Grand Rapids: Eerdmans/Edinburgh: Clark, 1994), 2:369.

ered, from typology, or indirect identification via Wisdom (as can be seen in Philo), to a simple identification.[21]

It is certainly striking that Philo employs an allegorical exegesis of this rock, identifying it as Wisdom.[22] It is then very likely that Paul is tapping into preexisting speculation as to whether there was some kind of personal or personified identity behind this rock. What the interaction with this exegetical tradition should not obscure, however, is the extent to which Paul really did think of Christ as active in Israel's wilderness experience here.

Paul's argument does not really work if it is not Christ who is providing the water. In 1 Cor. 10.4-5, Paul is arguing that the Israelites also had Christ accompanying them in the wilderness, but that did not prevent them from being overthrown there. The point Paul goes on to make is that the Corinthians ought not to fall into the same trap: "we should not test Christ, as some of them did" (v. 9).[23] In this later statement it is more difficult to avoid the obvious implication that Paul saw Christ as not only involved in creation, but also continually involved in OT history. It seems that Witherington and Thiselton are correct in their conclusions that "the divine Christ was really a part of Israel's history, providing them with life-giving water,"[24] or, at greater length:

> If we insist on pedantic questions of nomenclature, Paul makes (i) *theological or ontological truth claims* about the agency of the preexistent Christ; (ii) utilizes a *typological context of historical parallels* between *events* in the experience of Israel and *events* in the experience of the church at Corinth; and further *using a suggestive semiotic*, (iii) *may* well be drawing *a cluster of symbolic resonances* as well (if some of the traditions which emerge in Philo and rabbinic sources were widespread as early as Paul's letter).[25]

21. For bibliography, see A. C. Thiselton, *The First Epistle to the Corinthians* (NIGTC; Grand Rapids: Eerdmans, 2000), 720-22.

22. Philo, *Leg. All.* 2.86, on which see H. Conzelmann, *Der erste Brief an die Korinther* (KEK; Göttingen: Vandenhoeck und Ruprecht, [12]1981), 204-5.

23. On the textual issue, see G. Fee, *The First Epistle to the Corinthians* (NICNT; Grand Rapids: Eerdmans, 1987), 457. He calls the "Christ" reading "almost certain," noting that "It easily has the best external support" (457 n. 34). It is given a rating of "B" in Nestle-Aland, and so it is a shame that many English translations are reluctant to use it.

24. B. Witherington, *Conflict and Community in Corinth: A Socio-Rhetorical Commentary on 1 and 2 Corinthians* (Grand Rapids: Eerdmans, 1995), 218, quoted in Thiselton, *The First Epistle to the Corinthians,* 729.

25. Thiselton, *First Epistle to the Corinthians,* 730. Italics original!

Conclusion

In summary, then, Paul employs Christ's preexistence in a number of different contexts. Furthermore, he mentions the idea throughout his letters, perhaps even as early as AD 48-49. What is most striking is that he very often *assumes* it, rather than arguing for it.[26]

What place should be assigned to Paul's employment of Wisdom christology? First, Paul clearly does employ wisdom motifs in his christology. However, early Jewish wisdom speculation is not *decisive* for Paul's employment of preexistence. 1 Corinthians 15, for example, is not shaped by it, nor is the Philippians hymn. The significance of preexistence for Paul is demonstrated, as we have seen, by its appearance in a number of different contexts, such as atonement, Israel's history, and the supremacy of Christ over all things by virtue of his role in creation. Habermann makes the key observation that Jesus Christ is always the criterion for preexistence in Paul, rather than there being a shadowy preexistent entity which is in a secondary sense christological.[27] Kammler's observation is correct, then, that "the preexistence of Christ in Paul . . . is conceived as *absolute, real* and *personal*."[28]

Because of Paul's widespread influence in earliest Christianity, it is difficult to imagine that these conceptions of preexistence were not also held much more widely: Paul's churches and coworkers are the most obvious contenders for sharing Paul's christology. As will be mentioned further at the end of this chapter, these coworkers may well have included one of the Gospel writers.

II. Hebrews

1. Date

The first question to be addressed here concerns the date of Hebrews, since some justification is needed for including it among our snapshots from pre-70 Christianity. There does seem, however, to be a growing consensus (in

---

26. As is commonly the case with much of his christology. See for example, M. Hengel, "Präexistenz bei Paulus?" 492, and Byrne, "Christ's Pre-existence," 315.

27. J. Habermann, *Präexistenzaussagen im Neuen Testament* (Europäische Hochschulschriften; Frankfurt am Main: Lang, 1990), 421.

28. H.-C. Kammler, "Die Prädikation Jesu Christi als 'Gott' (Röm 9,5b)," *ZNW* 94 (2003), 164-80 (176): "Die Präexistenz Christi ist bei Paulus wie auch sonst im Neuen Testament als eine *absolute, reale* und *personale* gefasst."

Anglo-American scholarship, at least) that the epistle does predate the destruction of the Temple.[29] Various arguments about persecution are always of limited value in dating NT documents; it is often very difficult to correlate the localized persecutions mentioned in NT books with the "official" persecutions such as that of Domitian.[30] That the recipients of the letter heard the Gospel from those who heard it from the Lord himself (Heb. 2.3) but were also expected to have been "mature" (in chapter 6) similarly does not give much indication of date.

One option for a date comes from the possible context of the *author,* if he is in the company of those "from Italy" (13.24). This probably does not mean that he is writing from Italy, but rather that he is sending greetings from Italian exiles (cf. Aquila and Priscilla in Acts 18.2).[31] This means that one possible "window" for the composition of the epistle would be AD 49-54.[32] Aquila and Priscilla, for example, have returned to Rome by the time Paul writes to them in AD 56-57. Dating the letter this early, however, must remain a possible, rather than an inevitable conclusion.

Other places in the letter support a pre-70 date, and here the discussion of the sacrificial system is much discussed. That the author talks in the present tense about those ministering at the altar (in passages such as Heb. 8.3-6; 13.10) is not in itself significant; as the commentaries note, the historic present is a standard enough way of speaking, also used by Josephus and Clement. Two points are relevant, however.

First, there is the lack of reference to the destruction of the Temple. Although this is an argument from silence, it is a very significant silence, since the destruction of the Temple would have helped the author's argument a great deal.

Second, the argument at points seems to presume that the Temple cult is still in operation. Heb. 10.1-2 is striking: "For this reason it can never, by the same sacrifices repeated *endlessly* year after year, make perfect those who draw near to worship. *Otherwise, would they not have stopped being offered?*" This is not cut and dried, since it could just mean that any sacrifices offered

29. For the contrary view, among German commentators see, e.g., H. F. Weiss, *Der Brief an die Hebräer* (KEK; Göttingen: Vandenhoeck und Ruprecht, 1991), 76.

30. Weiss, *Brief an die Hebräer,* 77, is far too optimistic in this regard.

31. As Robinson points out, it would be odd if an author in Italy were to describe those with him as "those from Italy"; the phrase fits much better as a description of their origin, as in Acts 18.2. See J. A. T. Robinson, *Redating the New Testament* (London: SCM, 1976), 206.

32. The former being the date of the exile, according to Orosius, and the latter the date of Claudius's death. This is of course following a line of argument which also touches on issues of the date of Romans.

would cease immediately since they would have fully accomplished their purpose.[33] Nevertheless, it would be an odd thing to say if the sacrifices actually had been forcibly brought to an end already. As Koester puts it: "The question expects that listeners will agree with the author, instead of pointing out that sacrifices have in fact ceased being offered because of the Temple's destruction."[34] Equally striking is 8.13: "By calling this covenant 'new' he has made the first one obsolete; and that which is decaying and growing old *is near to destruction.*" This also may well give an indication that the Temple is still standing, while at the same time, perhaps, that events in the land are looking extremely threatening for its continued operation.[35] This would then point to a date in the 60s.

These and other statements need not indicate positively that the Temple was still standing, but it seems a good assumption that many of them would sound rather odd after the Temple's destruction. On these grounds, the growing number of scholars who view Hebrews as pre-70 are almost certainly correct.[36] Both the first half of the 50s and the second half of the 60s are likely times, depending on whether one views the Italian exile situation or the imminent destruction of the Temple as the stronger factor.

2. Preexistence

As for the doctrine of preexistence in Hebrews, it is widespread, and occurs in a number of different forms.

First, Jesus Christ is presented at the outset as a co-agent in creation with God: he is the Son, whom God appointed heir of all things, "through whom he also made the ages" (Heb. 1.2). The plural of "ages" (αἰῶνας) here probably indicates reference both to *this* age (mentioned in 9.9) and "the age to come" (cf. 6.5).[37] A number of scholars speculate that the movement of

33. So similarly P. Ellingworth, *The Epistle to the Hebrews* (NIGTC; Grand Rapids: Eerdmans, 1993), 494.

34. C. Koester, *Hebrews: A New Translation with Introduction and Commentary* (Anchor; New York: Doubleday, 2001), 53. He goes on to note that this, too, is not entirely decisive, because of the author's lack of reference to the Temple itself.

35. F. F. Bruce reckons simply that the fact of the announcement of a new covenant spells the imminent demise of the old (*The Epistle to the Hebrews* [NICNT; Grand Rapids: Eerdmans, 1990], 179). H. Attridge, *The Epistle to the Hebrews* (Hermeneia; Minneapolis: Fortress, 1989), 229 n. 49, similarly rejects a reference to the Temple: "The author argues exegetically, not historically."

36. For lists, see Ellingworth, *Hebrews*, 33 n. 105; Koester, *Hebrews*, 54 n. 114.

37. Koester, *Hebrews*, 178.

thought goes from the eschatological action of God speaking in Christ *back* to the action of the Son in creation: "The author assumed that there was consistency in God's manner of speech, so that the way he spoke at the consummation of time corresponds to the way he spoke at the beginning of time."[38]

Ch. 1 continues in v. 6 to talk of God "bringing his first-born into the world," about which there is considerable controversy.[39] "World" can refer either to the earthly world or to the heavenly world. Indeed, the only other use of οἰκουμένη in Hebrews refers to the world to come (2.5). However, this is a rather unimaginative parallel, since 2.5 refers explicitly to "the world *to come*" (τὴν οἰκουμένην τὴν μέλλουσαν). It would be exceedingly odd, however, for "world" *on its own* to mean anything other than the present inhabited world. There is a genuine difficulty here, however, since the context does point strongly in favor of Christ's exaltation/ascent to heaven. However, reference simply to "world" on its own makes a reference to heaven very awkward, so the reference is probably incarnational.[40]

At the end of ch. 1, the author of Hebrews interprets the address of Ps. 102.25-28 to "the Lord" who "established the earth and made the heavens" as an address of God to Christ (v. 10); thus the Son, and not the Father alone, is also creator.[41] Attridge comments here that in Heb. 1.10, Christ is presented as "eternally sovereign over all things."[42]

Incarnational theology is also strongly in evidence in 2.14, 17 (which Koester compares with Christ's incarnational self-giving in Phil. 2.7)[43] and 5.7-8, which Attridge says "recalls the earlier reference to the incarnation in 2.17."[44] Christ is also described as an eternal being in 7.3, in the comparison

---

38. Koester, *Hebrews*, 186. Cf. also Weiss, *An die Hebräer*, 142, and E. Gräßer, *Der Brief an die Hebräer* (EKK; Zürich: Benziger, 1990), 1:57: both comment that this is the order and "nicht umgekehrt." But the sequence in the text does not necessarily reflect the order in which the author thought.

39. It might well refer to the exaltation, or to the second coming, or to the incarnation. For a summary of the debate, see A. Vanhoye, "L'οἰκουμένη dans l'épitre aux Hébreux," *Biblica* 45 (1964), 248-53. Koester, *Hebrews*, 192 covers some of the more recent discussion.

40. For examples of those taking the opposite view (i.e., "heaven"), see Vanhoye, "L'οἰκουμένη," 250-53; Weiss, *An die Hebräer*, 163-64; Gräßer, *Der Brief an die Hebräer*, 79.

41. Some have argued that such dialogue is itself evidence for preexistence on the grounds that it is dialogue between the Father and the pre-incarnate Son embedded in the OT narrative. The excursus at the end of this chapter argues, however, that this is probably not the case.

42. H. W. Attridge, *The Epistle to the Hebrews* (Hermeneia; Minneapolis: Fortress, 1989), 68. Similarly, Koester: "Heaven is included along with the earth in the created order that is contrasted with the eternal existence of Christ" (*Hebrews*, 195).

43. Koester, *Hebrews*, 232.

44. Attridge, *Hebrews*, 148.

with Melchizedek. Finally, it is possible — though ultimately unlikely — that 11.26 refers to the involvement of Christ in OT history. In this case, Moses "considered reproach for the sake of Christ as greater riches than the treasures of Egypt."[45]

There has been some debate, however, about whether there is any concept of *personal* preexistence in Hebrews. Lindars and Caird are skeptical on this point: "Neither the Fourth Gospel nor Hebrews ever speaks of the *logos* or Wisdom in terms which compel us to regard it as a person."[46] There seems, however, to be clear evidence of the action of the son in the incarnation in statements such as 10.7: "Behold, I have come to do your will, O God." It seems preferable to conclude in favor of personal preexistence rather than to assume that the eternal son is merely an abstraction. Caird's argument with respect to Hebrews here is only slightly more credible than it is for John's Gospel, where Jesus addresses the Father about "the glory that I had with you before the world existed" (John 17.5).

III. Jude

Finally, we come to Jude. Although less certain, Jude's evidence is valuable in that it may provide evidence from earliest *Palestinian* Christianity in a way that Hebrews and Paul do not. It also provides some distinctive evidence for preexistence that makes it unique in the NT.

1. The Date of Jude

The date of Jude depends on three factors: the authenticity of the prescript, the letter's relation to 2 Peter, and other internal evidence. Each of these naturally affects how the other is to be understood. In terms of authorship, it seems very probable that the *claim* is to authorship by Jude the brother of Je-

---

45. In favor, see the discussion by A. T. Hanson, "The Reproach of the Messiah in the Epistle to the Hebrews," in E. A. Livingstone, ed., *Studia Theologica VII: Papers Presented to the Fifth International Congress on Biblical Studies Held at Oxford, 1973* (Berlin: Akademie, 1982), 231-40. As Weiss notes, however, there is not really any solid evidence for the preexistence reading (Weiss, *Brief an die Hebräer,* 607).

46. Caird, *New Testament Theology,* 342-43. Hurst follows a similar line (and perhaps already does in Caird, *New Testament Theology!*). L. D. Hurst, "The Christology of Hebrews 1 and 2," in Hurst and N. T. Wright, eds., *The Glory of Christ in the New Testament* (Oxford: Clarendon, 1987), 151-64.

sus. Furthermore, Bauckham is surely right that there is no compelling evidence against authenticity.[47] In terms of the relation to 2 Peter, the majority of scholars now see the direction of dependence to be from Jude to 2 Peter rather than the other way around.

With respect to the internal evidence, Bauckham is again right to dispute both that an "early Catholicism" is reflected in v. 3, and that a retrospective nostalgia can be seen in v. 17 in the statement, "But you, brothers, remember the words spoken by the apostles of our Lord Jesus Christ, when they said to you. . . ."[48] This is an interesting statement, which as Bauckham rightly indicates, points to a date near the generation of the apostles rather than far subsequent to it: *Jude points to the fact that the audience (at least in part) heard the apostles warning them of the end of days.* On the other hand, I would dispute Bauckham's interpretation of "the apostles of our Lord Jesus Christ" here as the founding missionaries of the church being addressed: the phrase appears to be rather formal and to have an almost titular or technical sense, like, say, "the Twelve." It is more likely, then, that the church at one time received a delegation consisting of some of the Jerusalem apostles, perhaps. Bauckham comments that there is no reason to place the letter later than the 50s. Knight gives a broader range, commenting that if the letter is authentic, any time between 40 and 70 is possible.[49] One possibility arises from the fact that 1 Cor. 9.5 indicates brothers of the Lord as active in the mid-50s and so gives as plausible a setting as any for Jude's missionary and letter-writing activity. Since our evidence is so fragmentary, however, a precise timeframe of this kind cannot be more than a possibility.

2. The Text of Jude 5: "Jesus" or "Lord"?

As far as preexistence is concerned, the most important question has been the textual problem of Jude 5. Who is it that "saved the people [once] from Egypt, and thereafter destroyed those who did not believe"? Nestle-Aland, and therefore the majority of the English translations, have "the Lord" rather than "Jesus" as the subject of the sentence. However, this reading is given a rating of *D* in the apparatus to the UBS Greek New Testament: "The letter D, which occurs only rarely, indicates that the committee had great difficulty in arriving

---

47. R. J. Bauckham, *Jude, 2 Peter* (WBC; Waco: Word, 1983), 14-16.

48. Bauckham, *Jude, 2 Peter,* 13-14.

49. J. Knight, *2 Peter and Jude* (New Testament Guides; Sheffield: Sheffield Academic, 1995), 27.

at a decision."[50] We will comment further on the committee's opinions later. The argument in favor of reading "Jesus" as opposed to "the Lord" will be put in eight propositions:

i. The textual alternatives are "Jesus," "the Lord," "God," and "Christ, God." Hardly any scholars, however, have opted for either of the latter two, since they are so poorly attested. We are left with "the Lord" and "Jesus" as the serious options.

ii. The consensus is that, considered on purely *external* grounds, the reading "Jesus" is much more preferable. The minority report of the UBS Editorial Committee comments: "Critical principles seem to require the adoption of Ἰησοῦς, which admittedly is the best attested reading among Greek and versional witnesses."[51] Osburn, the author of the most substantial treatment of the problem, uses almost identical language: "the former reading has the best attestation among Greek and versional witnesses and . . . critical principles seem to require its adoption."[52] In addition to this manuscript evidence, there is a marginal comment in a minuscule manuscript (1739) attributing to Origen (d. 254) the comment: "Jude says in his epistle, 'For Jesus once saved the people from Egypt, and thereafter destroyed those who did not believe.'"[53]

iii. The principal reason for rejecting the reading "Jesus" is internal, in other words, the *a priori* unlikelihood of the writer saying that Christ was an agent in the exodus. Matthew Black, another Editorial Committee member, comments that "there does not seem to me to be any question about the right reading on internal grounds."[54] The problem with Black's argument, however, is that he considers the only two possibilities as "Lord" or "Joshua" (Ἰησοῦς). Despite the manuscript evidence, the majority of the committee (three of the five) decided that on sense grounds the reading Ἰησοῦς was "difficult to the point of impossibility."[55]

---

50. B. Aland, et al., *The Greek New Testament* (Stuttgart: UBS/Deutsche Bibelgesellschaft, ⁴1993), 3.

51. B. M. Metzger, *A Textual Commentary on the Greek New Testament* (London: United Bible Societies, 1971), 726. The minority is Metzger and Wikgren.

52. C. D. Osburn, "The Text of Jude 5," *Biblica* 62 (1981), 107-15 (107). For full details of the evidence, see K. Aland, ed., *Text und Textwert der Griechischen Handschriften des Neuen Testaments. I: Die Katholischen Briefe.* Volume I: *Das Material* (Berlin: de Gruyter, 1987), 205-9.

53. Quoted in Osburn, "The Text of Jude 5," 109.

54. M. Black, "Notes on Three NT Texts," in W. Eltester, ed., *Apophoreta. Festschrift für Ernst Haenchen zu seinem siebzigsten Geburtstag* (Berlin: Töpelmann, 1964), 39-45 (45).

55. Metzger, *Textual Commentary*, 726.

iv. A further reason offered by the Committee is that "nowhere else does the author employ Ἰησοῦς alone, but always Ἰησοῦς Χριστός."[56] However, this is a rather desperate argument: it is extremely hazardous to attempt to identify tendencies in nomenclature in a letter so short as Jude.

v. The final justification offered for the Committee's decision has been on the grounds of transcriptional error (the abbreviation "KC" read as "IC"). In the final analysis, however, transcriptional error should not be supposed if the reading best attested can be seen to make good sense, although it of course always remains a possibility.

vi. Even when there is considerable variation in manuscripts among *nomina sacra,* Ἰησοῦς does not usually figure in this variety. A brief examination of the *apparatus* to Nestle-Aland does not seem to give any indication of this, and Fossum wonders "*why* a copyist could feel able to substitute Ἰησοῦς for Kyrios."[57] Interestingly, Bauckham admits this, even though he takes the authentic reading to be κύριος:

> It should be noted initially that to some extent this textual situation is not unusual, since there are many places, especially in the Pauline corpus, where the text varies between two of the three words κύριος, θεός and Χριστός, and in some cases between all three. . . . What is exceptional in Jude 5 is the reading Ἰησοῦς, which there seems to be no evidence of scribes deliberately substituting for κύριος or θεός elsewhere.[58]

What this means is that "Jesus" is more likely to be original, since κύριος is more likely to be replaced by Χριστός or θεός. It is difficult to imagine why a scribe would change KC (κύριος) *to* IC (Ἰησοῦς).[59]

vii. On the other hand, there is every reason for a scribe to change IC to KC. One can imagine both orthodox and unorthodox clarifications. In the

---

56. Metzger, *Textual Commentary,* 726, an argument also noted in R. J. Bauckham, *Jude and the Relatives of Jesus in the Early Church* (Edinburgh: Clark, 1990), 308-9, and C. Landon, *A Text-Critical Study of the Epistle of Jude* (JSNTSS; Sheffield: Sheffield Academic, 1996), 73-74.

57. J. Fossum, "Kyrios Jesus as the Angel of the Lord in Jude 5-7," *NTS* 33 (1987), 226-43 (226).

58. Bauckham, *Jude and the Relatives,* 308.

59. Bauckham (*Jude and the Relatives,* 309) and Landon (*Text-Critical Study,* 72-73) appeal here to the Joshua-Jesus typology current in the second century, but it is difficult to see how this could lead to a modification from "Lord" to Ἰησοῦς when it is the exodus and the punishment in the wilderness that are in view: the Joshua typology does not work here.

first case, it might seem odd to an orthodox scribe (as it does to most modern scholars) to use the name "Jesus" in connection with an action prior to the incarnation. In this case, it would make sense for a scribe to clarify that it is not Jesus in his human nature who freed the Israelites but rather Jesus in his identity as the preexistent κύριος, and, in other manuscripts, as θεός.

viii. While this is perfectly possible, an *un*orthodox corruption of Scripture is somewhat more attractive. The Fathers talk frequently about this kind of practice. For example, a fragment preserved in Eusebius (*EH* 5.28) charges the Monarchians Artemon and Theodotus with changing biblical texts to prove their own doctrine, denying the divinity of Christ and that Christ is the Logos.[60] Osburn mentions a fragment of Origen's *Stromateis* (pre-232), which talks of people tampering with preexistence texts in his time, and a further work, *The Little Labyrinth,* which provides evidence of altering of such passages around 199-218 by Asclepiodotus, Theodotus, Hermophilus, and Apollonius. We can perhaps see this at work in 1 Cor. 10.9, from the textual *apparatus* there. Osburn concludes that in Jude 5 as well it is reasonable to suggest that this milieu was conducive to the alteration of Ἰησοῦς to κύριος or θεός.[61] It is easy to see, then, how Ἰησοῦς could give rise to the other readings which we have: it is more difficult to argue that the change would have gone the other way.[62]

The assumption in the NT guild is that considerable burden of proof rests on those who would dispute the Nestle-Aland reading. However, here we have a case in which two out of five of the committee — Bruce Metzger and Allen Wikgren — still argued for Ἰησοῦς, and so, as we noted above, the committee had great difficulty in deciding which reading to print in the Greek NT. Further, it seems that Matthew Black was operating with a very limited range of options (*either* "Lord" *or* "Joshua"). Wikgren (one of the minority) has produced a longer study of the problem which is far more penetrating than Black's inadequate note.[63] Similarly, the other major article, by Osburn, also

---

60. See Loeb edition, 1:516-25.

61. Osburn, "The Text of Jude 5," 115.

62. A further, very tentative observation: it is interesting that there seems to be some overlap between manuscripts which preserve the variants with "lower" christologies in 1 Corinthians 10 and the manuscripts which deviate from Ἰησοῦς in Jude 5, specifically in ℵ, C, 436, and 1175.

63. A. Wikgren, "Some Problems in Jude 5," in B. L. Daniels and M. J. Suggs, eds., *Studies in the History and Text of the New Testament in Honor of Kenneth Willis Clark* (Studies and Documents; Salt Lake City: University of Utah Press, 1967), 147-52.

argues for the reading "Jesus."[64] There is good reason, then, to follow the verdicts of the minority report of the committee, and of the two major studies of the problem, and to read "Jesus" as the subject.

One final observation. *Even if* the reading "Lord" is correct, there is still substantial evidence that Jude understands this as a reference to Jesus. All but one of the other usages in Jude of the title "Lord" are in connection with Jesus, although we need to bear in mind the caution above about drawing conclusions about usage on the basis of only 25 verses of text. Jude's reference to the activity of the heretics in v. 8 includes the fact that they "reject authority," more literally the lordly rule of Christ (κυριότητα), as well as slander heavenly beings. These heretics will be condemned "when the Lord comes with the tens of thousands of his holy angels to carry out judgment . . ." (vv. 14-15). Jesus is called "Lord" again in vv. 17, 21, and 25. Particularly striking, however, is the fact that the previous verse (v. 4) describes Jesus as "our *only* Master and Lord." This makes a potential subsequent reference to "the Lord" immediately afterward in v. 5 highly likely to be christological.[65] So even if the reading "Lord" is correct, it is quite possible — unless one presupposes an evolutionary christology whereby since Jude is "primitive" it could not display preexistence christology — that Jude refers to Jesus as active in history before his incarnation.

3. The Substance of Christ's Activity

The activity of the Lord Jesus here consists of three (or perhaps four) elements:[66] Jesus (a) "saved the people out of Egypt," then (b) "destroyed those who did not believe." Furthermore, (c) "angels who did not stay within their own position of authority, but left their proper dwelling, he has kept in eternal chains under gloomy darkness until the judgment of the great day" (Jude 5-6).

That Jesus "saved the people from Egypt" is in one sense a straightforward enough statement. The reference is clearly to the exodus from Egypt, which makes impossible the idea that the Ἰησοῦς in question is Joshua.[67] But

64. Landon's study (*Text-Critical Study*, 70-77) is also comparatively lengthy, but offers no new evidence or arguments.

65. I am grateful to my colleague Dr. Peter Williams for this observation.

66. In addition to literature already cited, see further F. Maier, "Zur Erklärung des Judasbriefes (Jud 5)," *BZ* 2 (1904), 391-97; A. F. J. Klijn, "Jude 5 to 7," in W. C. Weinreich, ed., *The New Testament Age: Essays in Honor of Bo Reicke* (Macon: Mercer University Press, 1984), 1:237-44.

67. Suggested already by Jerome, and later by E. E. Kellett, "Note on Jude 5," *ExpT* 15

is Jude identifying Jesus here straightforwardly with (a) "the Lord who brought you out of Egypt" (as per Deut. 6.21, etc.) or with (b) the angel of the Lord who went before and behind the Israelites (Exod. 14.19; 23.20)? Here Fossum argues for the identification of Jesus with an angelic figure. By contrast, on the basis of Jude's application to Christ of texts which refer to God (*1 Enoch* 1.9 in Jude 14-15), it is perhaps a more economical solution simply to view Jude as thinking in terms of the inclusion of Jesus within the divine identity. The angelic interpretation is not necessarily so different, however, since the distinction between the Lord and his angel in the Pentateuch is often rather blurred.

Jesus "thereafter destroyed those who did not believe." Here the reference is to those who died in the wilderness in Numbers 14.

Thirdly, he also bound in chains the angels who did not obey the authority over them. This is significant because the event referred to here predates even the exodus and the wilderness wanderings and identifies Jesus' activity in primeval time. Apart from the references to Christ as creator, this would be the only such case (of Christ's action in *primeval* time) in the NT.[68] Some have also included the destruction of Sodom and Gomorrah in this list of Christ's preexistent activities, although it is not clear that this is also in view.

The final point to be noted is that which causes the difficulty for all the textual critics in the first place: Jude appears to be the first Christian author to refer to the pre-incarnate Christ as "Jesus." In fact, however, this is not nearly so unusual as is commonly thought. As noted above, it is the person of Jesus Christ who is continuous with the preexistent one, such that Paul can talk specifically of "Christ Jesus" as the one "who being in the form of God . . . made himself nothing" (Phil. 2.6-7), and as the one "through whom all things were made" (1 Cor. 8.6). Jude's statement is really no different in kind, and it is interesting to note that all this is taking place in a text written by one whose "real intellectual background is in the literature of Palestinian Judaism."[69]

(1903-4), 381. Wikgren ("Some Problems in Jude 5," 148) is a little sympathetic to the interpretation, though he does not follow it. Osburn decisively demolishes it ("The Text of Jude 5," 112). Joshua neither rescued the people from Egypt, nor destroyed them in the wilderness, and most certainly did not bind the fallen angels: if Joshua is the subject of v. 5, then the verb τετήρηκεν in v. 6 is left without a subject.

68. Assuming that Luke 10.18 is not referring to a primeval event. See S. J. Gathercole, "Jesus' Eschatological Vision of the Fall of Satan," *ZNW* 94 (2003), 143-63.

69. Bauckham, *Jude 2, Peter* 7.

Conclusion

We have seen, then, that there is a widespread belief in the preexistence of Christ in pre-70 Christian communities.[70] Paul does not reflect at length on the preexistence of Christ, in part because he assumes his audiences to be both familiar with it and in agreement with him on the matter. Thus, it should be concluded that the Roman, Galatian, Corinthian, and Philippian Christians, as well as those in Colossae (and Laodicea as well: see Col. 4.16) were familiar with the doctrine of Christ's preexistence very probably before they received their epistles (and if not before, then certainly after). It may well be that motifs which we have picked up on were familiar aspects of Paul's missionary proclamation (especially points such as "God sent his Son") such that other Christian communities which Paul founded or taught in — but which did not receive an extant letter — would also be familiar with them: Antioch would undoubtedly be one example. If the undisputed letters of Paul which we have discussed above amount to about five hours worth of spoken material, it does not take much historical imagination to see that references to preexistence would have been frequent in Paul's teaching.[71] We should probably assume that in addition to Paul himself, those who were involved in ministry with him (and particularly in the coauthoring the letters we have discussed!) would be acquainted with his distinctive understanding of Christ's preexistence: Barnabas and Silas for long periods of time, those people who constitute the much discussed "us" in the "we" passages in Acts, Sosthenes (coauthor of 1 Corinthians), and Timothy (coauthor of 2 Corinthians, Colossians, and Philippians).

It would be even more significant for the interpretation of the Synoptic Gospels if any of them were composed by an associate of Paul. In the case of Mark, much twentieth-century scholarship was dominated by the view that Mark and Paul were entirely independent. Recently, however, Joel Marcus has commented that "now the tide appears to be shifting, and several scholars have recently contended that Mark should be situated in the Pauline sphere of activity."[72] Of course, there is an even stronger connection between the author of the Third Gospel and Paul, since the "we" passages in Acts strongly suggest that the Evangelist really was an associate of the apostle.[73]

---

70. If one were more ambitious, it would be possible at least to discuss the christologies underlying Jas. 5.10 and 1 Pet. 1.20 as well.

71. On this point, see Hengel, "Präexistenz bei Paulus?" 492.

72. J. Marcus, "Mark — Interpreter of Paul," *NTS* 46.4 (2000), 473-87 (474).

73. The burden of proof surely rests heavily on those who would argue for the alternative. For the most comprehensive treatment of this issue, see C.-J. Thornton, *Der Zeuge des Zeugen. Lukas als Historiker der Paulusreisen* (WUNT; Tübingen: Mohr, 1991).

The evidence from Hebrews and Jude is of course not so strong, not least because they cannot be so securely dated prior to AD 70. But on the basis of the arguments above, it is probable that, in addition to the Pauline churches, the community which received Hebrews also knew about the kind of preexistence spelled out in that letter. Further, Jude gives us an example of an early Jewish Christian who had a christology in which the preexistent Christ had repeatedly been active prior to his incarnation. Sometimes the impression is given of Paul as a lone early voice for preexistence, a one-off who anticipated the real flourishing of preexistence in the late first century. But it is hard to see how this would be the case, especially given how widespread Paul's influence was. In fact, the burden of proof is rather on those who would try to discover Christian groups who did *not* accept or know about the preexistence of Christ.

Excursus: "Prophetic Dialogue"[1] in Hebrews

Returning to the christology of Hebrews, there is the phenomenon of OT passages being put into the mouth of Christ, or being described as address from the Father to the Son. This has been seen by some commentators as necessarily involving speech by or to the *preexistent* Son. Passages typically important here are Heb. 1.5-13 and 2.12-13:[2]

> For to which of the angels did God ever say,
>   "You are my Son, today I have begotten you"?
> Or again, "I will be to him a father, and he shall be to me a son"? (1.5)

> For he who sanctifies and those who are sanctified all have one origin.
> That is why he (Jesus) is not ashamed to call them brothers, saying,
>   "I will tell of your name to my brothers;
>   in the midst of the congregation I will sing your praise."
> And again, "I will put my trust in him."
> And again, "Behold, I and the children God has given me." (2.11-13)

Hanson comments on these: "in 1.5, 1.7-13 we have the Father addressing the Son in Psalms. In 2.12, 13 we find the Son addressing the Father."[3]

---

1. This helpful designation comes from A. T. Hanson, *Jesus Christ in the Old Testament* (London: SCM, 1965), 139.

2. Commentators also note 5.5-6; 7.17, 21; and 10.5-9.

3. Hanson, *Jesus Christ in the Old Testament*, 140. This line presumes, of course, that 1.5 is a statement *to* the Son, rather than *about* the Son.

Opinion is, nevertheless, still divided over the validity of applying the prophetic dialogue model here. Some scholars see the reference as to an undefined address by God to the earthly Jesus,[4] and others understand the point to be the human Christ's encounter with Scripture.[5] A number of scholars, however, do see reference to preexistence in these "dialogues." A similar position to that of Hanson was also taken by T. F. Glasson.[6] More recently, Paul Ellingworth and Robert Gordon have also argued for speech by the preexistent Christ in some of these passages, as does Erich Gräßer: "The Letter to the Hebrews presupposes the basic 'Christian-ness' [Christlichkeit] of the OT, which corresponds to the eschatological approach to its use of Scripture, according to which the OT is the word of the preexistent Christ (2.12-13; 10.5-7)."[7]

The problem lies in identifying how much the author envisaged as he carried out his exegesis of the Septuagint. None of the authors mentioned above supply any particular evidence why these OT references should be understood as (a) statements made by the Father to the preincarnate Son (or *vice versa*), or (b) symbolic statements in a register different from Hebrews' regular theological expression, which express the status of Christ as divine Son and priest. One could, of course, appeal to the fact that the "plain sense" of the statements does point in favor of preexistence.

While understanding these uses of the OT in Hebrews as prophetic dialogue is in some ways attractive, the situation is a little more complex. In fact, in addition to the speech of Father and Son (and indeed Spirit, in 3.7), there is also speech between God and the Christian believer in 13.5-6:

> Keep your life free from love of money, and be content with what you have, for he has said, "I will never leave you nor forsake you." So we say with confidence, "The Lord is my helper; I will not fear; what can man do to me?"

---

4. G. B. Caird (L. D. Hurst, ed.), *New Testament Theology* (Oxford: Clarendon, 1994), 64: "God addresses the man Jesus." He goes on to argue that Heb. 10.5 is not about Jesus' birth but about the beginning of his adult ministry (67 n. 72). Here, however, the subject is "a body prepared" and is therefore specifically incarnational.

5. D. G. Peterson, *Hebrews and Perfection: An Examination of the Concept of Perfection in the Epistle to the Hebrews* (SNTSMS; Cambridge: Cambridge University Press, 1982), 147.

6. T. F. Glasson, "'Plurality of Divine Persons' and the Quotations in Hebrews I.6ff.," *NTS* 12 (1965-66), 270-72.

7. E. Gräßer, *Der Brief an die Hebräer* (EKK; Zürich: Benziger, 1990), 1:72: "Der Hebr setzt die prinzipielle 'Christlichkeit' des Alten Testaments voraus, entsprechend der eschatologischen Gesamtvoraussetzung seiner Schriftbenutzung, wonach auch das Alte Testament 'Wort des (präexistenten) Christus' ist (2,12-13; 10,5-7)."

The author clearly does not regard the conversation between God and the Christian here as predating the coming of Christ.[8] In the light of this example, it seems much more likely that the author regards the OT as a kind of script for a drama. Some of the content is located at specific events (e.g. Heb. 10.5-7). More specifically, some passages are concerned with expressing the Son's willingness to obey the Father in carrying out his purpose through incarnation, death and exaltation (2.13a; 10.7). More commonly, however, the OT language used is more concerned with describing the identity of the Son, as determined by the Father (1.5-13). In other words, Hebrews uses the OT as a dramatic script to construct imaginary lines or speaking parts for God, the Son, and Christian believers. Therefore, while it is clear that Hebrews elsewhere understands Christ as preexistent (1.1-4, etc.), it is risky to use prophetic dialogue texts to bolster such a view.

8. However, it is possible that here the author envisages the words of Ps. 118.6 as spoken by the "preexistent church," that is to say, by *Israel*. I am grateful to Richard Sturch for this observation.

CHAPTER 2

The Transcendence of Christ
in Matthew, Mark, and Luke

Introduction

The previous chapter aimed to provide evidence of the widespread dispersion of preexistence christology in earliest Christianity, with the implication that preexistence would be an idea which the Gospel writers might have found it difficult to avoid. The present chapter functions as the second half of the preparatory work for the exegesis of the relevant passages in the Synoptic Gospels, offering evidence that the Synoptic Gospels present Jesus as a transcendent, heavenly, divine figure.

This has already been identified by some recent scholarship, as was highlighted in the introduction. For example, L. Hurtado's work has argued that the claims made in the Synoptic Gospels "amount to considerably more than merely claiming royal-messianic status for Jesus."[1] Furthermore, Hurtado frequently uses the language of "transcendence" in connection with the christology of Matthew, Mark, and Luke.[2] This chapter aims to develop this paradigm further by clarifying exactly what it is that Jesus transcends, or goes beyond; "transcend" is a transitive verb. The focus here will not (yet) be on the issue of preexistence, which is of course itself a kind of transcendence,

1. L. W. Hurtado, "Pre–70 CE Jewish Opposition to Christ-Devotion," *JTS* 50 (1999), 35-58 (38).

2. Hurtado, "Jewish Opposition to Christ-Devotion," 39, 40, 44; idem, *Lord Jesus Christ: Devotion to Jesus in Earliest Christianity* (Grand Rapids: Eerdmans, 2003), 285, and, on the "Son of God" title, 287. See further the references under the index entry "Jesus' Titles: Son of God, in Synoptics."

the temporal transcendence of Jesus' earthly ministry not only after his death (post-existence), but also before his birth. Rather, the focus here will be on three elements: (I) Jesus' transcendence of the heaven-earth divide, (II) Jesus' transcendence of the God-creation divide, and (III) the pre- and post-resurrection Jesus as transcending space. The present chapter will only offer snapshots from the Synoptic Gospels since an exhaustive study is of course out of the question here. However, if this case is made, then there are perhaps further grounds for reading the material which will be discussed later as offering evidence for preexistence christology.

I. Jesus' Transcendence of the Heaven-Earth Divide

Perhaps the most useful evidence to prepare the way for the discussion of preexistence is the material in the Synoptics where Jesus transcends the heaven-earth divide. In Matthew, Mark, and Luke, Jesus is regarded *already in the earthly, pre-Easter situation* as having a heavenly identity; that is to say, he is a figure who is not merely firmly planted on earth, but is also operating at the same time in the heavenly sphere. The tension between Jesus' heavenly identity and his existence within the earthly realm is a point which will be revisited at the end of this section.

Jesus' Heavenly Identity as "Son" in the Transfiguration (Mark 9.2-8 par. Matthew 17.1-8; Luke 9.28-36)

As the commentators note, scholars have come to a very wide variety of interpretations of the transfiguration.[3] To take a very small selection, in the heyday of the *religionsgeschichtliche Schule,* Ernst Lohmeyer argued in one of the first scholarly articles on the transfiguration that it points to Jesus as a Hellenistic god-figure come down temporarily from heaven.[4] Marcus, by contrast, sees the focus in highlighting Jesus as the "prophet-like-Moses" of Deuteronomy 18.[5] Pesch sees it as a revelation of Jesus as the Son of Man.[6] Gundry talks of

---

3. See for example the comments by J. Gnilka, *Das Evangelium nach Markus. 2: Mk 8,27–16,20* (EKK II/2; Zurich: Benziger, 1979), 37.

4. E. Lohmeyer, "Die Verklärung Jesu nach dem Markus-Evangelium," *ZNW* 21 (1922), 185-215 (205).

5. J. Marcus, *The Way of the Lord: Christological Exegesis of the Old Testament in the Gospel of Mark* (Louisville: Westminster John Knox, 1992), 80-93.

6. R. Pesch, *Das Markusevangelium. 2: Kommentar zu Kapitel 8,27–16,20* (HTK; Freiburg: Herder, 1977), 73-74.

Jesus' divinity being revealed, but along OT rather than Hellenistic lines.[7] The importance of the transfiguration for our argument here lies in the fact that it gives ample evidence for Jesus' transcendence of his earthly existence, such that he is also envisaged simultaneously as a heavenly figure. The opening of the transfiguration in Mark 9.2-4 (and parallels), and the voice in v. 7 are the key elements here:

> And after six days Jesus took with him Peter, James and John, and led them up a high mountain by themselves. And he was transfigured before them, and his clothes became radiant, intensely white, as no one on earth could bleach them. And there appeared to them Elijah with Moses, and they were talking with Jesus. . . . And a cloud overshadowed them, and a voice came out of the cloud, "This is my beloved Son: listen to him."

In Mark 9.2, then, Jesus ascends a "high mountain," and by the action of God is transformed. A number of commentators interpret the mountain as something of a "suburb of heaven," or a "half-way house between earth and heaven."[8] This is preferable to the view that the mountain actually *is* heaven;[9] otherwise it is difficult to account, on the one hand, for the heavenly identities of Jesus, Elijah, and Moses, and — on the other — for the fact that Peter, James, and John remain unchanged.[10]

Verse 3 takes up the transformation of Jesus' clothes: they are whiter than any launderer *on earth* could wash them, hence they reflect a *heavenly* whiteness.[11] Bauckham has pointed out that shining garments are not necessarily evidence of a *divine* person, but are strongly resonant of *heavenly* identity. In discussing the motif in Jewish literature, he talks of

> . . . a standard set of descriptives that could be used to describe any heavenly being, including quite ordinary as well as quite exalted heavenly be-

---

7. R. H. Gundry, *Mark: A Commentary on His Apology for the Cross* (Grand Rapids: Eerdmans, 1993), 458.

8. Respectively, Gundry, *Mark,* 457, and J. Fossum, "Ascensio, Metamorphosis: The 'Transfiguration' of Jesus in the Synoptic Gospels," in idem, *The Image of the Invisible God: Essays on the Influence of Jewish Mysticism on Early Christology* (Novum Testamentum et Orbis Antiquus 30; Freiburg/Göttingen: Vandenhoeck und Ruprecht, 1995), 71-94 (72). Fossum does not actually endorse this definition, however, despite offering some parallels to the idea from the *Testament of Levi,* the *Ascension of Isaiah,* and the *Apocalypse of Peter.*

9. See Fossum, "Ascensio, Metamorphosis," 72-76.

10. *Pace* Fossum, "Ascensio, Metamorphosis," 91, it does not appear to be the case that "Peter has grasped that he is in heaven."

11. Pesch, *Markusevangelium,* 2:73.

ings. The basic idea behind all these descriptions is that heaven and its inhabitants are shining and bright. Hence the descriptions employ a stock series of images of brightness: heavenly beings or their dress are typically shining like the sun or the stars, gleaming like bronze or precious stones, fiery bright like torches or lightning, dazzling white like snow or pure wool.[12]

For a Markan parallel, the young man in a white robe in Mark 16.5 is clearly an angelic figure. In Matthew's and Luke's accounts of the transfiguration, furthermore, it is explicit that not only Jesus' clothes, but also his *face* was transformed: in Matthew it shines like the sun (Matt. 17.2), and in Luke, its appearance is altered as Jesus is praying (Luke 9.29). However, Mark's account should probably not be understood, by contrast, as a mere change in Jesus' clothing: the reference to Jesus being "transformed" in Mark 9.2 is probably *supplemented by* the reference to the clothes rather than *interpreted as* simply his clothes becoming dazzling. Furthermore, there is no evidence in any of this that "the radiance is connected with 'borrowed glory,'" as Kee puts it.[13] The narrative does not suggest that Jesus' glory in Mark 9.2-3 *really* belongs to someone else.

This heavenly character of Jesus is reinforced by verse 4, where Jesus talks to Elijah and Moses. In Luke's version, the heavenly identity of these two is emphasized by the reference to their appearance "in glory" (Luke 9.31). Pesch, in his discussion of Mark, is probably right to comment here: "The fact that Elijah and Moses speak with Jesus indicates . . . that Jesus belongs to their world."[14]

Where Pesch is almost certainly wrong, however, is in his insistence on the *merely* proleptic, or anticipatory, character of the transfiguration, and that there is little sense that this heavenly identity of Jesus belongs to Jesus in the present in his ministry.[15] Where his view falls down is in the fact that the

12. R. J. Bauckham, "The Throne of God and the Worship of Jesus," in C. C. Newman, J. R. Davila, and G. S. Lewis, eds., *The Jewish Roots of Christological Monotheism* (Leiden: Brill, 1999), 43-69 (51).

13. H. C. Kee, "The Transfiguration in Mark: Epiphany or Apocalyptic Vision?" in J. Reumann, ed., *Understanding the Sacred Text. FS M. Enslin* (Valley Forge: Judson, 1972), 135-52 (144).

14. Pesch, *Markusevangelium*, 2:74: "Daß Elija und Mose mit Jesus reden . . . zeigt an, daß Jesus ihrer Welt zugehört." The essential point is that Elijah and Moses appear *alongside* Jesus — there is of course even in the transfiguration pericope communication between God and the disciples, but it is communication from God *down to* the disciples.

15. Pesch, *Markusevangelium*, 2:72, 74; Kee in particular emphasizes this line ("Transfiguration in Mark," 144, 149-50). Cf. to some extent Gundry, *Mark*, 477.

heavenly identity of Jesus revealed in the transfiguration is so closely tied to his revelation as God's *Son:* the purpose of God's action in transforming Jesus in this way is to show the disciples what is actually the case, namely Jesus' divine sonship. For the readers of Matthew, Mark, and Luke, however, Jesus has been the divine Son throughout his ministry: already at the baptism, Jesus is the Son of God. As a result, it seems that Jesus' shining heavenly identity shown forth in the transfiguration is not merely proleptic of the resurrection or parousia in the future, but is also already present just as his identity as Son of God is already a present reality.

The Heavenly Hierarchy (Mark 13.32 par. Matthew 24.36)

This is further reinforced by the probable reference to Jesus' heavenly identity as Son in Mark 13.32 par. Matt. 24.36, in reference to the question of who knows the date of the end of the age: "About that day, and the hour, no one knows: not even the angels in heaven, nor the Son — only the Father." We will examine below the *divine* hierarchy of Father, Son and Holy Spirit in Matthew 28. The statement under discussion here is slightly different in that we seem here to have a hierarchy simply of *heavenly* beings: Father — Son — Angels.[16] The point of the statement is that we would perhaps *expect* the Son and the angels to know the date of the end: as heavenly beings, are they not privy to the secrets of the divine council? The answer is that, despite who they are, God has kept secret even from them when the end will come. The presupposition is, then, that Jesus is a heavenly being like God and the angels. These observations specifically connected with the "ignorance logion"[17] only apply to Mark and Matthew; Luke omits the saying.

Jesus in the Heavenly Council
(Luke 10.18-20; 22.31-32; 10.21 par. Matthew 11.25-26)

Similarly, there are other passages in the Gospels which presuppose the idea of a divine council. A topic which receives far too little attention in NT schol-

---

16. This is not quite the same as a "divine hierarchy," attributed to Mark by P. G. Davis, "Mark's Christological Paradox," *JSNT* 35 (1989), 3-18 (13).

17. Cf. the title of J. Winandy, "Le Logion de l'Ignorance (Mc, XIII,32; Mt., XXIV,36)," *RevB* 75 (1968), 63-79, who has good coverage of the issues. His argument that Jesus does not know the hour because he has not been commissioned to reveal it (cf. *4 Ezra* 4.51-52) is a good possibility. His contention that the Father has not yet fixed the date is less likely.

arship, it is of course very familiar to OT scholars. We will look first at two instances where Jesus is understood as a "member" of the heavenly council, although this is in itself not a particularly exalted function: prophets are pictured in the OT as receiving their commissions in the heavenly court. In conjunction with the other points we have observed, however, it is significant.

The statement "I saw Satan fall like lightning from heaven" (Luke 10.18) has received a considerable amount of scholarly attention already, as it has long been an exegetical puzzle. I have argued elsewhere at length that the vision is neither of a primeval event witnessed by the preexistent Christ nor of a fall of Satan within Jesus' ministry. It is, rather, a vision which the earthly Jesus sees of eschatological "end-times" events.[18] Although the introductory "I saw . . ." in the OT does not always indicate a vision of the future, the place where it occurs most frequently is in the book of Daniel, where the dreams and visions described point to *future* events.[19] Although the eschatological interpretation has been a minority position, it has found some adherents.[20] Green describes an important aspect of this reading: "Luke portrays Jesus as having a prophetic vision, then, whose content was the future (and ultimate) downfall of Satan."[21] But the principal point which has not been appreciated by scholars thus far is the fact that the final "fall of Satan" is something of a mixed blessing, at least in the short term. In fact, the substance of this vision is *the final descent of Satan to earth when he unleashes his wrath prior to his final destruction.* What this means for our purposes here is that Jesus is a seer of visions, which means that he has access to the heavenly council. This finds support from the other special knowledge which Jesus has in the pericope, such as the fact that "nothing will harm" the disciples (Luke 10.19). It must be remembered, on the other hand, that all this is quite in keeping with what a prophet could also know.

Beyond prophetic knowledge, however, is Jesus' knowledge the disciples' names "are written in heaven" (Luke 10.20). Here, Jesus' knowledge is closer to that possessed by exalted angelic figures. The contents of the book of life are, after all, a heavenly secret not to be made publicly known until the end.

More evidence comes in perhaps the most exalted reference to Jesus'

---

18. I have discussed it at length in S. J. Gathercole, "Jesus' Eschatological Vision of the Fall of Satan: Luke 10.18 Reconsidered," *ZNW* 94 (2003), 143-63. For some of the most important literature, see 143 n. 2.

19. J. Nolland, *Luke 9:21–18:34* (WBC; Waco: Word, 1993), 564.

20. S. R. Garrett, *The Demise of the Devil: Magic and the Demonic in Luke's Writings* (Minneapolis: Fortress, 1989), 49, is correct that the skepticism of most scholars about this possibility is unjustified.

21. J. B. Green, *The Gospel of Luke* (Grand Rapids: Eerdmans, 1997), 419, citing *Testament of Levi* 18.12; *Testament of Simeon* 6.6; *Testament of Zebulun* 9.8; *Testament of Solomon* 20.17.

knowledge in the heavenly council, the "thunderbolt from the Johannine heaven" in Matt. 11.25-26 par. Luke 10.21: "I thank you Father, Lord of heaven and earth, that you have hidden these things from the wise and understanding and revealed them to little children. Yes, Father, for such was your decree (εὐδοκία)." Here Jesus is represented as having insight into God's election. There may even be a hint of preexistence, but the point here is simply to highlight Jesus' intimacy with the Father in his knowledge of heavenly secrets. In this respect, there is a similarity with the assumption underlying Mark 13.32 par. Matt. 24.36, which we discussed above.

Even more striking is Luke 22.31-32a: "Simon, Simon, behold Satan has asked to sift you like wheat. But I have prayed for you, so that your faith might not fail. . . ."[22] This first verse has often been a *crux interpretum* because, after addressing Simon alone, Jesus says, "Satan has asked to sift *you (plural)*." But Botha's explanation seems satisfactory:

> [T]he fact that He addresses Simon personally in this verse is to fix especially Peter's attention to this warning. The Lord knows that Peter will deny Him and therefore he specially has to note this. Satan has asked to have all the apostles that he may sift them as wheat. Surely not only one of them — it makes no sense to sift only one corn-stalk.[23]

This saying again offers a very unusual insight into events in the heavenly world. Foerster contends that we have here a reference not only to Jesus' supernatural knowledge but also to his intervention in the divine council as heavenly intercessor, the opponent of Satan in the heavenly court. He prays not so much that Simon himself might have the strength to resist Satan; rather, *Jesus* is pitted against Satan, and somehow also knows that his intercession for Simon is effective.[24] In acting as an advocate of this kind, it seems likely that Jesus fulfills *even in the course of his earthly ministry* the role, familiar from Jewish apocalyptic and rabbinic literature, played by Michael.[25] The implications, then, are twofold: (1) Jesus is privy to events similar to those going on in the heavenly council in Job 1–2 and thus has some kind of presence there,[26] and (2) he functions already before Easter as a heavenly intercessor

---

22. For the most detailed treatment, see W. Dietrich, *Das Petrusbild der lukanischen Schriften* (BWANT; Stuttgart: Kohlhammer, 1972), 121-36.

23. F. J. Botha, "'Umas [*sic*] in Luke xxii.31," *ExpT* 64 (1952-53), 125; contra A. W. Argyle, "Luke xxii.31f.," *ExpT* 64 (1952-53), 222.

24. W. Foerster, "Lukas 22 31f.," *ZNW* 46 (1955), 129-33 (131-32).

25. Foerster, "Lukas 22 31f.," 131, 133.

26. The connection with Job is made frequently in the commentaries. See also Foerster, "Lukas 22 31f.," 130.

combating Satan. Crump is exactly right to note "Jesus' heavenly opposition to the adversary of God's people."[27]

Recognition of Jesus by Other Heavenly Figures

Perhaps of even greater significance are the numerous places in the Gospels where Jesus is identified as he really is by other heavenly figures:

> What have you to do with us, Jesus of Nazareth? Have you come to destroy us? I know who you are — the holy one of God! (Mark 1.24)

> The unclean spirits, when they saw him, fell down before him and cried out, saying, "You are the Son of God." (Mark 3.11)

Because these statements are not concerned with individual aspects of Jesus' knowledge in the heavenly council, but with his *identity,* they emphasize that Jesus has heavenly identity throughout his ministry, and not only when he receives moments of prophetic inspiration. The point here is not that the titles "holy one of God" or "Son of God" themselves require a heavenly sense but that Jesus' identity is noticed by the demons very clearly. Although the demons are indwelling people in the events narrated, it is clearly as heavenly beings that they identify who Jesus is.

The ultimate heavenly figure who identifies Jesus is of course God, not only in the transfiguration, as we have seen, but also in the baptism of Jesus (Mark 1.9-11 par.). In the discussion of the voice from heaven, attention has been focused on both the election of the Son and on the title "Son of God" itself. In terms of the election expressed in "in you I am well pleased" (Mark 1.11), it is unlikely that preexistence is necessarily implied. As Marcus puts it, the question of preexistence is left open[28] since election in itself does not of course mean preexistence. Mark 1.11 "implies God's preexistent *choice* of the Messiah"[29] and is "a confirmation of His already existing filial conscious-

27. D. Crump, "Jesus, the Victorious Scribal Intercessor in Luke's Gospel," *NTS* 38 (1992), 51-65 (65).

28. J. Marcus, *Mark 1–8: A New Translation with Introduction and Commentary* (Anchor; New York: Doubleday, 2000), 162: εὐδόκησα refers "to a past divine choice of Jesus being ratified at his baptism." See also Marcus, *Way of the Lord,* 56-57.

29. Marcus, *Way of the Lord,* 75. Contra G. Sevenster, "Christologie," *RGG*[3] I, col. 1753, and J. Schreiber, "Die Christologie des Markusevangeliums," *ZTK* 58 (1961), 154-83 (167 n. 5). See also J. Schreiber, *Die Markuspassion. Eine redaktionsgeschichtliche Untersuchung* (BZNW 68; Berlin: de Gruyter, 1993), 219, 254-56, 375 n. 61.

ness."[30] In this respect, the recognitions of Jesus' identity by the demons are in line with this divine verdict announced at the opening of the Gospel: Jesus' identity in relation to the Father is fully seen in the course of his ministry only by other heavenly figures. As such, he is not merely a temporary visitor to the heavenly council, like the prophets, but rather a *permanent* member.

Conclusion

To conclude, then, Jesus is portrayed in the Synoptic Gospels as having a heavenly identity — participating in the heavenly realms — already before Easter. This is apparent in the transfiguration, where he is seen in radiant glory in the company of Elijah and Moses. He is also sandwiched between God and the angels in Mark 13.32 par. Despite the limitations on his knowledge of the date of the end here, he is otherwise privy to the divine secrets in his knowledge of the downfall of Satan, the divine decree (God's εὐδοκία), and the identity of the elect. He even functions for Simon Peter as the counterpart to Satan, pleading against the accuser in Simon's defense. The heavenly identity of Jesus is emphasized by the fact that it is God and the demons who recognize who he truly is — one of their own kind.

There is a tension here, of course. It is not *simply* the case that one can describe Jesus as a heavenly figure without qualification. Jesus is never described as being "in heaven" in the way that the Father and the angels are,[31] but is very much "on the earth" (Mark 2.10; Luke 12.49; Luke 12.51 par. Matt. 10.34). This is not the place to attempt to resolve the tension between this heavenly identity of Jesus and the fact that he is also emphatically on earth. It should merely be noted at this point that it is strongly suggestive for a theology of Christ's preexistence, the key point which will be developed in the subsequent chapters of this book.

II. Jesus' Transcendence of the God/Creation Divide

Again, in advance of the discussion of the more divine aspects of Jesus' identity, it will be necessary to remember the fact that Jesus' truly human, earthly

---

30. C. E. B. Cranfield, "The Baptism of Our Lord: A Study of St. Mark 1:9-12," *SJT* 9 (1955) 53-63 (62).

31. The "Father in heaven": Matt. 5.16, 45; 6.1, 9; 7.11, 21; 10.32-33; 12.50; 16.17; 18.10, 14, 19; 23.9; Mark 11.25-26. The "angels in heaven": Mark 12.25 par. Matt. 22.30; Mark 13.25 (?); 13.32; Luke 15.7 (?).

nature is not in dispute. An economical statement of Jesus' humanity in Mark's Gospel comes in Davis's helpful summary: "the Spirit 'drives' Jesus into the wilderness (1.12); he becomes angry (3.5; 10.14); his sanity is doubted (3.21); he is sometimes unable to perform miracles."[32] Davis may be correct in saying that the human emotions and limitations of Jesus are more prominent in Mark's Gospel. But they are by no means absent from the other Evangelists; indeed, there are some ways in which Matthew and Luke include further material which points to Jesus' full humanity. At the outset, Matthew includes Jesus in a genealogy with the titles "Son of David, Son of Abraham" (Matt. 1.1). To take another example, Jesus is hungry in Matt. 4.2 par. Luke 4.2, so he is clearly no visiting angel like Raphael in the book of Tobit, who only pretends to eat food.[33] On the other hand, this by no means detracts from the picture of Jesus in the Synoptics as one who bridges the God-humanity divide.

Election (Mark 3.13 par. Luke 6.13; Mark 13.27 par. Matthew 24.31; Matthew 11.27 par. Luke 10.22)

The most strikingly exalted christological element in the Synoptic Gospels is the presentation of Jesus as one who *elects*. The portrait in Mark is not so strong as in Matthew, but it is still present. Mark 3.13 contains the first reference: "Jesus went up on a mountainside and *called to him those he wanted*, and they came to him." This double use of choosing language ("called" *and* "wanted") underlines Jesus' role as the agent of election. Luke instead has Jesus addressing his disciples and choosing from them twelve, whom he named apostles (Luke 6.13). In both cases, Jesus then goes on to call twelve apostles, who (as has been widely recognized) are in some way intended to be the nucleus of a restored Israel. There are of course alternative explanations of the twelve, but whichever position one takes on this question, the christological implications are similar.[34] As Hooker has put it:

> The twelve represent the whole nation, since Israel consisted of twelve tribes. The tradition is united in affirming that Jesus appointed twelve men in addition to himself: in other words, Jesus is seen as in some sense

---

32. Davis, "Mark's Christological Paradox," 6. What is inappropriate here, however, is to cite the second element (anger) as a specifically human rather than divine emotion.

33. See Tobit 12 for Raphael's denial that he ate with Tobias on his journey.

34. On "the twelve" see the bibliography in R. A. Guelich, *Mark 1–8:26* (Waco: Word, 1989), 153-54, and the comment on 158. Here, Guelich also treats the issue of whether those "called" and "chosen" are actually the twelve.

standing over against the nation. Had he chosen eleven men to join him, he would still have been gathering together a nucleus of the true Israel (as did John the Baptist); but if the tradition is correct, then his choice of twelve men represents an implicit claim regarding his own status.[35]

Again, whatever language one prefers to use to talk of the twelve, the relationship between Jesus and the twelve and what they symbolize is the same. There are striking echoes in Mark 3.13-14, then, of OT election language. Within this context, it is easy to understand the reference in Mark 13.27 to the people of God as "his (i.e., the Son of Man's) elect." Craig Evans notes here how extraordinary it is that the Son of Man has his own angels; similarly interesting is the point that he has his own elect people.[36]

If Jesus exercises some form of election in Mark's Gospel, this is even more strikingly clear in Matthew and Luke. Perhaps the clearest reference to Jesus' divine identity comes in Matt. 11.27 par. Luke 10.22 in the fact that ". . . no one knows the Father except the Son and *those to whom the Son chooses to reveal him.*" Interestingly, this function of the Son as the one who chooses does not get nearly as much attention from commentators as the other features of this much-discussed verse.[37] This role of the Son in election, however, places him squarely on the divine side of reality: it is difficult to conceive of anyone but a divine figure having this role. This is not merely a function as an eschatological figure who judges Israel and the nations at the end on the basis of their response to the kingdom; rather, Jesus stands over against the whole of humanity in the initiation of salvation, in his authority to reveal himself and the Father to individuals. It is the will of Jesus, in coordination with the decree of the Father, which determines to whom the truth and power of the kingdom are revealed. As ever, though, this identity is constantly determined by the Father, as the first statement makes clear: "All things have been committed to me by my Father. . . ." Furthermore, the electing action of the Son is clearly coordinated with that of the Father, since the statement of Jesus' "choosing to reveal" stands in parallel with the point that it is the Father's choice that he, the Father, has chosen to reveal himself

---

35. M. D. Hooker, *The Gospel according to Mark* (Black's NT Commentary; London: Black, 1991), 111.

36. C. A. Evans, *Mark 8:27–16:20* (WBC: Nashville: Nelson, 2001), 329. On the angels, see also P. T. Coke, "The Angels of the Son of Man," *SNTSU* 3 (1978), 91-98, who argues that: "The role of the angels and the role of Jesus' followers were similar: to prepare the way of the Lord, preach the gospel of the victory of God in Jesus, and to gather God's elect" (96).

37. See, for example, C. Deutsch, *Hidden Wisdom and the Easy Yoke: Wisdom, Torah and Discipleship in Matthew 11:25-30* (JSNTSS; Sheffield: JSOT, 1987), 38-39.

to the foolish but not to the wise (Matt. 11.25-26 par. Luke 10.21). To anticipate our conclusion to this section, these motifs combine to identify Jesus as sharing, with the Father, in the identity of God.[38] One scholar who does recognize that the election theme is a particularly noteworthy aspect of Matt. 11.27 is Hagner: "This in principle places Jesus on the side of the Father in contrast to all humanity."[39]

Following on from this (though only in Matthew) is the striking role which Jesus assigns himself in the construction of the eschatological people of God later on in the Gospel: "*I* will build *my* church," he says (Matt. 16.18). It is his action, and his church, because he has chosen it.

Jesus' Authority to Forgive: Mark 2.1-12 par.; Luke 7.49

Mark 2.1-12 is probably the most popular passage in the Synoptic Gospels used in support of a divine christology. This is not without some justification. In the course of this event of the forgiveness and healing of the paralytic, verses 5, 7, and 10-11 are particularly relevant:

> And when Jesus saw their faith, he said to the paralytic, "Child, your sins are forgiven."

> "Why does he speak like this? He is blaspheming! Who can forgive sins but God alone?"

> "But so that you may know that the Son of Man has authority on earth to forgive sins" — he said to the paralytic — "I say to you, rise, pick up your bed and go home."

The standard explanations dispute that Jesus is claiming a divine prerogative here and have generally been twofold. First, it has been suggested that Jesus' statement is merely a kind of priestly absolution: "Jesus' words need not be any more than an authoritative declaration that the man's sins had been forgiven *by God*."[40] However, all those who have made the suggestion have yet to provide evidence that the Jewish priest ever himself pronounced the people

---

38. Some scholars see Wisdom as the primary template for the portrait of Jesus, a point to which we will return in a later chapter. It suffices to say at this stage that while Jesus shares some of the characteristics of Wisdom, it is only the portrait of God himself in the OT which offers a clear parallel to the depiction of the Son here.

39. D. A. Hagner, *Matthew 1–13* (WBC; Waco: Word, 1993), 320.

40. D. E. Nineham, *The Gospel of Saint Mark* (Harmondsworth: Penguin, 1969), 93.

forgiven.[41] Second, the argument goes that there is a kind of divine *agency* at work here, whereby Jesus carries out a divine function without any sense of him actually being himself God. On this model, the action identifies Jesus as having a *prophetic* authority derived from God. So, for example, O'Neill: "the claim to forgive sins was a claim to pronounce validly that *God* had forgiven the sinner. Even if the scribes held that the sickness was God's direct punishment of sin, they could not have denied God's right to reverse his verdict, and to announce that reversal through a prophet."[42] The two objections, then, are in fact very similar.

However, an important critique of, and constructive alternative to, these explanations has been provided by Hofius.[43] Hofius argues that when Jesus says, "Your sins are forgiven," he is not declaring merely that "*God* has forgiven your sins" — it is not merely a passive of divine action. There are two particularly important elements to this. First, there is a strong parallel between what is true of God in the scribes' statement — that he "can forgive sins" — and what is claimed by Jesus — that the Son of Man "has authority to forgive sins." The "can" (δύναται) and the "has authority" (ἐξουσίαν ἔχει) are virtual synonyms.[44] Secondly, it is by no means clear from the expression "on earth" that the Markan Jesus intends to contrast what God is doing in heaven with what the Son of Man does on earth, as if God could not himself act on earth: Hofius lists a long string of passages in which God acts directly *on earth*.[45] As a result, there appears to be a claim about Jesus' divine identity here in the Synoptic Gospels. This is, needless to say, reinforced by the reaction of the scribes, which will be treated in more detail below.

Finally, this theme of Jesus as the one with authority to forgive sins is actually amplified in Luke, since he appends to the story of the sinful woman the statement of Jesus "your sins are forgiven" and the corresponding reaction of others present: "Who is this, who even forgives sins?" (Luke 7.49).[46]

41. For a decisive demonstration of the paucity of the evidence for this view, see O. Hofius, "Vergebungszuspruch und Vollmachtsfrage. Mk 2,1-12 und das Problem priesterlicher Absolution im antiken Judentum," in idem, *Neutestamentliche Studien* (WUNT; Tübingen: Mohr, 2000), 57-69.

42. J. C. O'Neill, "The Charge of Blasphemy at Jesus' Trial before the Sanhedrin," in E. Bammel, ed., *The Trial of Jesus: Cambridge Studies in Honour of C. F. D. Moule* (London: SCM, 1970), 72-77 (73).

43. O. Hofius, "Jesu Zuspruch der Sündenvergebung. Exegetische Erwägungen zu Mk 2,5b," in idem, *Neutestamentliche Studien*, 38-56.

44. Hofius, "Jesu Zuspruch der Sündenvergebung," 41.

45. Hofius, "Jesu Zuspruch der Sündenvergebung," 42.

46. The reaction here, however, seems to be more positive than in the similar story of the healing of the paralytic in Luke 5.

Blasphemy (Mark 2.1-12 par.; Mark 14.63-64 par.)

Closely connected with the divine claim on Jesus' part in his forgiveness of the paralytic's sins is the resulting accusation of blasphemy, an accusation which is leveled again at the trial at the end of Jesus' life. The contribution of this theme for our purposes is that it shows that it is not simply from a modern standpoint that Jesus appears to be making divine claims. Rather, what the Synoptic Evangelists say underscores the fact that such claims would also have been heard in this way from the standpoint of first-century Judaism. Mark 2.1-12 and 14.63-64 will benefit from being treated together here.[47]

Bock and Evans have together collected an enormous amount of background material on the blasphemy charge.[48] The Jewish evidence can perhaps very roughly be divided into three types of material. First, there are the texts which talk of explicit attacks on God — cursing God, despising God, or even in some circumstances opposing the *people* of God or the Torah in a way that is tantamount to opposing God himself. Second, there is the frequent criticism of the practice of *pronouncing the divine name,* which also incurs the sentence of death just as readily as actually cursing God. Thirdly, there is material in which some divine prerogative is usurped. All instances of blasphemy incur the death penalty, although by the time of the compilation of the Mishnah, only *pronouncing the divine name* is subject to capital punishment.[49]

In Mark 2, it is clearly the third of these three options which incurs the objection that Jesus has acted blasphemously: "Why is he speaking in this way? He is blaspheming! Who can forgive sins but God alone?" (v. 7). Two elements are implicit in the charge. First, there is the specific charge against Jesus' statement about *forgiveness.* Logically, of course, sin is an offense against God, in some sense exclusively so.[50] To this extent, then, only God can for-

---

47. On both blasphemy passages, including discussion of Matthean redaction, see Hurtado, "Jewish Opposition to Christ-Devotion," 37-39.

48. See especially C. A. Evans, "In What Sense 'Blasphemy'? Jesus before Caiaphas in Mark 14:61-64," *SBLSP* 30 (1991), 215-34; however, see the brief but very detailed and helpful collection of material in Evans, "Excursus: Blasphemy," in idem, *Mark 8:27–16:20,* 453-58; D. L. Bock, *Blasphemy and Exaltation in Judaism and the Final Examination of Jesus* (WUNT; Tübingen: Mohr, 1998); n.b. also A. Y. Collins, "The Charge of Blasphemy in Mark 14.64," *JSNT* 26 (2004), 379-401.

49. Even then the death penalty is still probably only a hypothetical reality in Mishnaic law.

50. Although the returning prodigal can confess his sin against heaven and against his earthly father (Luke 15.21), the Psalmist declares — even after adultery and murder — that "against you alone have I sinned" (Ps. 51.4).

give.[51] Second, underlying it is a general idea that claiming to do something which is the sole preserve of "God alone" constitutes blasphemy. Jesus, far from rebutting the charge of having claimed divine identity, in fact encourages the idea by performing the healing as confirmation. As noted earlier, it does not appear that the narrative audience in Mark 2 perceived Jesus to be claiming a priestly or prophetic role in declaring forgiveness.

Some of the problems surrounding the blasphemy charge in Mark 14 are alleviated when we take into account this prior charge of blasphemy for usurping a privilege of "God alone," although the charge here is slightly more complicated than in Mark 2. The key part of the narrative is as follows:

> . . . Again the High Priest asked him and said to him, "Are you the Christ, the Son of the Blessed One?" And Jesus said, "I am, and you will see the Son of Man seated at the right hand of power, and coming with the clouds of heaven." The High Priest tore his garments and said, "What further witnesses do we need? You have heard the blasphemy! What do you think?" And they all condemned him as worthy of death. (Mark 14.61-64)

Scholars have often commented that since there is nothing intrinsically blasphemous in claiming to be Messiah, it is unlikely that this is the reason for the charge here.[52] Similarly, it is unlikely that the "I am" in 14.62 is the blasphemy, since it is probably merely Jesus' answer to the High Priest's question.[53] More plausible is Bock's suggestion that one element of the blasphemy is Jesus' implicit attack on those who are currently ordained in the divinely instituted priesthood.[54] For the criminal in the dock to claim that he will return to condemn the High Priest could very easily be understood as blasphemy. However, this would not have any significant christological implications, since anyone could conceivably launch an attack on the High Priest.

For our purposes, the more important component in the charge in

51. Hofius, "Jesu Zuspruch der Sündenvergebung," 40 n. 11, notes an extremely close parallel in Midrash Psalms to the idea expressed by the scribes, in which David says to God, "No one can forgive sins but you alone."

52. Contra what is implied at points in O'Neill, although for him this is very closely tied to the claim on Jesus' part to divine honors. See O'Neill, "The Charge of Blasphemy at Jesus' Trial," 72-77. On the other side, see O. Hofius, "βλασφημία κτλ," in *EDNT* 1:219-21 (221): "The messianic claim as such was hardly an occasion for condemnation on the basis of blasphemy."

53. Likewise, "I am" (ἐγώ εἰμι) is not necessarily a representation of the divine name in *m. Sanhedrin* 7.5: Evans, "In What Sense 'Blasphemy'?" 218; C. Williams, *I Am He: The Interpretation of 'Anî Hû' in Jewish and Early Christian Literature* (WUNT; Tübingen: Mohr, 2000), 247.

54. Bock, *Blasphemy and Exaltation*, 206-9.

Mark 14.63-64 consists in Jesus' claim *to a heavenly throne.*[55] In this case, it is not clear whether he is laying claim to a second throne at the right hand of God or to a share in the one throne of God.[56] In this respect, the key point of the blasphemy charge from the High Priest fits well with the sense of blasphemy in both Mark 2 and the material on the blasphemy law in Jewish tradition about usurping a divine prerogative. Evans draws attention to a passage in the Talmud (*b. Sanhedrin* 38b) at this point which is particularly instructive.[57] Here Rabbi Akiba interprets "thrones were set up" (Dan. 7.9) as referring to one throne for God and one for David. Rabbi Jose responds, however, by saying: "Akiba, how long will you profane the Shekinah? Rather one (throne) is for justice and one is for mercy." One could certainly draw the conclusion here that if Akiba was almost accused of blasphemy for suggesting that David had a throne alongside God, how much more would Jesus have been accused of full-blown blasphemy if he actually claimed that he would *himself* sit on a throne at the right hand of God?

In conclusion, Mark 2 and 14 and their parallels in Matthew and Luke make it fairly clear that Jesus' claims were in certain cases to prerogatives belonging uniquely to God in the OT and Jewish tradition. The contention between Jesus and his opponents on these issues does not consist in the accuracy of the accusations. Rather, there is agreement on the actual content, and the dispute is over their truthfulness.

Jesus' Sea Miracles: Mark 4.35-41; 6.45-52 par.

As we saw in the case of Jesus' forgiveness of sins above, there is particular dispute among scholars in cases where Jesus seems to be saying or doing something which is a particular prerogative of Yahweh in the OT. Is he acting as one uniquely endowed by God in a *representative* function, or is he in fact acting simply *as* God himself?

The sea miracles have been identified as particularly significant in their

---

55. Evans, "In What Sense 'Blasphemy'?" 221; Bock, *Blasphemy and Exaltation,* 200-206; Collins, "The Charge of Blasphemy in Mark 14.64," 399. Bock and Collins also draw attention to Jesus' claim to "come with the clouds of heaven" as blasphemous. This is a strong possibility, although the advantage of the throne theme above is that we have a concrete parallel in the rabbinic discussions of Akiba's profanation.

56. On this question see Bauckham, "The Throne of God and the Worship of Jesus," 43-69, and now D. D. Hannah, "The Throne of His Glory: The Divine Throne and Heavenly Mediators in Revelation and the Similitudes of Enoch," *ZNW* 94 (2003), 68-96.

57. Evans, *Mark 8:27–16:20,* 456.

demonstration of Jesus' rule over creation.[58] For example, Hurtado says of the first miracle pericope in Mark 4 (and the response "Who is this?") that "Jesus has shown godlike superiority over the elements."[59] Similarly, Marcus writes on Mark 6.45-51: "the overwhelming impact made by our narrative is an impression of divinity."[60] Some scholars also use the language of epiphany in connection with both events.[61] This does not seems to me, however, to be very productive: it seems usually to refer to a vague sense of divine presence, and a sense of the "numinous" (a similarly imprecise term) felt by others present.

Calming the Storm: Mark 4.35-41
par. Matt. 8.23-27; Luke 8.22-25

The trigger for Jesus' working of this particular miracle is that the disciples are afraid of death in Mark 4.38, and as a result Jesus calms the storm in 4.39:

> And a great windstorm arose, and the waves were breaking into the boat, so that the boat was already filling. . . . And they said to him, "Teacher, do you not care that we are perishing?" And he awoke and rebuked the wind and said to the sea, "Quiet! Be still!" And the wind ceased and there was a great calm.

Commentators often refer to Psalm 107 (106 LXX) in this connection:[62]

> He commanded and raised the stormy wind
>   Which lifted up the waves of the sea.

58. Davis, "Mark's Christological Paradox," 7-8.

59. Hurtado, *Lord Jesus Christ*, 285-86.

60. Marcus, *Mark 1–8*, 432, quoted in Hurtado, *Lord Jesus Christ*, 286.

61. Guelich, *Mark 1–8:26*, 351; Hurtado, *Lord Jesus Christ*, 285. On the walking on the water specifically, see A. Y. Collins, "Rulers, Divine Men, and Walking on the Water (Mark 6:45-52)," in L. Bormann, K. Del Tredici, and A. Standhartinger, eds., *Religious Propaganda and Missionary Competition in the New Testament World: Essays Honoring Dieter Georgi* (Leiden: Brill, 1994), 207-27; J. P. Heil, *Jesus Walking on the Sea: Meaning and Gospel Functions of Matt 14:22-33, Mark 6:45-52 and John 6:15b-21* (Rome: Biblical Institute Press, 1981), 8-30; P. J. Madden, *Jesus' Walking on the Sea: An Investigation of the Origin of the Narrative Account* (Berlin: de Gruyter, 1997), 86-88.

62. For the most comprehensive treatment of the influence of Psalm 107 on Mark, see R. Meye, "Psalm 107 as 'Horizon' for Interpreting the Miracle Stories of Mark 4.35–8.26," in R. A. Guelich, ed., *Unity and Diversity in New Testament Theology: Essays in Honor of George E. Ladd* (Grand Rapids: Eerdmans, 1978), 1-13. However, the case is probably pressed too far for the miracles throughout Mark 4.35–8.26, although Meye's comments are entirely appropriate for Mark 4.

Their courage melted away in their evil plight. . . .
They reeled and staggered like drunken men
   And were at their wits' end.
Then they cried to the Lord in their trouble,
   And he delivered them from their distress.
He made the storm be still,
   And the waves of the sea were hushed.

In Mark 4, then, Jesus makes the strange transition from a Jonah-like figure who sleeps while the rest of the sailors are in peril (Jonah 1.5) to a divine figure who calms the storm like God in Psalm 107. But a point of contrast is present in the comfort which the people of God receive by his activity in Ps. 107.30: "Then they were glad that the waters were quiet. . . ." If anything, Jesus' action in Mark 4 seems to make the disciples even more afraid than before: "they were terrified" (4.41)! Matthew on the other hand has the disciples in amazement, which is closer to Psalm 107, and Luke has them both amazed *and* terrified.[63] The conclusion in all three Gospels is the same, however: "Who is this, that the wind and the sea obey him?" a question which is left unanswered.

Walking on the Sea: Mark 6.45-52 par. Matt. 14.22-33

In the second miracle, the difference is that the storm is not quite so serious; the miracle is Jesus' walking on the sea, accompanied by his Johannine sounding "I am" (Mark 6.50).[64] The walking on water motif is noteworthy, because it seems to be connected (like the forgiveness of sins) with a *uniquely* divine prerogative in the only real OT parallel to the event in Mark:

> God who alone stretched out the heavens, *walking on the sea* (περιπατῶν . . . ἐπὶ θαλάσσῃ) as if on dry land. . . . (LXX Job 9.8)

> . . . At about the fourth watch of the night, he came to them *walking on the sea* (περιπατῶν ἐπὶ τῆς θαλάσσης), and he wanted to pass by them. But they saw him *walking on the sea* (ἐπὶ τῆς θαλάσσης περιπατοῦντα). . . . (Mark 6.48-49)

---

63. Both Matt. 8.23-27 and Luke 8.22-25 have the reaction ἐθαύμασαν, to which compare the θαυμάσια of LXX Ps. 106.24, 31.

64. For exhaustive treatments of this miracle, see Madden, *Jesus' Walking on the Sea*, which is excellent on the history of research into the passage, and Heil, *Jesus Walking on the Sea*, who has more on the exegetical side.

Jesus is clearly being identified here in a way that is reminiscent of God in Job. Moreover, one of the most striking points about the Job passage is that it is probably discussing how God *alone* stretches out the heavens and walks on the sea. As Ritt rightly says of Mark's statement here, "it appears almost verbatim in the response of Job about God's power." The reference to walking on the sea is a "theophany[65] motif which is taken over from Yahweh to Jesus."[66] In addition to the striking parallels here, there is the high christological claim implicit in Jesus' statement "I am" (Mark 6.50). Even though it could conceivably be interpreted merely as a statement of self-identification ("It's me!") in response to the disciples' idea that they were seeing a ghost, it is highly likely that there is an implication of divine identity as well here. As Collins concludes her treatment of the pericope: "Mark, in this context at least, wished to say something about the difficulty of perceiving the divinity of Jesus."[67] Williams, in the most recent and comprehensive study of the "I am" motif, agrees.[68]

Matthew's version of this pericope (which is not paralleled in Luke) has two interesting supplements. The first is the fact that Jesus' power over the sea means that he can even offer power to Peter to do the same, although Peter's faith fails him.[69] The second concerns the christological claims, which are even more striking than those already in Mark: "Those in the boat worshiped him, saying, 'Truly you are the Son of God'" (Matt. 14.33). We will return to this theme of worship later on. For the moment, however, the combination of the two passages showing Jesus' mastery of the sea points very strongly to a close identification of him with Yahweh in the OT.

65. Theophany is a slightly more productive category than epiphany since it specifies the identity of the person appearing, rather than pointing in a very vague way to an appearance of a spiritual being to an earthly figure who senses the presence of the numinous.

66. H. Ritt, "Der 'Seewandel Jesu' (Mk 6, 45-52 par). Literarische und theologische Aspekte," *BZ* 23 (1979), 71-84 (79): "es erscheint fast wörtlich in der Gegenrede des Ijob über Gottes Macht . . . ein Theophaniemotiv, das von Jahwe auf Jesus übertragen wird."

67. Collins, "Rulers, Divine Men, and Walking on the Water," 227. Similarly also J. D. M. Derrett, "Why and How Jesus Walked on the Sea," *NovT* 23 (1981), 330-48 (330-31): "his actions, however curious in practical, historical terms, are, properly understood, manifestations of YHWH personally present on earth."

68. Williams, *I Am He*, 214-28, and see 216 n. 16 for other scholars taking this view.

69. This is in accordance with the common Matthean theme of Jesus' power extending also to the disciples, particularly in connection with some of the references to the Son of Man. On the Matthean addition here, see in particular G. Braumann, "Der sinkende Petrus. Matth. 14,28-31," *TZ* 22 (1966), 403-14, although one need not share the assumption expressed throughout the article that the pericope mirrors certain aspects of the life of the Matthean community.

The "Name" of Jesus

Thus far, the majority of the discussion has been concerned with Jesus' exercise of divine functions. Some of these could conceivably be interpreted simply as Jesus acting *on God's behalf*. As we have seen, however, this runs into difficulty when the functions are specifically predicated in the OT as *uniquely* God's. Reinforcing the close identity of Jesus with God in the Synoptic Gospels is the material on Jesus' "name," particularly where Jesus' name is used in a strikingly similar way to the usage of the name of Yahweh in the OT. Since a "name" is a matter of identity and not merely function, this perhaps provides particularly helpful evidence for our purposes. The material can be divided for convenience into (i) Jesus' requirements of meeting and baptism "into his name," and (ii) the wider use of the name of Jesus in such a way that it stands in for the name of Yahweh.

(i) Twice in Matthew's Gospel Jesus assumes that meeting together and baptism take place "in his name":

> For wherever two or three are gathered in my name, there am I among them. (Matt. 18.20)

> Therefore go and make disciples of all nations, baptizing them in the name of the Father, and of the Son, and of the Holy Spirit. (Matt. 28.19)

We will see below in discussion with Ruck-Schröder the significance of the interchangeability of the OT expression "in the name of the Lord" with "in the name of Jesus." But also important to consider is Hartman's observation on the actual *meaning* of the formula:

> There is, however, a Jewish-rabbinic usage of the phrase "into the name" which seems to solve the problem of the original wording and meaning of the baptismal formula. As mentioned above, the expression is basically a general one, "with regard to," "having in mind." But it is also used in a particular kind of context which is of interest in our case, contexts concerning religious rites. The rites are performed "into the name" of the god, to whose cult the rite belongs or who is otherwise associated with the rite in question. This god is the fundamental referent of the rite; he/she is the one whom the worshipper "has in mind" or "with regard to" whom the rite is performed and who thus makes it meaningful.[70]

70. L. Hartman, *"Into the Name of the Lord Jesus": Baptism in the Early Church* (Edinburgh: Clark, 1997), 42.

Hartman cites a number of examples in Jewish texts (referring either to Jewish worship or to Samaritan or gentile idolatry) in which the expression is used in this way.[71] For our purposes, we can confine ourselves to the only two instances in the Synoptic Gospels, Matthew 18.20 and 28.19. In these cases, *meeting* and *baptism* are the two ritual acts of worship which have Jesus as their ultimate reference point and object. The baptismal formula in Matthew 28 has been much discussed. But Matthew 18 is even more striking in terms of its christology since, within the narrative of Matthew's Gospel, it takes place within the course of Jesus' ministry. When he says, "for where two or three are gathered 'into' my name," he is referring to gatherings of disciples that are ultimately organized in orientation to him.[72] Perhaps the most significant of Hartman's Jewish parallels is that which has exactly the same ritual context of Matthew 18 — *m. 'Abot* 4.11: "every assembling together that is 'into the name of' Heaven (כל כנסיה שהיא לשם שמים) shall in the end be established, but any that is not into the name of Heaven shall not in the end be established." It is highly likely that both here and in Matthew 18 we have the same sense of a gathering which is to take place for the honor of God/Jesus, with God/Jesus as the ultimate reference point to whom the gathering should be oriented.

As a result, while there is perhaps a certain ambiguity whether the spontaneous reactions to Jesus in the course of his ministries were equivalent to the worship due to the one God, the use of the "into the name of" formula in Matthew 18 is decidedly clearer.

(ii) In an excellent recent monograph on the subject, Adelheid Ruck-Schröder has highlighted a number of the key aspects of the "name" of Jesus more broadly in the NT.[73] She comments rightly (in the context of a discussion of Matthew) that the statements referring to the name of Jesus can be understood as an interpretation of the name of God in the last days.[74] However, one element probably requiring correction is her location of this argu-

---

71. See, e.g., *m. Niddah* 5.6; *m. Hullin* 2.8; 4.11. Hartman, *"Into the Name of the Lord Jesus,"* 42-43. For further examples, see L. Hartman, "Into the Name of the Lord Jesus: A Suggestion Concerning the Earliest Meaning of the Phrase," *NTS* 20 (1974), 432-40.

72. For the possibility that Matt. 18.20 and the rabbinic parallels extend even beyond formal gatherings, see J. Sievers, *"Shekinah* and Matthew 18.20," in A. Finkel and L. Frizzell, eds., *Standing before God: Studies on Prayer in Scriptures and in Tradition with Essays in Honor of John M. Oesterreicher* (New York: Ktav, 1981), 171-82 (177).

73. A. Ruck-Schröder, *Der Name Gottes und der Name Jesus. Eine neutestamentliche Studie* (WMANT; Neukirchen: Neukirchener, 1999).

74. Ruck-Schröder, *Der Name Gottes und der Name Jesus,* 263: ". . . können die Aussagen über den Namen Jesus bei Matthäus als Auslegung des Namens des Gottes Israels 'am Ende der Zeiten' verstanden werden."

ment within discussion of Jesus' *functional* relation to God.[75] In fact, the "name" of Jesus is perhaps a key point at which functional approaches to christology break down: a "name" more than anything else is concerned precisely with identity. As a result, it offers a peculiarly good confirmation of Bauckham's thesis that *identity* is a better general term to describe the relation between Jesus and God than function or even nature. Three of the most important examples in the Synoptic Gospels are as follows:

> Many will come in my name, saying, "I am he!" and they will lead many astray. (Mark 13.6 par. Matt. 24.5; Luke 21.8)

> On that day, many will say to me, "Lord, Lord, did we not prophesy in your name, and cast out demons in your name, and do many mighty works in your name?" (Matt. 7.22)

> . . . and in his name the nations will hope. (Matt. 12.21)

The majority opinion is probably right that the future figures envisaged in Mark 13.6 are claiming to be Jesus at his promised return.[76] The combination of "in my name" and "it is I (ἐγώ εἰμι)" points to an identification with Jesus himself. The obvious reference point here, however, is Ps. 118.26: "Blessed is he who comes in the name of Yahweh." When Jesus draws attention to the fact that "many will come in my name," he is clearly drawing an analogy between coming in his own name and the coming in the name of Yahweh mentioned in the Psalm.

Matt. 7.22, quoted second above, is similarly important because it envisages early Christian prophecy taking place "in the name of Jesus." Again, there is a very clear OT reference point, indicating that the name of Jesus stands in for the name of Yahweh:

> I will raise up for them a prophet like you from among their brothers. And I will put my words in his mouth, and he will speak to them all that I command him. And whoever will not listen to my words that *he shall speak in my name*, I myself will require it of him. But *the prophet who presumes to speak a word in my name* that I have not commanded him to speak, *or, who speaks in the name of other gods*, that same prophet shall die. (Deut. 18.18-20)

---

75. Ruck-Schröder, *Der Name Gottes und der Name Jesus*, 263.

76. Pace Ruck-Schröder, who argues that the claim is that eschatological salvation is present (*Der Name Gottes und der Name Jesus*, 110-11).

Since prophecy in Deuteronomy here should be speaking "in the name of Yahweh," the move made in Matt. 7.22 is unmistakable.

With Matt. 12.21, the situation is slightly more complex, but the evidence is just as important. The promise that "the nations will put their hope in his name" is curious because neither the Hebrew text of Isa. 11.10 nor the LXX refers to hoping "in his name." Be that as it may, the expression clearly echoes the numerous places in the OT where God's name is almost synonymous with his presence and power, in particular the expression of confidence in God's faithfulness in Ps. 52.9: "And *I will hope in your name,* for it is good, in the presence of your saints" (cf. Isa. 50.10; Jer. 7.14). As Beaton notes, "the inclusion of the name of Jesus is an element in Matthew's development of a high Christology."[77] Specifically, the nations hoping in Jesus' name finds its closest parallel in the Psalmist's confession in Psalm 52, except that, again, the name of Jesus stands in for the name of Yahweh.

Also noteworthy are Mark 9.38 par. Luke 9.49 and Luke 10.17 in that they too point to the power of Jesus in his name. In both cases, the reference is to casting out demons in the name of Jesus. As Ruck-Schröder rightly points out, there is probably a double sense here of the demons submitting "at the invocation of" and "at the power which is present in" Jesus' name.[78] Hurtado refers to the "theurgic" use of Jesus' name (i.e., that whereby divine power is exercised) at this point.[79]

Matt. 28.19 aside, the use of the "name" of Jesus in the Synoptics might be explained by reference to a kind of *extension* of the name of Yahweh in the OT: this would suffice as a summary of the christological implications of the "name" theology in Mark and Luke. But 28.19 can only be understood as referring to an explanation or "trifurcation" of the single divine name which has been revealed by the risen Jesus. (A parallel would be the way in which Paul in 1 Cor. 8.6 "splits" the *Shema*'s "the Lord our God, the Lord is one" into "one God, the Father" and "one Lord, Jesus Christ.") As we noted above, the Synoptics' use of the name of Jesus is "an interpretation of the name of God in the last days," as Ruck-Schröder puts it.

77. R. Beaton, *Isaiah's Christ in Matthew's Gospel* (SNTSMS; Cambridge: Cambridge University Press, 2002), 147-48; cf. 154.

78. Ruck-Schröder, *Der Name Gottes und der Name Jesus,* 193. Her thesis here, however, that Mark and Luke are polemicizing against non-Christians who are using the name of Jesus as a means for healing is rather implausible and speculative.

79. "These practices reflect a view of Jesus as possessing transcendent authority that can be mediated through his name, which thus functioned in a way similar to a divine name." Hurtado, "Jewish Opposition to Christ-Devotion," 39. See also the discussion here of Matt. 7.22; 10.16-25 (especially vv. 18 and 22), as well as of the Luke-Acts material (39 n. 18, 42-43).

Responses to Jesus of Obeisance/Devotion/Worship

How to describe the responses of the disciples at the moments of their highest appreciation of Jesus has been controversial.[80] Particularly, argument has been focused around the meaning of the Greek word προσκυνεῖν. Moule has rendered it as "obeisance";[81] Hurtado has continued to use the language of "devotion";[82] Bauckham is happy to translate the word as "worship" in many instances, particularly in Matthew.[83] The question, however, is not particularly which term is used, but whether one is to understand the obeisance/devotion/worship offered to Jesus *as that which is specifically due, and also offered, to the one God.* There is little evidence of this in Mark's Gospel, where the language of προσκυνεῖν is not present, although we do see the leper (Mark 1.40) and the rich man (10.17) falling on their knees before Jesus, and Jairus similarly falls at Jesus' feet (5.22). Matthew and Luke, however, offer a somewhat clearer picture.

Matthew uses προσκυνεῖν repeatedly. It occurs in connection with the reverence of the Magi toward Jesus (ch. 2) and in Matthew's supplement to the second Markan sea miracle (14.33) where, after Jesus walks across the water and calls Peter to do the same (verses 28-32), the disciples "worship" him, confessing him as "Son of God." As Hurtado rightly notes, this goes beyond simple respect for a superior.[84] Even if such expressions of devotion or obeisance to the pre-resurrection Jesus cannot be straightforwardly read as offerings of the worship due to the one God,[85] it is probably still correct to say that Matthew presents pre-Easter *proskynesis* as anticipating that which is offered to the risen Jesus.

After the resurrection, then, the picture is perhaps slightly clearer. The final reference to the worship of Jesus, in Matt. 28.17, is immediately prior to the ascension: "And when they saw him, they worshiped him, but they

---

80. For the recent debate, see the discussion throughout Newman, et al., eds., *The Jewish Roots of Christological Monotheism,* and Hurtado, *Lord Jesus Christ.*

81. C. F. D. Moule, *The Origin of Christology* (Cambridge: Cambridge University Press, 1977), 175.

82. Hence the title of his *JTS* article, "Pre–70 CE Jewish Opposition to Christ-Devotion," and the subtitle of his 2003 magnum opus, *Devotion to Jesus in Earliest Christianity.* On προσκυνεῖν, see Hurtado, "Jewish Opposition to Christ-Devotion," 40-42.

83. Bauckham, "The Throne of God and the Worship of Jesus," 67-68. Especially interesting is the idea of the relation between the worship of Jesus and Matt. 4.10.

84. The other places in Matthew are 8.2; 9.18; 15.25; and 20.20.

85. Cf. the conclusion of R. T. France, "The Worship of Jesus: A Neglected Factor in Christological Debate?" in H. H. Rowdon, ed., *Christ the Lord: Studies Presented to Donald Guthrie* (Leicester: Inter-Varsity, 1982), 17-36 (26-27).

doubted. . . ." Then follows the references to all power having been given to Jesus (28.18) and his location in the heavenly hierarchy (28.19). So an extremely exalted response from the disciples here makes good sense (cf. also 28.9).

Luke, like Mark, has the instance of Jairus falling at Jesus' feet (Luke 8.41); similarly, the leper falls on his face (5.12), and the Samaritan leper does both (17.16). This evidence is somewhat ambiguous, however, since there are parallels of such prostration before other human beings (e.g., Gen. 33.3). Sometimes it is disapproved of, however, and Moule is probably right to say that "it seems to have been regarded as an exceptional and extravagant gesture when offered to a man."[86] Strikingly, in the last two verses of the Gospel, devotion to Jesus and worship of God are presented alongside one another: "And they worshiped (προσκυνήσαντες) him (Jesus), and went back to Jerusalem with great joy. And they went on blessing God continually in the temple" (Luke 24.52-53). This still does not fully answer the question of what Luke means, however.

An interesting perspective on Luke's references to prostration and *proskunein* can be seen in Acts 10.25-26:

When Peter entered, Cornelius met him and fell down at his feet and worshiped (προσεκύνησεν) him. But Peter lifted him up, saying, "Stand up, for I too am a man."

In the light of this (Luke would no doubt agree with Peter's verdict), it would appear that the prostration and *proskynesis* offered to Jesus in the Gospel narrative is regarded by Luke as entirely appropriate because Jesus is not *merely* a man, but rather transcends humanity by virtue of his divine identity.

Jesus' Supernatural Knowledge

Jesus' supernatural knowledge can be subdivided into two distinct types: his knowledge of human hearts and his very detailed knowledge of future events. First, then, Jesus shows signs of being able to "mind-read" and does so with considerable regularity.[87] Hofius and Marcus may be right in suspecting a

---

86. Moule (*Origin of Christology*, 175) supplies the examples of Josephus, *Antiquities* 10.211 and Philo, *De Decalogo* 64.

87. P. Rolland, "Jésus connaissait leurs pensées," *ETL* 62 (1986), 118-21, gives the following as examples: Matt. 9.4; 12.25; Mark 2.8; Luke 5.22; 6.8; 9.47; 11.17; cf. Matt. 22.18; Mark 12.15; Luke 20.23 (118). Luke 7.39-40 should perhaps be added to this list, and Mark 8.17? Rolland's study is so brief because it takes the "mind-reading" sayings as a case-study for his particular view of the Synoptic problem. A more substantial treatment of the theological issues is certainly a desideratum.

considerably exalted christology here. As Marcus puts it: "The fact that he can discern and expose the scribes' inmost thoughts already supports this more-than-human status, especially since God is described in the OT as the one who knows people's hearts."[88] To take the example of Matt. 12.25 (cf. Luke 11.17), "he knew their thoughts," Rolland comments that it is drawn directly from Job 21.27 and Ps. 94.11, concluding that Jesus' knowledge of the secrets of hearts is a "divine privilege, according to Psalm 94.11."[89] In itself, this phenomenon might not go beyond what was expected of a prophet, but it is the regularity with which Jesus demonstrates such knowledge that is striking.[90]

Similarly, some commentators interpret the events of Luke 19.29-34 (Jesus' knowledge of the colt being tied up) and 22.7-13 (Jesus' knowledge of the man carrying the jar of water and of the room prepared for the Passover) in the same way. Eckey, for example, takes these as instances of Jesus' divine foreknowledge, and this certainly seems correct in the latter case.[91]

Jesus as the Sender of Prophets

The unique identity of Jesus is further seen in his relation to early Christian prophets. In Matt. 5.11-12 Jesus draws an analogy between his disciples and the OT prophets; as we have seen, the reference in Matthew 7 to those who speak in Jesus' name is similar in this respect. In Matthew 23, however, the point is even stronger: Jesus has come as the eschatological manifestation of God who is to send a last cohort of prophets to their deaths at the hands of the present generation. This will have the function of confirming that generation in their guilt, and precipitating their final condemnation. Jesus is re-enacting in this final generation a drama in which God has been calling Israel to repentance throughout OT history. And in this drama, Jesus plays the part of God:

> Therefore, behold, I send to you prophets and wise men and scribes: some of them you will kill and crucify, and some of them you will scourge in your synagogues, and pursue from city to city. This is in order that all

---

88. Marcus, *Mark 1–8*, 222, referring to such passages as Psalm 139; Prov. 24.12; and others (cf. also Acts 1.24). Hofius, "Jesu Zuspruch," 43 n. 19, considers the evidence as strongly pointing to Jesus as God.

89. Rolland, "Jésus connaissait leurs pensées," 118, 121: "privilège divin d'après Ps 94,11."

90. See especially the reaction of the Samaritan woman in John 4.19; cf. also Luke 22.64.

91. W. Eckey, *Das Lukasevangelium unter Berücksichtigung seiner Parallelen*. Volume II: *11,1–24,53* (Neukirchen-Vluyn: Neukirchener, 2004), 804.

the righteous blood poured out on the earth — from the blood of Abel the righteous, to the blood of Zechariah the son of Barakiah, whom you killed between the sanctuary and the altar — might come upon you. Truly I say to you, all this will come upon this generation. (Matt. 23.34-36)

We will discuss this passage in more detail in Part III, but the essential point for our purposes here is that the role which Yahweh played in the OT as sender of prophets is the same role to which Jesus lays claim in his generation — we therefore have here a very exalted christology.[92] The reference to Jesus in Matthew as the sender of prophets places him on the divine side of reality rather than on the created, human side. He belongs with God (and Wisdom) in this sense, but it is more likely that the Matthean version of the saying is making a more immediate connection between Jesus and God than between Jesus and Wisdom. It need hardly be said that *God* is the one most commonly depicted as the sender of the prophets, although some scholarly exegesis with its emphasis on Wisdom seems to forget this!

Divine Hierarchy (Matthew 28.19)

We have seen already how in Mark 13.32 Jesus stands between God and the angels in a heavenly hierarchy; in Matt. 28.19, however, we have a *divine* hierarchy of Father, Son, and Spirit: all three persons participate in the divine name invoked in baptism.

Already within the context of earliest Christianity, there is significance in the *order* of the names, however. Very common in the Synoptics is the implication of the Father's authority over the Son and the corresponding obedience of the Son to the Father.[93] All things are given to the Son by his Father (Matt. 11.27 par. Luke 10.22; Matt. 28.18), and he continues to depend on the Father in prayer (e.g., Mark 1.35). Perhaps most clearly of all, the Son is frequently described as *sent by* the Father: once or twice in Mark, twice in Mat-

92. As Hare puts it, "the daring Christological claim implicit in 23.34 ought not to be overlooked." D. R. A. Hare, *The Theme of Jewish Persecution of Christians in the Gospel according to St Matthew* (SNTSMS 6; Cambridge: Cambridge University Press, 1967), 140 n. 3, cited in M. J. Suggs, *Wisdom, Christology and Law in Matthew's Gospel* (Cambridge: Harvard University Press, 1970), 58-59.

93. Contra H. D. Buckwalter, *The Character and Purpose of Luke's Christology* (SNTSMS; Cambridge: Cambridge University Press, 1996), passim, though see especially 187-91. Buckwalter's target is the concept of subordination, but in his critique he does not do justice to this emphasis on the Father's determination of the Son's identity.

thew, four times in Luke.[94] Sending clearly presupposes an authority of the sender over the envoy.[95]

In terms of the Son's authority over the Spirit, in John and Acts it is evident that the Son sends the Spirit (John 15.26; cf. 14.26; Acts 2.33). Jesus' sending of the Spirit at Pentecost would have been understood as the fulfillment of John the Baptist's promise (common to all four Gospels) that Jesus would baptize with the Holy Spirit.[96] This itself presupposes divine identity: as Jenson rightly notes, "No prophet as such can do this. To give the Spirit is to act from the position of God."[97] But if the Son is the one who *sends* the Spirit, then this again would presuppose a relationship of hierarchy within a Jewish context. As a result, it can be concluded that the order Father-Son-Spirit in Matt. 28.19 is not incidental; rather, it is born out of the early Christian thinking that the Father has authority over the Son, who in turn has authority over the Spirit.[98]

"Why Do You Call Me Good? No One Is Good except God Alone."[99]

The pericope Mark 10.17-22 has long been a source of considerable dispute. Already in 1908, Friedrich Spitta described it as "discussed a hundred times over."[100] It attracted three articles in the *Zeitschrift für die Neutestamentliche Wissenschaft* by the time the journal was ten years old.[101] Drawing christo-

94. On these, see chapter 7 below. (The ambiguity of "once or twice in Mark" concerns the question of whether to include Mark 12.6.)

95. The relation between the centurion and his soldiers in Luke 7.8 is a good illustration: "For I too am a man set under authority, with soldiers under me: I say to one, 'Go,' and he goes; and to another, 'Come,' and he comes. . . ." I am grateful to Dr. Audrey Dawson for suggesting this example.

96. Matt. 3.11; Mark 1.8; Luke 3.16; John 1.33.

97. R. W. Jenson, *Systematic Theology,* Volume 1: *The Triune God* (Oxford: Oxford University Press, 1997), 88.

98. Beale comments that in the case of Rev. 1.4, "The reason for the unusual placement of the Spirit before Christ is not clear." G. K. Beale, *Revelation* (NIGTC; Grand Rapids: Eerdmans, 1999), 189. But it is most likely to be because the author was planning an extended praise to Christ, which in fact spans the whole of vv. 5-7. The Father and the Spirit get eight words each, while Christ — in final position — gets fifty-three.

99. There is nothing in particular here pointing to preexistence, contra J. Schreiber, *Die Markuspassion,* 237-38.

100. F. Spitta, "Jesu Weigerung, sich als 'Gut' bezeichnen zu lassen," *ZNW* 9 (1908), 12-20 (12).

101. For these references and a substantial bibliography of other works, see F. Bovon, *Das Evangelium nach Lukas (Lk 15,1–19,27)* (EKK III/3; Düsseldorf/Zurich: Benziger/Neukirchener, 2001), 227-28.

logical conclusions from the question and statement of Jesus here has been something of a hazardous enterprise; nevertheless, a tentative attempt will be made here.[102] Our exegesis here applies to the Markan and the Lukan versions of the saying, which are identical; the parallel in Matt. 19.17 is not so significant for our purposes.

It will be helpful, for the purposes of a foil, to note features of R. Pesch's interpretation. He identifies as important the transition from v. 18 ("no one is good but God alone") to v. 19 ("you know the commandments: do not murder," etc.). As a result, he concludes that "The fact that the one God . . . is alone good means that Jesus can only point to God's commandments in his answer to the question of what action is commanded."[103] This is half right, but unfortunately at the same time misses the key point. As Gundry has observed, what is most striking is that having established the one good God as the one who defines what is required of human beings, in the final analysis *Jesus* is the one who defines what is ultimately commanded: "'One thing you lack,' he said. 'Go, sell everything you have, and give to the poor, and you will have treasure in heaven. Then come, follow me'" (Mark 10.21). In fact, then, Pesch has ended up saying precisely the reverse of what Jesus says. If God alone is good and able to give commandments, then Jesus does so as well. By implication, then, he is also good. And he is good not in the sense implied by the rich man, but in the absolute, divine sense as used by Jesus himself.[104]

No exegesis of Mark 10.18 (including that offered above) is devoid of problems. In the light of the considerations above, however, it is suggested as a strong possibility that Jesus' contrast between himself and God in v. 18 is only a temporary rhetorical strategy: from the pericope as a whole, it can be seen that Jesus is in fact making a subtle, implicit claim to solidarity with God and his goodness. As in 2.7, we have the phrase ". . . except God alone," and in both places Jesus does not constitute a *second* exception alongside God but rather stands, in his goodness, on the divine side of reality over against humanity.[105]

---

102. The position outlined below follows, to some extent, the reading of Gundry, *Mark*, especially 553.

103. Pesch, *Markusevangelium*, 2:138: "Dass allein der einzige Gott . . . gut ist, bedeutet, daß Jesus in seiner Antwort an die Frage nach dem gebotenen Tun nur auf Gottes Gebote verweisen kann."

104. Lohmeyer comments that the problem is with calling Jesus a "good *teacher*," using "good" in the absolute sense. E. Lohmeyer, *Das Evangelium nach Markus* (KEK; Göttingen: Vandenhoeck und Ruprecht, [17]1967), 209.

105. The blessing of the children in Mark 10.13-16 and the reference to Jesus "loving" the man in 10.21 are perhaps in the Evangelist's mind as further pointers to Jesus' goodness.

"Depart from Me, for I Am a Sinful Man."[106]

Incorporated into the Lukan account of the miraculous catch of fish (Luke 5.1-11; cf. John 21.1-14) is an instance in the Gospels of the OT motif in which a human being recoils from the divine presence on account of his own sinfulness. Simon reacts to Jesus' activity in Luke 5.8 with "Depart from me, for I am a sinful man, Lord." Joel Green points to the correspondence between Luke 5.1-11 and Isaiah 6 in particular, noting the four stages in each narrative:[107]

	Luke 5.1-11	*Isaiah 6.1-10*
Epiphany	vv. 4-7	vv. 1-4
Reaction	v. 8	v. 5
Reassurance	v. 10b	v. 7
Commission	v. 10b	vv. 8-10

As Bovon also puts it, "The appearance of the numinous uncovers the sins of human beings and is dangerous to them. Simon's reaction corresponds to the Hebrew Bible theophanies: one cannot see God without dying."[108]

We appear to have in Luke 5.8 an extremely exalted christological claim. One aspect of this is that there is a fundamental distinction between Jesus and sinful humanity. The second is that he should somehow not come into the presence of that sinful humanity and be contaminated by it. The very strong suggestion here is again that Jesus stands on the divine side of reality.[109]

Matthew's "Emmanuel"

As a result, it is entirely understandable that Matthew should describe Jesus as "Emmanuel," God with us. In the light of the considerations above, this should probably be understood as highlighting Jesus' identification with God

---

106. This motif seems to be rather under-researched: the only — very brief and inadequate — study I have been able to find is A. J. Matthews, "Depart from Me; For I Am a Sinful Man, O Lord," *ExpT* 30 (1918-19), 425.

107. Green, *The Gospel of Luke*, 233. He also points to the parallel with Exod. 3.5-6.

108. F. Bovon, *Luke 1: A Commentary on the Gospel of Luke 1:1–9:50* (Hermeneia; Minneapolis: Fortress, 2002), 170.

109. A similar, though less extreme reaction comes from the centurion who requests that Jesus heal his servant: "Lord, I am not worthy to have you come under my roof, but only say the word, and my servant will be healed" (Matt. 8.8; cf. Luke 7.6).

in a *hard* sense. David Kupp's study of the Emmanuel theme describes Jesus as the "God-with-us Messiah," and yet, "Matthew never openly asserts that Jesus is divine. Although I have used the term 'divine presence' continuously in connection with Jesus, it does not require that Jesus is God."[110] This is problematic, however: the fact that Kupp is happy to talk of the worship of Jesus highlights the incoherence here.[111] This *soft* sense of Jesus as divine presence does not quite do justice to Jesus' role in election or his place in the divine hierarchy.

Conclusion

As noted, often the events above are characterized in rather vague terms as "epiphanic" or the like. As has already been argued, however, this category is rather unproductive. A number of the instances noted show Jesus specifically carrying out divine functions, that is, doing the work attributed to God in the OT. Two factors, however, mean that this cannot be reduced to evincing a functional christology in which Jesus is merely an agent of God. First, a number of these functions belong exclusively and uniquely to God alone in the OT and Jewish tradition, either implicitly (electing God's people) or explicitly (forgiving sins, walking on the sea, etc.). That these divine prerogatives could not normally be claimed is echoed in the fact that, on the one hand, Jesus is accused of blasphemy, and, on the other, receives worship in Matthew and Luke. Secondly, the Synoptic Gospels all use the formula "in the name of Jesus" in such a way that it stands in for the OT formula "in the name of Yahweh." As such, as we have noted, we have much more than a functional christology, and rather a christology of divine identity, since a name is about identity.[112] Jesus is not seen as *exhausting* the divine identity, nor is he depicted as a second being worthy of worship in addition to God. The language of "inclusion within the divine identity" is helpful in that it avoids these two extremes. Both in claiming prerogatives otherwise uniquely divine and in sharing the identity of God, then, the Jesus of the Synoptics clearly transcends, goes beyond, the God-creation divide.

110. D. D. Kupp, *Matthew's Emmanuel: Divine Presence and God's People in the First Gospel* (SNTSMS; Cambridge: Cambridge University Press, 1996), 220.

111. Kupp, *Matthew's Emmanuel*, 227, 228.

112. R. J. Bauckham has advanced the case for preferring "identity" over "function" or "nature" in his *God Crucified: Monotheism and Christology in the New Testament* (Grand Rapids: Eerdmans, 1999), and there is a succinct statement in Bauckham, "The Throne of God and the Worship of Jesus," 45 n. 4.

The passages we have discussed here have no direct, explicit reference to preexistence. However, if there is clear reference to the divine identity of Jesus, it is questionable whether in the context of early Judaism and Christianity that would have been conceivable without preexistence. At the very least, then, the reader of the Synoptic Gospels ought not to be suspicious of potential evidence for preexistence in the writings of Matthew, Mark, and Luke.

III. The Pre- and Post-Resurrection Jesus as Transcending Space

As we noted in the introduction above, the term "transcendent" is sometimes used rather loosely in theological study, but we can at least identify two cases in Matthew's Gospel where Jesus is described in such a way that he is envisaged as transcending geographical space; that is, that he is not tied to his local presence. We will see further in our discussion of preexistence proper that Matthew also refers elsewhere to Jesus' transcendence of *time* as well. But it is spatial transcendence that is our concern here.

The first case is Matt. 18.15-20, where Jesus outlines the procedure for dealing with the wayward brother who sins (vv. 15-17). Then comes the mysterious statement that "whatever you bind on earth will be bound in heaven, and whatever you loose on earth will be loosed in heaven" (v. 18), which is explained in the next verse as meaning that when a request is agreed on, it will be accomplished by God in heaven. There is a further basis for this in v. 20: "for where two or three are gathered in my name, I am there in their midst." This statement is surprising because, while we might expect such a statement from the risen Jesus, it seems here that from Matthew's perspective Jesus even accompanies groups of his disciples and thereby transcends space in the course of his *earthly* ministry. As is commonly noted, there is almost certainly a reference here on Jesus' part to his being "the locus of the Shekinah,"[113] which was attributed in some strands of Jewish tradition to the Torah (most famously, *m. 'Abot* 3.2). G. Barth's suggestion is a nice possibility: "the place of the Torah is taken by the name of Jesus; the place of the Shekinah by Jesus himself."[114] Matt. 18.15-20 is thus excellent evidence of Hurtado's contention

---

113. R. G. Hamerton-Kelly, *Preexistence, Wisdom, and the Son of Man: A Study of the Idea of Preexistence in the New Testament* (SNTSMS 21; Cambridge: Cambridge University Press, 1973), 70.

114. G. Bornkamm, G. Barth, and H.-J. Held, *Tradition and Interpretation in Matthew* (London: SCM, 1963), 135, cited in Hamerton-Kelly, *Preexistence*, 70. For similar comments, see Sievers, "*Shekinah* and Matthew 18.20," 177-78.

that Jesus is a transcendent character in Matthew's Gospel, in this case specifically transcending his bodily space.

Secondly, the risen Jesus announces this also to be true of his presence with his disciples *throughout the world* and *in perpetuity:*

> Then Jesus came to them and said, "All authority in heaven and on earth has been given to me. Therefore go and make disciples of all nations, baptizing them in the name of the Father and of the Son and of the Holy Spirit, and teaching them to obey everything I have commanded you. And surely *I am with you always, to the very end of the age.*" (Matt. 28.18-20)[115]

Here the promise of Matt. 18.20 is reiterated and extended indefinitely into the future. Further, because of the implication of the worldwide mission of the disciples in 28.19, the promise extends throughout the world in 28:20: "wherever" in 18:20 would probably not have been heard at that point in the Gospel as encompassing such a scope.

The key point here, then, is that there is no disjunction on this point of Jesus' transcendence of geographical space between his earthly ministry and his risen glory. The promise in Matt. 28.18-20 is not significantly different from the promise Jesus makes in 18.20, even before his resurrection. Matthew presents Jesus here, then, as transcending his local presence; this is only a short step away from preexistence, which is the transcendence of Jesus' *temporal* presence in the world between his birth and ascension. This, again, is what we will see perhaps most strikingly in Jesus' lament over Jerusalem in Matt. 23.37.

Conclusion

We have seen, then, a considerable degree of consistency in the portrayals of Jesus in each of the Synoptic Gospels, although there are differences in emphasis. Almost always, however, the material in Mark is incorporated into one or (more usually) both of the other two, so that it is difficult to describe distinctively Markan emphases. Luke, on the other hand, has an extra "forgiveness" saying (Luke 7.49), and some significant special material which emphasizes Jesus' heavenly identity (10.18-20; 12.49; 22.31-32). In fact, however, it is the first Gospel which has the strongest emphasis on Jesus' transcendence —

---

115. For exhaustive exegesis and bibliography on this passage, see U. Luz, *Das Evangelium nach Matthäus.* Volume 4: *Mt 26–28* (Zurich: Benziger, 2002), 427-59.

a phenomenon we will see again when we explore the theme of preexistence in later chapters. Matthew alone has the material about Jesus' transcendence of space and the requirement to meet *in his name* (Matt. 18.18-20), as well as the *Emmanuel* motif, the mention of Jesus as sender of prophets, and the supplement to the walking-on-water account which contains just one of many references in the Gospel to reverence (προσκυνεῖν) of Jesus. Matthew also has the "thunderbolt from the Johannine heaven" (Matt. 11.27 par. Luke 10.22) in common with Luke, but it is hoped that this chapter has shown that a heavenly christology is not a distinctively Johannine phenomenon: there are plenty of thunderbolts throughout Matthew, Mark, and Luke as well.

In very brief summary, then, we have seen a clear identification of Jesus as transcending the God-creation divide, the heaven-earth divide, and as transcending the confinements of his earthly ministry. This is held together with his genuine humanity, and subordination to the Father: all the power and status which the Son has is as a result of the Father's determination. Nevertheless, the extremely exalted portrait of the Son here should, as has been mentioned, cause readers of the Synoptic Gospels to be less suspicious of potential evidence for preexistence than has been the case in the past generation of scholarship. In fact, the converse is true. As was noted in the conclusion to the first chapter, it would in fact be strange in the light of the material here if Jesus were not regarded as preexistent. He would then be a divine, heavenly, space-transcending figure who was somehow not preexistent. The following chapters aim to show that this final ingredient — preexistence — is in fact an integral part of the christologies of Matthew, Mark, and Luke.

PART TWO

The Advent and Mission of Jesus

CHAPTER 3

The "I Have Come" + Purpose Formula
in Matthew, Mark, and Luke

The "I have come" sayings in the Gospels have throughout the history of the church been proof texts for the preexistence of Jesus. This is particularly true of the Johannine versions, where the "coming" in question is further specified as a coming "down from heaven" (John 6.38, 42), or "into the/this world" (9.39; 12.46; 16.28; 18.37). There is also an overwhelming *scholarly* consensus that these Johannine sayings — because of the references to "heaven" and "the world" and the setting within John's logos christology more broadly — imply preexistence. On the other hand, the standard view is that the similar sayings in Matthew, Mark, and Luke do *not* presuppose preexistence. Part Two of the present study (chapters 3-7) aims to challenge this and will argue that *the Synoptic "I have come" sayings also bear witness to an understanding of the preexistence of Christ on the part of the Evangelists.* In fact, they are the strongest evidence for such a christology in the first three Gospels.

This brief preliminary chapter sets out three initial considerations: I. the object of study, that is, a brief identification of the "coming" sayings under discussion; II. a discussion of the common elements of the *"I have come" + purpose* formula; and III. the fact that on the surface this "I have come" + purpose formula might plausibly be interpreted as referring to a coming from preexistence in heaven. We will then conclude by noting how this fits into the broader argument of Part II as a whole.

I. The Object of Study

In addition to the "I have come" sayings, we will also examine here the two "the Son of Man has come . . ." sayings (Mark 10.45/Matt. 20.28; Luke 19.10). These have often been grouped together with the "I have come" sayings since, as far as the Gospel writers are concerned, Jesus and the Son of Man are clearly one and the same. Also included in the discussion are two questions addressed by demons to Jesus. While not attributed to Jesus himself, these questions nevertheless attest to the Evangelists' view that Jesus has come with a purpose. This gives us a total of ten sayings. First, from the demons:

1. "What have we to do with you, Jesus of Nazareth? *Have you come to destroy us?* I know who you are: the holy one of God!" (Mark 1.24 par. Luke 4.34)
2. "What have we to do with you, Son of God? *Have you come here to destroy us* before our due time?" (Matt. 8.29)

Then the "I have come" sayings:

3. "Let us go elsewhere into the nearby villages, so that I may also preach there. *For this reason I have come forth.*" (Mark 1.38; cf. Luke 4.43)
4. "It is not the healthy who need a doctor, but those who are sick. *I have not come to call the righteous, but sinners.*" (Mark 2.17 par. Matt. 9.13; Luke 5.32; Luke adds *"to repentance"*)
5. "*Do not think that I have come to abolish* the Law or the prophets. *I have not come to abolish them, but to fulfill them.*" (Matt. 5.17)
6. "*I have come to cast fire onto the earth,* and how I wish it were already kindled." (Luke 12.49).
7. "*Do not think that I have come to bring peace on the earth; I have not come to bring peace but a sword/division*" (Matt. 10.34 par. Luke 12.51)
8. "*For I have come to divide* man against father and daughter against mother, and daughter-in-law against mother-in-law. . . .*"* (Matt. 10.35)

Then "the Son of Man came":

9. "For even *the Son of Man came not to be served, but to serve, and to give his life* as a ransom for many." (Mark 10.45 par. Matt. 20.28)
10. "For *the Son of Man came to seek and to save* what was lost." (Luke 19.10).

These ten statements will be adduced here as evidence, in varying degrees of importance, for a preexistence christology in the Synoptic Gospels. There are of course many other references to Jesus moving around, where the verb "to come" and its cognates are used in connection with him, but these are the instances where there are potential christological implications in the references to Jesus' coming with a purpose.

II. The "I Have Come" + Purpose Formula

The reason the "I have come" sayings have attracted a certain amount of attention is that they are *summaries of Jesus' mission as a whole.* Although some have argued that one or two of the sayings above refer to Jesus coming to a particular location (e.g., Capernaum), no scholar has attempted to defend the indefensible by arguing that all of them have this sense. It is generally agreed that the sayings as a whole concern the entirety of Jesus' earthly ministry, and that the goals of his coming are his life's work.

In connection with this, a number of scholars have identified the fact that the "I have come" sayings of Jesus are very often accompanied by purpose clauses.[1] This is not exclusively the case, however, since we will also argue that Mark 1.38 ("for this reason I have come forth") also belongs among the "I have come" sayings. Although it does not follow the pattern "I have come" + infinitive, it clearly still has a reference to coming in connection with purpose. Similarly, there is variation in that, as we have said, the Gospels sometimes uses the first person form and sometimes use "the Son of Man" with a third person verb. Again, while in the majority of cases the verb used is the common verb for "come" in Greek (ἔρχομαι), in one case a synonym is used (παραγίνομαι in Luke 12.51), and on another occasion the compound verb "I have come *forth*" (ἐξέρχομαι) is used. Nevertheless, the consensus view that these sayings all belong together is certainly correct.

In this sense, it is appropriate to talk of the "I have come" + purpose pattern as a formula. It is important to distinguish this from the view that "come" is a technical term, a line of argument which we will criticize in the following chapter. A *formula* simply consists of a regular pattern of language: in a Christian marriage, for example, the minister may say, "I pronounce you man and wife"; this is a formula, even though none of its constituent words is on its own a technical term. As for the "I have come" sayings, it is the regular-

---

1. See for example, V. Hampel, *Menschensohn und historischer Jesus. Ein Rätselwort als Schlüssel zum messianischen Selbstverständnis Jesu* (Neukirchen-Vluyn: Neukirchener, 1990), 210: "Sieht man zunächst noch von der (Schein-) Ausnahme Mt 11,19ab par Lk 7,34 ab, sind sie alle infinitivisch konstruiert, wobei die Infinitive die finale Bestimmung ausdrücken. . . ." The "apparent exception" of Matt. 11.19 is discussed in an excursus at the end of this chapter.

ity of the pattern in the Gospels which makes it a formula: it certainly occurs frequently enough for it to be classified as such.

This is confirmed by the fact that it subsequently generated further instances of the formula that were attributed to Jesus in antiquity. In the *Sophia of Jesus Christ* from Nag Hammadi, for example, the Christ figure makes the following statements:

> I have come from the boundless one so that I might tell you all things. (*NHC* III 96,19-21)

> I have come from the Self-Begotten and the first endless light so that I might reveal everything to you. (*NHC* III 106,6-9)

> I have come from the first who was sent so that I may reveal to you him who is from the beginning. (*NHC* III 118,15-19)[2]

One of the most notorious cases is the saying, "I have come to destroy the works of the woman," attributed to Jesus in the Greek *Gospel of the Egyptians* (probably second century AD).[3] There is also the famous variation on Matt. 5.17 in the Talmud: "I came neither to destroy the Law of Moses nor to add to the Law of Moses" (*b. Shabbat* 116b).[4]

III. The *Prima Facie* Plausibility of the Preexistence Interpretation

The controversial point to be emphasized in the present chapter is that there is a strong *prima facie* case for seeing preexistence implied in the Synoptic "I have come" sayings. Specifically, because the sayings talk of coming *with a purpose,* they imply that the coming is a deliberate act. A deliberate act requires a before-and-after, and, in the case of a "coming," an origin from which

2. Translations are by D. M. Parrott in M. W. Meyer, ed., *The Nag Hammadi Library in English* (Leiden: Brill, 1977), 211, 218, and 227 respectively.

3. That the *Gospel* is cited by Clement of Alexandria shows that he knew it in the late-second/early-third century. The text of this fragment is from Clement, *Stromateis* 3.63. See the translation in W. Schneemelcher, ed., *New Testament Apocrypha*, volume 1: *Gospels and Related Writings* (Louisville: Westminster John Knox, 1991), 209. Origen also mentions the *Gospel* (Schneemelcher, ed., *New Testament Apocrypha*, 1:45).

4. There is also the reference in the *Gospel of the Ebionites* to Jesus saying, "I have come to do away with sacrifices" (Schneemelcher, *New Testament Apocrypha*, 1:170). See also K. Berger, *Die Auferstehung des Propheten und die Erhöhung des Menschensohnes. Traditionsgeschichtliche Untersuchungen zur Deutung des Geschickes Jesu in frühchristlichen Texten* (SUNT 13; Göttingen: Vandenhoeck und Ruprecht, 1976), 527, for further instances from late antiquity.

the speaker has come.[5] Hence the *usual* sense which one would attach to the statement "I have come to do such-and-such" would be that the person was previously not carrying out the task, but has come *from* somewhere in order to carry it out. Furthermore, if the person is referring to his whole earthly activity as the goal of the coming, the place of origin is logically somewhere outside of the human sphere. This is of course not watertight, since there may be some kind of idiom in operation. As a result, it is necessary to test this hypothesis, by examining the formula in its Jewish context to see what the most likely meaning for the phrase would be. But at this point, the *prima facie* sense should at least be open for discussion.

Conclusion, and the Argument of Part II

We have noted already, then, the first element of our larger argument in Part II:

- The preexistence interpretation of the "I have come" sayings has prima facie plausibility on simple logical grounds (chapter 3).

The next three chapters will attempt to confirm this hypothesis in three stages, arguing that

- None of the other scholarly options can be considered plausible (chapter 4).
- The "I have come" + purpose formula of the Gospels is most closely, and most abundantly, paralleled in announcements by angels of their comings from heaven (chapter 5).
- The preexistence interpretation is confirmed by the content and literary context — in particular, the heavenly and dynamic features — of the "I have come" sayings in the Synoptics (chapter 6).

The first point, then, we have already noted — the logical implications of the "I have come" + purpose formula. Secondly, the next chapter will have the negative function of showing that explanations of the "I have come" sayings as highlighting (for example) the *prophetic* or *Messianic* dimensions of Jesus'

---

5. Cf. the comments in connection with the Son of Man sayings in D. Macleod, *The Person of Christ* (Contours of Christian Theology; Leicester: Inter-Varsity, 1998), 45-70. Macleod says of Mark 10.45 and Luke 19.10 that "[t]he point is not simply that the Son of Man is in the world because he came into it . . . but that these passages ascribe to him a deliberate intention in coming" (59-60).

ministry are not persuasive. In chapter 5, the case will be made that qualitatively the closest and quantitatively the most numerous parallels to the "I have come" sayings of Jesus are those spoken by angels in rabbinic and other early Jewish literature. Angels also frequently announce their comings from heaven by a statement, "I have come" + purpose. This is significant because one does *not* find ordinary humans (even including figures as great as prophets) talking about their lives' work in such terms. Finally, we will proceed in chapter 6 to explain how the preexistence interpretation also makes good sense of the content of the "I have come" sayings in their literary contexts in Matthew, Mark, and Luke. We will see that the heavenly dimensions of Jesus' tasks delineated in these sayings strengthen the argument.

EXCURSUS: THREE RED HERRINGS

Other passages in the Gospels have been argued by some as meriting inclusion among the "coming" sayings in the Gospels, and alluding to preexistence. There are three chief contenders, but we will offer reasons below that they should not be included.

> The Son of Man has come eating and drinking, and they say, "Look at the man — a glutton and a drunkard, a friend of tax-collectors and sinners. (Matt. 11.19a par. Luke 7.34)

The setting of this saying as part of the sequel to Jesus' parable of the children has been much discussed elsewhere, and the details need not detain us.[1] After this parable, Jesus describes the behavior of both himself and John in Matt. 11.18-19a. As Harnack noted long ago, the emphasis here is not on the missions or advents of John and Jesus, but in each case on the *modus vivendi*.[2]

---

1. See S. J. Gathercole, "The Justification of Wisdom (Mt. 11.19b/Lk 7.35)," *NTS* 49 (2003), 476-88 (479-80). F. W. Beare's summary (*The Gospel according to Matthew* [Oxford: Blackwell, 1981], 261) is on the mark: "The general point of the parable is clear. The same people who criticize John for his austere manner of life are now criticizing Jesus for his lack of austerity." For a longer description of the setting, see P. M. Casey, *An Aramaic Approach to Q: Sources for the Gospels of Matthew and Luke* (SNTSMS; Cambridge: Cambridge University Press, 2002), 129-32, and F. Mussner, "Der nicht erkannte Kairos (Mt 11,16-19 = Lk 7,31-35)," *Biblica* 40 (1959), 599-612 (599-600). For the technical details of the games, see J. Jeremias, *The Parables of Jesus* (New Testament Library; London: SCM, 1963), 160-62.

2. A. Harnack, "'Ich bin gekommen.' Die ausdrücklichen Selbstzeugnisse Jesu über den Zweck seiner Sendung und seines Kommens," *ZTK* 22 (1912), 1-30 (3 n. 1). He is correct, then, in

Like Harnack, Warren Carter is right to exclude Matt. 11.19 from the "I have come" sayings on several grounds, most importantly that "in this statement, participles (μήτε ἐσθίων, μήτε πίνων), not an infinitive, are used after the finite verb ἦλθεν, thus creating an observation, not a declaration of purpose."[3] So it is not accurate to classify Matt. 11.19a par. Luke 7.34 among the sayings under discussion here.[4]

> The Son of Man has not come to destroy souls, but to save them. (Luke 9.55)[5]

This saying probably does not belong to the original text of Luke. In terms of its content, there is no problem with Lukan authorship: the antithetical formulation in connection with the coming of Jesus ("The Son of Man came not to . . . but to . . .") is very standard, and the content of Jesus' mission described here is common enough. There is nothing which betrays later phraseology: the reference to "souls" is a standard Jewish way of referring to "people," as parallels such as Rom. 2.9 show. It is even possible that the plural "souls" might point in the direction of Lukan authorship.[6] So, the internal evidence is unproblematic. The manuscript evidence for attestation of the saying, however, is weak. As is noted in the commentaries, this Son of Man saying is absent both from early manuscripts and from a number of uncials. Nestle-Aland's wise decision to omit the logion is based on the lack of attestation in $\mathfrak{P}^{45}$, $\mathfrak{P}^{75}$, ℵ, A, B, C, L, W, Δ, Ξ, and Ψ. Only Θ, $f^{1, 13}$, lat, syr[c, p], bo[pt] witness in

---

not including this saying among the ἦλθον sayings. See also W. Carter, "Jesus' 'I Have Come' Sayings in Matthew's Gospel," *CBQ* 60 (1998), 44-62 (46 n. 7), who makes the same point. I have discussed this point in Gathercole, "The Justification of Wisdom," 479-80.

3. Carter, "Jesus' 'I Have Come' Sayings in Matthew's Gospel," 46 n. 7.

4. It is also possible that the sense is not that they "came," but rather that they "went about" in their respective manners, a common meaning of ἔρχομαι + present participle. See, e.g., Mark 1.14, 39; Luke 2.16; 24.1; John 9.7. Contrast D. Verseput, *The Rejection of the Humble Messianic King: A Study of the Composition of Matthew 11–12* (Europäische Hochschulschriften: Frankfurt am Main/New York: Lang, 1986), 109, who talks of the "theological manner" of Matthew's expression in his use of ἦλθεν; similarly F. Christ, *Jesus Sophia. Die Sophia-Christologie bei den Synoptikern* (ATANT 57; Zurich: Zwingli, 1970), 68.

5. For detailed treatment of the textual issues involved in this verse, see Harnack, "Ich bin gekommen," 14-16; B. B. Warfield, "Jesus' Mission, according to His Own Testimony," *Princeton Theological Review* 13 (1915), 513-86 (514-17); B. M. Metzger, *A Textual Commentary on the Greek New Testament* (London: United Bible Societies, 1971), 148-49; J. M. Ross, "The Rejected Words in Luke 9$^{54-56}$," *ExpT* 84 (1972-73), 85-88.

6. While not endorsing Lukan authorship of the saying, I. H. Marshall, *The Gospel of Luke: A Commentary on the Greek Text* (NIGTC; Grand Rapids: Eerdmans, 1978), 407, points out the evidence on this point.

its favor, although Marcion also does.[7] Some scholars, most notably C. H. Dodd, have regarded the saying as authentically dominical while not authentically Lukan. Since our concern is with the final form of the Gospels, however, we will not pursue this discussion here. We can simply conclude that Luke 9.55 does not belong to the original text of the Gospel.

> The One who had come forth began to preach continually, and proclaimed the word widely, such that he could no longer go into a city in the open. He rather stayed outside in desert places, and they came to him from all around. (Mark 1.45)

An intriguing proposal for this verse has been put forward by the distinguished text critic J. K. Elliott along the following lines.[8] First, the subject of the sentence is not the leper disobeying the command of Jesus, but rather Jesus himself. Elliott argues this on the grounds that "It is doubtful . . . whether δέ would be a sufficiently strong adversative to denote a contrast between Jesus' injunction to silence in i 44 and the 'but on the contrary the leper went out . . .' in i 45."[9] He notes further problems with the usual rendering: (a) Jesus has been the subject thus far, and there is nothing to suggest a change of subject for "he began to preach"; (b) it would require a change in subject midway through Mark 1.45; (c) if the "spreading the *logos*" is the work of the leper, then the sense of *logos* here would be "tale," a sense otherwise unattested in Mark;[10] and (d) also unattested in Mark is anyone other than Jesus, John, and the apostles "preaching." In conclusion, Elliott states that "consideration of the linguistic details gives strong support for the suggestion that there is no change of subject in i.43-45 and that it is Jesus who is the subject of ἤρξατο."[11] Further, in other miracle stories, no comment is made about whether Jesus' injunction to silence is heeded; or rather, the exceptions can be explained. The result is that Mark 1.45 is an "unconnected verse" (unconnected to the

---

7. In addition to the apparatus in Nestle-Aland, see D. L. Bock, *Luke* (BECNT; Grand Rapids: Baker, 1996), 2:973, and J. Nolland, *Luke 9:21–18:34* (WBC; Waco: Word, 1993), 533.

8. J. K. Elliott, "Is ὁ ἐξελθών a Title for Jesus in Mark 1.45?" *JTS* 27 (1976), 402-5. A plank in Elliott's argument is also found in his "The Conclusion of the Pericope of the Healing of the Leper and Mark i.45," *JTS* 22 (1971), 153-57. For a similar position on the grammatical points, see G. D. Kilpatrick's two notes "Mark i 45 and the Meaning of λόγος," *JTS* 40 (1939), 389-90, and "Mark i 45," *JTS* 42 (1941), 67-68. On the λόγος issue, see also A. Feuillet, "Témoins oculaires et serviteurs de la Parole (Luc 1.2b)," *NovT* 15 (1973), 241-59 (especially 249).

9. Elliott, "Conclusion of the Pericope," 154.

10. Kilpatrick, "Mark i 45," *JTS* 42 (1941), 67, notes "the marked regularity of usage over at least twenty-two instances."

11. Elliott, "Conclusion of the Pericope," 155.

leper incident, that is) and "a characteristic Marcan summary such as is found at i.39 and ii.13."[12]

The next stage of the argument, which Elliott pursued later, was to say that "the One who had come forth" is a title of Jesus, or better, a "description of Jesus coined by Mark on the analogy of ὁ ἐρχόμενος under the influence of εἰς τοῦτο γὰρ ἐξῆλθον at i.38."[13] Hence, the designation is a reference to "the incarnate Jesus," the one who has come "from heaven."[14]

While intriguing, Elliott's proposal should probably be rejected. Mark commonly begins sentences with verbal participles, not least in the surrounding context of 1.45 (e.g., 1.41, 43; 2.1, 4, 5, 8). But "the One who had come forth" is unattested elsewhere as a title or designation of Jesus. Elliott's possible explanation of this, that the term implies that Jesus' ministry was completed in his lifetime and was thus of limited appeal, is not convincing.[15] The principal linguistic problem with the idea is that the δέ in ὁ δὲ ἐξελθών, while not constituting a strong adversative, probably does indicate a change of subject, from Jesus to the leper.[16] This has been emphasized further by the most recent detailed study by Swetnam.[17]

---

12. Elliott, "Conclusion of the Pericope," 156-57.

13. Elliott, "Is ὁ ἐξελθών a Title?" 405.

14. Elliott, "Is ὁ ἐξελθών a Title?" 404.

15. Elliott's point would only work if a rise in interest in the second coming led to a corresponding diminution of focus on preexistence and advent, which seems highly implausible.

16. C. R. Kazmierski, "Evangelist and Leper: A Socio-Cultural Study of Mark 1.40-45," *NTS* 38 (1992), 37-50 (49).

17. J. Swetnam, "Some Remarks on the Meaning of ὁ δὲ ἐξελθών in Mark 1,45," *Biblica* 68 (1987), 245-49.

CHAPTER 4

False Perspectives on the "I Have Come" Sayings

We noted in the previous chapter the *first* component of the fourfold argument of Part II, namely that the preexistence interpretation of the "I have come" sayings has *prima facie* plausibility on simple logical grounds. We now proceed to the second element of the agenda, that *none of the other scholarly options can be considered plausible.* This particular chapter, then, has a primarily negative function. Since the argument pursued with respect to the "I have come" sayings in these chapters is somewhat controversial, it will advance the case considerably if it can be shown that other explanations of the "I have come" sayings in the Gospels are in fact without any basis.

We will first survey the most important literature from the past on the "I have come" sayings. Secondly, the main part of the chapter will critique previous understandings of the sayings. Finally, we will offer criticisms of previous attempts — correct for the wrong reasons — to find preexistence in the "coming" sayings.

I. The Major Treatments

The "I have come" sayings have attracted scholarly attention in the last century or so because of their clear significance for the illumination of the purpose of Jesus in his ministry. Adolf Harnack's 1912 article noted that no less than four of the "I have come" sayings[1] which he treats give Jesus' ministry a

---

1. Harnack does not include Mark 1.38 in his discussion, but does discuss Luke 9.55. He

soteriological focus, with the other key aspect being the designation of Jesus as a Mosaic law-giver.[2] The significance of Harnack's article in the history of research, however, has been not so much in his conclusions as in his identification of the "I have come" sayings (with the similar Son of Man sayings in Mark 10.45 and Luke 19.10) as a more or less coherent object of study.

This was confirmed by B. B. Warfield's book-length article in response to Harnack.[3] On the other hand, Warfield objects to Harnack's equivocation over the messianic character of the sayings. For Warfield, this dimension is anchored not primarily in the "coming" alone (although he does connect it with the "coming one" title), but in the combination of the "coming" with the messianic ministry implied in the proclamation of the kingdom (as in Mark 1.38).[4] In combination with the "Son of Man" title, the "coming" sayings even imply preexistence.[5] Generally, however, Warfield refers to "I have come" as a "technical term" which makes "solemn reference to [Jesus'] divine mission."[6]

The only treatment longer than that of Warfield is the monograph on the sayings by E. Arens.[7] While he does not know of Warfield's article, Harnack is a particular target for Arens. He is especially critical of the way in which Harnack isolated the "I" sayings from their contexts and so he sets out to analyze both their original *Sitz im Leben* and their literary settings in the Synoptic Gospels.[8] He also attempts to counter the suspicion thrown by Bultmann on the historicity of the sayings, in which they were attributed to later reflection by the church. By contrast, Arens builds on the work of Jeremias in seeing an Aramaic idiom underlying the sayings.[9] In their present

---

treats Matt. 10.34-35 together, and also includes Matt. 15.24 ("I have only been sent to the lost sheep of the tribe of Israel"). See his list in "'Ich bin gekommen.' Die ausdrücklichen Selbstzeugnisse Jesu über den Zweck seiner Sendung und seines Kommens," *ZTK* 22 (1912), 1-30 (3-4).

2. On the conclusion of the soteriological focus of Jesus' coming, see Harnack, "Ich bin gekommen," 23, and for the issue of Jesus as law-giver, see p. 25.

3. B. B. Warfield, "Jesus' Mission, according to His Own Testimony," *Princeton Theological Review* 13 (1915), 513-86. I am grateful to Don Garlington for alerting me to this article, which has not been cited in any of the subsequent discussion of the "I have come" sayings.

4. Warfield, "Jesus' Mission," 534-35; cf. also 565. On the connection with "the coming one," see 539.

5. Warfield, "Jesus' Mission," 568.

6. On the "technical term," see Warfield, "Jesus' Mission," 528. For the quotation, see 522.

7. E. Arens, *The ΗΛΘΟΝ-Sayings in the Synoptic Tradition: A Historico-Critical Investigation* (Orbis Biblicus et Orientalis 10; Freiburg/Göttingen: Universitätsverlag Freiburg/Vandenhoeck und Ruprecht, 1976).

8. See the comment in Arens, *ΗΛΘΟΝ-Sayings,* 14.

9. Arens, *ΗΛΘΟΝ-Sayings,* 265-70. I have analyzed Arens's treatment in detail in S. J. Gathercole, "On the Alleged Aramaic Idiom behind the Synoptic ἦλθον Sayings," *JTS* 55 (2004), 84-91.

contexts, the "I have come" sayings also have epiphanic and, to some extent, messianic overtones as well.[10]

There is also a substantial article by J.-A. Bühner in a privately printed collection of Tübingen essays.[11] While this is extremely difficult to get hold of, much of the material is incorporated into his later monograph on the sending motif in John's Gospel.[12] The general argument, which will be further explored later, consists in the fact that "I have come" sayings, like their counterparts which have "sending" terminology, are essentially announcements by *messengers*. However, the greatest contribution which Bühner makes for our purposes is in his discovery of some parallel "I have come" sayings from the OT, early Judaism, and elsewhere in antiquity. One of the chief aims in the present (and next) chapter of our study here is to examine these and other parallels.[13]

In addition to these lengthy treatments, several scholars have also offered briefer accounts which have focused on the implications of the Synoptic "I have come" sayings for other areas of research.[14] We will not explore these in detail, however. Rather, it is time to categorize the various attempts (seven in all) to explain the "I have come" sayings and to identify their deficiencies.

10. Arens, *HΛΘON-Sayings*, 346.

11. J.-A. Bühner, "Zur Form, Tradition und Bedeutung der ἦλθον-Sprüche," *Das Institutum Judaicum der Universität Tübingen* (1971-72), 45-68.

12. See J.-A. Bühner, *Der Gesandte und sein Weg im vierten Evangelium. Die kultur- und religionsgeschichtlichen Grundlagen der johanneischen Sendungschristologie sowie ihre traditionsgeschichtliche Entwicklung* (WUNT 2; Tübingen: Mohr, 1977), 138-54.

13. The concern of the next chapter will be to make constructive use of some of Bühner's parallels and supplement them with numerous further examples.

14. J. P. Miranda, *Der Vater, der mich gesandt hat. Religionsgeschichtliche Untersuchungen zu den johanneischen Sendungsformeln, zugleich ein Beitrag zur johanneischen Christologie und Ekklesiologie* (Frankfurt/Bern: Lang, 1972), 43-48; H. Stettler, *Die Christologie der Pastoralbriefe* (WUNT; Tübingen: Mohr, 1998), 51-54; Gathercole, "On the Alleged Aramaic Idiom," 84-91. There is not space here to note comments any briefer than these treatments. W. Carter, "Jesus' 'I have come' Sayings in Matthew's Gospel," *CBQ* 60 (1998), 44-62, deserves mention here, although his focus is on the narrative function of the sayings and the significance of the purposes, rather than the meaning of the *coming*. Also indirectly relevant is G. D. Kilpatrick, "ACTS VII. 52 ΕΛΕΥΣΙΣ," *JTS* 46 (1945), 136-45. Kilpatrick comments that while in Christian usage from Acts to Irenaeus the term relates to the prophesied coming of Christ, the same term is used of Michael in *Testament of Abraham* A 16.

II. False Perspectives

Idiom of a Hellenistic Prophet

First, we come to the argument of Rudolf Bultmann, who asserted not only that the "I have come" sayings are not authentic sayings of Jesus, but also that they do not fit in a Palestinian context at all. Rather, they have resonances of statements made by *Hellenistic prophetic figures*.[15] It will be necessary to examine some of the evidence adduced by Bultmann and others subsequent to him to see if there is such a thing as the Hellenistic "prophetic style."

One of the key parallels adduced by scholars to point to the absence of any extraordinarily incarnational claim on the part of Jesus is a statement of Josephus in *Jewish War*.[16] Otto Michel's study is often cited as important in this regard.[17] The context is of Josephus's capture by the Romans and his being conducted to Vespasian as a prisoner. The key statement consists of Josephus's claim "I have come" and the corresponding statement that he has been sent by God:

> You imagine, Vespasian, that in the person of Josephus you have taken a mere captive; but I have come to you as a messenger of greater things (ἐγὼ δὲ ἄγγελος ἥκω σοι μειζόνων). Had I not been sent on this errand by God (μὴ γὰρ ὑπὸ θεοῦ προπεμπόμενος), I knew the law of the Jews and how it becomes a general to die. (*War* 3.400).

Like Bultmann, Michel thinks Josephus is tapping into a Hellenistic mode of prophetic self-presentation in which it was not out of the ordinary to say "I have come" and to claim to be on a divine mission. As a result, he regards this saying as a helpful parallel to the "I have come" sayings as they stand in the Gospels.[18] There are, however, two problems with drawing a strong parallel between Josephus's statement and the Synoptic "I have come" sayings.[19]

---

15. R. Bultmann, *History of the Synoptic Tradition* (Oxford: Blackwell, 1968), 156-57 n. 3. Bultmann does make a curious comment about Matt. 5.17 in the second edition's addenda (p. 412), which seems to be in some tension with what he says about "the hellenistic prophet."

16. Arens, *ΗΛΘΟΝ-Sayings*, 21 n. 9; J. Marcus, *Mark 1–8: A New Translation with Introduction and Commentary* (New York: Doubleday, 2000), 204; J. D. G. Dunn, *Christology in the Making: An Inquiry into the Origins of the Doctrine of the Incarnation* (London: SCM, 1980), 89. Dunn, however, also regards the "coming" sayings as transcending prophetic categories (Dunn, "New Testament Christology," in idem, *Christ and the Spirit*, Volume 1: *Christology* [Grand Rapids: Eerdmans, 1998], 6-7, on Mark 2.17 etc.).

17. O. Michel, "Ich komme," *TZ* 24 (1968), 123-24.

18. Michel, "Ich komme," 123.

19. There is no problem with the fact that the words are different; ἥκω and ἦλθον are sufficiently synonymous.

First and most striking, Josephus is merely talking about an episode in his life whereas, when Jesus talks about himself as having come, he is summing up his whole life and ministry. Josephus certainly claims that there is a theological character to his visit to Vespasian, that he has been providentially "sent by God." Yet, as has not been sufficiently recognized, *Josephus says he has come for a task which is only one event in his life.* Here, the parallel with the sayings of Jesus breaks down, and breaks down at a crucial point, as far as our argument is concerned. There is a crucial distinction between Josephus's report of his journey from his hiding place to Vespasian, and Jesus' summary of the purpose of his entire life and earthly ministry.

Secondly, there are significant problems with the idea that there is an established tradition of "prophetic self-presentation" which Michel claims to have identified. The only other example he cites is a single instance in Origen, *Contra Celsum* 7.9, in which Origen allegedly reports Hellenistic prophets saying such things as "I have come because the world is perishing."[20] Again, this has the effect among scholars of showing that "I have come" carries no sense of a descent from the heavens, since, as with Josephus, the expression merely demonstrates a claim to prophetic status.[21]

But this twists Origen's meaning by removing it entirely from its context. In fact he makes precisely the opposite point, as can be seen from the section in its entirety:

> But as Celsus promises to give an account of the manner in which prophecies are delivered in Phoenicia and Palestine, speaking as though it were a matter with which he had a full and personal acquaintance, let us see what he has to say on the subject. First he lays it down that there are several kinds of prophecies, but he does not specify what they are; indeed, he could not do so, and the statement is a piece of pure ostentation. However, let us see what he considers the most perfect kind of prophecy among these nations. "There are many," he says, "who, although of no name, with the greatest facility and on the slightest occasion, whether

---

20. This passage has also been an important part of history-of-religion discussion of the title "Son of God": A. E. J. Rawlinson already refers to it as "famous" in his 1926 Schweich lectures (*The New Testament Doctrine of the Christ* [London: Longmans, Green, 1929], 69), just as Reitzenstein identified it in 1904 as "bekannt" (*Poimandres. Studien zur griechisch-ägyptischen und frühchristlichen Literatur* [Leipzig: Teubner, 1904], 222).

21. Thus Michel; so also Bultmann, who regards "I have come" as unlikely for a Jewish prophet and notes the Origen text as resting "on the tradition of the prophetic style" (*History of the Synoptic Tradition*, 156-57, n. 3).

within or without temples, assume the motions and gestures of inspired persons; while others do it in cities or among armies, for the purpose of attracting attention and exciting surprise. These are accustomed to say, each for himself, 'I am God; I am the Son of God; or, I am the Divine Spirit; I have come because the world is perishing, and you, O men, are perishing for your iniquities. But I wish to save you, and you shall see me returning again with heavenly power. Blessed is he who now does me homage. On all the rest I will send down eternal fire, both on cities and on countries. And those who know not the punishments which await them shall repent and grieve in vain; while those who are faithful to me I will preserve eternally.'" Then he goes on to say: "To these promises are added strange, fanatical, and quite unintelligible words, of which no rational person can find the meaning: for so dark are they, as to have no meaning at all; but they give occasion to every fool or impostor to apply them to suit his own purposes."[22]

Two key points are to be noted here. First, it is not Origen's own words which are cited but a quotation from Celsus. This is significant because Origen argues in the following chapter that Celsus's data about prophets is highly questionable: "And it seems quite clear that Celsus is speaking falsely, when he says that those prophets whom he had heard, on being pressed by him, confessed their true motives, and acknowledged that the ambiguous words they used really meant nothing" (7.11). In his translation of the *Contra Celsum*, Henry Chadwick endorses Origen's verdict: following W. L. Knox, he takes the view that Celsus is clearly parodying early Christian teaching.[23] In fact, almost all scholars see some kind of misunderstanding or parody of Christian preaching on Celsus's part here.[24] My aim here is to make a similar point to that made by Knox in his rebuke of E. Fascher for making "the very unsafe assumption that Celsus' 'prophets' from Palestine can be quoted as parallels" to anything in the New Testament.[25]

Secondly, Celsus is reporting that he has come across those who claim

22. A. Roberts, J. Donaldson, eds., *The Ante-Nicene Fathers*, Volume 4 (Grand Rapids: Eerdmans, 1994), 614.

23. H. Chadwick, *Origen: Contra Celsum* (Cambridge: Cambridge University Press, 1953), 402-3 n. 6; W. L. Knox, *Some Hellenistic Elements in Primitive Christianity* (London: British Academy, 1944), 83 n. 2.

24. Rawlinson, *New Testament Doctrine of the Christ*, 70: "Celsus of course had read the Gospels, and the claims which he thus puts in the mouth of the typical Syrian prophet are to a large extent a deliberate parody of the claims made by the church on behalf of our Lord."

25. Knox, *Some Hellenistic Elements*, 83 n. 2, responding to E. Fascher, *Prophētēs. Eine sprach- und religionsgeschichtliche Untersuchung* (Giessen: Töpelmann, 1927), 203.

not merely to be prophets, but to be divine:[26] "They are accustomed to say, each for himself, 'I am God; I am the Son of God; or, I am the Divine Spirit; I have come because the world is perishing.'" Celsus's three alternatives here clearly follow a trinitarian sequence: God, Son of God, divine Spirit. Origen reinforces this in his response to Celsus in the next chapter:

> But if he were dealing honestly in his accusations, he ought to have given the exact terms of the prophecies, whether those in which the speaker is introduced as claiming to be God Almighty, or those in which the Son of God speaks, or finally those under the name of the Holy Spirit. (7.10).

So for Origen, Celsus's speakers are claiming to have come from heaven as Father, Son, or Holy Spirit. Clearly, then, using the *Contra Celsum* passage here as a parallel to the "I have come" sayings of Jesus in support of a prophetic interpretation of those sayings is impossible.

Other alleged parallels are adduced by Bultmann, who makes reference to Solon's statement that he has come (ἦλθον) as a herald to deliver a poem.[27] The context, however, makes it explicit that Solon has come "from beloved Salamis," and so this is a straightforward coming from "a" to "b."[28] Similarly, in the second edition of *History of the Synoptic Tradition,* Bultmann adds a reference to Pindar's second Pythian ode.[29] But while the inspired poet does exclaim "I come" (ἔρχομαι) in line 4, it is "from Thebes" (ἀπὸ Θηβῶν) that he has come.[30] The primary sense, then, is of a local "coming" rather than particular epiphanic or prophetic connotations. In which case, that the coming re-

26. One could add to this a number of parallels adduced by Weinreich. In 1915, he published a series of commentaries on Greek papyri, including one which he calls "The not-unknown God, Phoebus," dating from AD 117. See O. Weinreich, "Οὐκ ἄγνωστος Φοῖβος θεός," *Archiv für Religionswissenschaft* 18 (1915), 34-45. In this papyrus, Phoebus (Apollo) announces his arrival with a similar formula to that found in Josephus: ἥκω σοί, ὦ δῆμε. What is more interesting, however, is that he provides a number of parallels, largely drawn from plays in which a god speaks the prologue setting the scene, but begins by announcing his own arrival from wherever he has come. In some examples from Euripides, Hermes introduces the *Ion;* Poseidon the *Troades;* and Dionysus the *Bacchae.* The mortal exception to this is Polydore who introduces the *Hecuba,* but he is a ghost who has "come" from the underworld. Weinreich, "Οὐκ ἄγνωστος Φοῖβος θεός," 39. Weinreich goes on (pp. 40-41) to offer further parallels from the prologues of Plautus's plays.

27. Bultmann, *History of the Synoptic Tradition,* 156-57 n. 3.

28. For text and English translation, see I. M. Linforth, *Solon the Athenian* (Berkeley: University of California Press, 1919), 150-51 (poem XX): "Αὐτὸς κήρυξ ἦλθον ἀφ' ἱμερτῆς Σαλαμῖνος."

29. Bultmann, *History of the Synoptic Tradition,* 412.

30. Pindar, *Pythian Odes* 2.3-4.

lates to one episode in the poet's life makes the reference singularly inappropriate as a parallel to the "I have come" sayings of Jesus.

There are numerous other examples which are clearly dependent on either Synoptic or Johannine "I have come" sayings.[31] But on the basis of those above which are with some exceptions independent of the Gospel traditions, we can reach some conclusions. It seems that the identification by Bultmann and Michel of a Hellenistic mode of prophetic self-presentation (a "hellenistische Präsentationsstil") has yet to be demonstrated. The typical problem here is that scholars simply adduce one or two parallels, but often the parallels have very little in common with each other. The examples from Josephus and Origen are not of the same kind, and Bultmann's references to Solon and Pindar are very different again. The case that there is some kind of Hellenistic "type" of prophetic self-presentation here is thus very shaky.

"I Have Come," an Aramaic Idiom for "I Am Here . . ."?

The trigger for the emphasis on the Aramaic background to the "I have come" sayings was the attack on their authenticity by Bultmann which we have already mentioned.[32] While this proposal of Bultmann has had considerable influence,[33] Jeremias argued in reply that Bultmann's objection "is quite inappropriate for the underlying Aramaic *'atayit,* which can simply mean 'I am there,' 'I will,' 'it is my task.'"[34] In a now famous article Jeremias identifies

31. See the examples given by Bultmann from Mandaean and Manichaean sources in his "Die Bedeutung der neuerschlossenen mandäischen und manichäischen Quellen für das Verständnis des Johannesevangeliums," *ZNW* 24 (1925), 100-146 (104-7).

32. In fact it was Wrede who first made the argument, but it is most associated with Bultmann. See W. Wrede, *The Messianic Secret* (Cambridge: Clarke, 1971), 223 n. 26 = *Das Messiasgeheimnis in den Evangelien. Zugleich ein Beitrag zum Verständnis des Markusevangeliums* (Göttingen: Vandenhoeck und Ruprecht, 1963), 222 n. 2.

33. See, for example, E. Käsemann, "Die Anfänge christlicher Theologie," in idem, *Exegetische Versuche und Besinnungen* (Göttingen: Vandenhoeck & Ruprecht, 1970), 82-104 (96) = "The Beginnings of Christian Theology," in idem, *New Testament Questions of Today* (Philadelphia: Fortress, 1969), 82-107 (97-98); Miranda, *Der Vater, der mich gesandt hat,* 44-45; A. Hultgren, *Jesus and His Adversaries: The Form and Function of the Conflict Stories in the Synoptic Tradition* (Minneapolis: Augsburg, 1979), 109-11.

34. J. Jeremias, *New Testament Theology* (London: SCM, 1971), 83. See also idem, "Das Lösegeld für viele," in idem, *Abba: Studien zur neutestamentlichen Theologie und Zeitgeschichte* (Göttingen: Vandenhoeck und Ruprecht, 1966), 216-29 (224); idem, *Jesus' Promise to the Nations* (London: SCM, 1968), 23-24.

some of the Aramaic parallels he has in mind.[35] His chief argument lies in his noting rabbinic parallels in which the phrase "come to" apparently has the sense of to intend, want, have the task of, etc. Applied to the Gospels, then, this would mean that the relevant sayings of Jesus meant "my task is not to call the righteous, but sinners" or "my task is to cast fire on the earth." This line is still taken in more recent scholarship: Jeremias is followed by Arens in his book on the "I have come" sayings[36] as well as by other, particularly German language, commentators.[37] Jeremias is principally concerned with defending, against Bultmann, the authenticity of the sayings. Since our concern is the final form of the Greek Gospels, this debate will not be pursued here.

There are numerous problems with Jeremias's hypothesis, as I have argued elsewhere.[38] But even if this idiom did underlie the statements made by the historical Jesus, would it apply to the Greek texts of the Evangelists? As far as the Greek texts of the Gospels are concerned, Jeremias himself is not at fault: his concern is with the original Aramaic words of Jesus, and with their authenticity. Problems do occur, however, when commentators such as Grundmann, Wiefel, and Bovon import the meaning of the hypothetical Aramaic idiom into the Greek "I have come" sayings. Bovon, for example, translates the Greek of Luke 5.32 as: "I am not here ('Ich bin nicht da') to call the righteous to repentance, but sinners."[39] Wiefel makes a very similar move.[40] Schürmann is right to disagree with the validity of the Aramaic parallels at this point, on the grounds that they are surely irrelevant to the interpretation

---

35. J. Jeremias, "Die älteste Schicht der Menschensohn-Logien," *ZNW* 58 (1967), 159-72 (167).

36. Arens, *ΗΛΘΟΝ-Sayings*, 21, 54-55.

37. W. Grundmann, *Das Evangelium nach Markus* (Theologischer Handkommentar zum Neuen Testament; Berlin: Evangelische, 1968), 63 n. 10a; F. Bovon, *Das Evangelium nach Lukas. 15-19,27* (EKK; Zurich: Benziger, 2001), 277; P. Stuhlmacher, "Existenzstellvertretung für die Vielen. Mk 10,45 (Mt 20,28)," in idem, *Versöhnung, Gesetz und Gerechtigkeit. Aufsätze zur Biblische Theologie* (Göttingen: Vandenhoeck und Ruprecht, 1981), 27-42 (36) = "Vicariously Giving His Life for Many, Mark 10:45 (Matt. 20:28)," in idem, *Reconciliation, Law, and Righteousness: Essays in Biblical Theology* (Philadelphia: Fortress, 1986), 16-29 (22); S. Kim, *The "Son of Man" as the Son of God* (Tübingen: Mohr, 1983), 42-43; Stettler, *Die Christologie der Pastoralbriefe,* 52. For further examples, see Gathercole, "On the Alleged Aramaic Idiom behind the Synoptic ἦλθον-Sayings," 84-85.

38. Gathercole, "On the Alleged Aramaic Idiom behind the Synoptic ἦλθον-sayings," 84-91.

39. F. Bovon, *Das Evangelium nach Lukas.* Volume 1: *Lk 1,1–9,50* (EKK; Zurich: Benziger, 1989), 252: "Ich bin nicht da, Gerechte zur Umkehr zu rufen, sondern Sünder."

40. W. Wiefel, *Das Evangelium nach Lukas* (Theologischer Handkommentar zum Neuen Testament; Berlin: Evangelische, 1988 [new edition]), 248: "Das παρεγενόμην (= ich bin da), entspricht dem ἦλθον (beides = aram. *atet*)," following W. Grundmann, *Das Evangelium nach Lukas* (Theologischer Handkommentar zum Neuen Testament; Berlin: Evangelische, 1969), 271.

of the Greek text.[41] So this idiomatic interpretation of the "I have come" sayings should also be dismissed.

"I Have Come" — from Nazareth?

This explanation sees the references to Jesus' coming as a coming out of obscurity in Nazareth into his public ministry. However, while it has been adopted by a few scholars for the cases in the early chapters of Mark, no scholar to my knowledge has attempted to explain all the sayings this way.[42]

In fact, even for the early chapters of Mark this is a questionable approach. Support might come from the use of "come" (ἔρχομαι) with Jesus as the subject in Mark 1.9: "Jesus came from Nazareth in Galilee and was baptized by John in the Jordan." However, the first references in Mark's Gospel to Jesus' coming specifically with the purposes entailed by his mission are in 1.24 and 38. Throughout Mark 1.21-38, Jesus is in Capernaum, and it hardly marks an emergence from obscurity for Jesus to start his ministry only twenty-five miles from Nazareth in another small village. (A recent estimate has put the population of Capernaum at about 1000.)[43] Similarly, there is no real basis for the idea that "coming" language can be understood idiomatically as "coming out of obscurity."

In addition, this would not work very easily for the narrative of Matthew's Gospel: as mentioned above, there have not been any serious attempts to argue for the "from Nazareth" view here. When Jesus comes "from Galilee" in Matthew 3.13, it is specifically "to be baptized by John." Furthermore, the "I have come" sayings in Matthew's Gospel are quite unsuited to an implicit reference to coming from Nazareth, as will be seen in chapter 6.

Again, in Luke, there is no reference to Jesus coming forth from Nazareth. The beginning of Jesus' adult life is announced rather suddenly in Luke 3.21: "When all the people were being baptized, Jesus was also baptized. . . ." As with Matthew's "I have come" sayings, reference to a coming from Nazareth would be quite inappropriate to the content of the Lukan sayings. Again, this will be explored further in chapter 6.

41. H. Schürmann, *Das Lukasevangelium.* Volume 1: *Kommentar zu Kap. 1,1–9,50* (Herders theologischer Kommentar zum Neuen Testament; Freiburg: Herder, 1969), 292 n. 35.

42. On Mark 1.38 and 2.17, see R. H. Gundry, *Mark: A Commentary on His Apology for the Cross* (Grand Rapids: Eerdmans, 1993), 94, 130.

43. J. C. H. Laughlin, "Capernaum from Jesus' Time and After," *BAR* 19 (1993), 54-63, 90 (57). The attempt by Meyers and Strange to argue for a much larger population has received heavy criticism. I am grateful to Stephen Catto for supplying me with this information.

Jesus Coming as a Prophet of Israel

In his *The Holy Spirit and the Gospel Tradition,* C. K. Barrett identifies a number of features which contribute evidence for the prophetic identity of Jesus: predictions, symbolic actions, an authoritative tone, pneumatic inspiration, calling for national repentance, and the like. In addition to a long list of passages in support borrowed from C. H. Dodd, Barrett follows the lead of Bultmann and adds the "I have come" sayings because of their "particularly authoritative nature."[44] The principal difference from Bultmann, however, lies in the fact that Barrett sees the "I have come" sayings as pointing to a prophetic identity *along OT lines* rather than as a Hellenistic prophet. A number of modern commentators follow this line, such as Pesch, Davies/Allison, and Johnson. For Pesch, "coming" language can refer to Jesus' "prophetic consciousness of being sent."[45] Davies and Allison, in defending the authenticity of the sayings, note that "if Jesus spoke of his purpose in coming into the world, this would be consistent with his self-conception as a prophetic figure and his conviction that his commission was of heavenly origin."[46] According to Johnson, the "I have come" saying in Luke 12.49 "suggests a prophetic passion and urgency" and 12.51 refers to a "prophetic visitation."[47] Earlier, Johnson talks of Jesus' activity of "calling" in Luke 5.32 as referring to a "prophetic call."[48] Suggs takes a similar view of the sayings.[49] We will examine the two pieces of evidence most commonly adduced for this understanding.

First, the alleged tradition-historical evidence. Bühner gives some instances of "I have come" statements from *prophetic* messengers. There is a very ancient Egyptian example which need not detain us.[50] At the other end

44. C. K. Barrett, *The Holy Spirit and the Gospel Tradition* (London: SPCK, 1966), 95.

45. R. Pesch, *Das Markusevangelium.* Volume 1: *Einleitung und Kommentar zu Kap. 1,1–8,26* (Herders theologischer Kommentar zum Neuen Testament; Freiburg: Herder, 1976), 249-50 n. 13: "prophetisches Sendungsbewusstsein."

46. W. D. Davies and D. C. Allison, *A Critical and Exegetical Commentary on the Gospel according to Saint Matthew.* Volume 1: *Introduction and Commentary on Matthew I–VII* (ICC; Edinburgh: Clark, 1988), 483 (on 5.17).

47. L. T. Johnson, *The Gospel of Luke* (SacPag 3; Collegeville: Liturgical, 1991), 209 and 208 respectively *(sic)*. He also comments on the "prophetic challenge" and "prophetic background" to Luke 12.49, although this perhaps focuses on the Elijah background (209).

48. Johnson, *Luke,* 97.

49. M. J. Suggs, *Wisdom, Christology and Law in Matthew's Gospel* (Cambridge: Harvard University Press, 1970), 50.

50. Pap. Turin, Pleyte Rossi 137 *(non vidi),* cited in O. Firchow, "Die Boten der Götter," in idem, ed., *Ägyptologische Studien. FS Hermann Grapow* (Berlin: Institut für Orientforschung, 1955), 87: "I am the messenger of Toth, who comes to bring (life and health?)."

of the scale there is a very modern example, where Elijah comes to warn a bridegroom who is in danger of dying: this will be discussed further in the following chapter.[51] The first main example comes in 1 Samuel 16:

> The Lord said to Samuel, "How long will you mourn for Saul, since I have rejected him as king over Israel? Fill your horn with oil and be on your way; I am sending you to Jesse of Bethlehem. I have chosen one of his sons to be king." But Samuel said, "How can I go? Saul will hear about it and kill me." The Lord said, "Take a heifer with you and say, *'I have come to sacrifice to the Lord.'* Invite Jesse to the sacrifice, and I will show you what to do. You are to anoint for me the one I indicate." Samuel did what the Lord said. When he arrived at Bethlehem, the elders of the town trembled when they met him. They asked, "Do you come in peace?" Samuel replied, "Yes, in peace; *I have come to sacrifice to the Lord.* Consecrate yourselves and come to the sacrifice with me." Then he consecrated Jesse and his sons and invited them to the sacrifice.

Of course, Samuel is a prophet, and Bühner is right to classify this statement among references to prophets. But it is not specifically a "prophetic advent" which is highlighted here. As Fokkelman has noted, immediately after the account of Samuel in 1 Sam. 16.1-5, the other participants in the sacrifice all "come" as well:

> "*bo'* ["come"] occurs seven times . . . and then an eighth time. . . . The prophet is always the subject for the first four times that it appears in the text, but the last four times it is always his guests, twice a group from Bethlehem (5d, 6a) and twice an individual (11h, 12a). We realize that this last arrival, that of David himself, is a climax by opening the decisive moment of the plot. The prophet recognizes that himself in v.11h: "we will not sit down [to the sacrificial feast], until he has come here." . . . In every case, the movement of the coming is aimed at one and the same place, that of the sacrifice ceremony. Both Samuel's long journey from Ramah and the short movement of those invited from Bethlehem have that end objective. The narrated space thus has one distinct middle point, the place of sacrifice, through the whole story.[52]

---

51. Bühner, *Der Gesandte und sein Weg,* 142.
52. J. P. Fokkelman, *Narrative Art and Poetry in the Books of Samuel: A Full Interpretation Based on Stylistic and Structural Analyses.* Volume II: *The Crossing Fates (I Sam. 13–31 & II Sam. I)* (Assen/Dover: Van Gorcum, 1986), 119.

So in fact, it is *David's* coming which is the highlight in 1 Samuel 16. Furthermore, coming to sacrifice is hardly a role particularly associated with *prophets.*

Bühner's second principal example comes in a rabbinic story in Pesikta Rabbati 20 of Moses' ascent to heaven to receive the Torah for Israel. The angel Kemuel tries to stop Moses from approaching God, but Moses gives his justification:[53]

> At the time that Moses was to go up on high, a cloud came and lay down in front of him. Moses did not know whether he was to mount it or to take hold of it. Thereupon the mouth of the cloud flew open and he entered it, as is said *And Moses entered into the midst of the cloud* (Exod. 24.18) — *into the cloud which covered the Mount* (Exod. 24.15). And the cloud covered Moses and carried him up. As he was preparing to walk on the firmament, the angel Kemuel, he that is in charge of the twelve thousand destroying angels that are seated at the gate of the firmament, met him. He rebuked Moses and said to him: "What dost thou among the holy ones of the Most High? Thou comest from a place of all foulnesses: what wouldst thou in a place of purity? Born of a woman in heat, what wouldst thou in a place of fire that is pure?" Moses replied: "I am Amram's son — *I am he who has come to receive the Torah for Israel.*"

As Bühner puts it, "as the context shows, Moses appeals with this statement to the commission from God for his daring undertaking to climb up into heaven."[54] But there is no emphasis in the passage on Moses' prophetic status. Moreover, this is no ordinary prophetic coming; here Moses is going from earth to God. While Moses is of course sometimes characterized as a prophet in early Judaism, there is no sense of his prophetic identity here. Rather, two other aspects are in focus. There is the view of the angel, first of all, that the problem with Moses is that he is a *human being.* As Groezinger has noted, this taps into the Jewish tradition of the rivalry between angels and humans.[55] On the other hand, Moses' own view is put forward in response: he is the one who has been commissioned by God to receive the Torah. That is to say, Moses points to his *unique* status as the one who has the function of receiving the Torah. He is not depicted as one in a line of prophets, even as the beginning of that line.

53. *Pesikta Rabbati* 20; see W. G. Braude, ed. *Pesikta Rabbati: Discourses for Feasts, Fasts and Special Sabbaths* (New Haven: Yale University Press, 1968), 1:406.
54. Bühner, *Der Gesandte und sein Weg,* 142.
55. K.-E. Groezinger, *Ich bin der Herr, dein Gott! Eine rabbinische Homilie zum Ersten Gebot (PesR 20)* (Frankfurter Judaistische Studien; Frankfurt: Lang, 1976), 148. On the theme, see further P. Schäfer, *Rivalität zwischen Engeln und Menschen. Untersuchungen zur rabbinischen Engelvorstellung* (Berlin: Gruyter, 1975).

As noted above, Bühner is not incorrect to classify these statements as "I have come" sayings in the mouths of prophets. However, neither Samuel nor Moses makes these statements *in their capacity as prophets* in any sense. As a result, it would be wrong to conclude from Bühner's observation that there is a traditional association of the "I have come" formula with prophets. Again, both instances are of figures describing specific episodes rather than summarizing their whole ministries. Bultmann's judgment that no prophet inaugurates his prophetic ministry or summarizes his career with "I have come" in the OT can probably be extended to post-biblical Judaism as well.[56]

The second way in which the "I have come" statements are placed in a prophetic class is by the argument that "I have come" simply corresponds to the passive of divine action "I have been sent." One example of this is the "I have come" saying in Mark 1.38, which is paraphrased by Luke as "I have been sent . . ." (Luke 4.43). Marshall and Klostermann, for example, make reference to Luke's correct interpretation of Mark 2.17 here.[57] W. Grimm's statement articulates what underlies a number of interpretations: "both forms," namely, "coming" and "being sent," "are totally synonymous and interchangeable."[58] Along similar lines, many commentators simply gloss references to Jesus' coming in terms of his mission.

J.-A. Bühner's study, however, is important in that it identifies some key ways in which the "I have come" sayings are formally different from statements of being sent. He notes that to say "I have come" points more directly to the responsibility and personal action *of the envoy,* rather than appealing to the action of the *sender.*[59]

Bühner sets the "I have come" sayings in a tradition-historical context of the arrival of a messenger so that they fit into the genre of "self-introduction": "'I have come' language belongs to the sphere of the report, which the messen-

---

56. Bultmann, *History of the Synoptic Tradition,* 156 n. 3. Bultmann notes that "the O.T. never speaks of prophets coming or having come in the technical sense, much less does any prophet say, 'I have come.'"

57. I. H. Marshall, *The Gospel of Luke: A Commentary on the Greek Text* (NIGTC; Grand Rapids: Eerdmans, 1978), 198; E. Klostermann, *Das Markusevangelium* (Handbuch zum Neuen Testament; Tübingen: Mohr, [5]1971), 19.

58. W. Grimm, *Weil ich dich Liebe* (Bern: Lang, 1976), 83: ". . . beide Formen völlig gleichwertig und austauschbar sind."

59. However, Bühner also identifies the way in which "I have come" sayings can also do this, although an additional reference to coming *from another* (e.g., "from God") is required here. Bühner identifies this in a number of instances in John's Gospel (e.g., 5.43; 7.28; 8.42); another example is the statement of Raphael in Tob. 12.18: "I have not come by my own grace, but by the will of God." See Bühner, *Der Gesandte und sein Weg,* 147-52.

ger makes before his addressee in order to introduce himself."[60] To paraphrase what Bühner goes on to say, the "I have come" saying forges a link between sender, envoy, and addressee in order to prepare for the message in such a way that the intention of the sender, the legitimacy of the envoy, and the address of the message be evident. On the other hand, "being sent" and "coming" are not identical, but rather constitute the two poles of the envoy's journey ("die beide Endpunkte des Botenweges"). Bühner rightly notes that in the sayings the sender is only there in the background: the focus is more on the envoy himself.[61] When seen in this light, the "I have come" sayings have considerably more significance than that seen in "the radically reductionist thesis of Jeremias and Arens."[62] While Bühner emphasizes here the dimension of the envoy's personal responsibility in his address to the recipient, that responsibility is not confined to this sphere; it also includes the action of coming.

In conclusion, it is of course not mistaken to explain Jesus' coming in terms of his being sent, but it is not entirely *sufficient:* within the structure of the "I have come" sayings we can see that Jesus' coming is not simply a passive event; rather, Jesus draws attention to his own action as instrumental in the coming. In fact, even if Grimm were correct to emphasize the interchangeability of "I have come" and "I have been sent," the question of the christological implication is still an open one: angels, prophets, messiahs and other figures are all "sent," and so sending on its own cannot be tied to a particular office. As a result, there is certainly insufficient evidence to place the "I have come" sayings of Jesus in a class of prophetic announcements.

Jesus Coming as Messiah

Some, however, have attempted to provide a slightly different account of the sayings by pointing to a *messianic* character for the statement "I have come."[63] Schneider's article in *TDNT* takes a strong line: in talking of the "I have come" sayings, he gives the summary statement that "They derive from the Messianic self-understanding of Jesus and are to be explained

---

60. Bühner, *Der Gesandte und sein Weg,* 145: "Das 'ich bin gekommen' hat seinen Platz im Bericht, den der Bote vor dem Adressaten gibt, um sich vorzustellen."

61. The point is also made in Warfield, "Jesus' Mission," 581.

62. Bühner, *Der Gesandte und sein Weg,* 140: "die radikale Reduktionsthese von Jeremias und Arens."

63. Harnack, "Ich bin gekommen," 1, sees messianic elements in some, though by no means all, of the sayings.

thereby."[64] Grimm has an elaborate argument for a strong connection between the "I have come" sayings and the Lord's anointed in Isaiah 61 and so takes the sayings in a strongly messianic sense, although this has not won wide acceptance.[65]

The principal argument made by some scholars (most recently, Bovon) attempts to connect the "I have come" sayings with the title of "the coming one" (ὁ ἐρχόμενος), a designation of the Messiah, the eschatological prophet.[66] Bovon states that the references to "coming" have an eschatological ring to them, because "the coming one" was a designation of the Messiah.[67]

However, the problem here is that the "I have come" sayings do not in fact *emphasize* the coming per se; the focus in these statements is invariably on the *goal* of the coming, rather than on the coming as the fulfillment of the expectation that someone would come. In this respect, the "I have come" sayings differ from the sayings in which Jesus specifically announces his *presence* in fulfillment of prophecy:

> I say to you that one greater than the Temple is here. (Matt. 12.6)

> The men of Nineveh will rise at the judgment with this generation and condemn it, because they believed Jonah's preaching. But behold, one greater than Jonah is here. (Matt. 12.41 par. Luke 11.32)

> The queen of the south will be raised at the judgment with this generation and condemn it, because she came from the ends of the earth to hear the wisdom of Solomon. But behold, one greater than Solomon is here. (Matt. 12.42 par. Luke 11.31)

It is clear, then, how these sayings focus on Jesus' presence *per se* (perhaps directly corresponding to the expectation of a "coming one") in a way that the "I have come" sayings do not.

As a result, it is difficult to see how the "I have come" sayings would originate specifically in Jesus' *messianic* self-consciousness (again, as distinct from an angelic, divine, or prophetic self-consciousness). There are perhaps more grounds for paying attention to the importance of a messianic self-

64. G. Schneider, "ἔρχομαι κτλ," *TWNT* 2:665 (= *TDNT* 2:668): "Sie entstammen dem messianischen Selbstbewusstsein Jesu und erklären sich aus diesem Selbstbewusstsein."

65. Grimm, *Weil ich dich liebe,* 86.

66. "Das Verb ἔρχομαι hat hier messianische Bedeutung." Bovon, *Evangelium nach Lukas,* 1:259, on Luke 5.32.

67. F. Bovon, *Das Evangelium nach Lukas.* Volume 2: *Lk 9,51–14,35* (EKK; Zürich: Benziger, 1996), 349.

consciousness when the various *purposes* for the coming are taken into account: coming "not to abolish the law but to fulfill it," "to teach," or "to cast fire on the earth" could perhaps be argued to be messianic functions.[68] But again, there is little to point to *specifically* messianic functions, and it is hard to see how the concept of messiahship in particular could account for all the goals of the advent. The messianic interpretation falls foul of the same problem as both of the prophetic interpretations: they rely heavily on "coming" being a technical or semi-technical term as opposed to referring to a coming from "a" to "b." Hampel, for example, describes "I have come" specifically as a "terminus technicus," as does Warfield.[69] This, however, is difficult to sustain. Some evidence for this can be seen in the excursus at the end of this chapter.

The "I Have Come" Sayings as Statements of "Epiphany"

It could be argued that Jesus' announcement of his advent has "epiphanic" connotations. This line of interpretation is adopted by, among others, Dibelius, Mussner, and to some extent Arens: Arens glosses "I have come" as referring to "Jesus' epiphanic coming."[70] Mussner, interestingly, sees such an interpretation as another way to counter Bultmann's retrospective reading "for the verb 'to come' is not used here in a retrospective sense, but 'epiphanically.'"[71] There are two principal difficulties here, however.

First, there is again the problem with interpreting "come" as a kind of technical term. Secondly, as we have noted already, there is a distinct lack of clarity as to what "epiphanic" actually means — it almost always has a rather vague sense. Consider for example the definition by Heil, based on the classic study by Pax:

> A broad definition of the literary genre of "epiphany" is the following: A disposition of literary motifs narrating a sudden and unexpected manifestation of a divine or heavenly being experienced by certain selected persons, in which the divine being reveals a divine attribute, action or message. The essential characteristic of an epiphany is that it reveals some aspect of God's salvific dealings with his people.[72]

68. As does Grimm (*Weil ich dich liebe*, 85-86).
69. V. Hampel, *Menschensohn und historischer Jesus* (Neukirchen-Vluyn: Neukirchener, 1990), 337; Warfield, "Jesus' Mission," 528.
70. Arens, *The HΛΘON-Sayings*, 252.
71. F. Mussner, "Der nicht erkannte Kairos (Mt 11,16-19 = Lk 7,31-35)," *Biblica* 40 (1959), 599-612 (603 n. 3): ". . . denn das Verbum ἔρχεσθαι wird hier nicht in rückschauender Betrachtung, sondern 'epiphanisch' gebraucht."
72. J. P. Heil, *Jesus Walking on the Sea: Meaning and Gospel Functions of Matt 14:22-33,*

There is confusion in this definition already over the question of whether the figure is "divine or heavenly" (first), or specifically "divine" (as later). This aside, the motif is still not a productive one: it is difficult to see how such a general definition would actually contribute to the understanding of the "I have come" sayings. The problem here is not so much one of accuracy as of usefulness.

"I Have Come": Words of a Leader?

Finally, one can easily dismiss as baseless the contention made by L. von Sybel. He argued in 1927-28 that "any leader ('jeder führende Mann') could use such expressions, without lapsing into eccentricity or presumption."[73] There is, however, little evidence for this, unless one wants to interpret the sayings of Jesus against the background of Julius Caesar's dictum "veni, vidi, vici."[74] Here again, however, one would face the same problem as was the case with the Josephus parallel: a reference to a specific episode in Caesar's life (his operations in Asia Minor) makes a poor parallel with the "I have come" sayings of Jesus, which sum up his earthly life and ministry as a whole. In conclusion, then, none of the previous attempts to attribute to the "I have come" sayings a kind of technical or idiomatic meaning have been successful.

III. Previous Arguments for Preexistence

On the other hand, some scholars have identified the "coming" sayings as indicative of the preexistence of Christ. Some simply state the point without further argument.[75] Others make the point more hesitantly, yet still without evidence.[76] More positively, Frenschkowski follows the point made by

---

Mark 6:45-52 and John 6:15b-21 (AnBib; Rome: Pontifical Biblical Institute Press, 1981), 8. He follows here E. Pax, *EPIPHANEIA. Ein religionsgeschichtlicher Beitrag zur biblischen Theologie* (Munich: Zink, 1955).

73. L. von Sybel, "Vom Wachsen der Christologie im synoptischen Evangelien," *TSK* 100 (1927-28), 362-401 (382).

74. Plutarch, *Caesar* 50.3: ἦλθον, εἶδον, ἐνίκησα"; cf. Suetonius, *Divus Julius* 37. Plutarch gives the words as Caesar's brief letter reporting his victory to a friend; in Suetonius's reference, the words were displayed in Caesar's triumph.

75. T. de Kruijf, *Der Sohn des lebendigen Gottes. Ein Beitrag zur Christologie des Matthäus-Evangeliums* (AnBib; Rome: Pontifical Biblical Institute Press, 1962), 146.

76. F. Christ, *Jesus Sophia. Die Sophia-Christologie bei den Synoptikern* (ATANT 57; Zurich: Zwingli, 1970), 68, says that they perhaps imply preexistence. Davies says that the references to coming-sent language are "hints . . . but these are only hints." P. E. Davies, "The Projection of Pre-Existence," *Biblical Research* 12 (1967), 28-36 (33).

Bultmann that no OT prophet ever made the claim "I have come." He then pushes the argument for preexistence further, however, in talking of "the semantic field of the 'coming' of Jesus, which has no analogy in OT and Jewish accounts of prophets."[77] The problem here, however, is that "coming" in itself *is* used more broadly; it is the "I have come" + purpose formula as a summary of one's life's work which is not seen in prophetic contexts.

Lagrange makes the slightly different point that it is not just that the Gospel writers use the term "coming" in relation to Jesus, but that the "I have come" is *absolute* and not qualified by any local marker. Jesus is not specified as having come *from* somewhere *to* somewhere else: "because it is not said that 'I have come among you,' but simply 'I have come,' one can supplement it with the idea of 'into the world,' and it is probable that Jesus alludes in this way to his own preexistence."[78] This is also a problematic argument, however, since the Qumran literature also describes Messiahs (CD-B 19.10-11; 1QS 9.11; 1QSa 2.14?), prophets (1QS 9.11), and other figures "coming" without local specification. Similarly, John the Baptist is also said to have "come" in the Synoptic Gospels (Mark 9.12-13; Matt. 21.32) without any local reference. Nevertheless, despite the unsatisfactory nature of these two attempts by Frenschkowski and Lagrange, I will argue that they are right for the wrong reasons by focusing, instead, on the parallels with angelic sayings, and in particular on the fact that the "I have come" sayings are accompanied by statements of *purpose*.

Conclusion

Neither previous arguments for preexistence, then, nor the alternative views discussed above have sufficient warrant to be accepted. In particular, the "I have come" + purpose formula is not used by people to refer to their lives' work as a whole, nor is it based on an idiom or technical usage of another kind. Not even prophetic or messianic figures employ it to sum up their destinies. Furthermore, we will see below in chapter 6 that, in addition to lacking evidence from Jewish tradition, the technical or idiomatic explanations also do not work particularly well as explanations of the "I have come" sayings of Jesus in their contexts in the Synoptic Gospels.

77. M. Frenschkowski, *Offenbarung und Epiphanie* (WUNT; Tübingen: Mohr, 1995), 1:198: ". . . das Wortfeld vom 'Kommen' Jesu, das keine Analogien in der atl. und jüdischen Prophetenbiographie hat."

78. M. Lagrange, *Évangile selon saint Marc* (Études Bibliques; Paris: Lecoffre, 1911), 45: "comme il n'y a pas 'je suis venu parmi vous,' mais 'je suis venu' tout court, on peut suppléer par la pensée 'dans le monde' et il est probable que Jésus fait ainsi allusion à sa propre préexistence."

On the other hand, we have prepared the way for providing a proper basis for understanding the sayings as implying the preexistence of Jesus. We proceed, then, in the next two chapters, to establish the following two points: that the *"I have come"* + *purpose* formula of the Gospels is most closely, and most abundantly, paralleled in announcements by angels of their comings from heaven (chapter 5), and that the preexistence interpretation is confirmed by the content and literary context — in particular, the heavenly and dynamic features — of the "I have come" sayings in the Synoptics (chapter 6). Our next concern, then, will be to establish the key linguistic evidence for the *"I have come"* + *purpose* formula being characteristic of heavenly figures.

EXCURSUS: "COMING" LANGUAGE IN THE DEAD SEA SCROLLS

The popularity of seeing in the "I have come" sayings a reference to a specific office of Jesus (whether prophetic, messianic, or whatever) should not obscure the fact that it is an extremely *odd* idea. To illustrate further the difficulty of pinning a specific office to the "I have come" sayings, we can look briefly at the use of "come" *(bo')* and its synonyms at Qumran as a helpful analogy. Most of this work has already been done in the various classical Hebrew dictionaries. The verb can of course refer to the advent of the Messiah, as scholars frequently observe: "until the messiah of righteousness comes (בוא)" (4Q252 5.3); "when there comes the Messiah of Aaron and Israel . . ." (בוא משיח אהרן וישראל, CD-B 19.10-11). But the same also applies to "the prophet": "until there shall come the prophet (עד בוא נביא) and the Messiahs of Aaron and Israel" (1QS 9.11). This is also the case with the "interpreter of the Law": "The star is the interpreter of the Law who shall come to Damascus" (הבא דמשק, CD 7.18-19). It can refer equally commonly to God himself: "And may they praise the name of Yahweh, *because he comes to judge every creature*" (כי בא לשפט את כל מעשה, 4Q88 9.5-6).

A number of other verbs are used in closely synonymous ways, in particular *'amad* (עמד, e.g., CD 12.23; CD-B 20.1) and *qûm* (קום). *Qûm* is often used in connection with prophets, as in 4Q375 1 1.4-5, presumably under the influence of Deut. 18.15, 18. Both of these verbs can also be used of false prophets or wicked agents of Belial (4Q339; CD-A 5.18).

Bo' is also used of the arrival of divinely ordained periods of time: "because all the ages of God will come at the right time (כיא כול קיצי אל יבואו לתכונם), as he established for them in the mysteries of his prudence" (1QpHab 7.12-13); "the time of righteousness is coming (באה) and . . . the age of peace is coming

(בא)" (4Q215a 1 2.5-6). It is also used of calendrical occurrences: ". . . and after it shall come (יבוא) the fifth week" (4Q247 fr. 1 2). Similarly, the term occurs when a certain festival or day "comes" or "falls" at a certain time, as throughout 4Q317, for example. In a different sense, the verb is used of phases of the moon: "On the eleventh twelfth of it, it is visible for four, and so it enters (תבוא) the night. On the thirteenth of it, it is visible for five, and so it enters (תבוא) the night. On the fourteenth of it, it is visible for six, and so it enters (תבוא) the night . . ." (4Q317 1 2.15-18, and *passim* in 4Q317).

Sometimes *bo'* (בוא) functions as an opposite of *yatsa'* (יצא) in contrasts of "coming in" and "going out," as in the pairings in the OT where "your going out and coming in" is a merismus for one's entire activity (1 Sam. 29.6; 2 Sam. 3.25; 2 Kgs. 19.27; Ps. 121.8; Isa. 37.28). The verbs can be used of angels in the heavenly court: "When the divinities of knowledge enter (במבואי) through the gates of glory, and in all the departures (מוצאי) of the holy angels to their domains, the gates of the entrance (מבוא) and the gates of the exit (מוצא) make known the glory of the king" (4Q405 23 1.8-9).

As in English and most other languages, "come" is extremely common in Hebrew and Greek, and so it is dangerously inaccurate to attribute a specific technical meaning to it. Even if "coming" is used commonly of expected figures, such language certainly does not point to a particular figure.

CHAPTER 5

Use of the "I Have Come" + Purpose
Formula by Angels

Thus far, in the previous two chapters, we have established the following parts of the argument:

- The preexistence interpretation of the "I have come" sayings has *prima facie* plausibility on simple logical grounds (chapter 3).
- None of the other scholarly options can be considered plausible (chapter 4).

We have seen, then, that the *"I have come" + purpose* formula *was not used by people generally, or even by those specially commissioned by God, to sum up their lives' work.* So, the formula does not even have any particular messianic or prophetic connotations. Having cleared the ground, then, we proceed here in this chapter to the third element of our argument:

- The "I have come" + purpose formula of the Gospels is most closely and most abundantly paralleled in the announcements by angels of their comings from heaven.

The attempt here, then, is to provide a background for the Synoptic "I have come" sayings which has a much firmer basis than the prophetic, idiomatic, messianic, or other senses which we critiqued in chapter 4. This chapter contends that *angelic* statements provide both more appropriate and more abundant evidence than any of the other theories reviewed earlier. *Crucially, angels do sum up their earthly activity in a particular visit with the "I have come" +*

purpose formula. The reference to a *particular visit* here is important: an angel announcing "I have come to . . ." is clearly not summarizing its *whole existence.* Similarly, we will examine later an instance when the heavenly Elijah, many centuries after his ascension, uses the formula to summarize the specific reason for a particular visit to the earthly realm, and not the raison d'être of his whole being, earthly and heavenly. Similarly, in the case of Jesus, in the Synoptic Gospels he is summarizing the reason for his *first* coming, not for his whole existence, which would also include his second coming, something which is not in view in the "I have come" sayings. The language of the Synoptic Gospels bears a striking resemblance to that of the angels and Elijah: in each case, these figures use this language *because they have come with prior intent from a preexistence in heaven.* The formula is not used by ordinary earthly individuals to summarize their human lives; rather, the angelic parallels are much closer to the sayings in the Synoptic Gospels.

Section I of this chapter offers further justification for the use of angelic parallels and attempts to ward off some potential objections. Then, we examine twenty-four examples of angelic statements in which the *"I have come"* + *purpose* formula is found. As noted above, the focus will not be exclusively on angels; we will also see the same formula applied in one instance to a visit from heaven of Elijah, who comes — like an angel — to bring news to someone. Finally, we will see that the formula is also occasionally used in connection with God. A number of the examples are early, but a number also come from later in the Rabbinic period, so the purpose is to show that there is a strong, and long-running tradition, rather than to pinpoint sources which are exactly contemporaneous with Matthew, Mark, and Luke.

I. Why Angels?

To seek analogies between the comings of Jesus and angels may initially seem an unpromising line of inquiry; in fact, however, there is a very close relationship. Jesus sums up his whole ministry with the formula "I have come" + purpose. When he does this, he refers not to an individual incident in his life which is inaugurated by this coming but to the entirety of his mission from God. Angels, similarly, frequently sum up their missions with the "I have come" + purpose formula, referring to their *prior intent* in coming. The language of such announcements refers to their intrusion into the earthly, human realm. Correspondingly, if the language of coming with a purpose in Jesus' use of the "I have come" formula is not to be understood idiomatically, it must be a "coming," *with prior intent,* to embark on the entirety of his ministry "on earth" (Mark 2.10; cf. Luke 12.49, 51). As such, the structure of angels' comings from heaven to earth — to fulfil a divinely ordained function that is the purpose of the mission — fits extremely well with the language of Jesus' "coming" sayings.

Returning to the point made in chapter 3, the *prima facie* sense of the sayings in the Synoptic Gospels is that Jesus has come from A to B with a purpose from God. We have seen in chapter 4, and will show further in chapter 6, that this coming cannot be explained as a coming from Nazareth, since — among other things — this would make no sense as a place of origin for Jesus coming "to cast fire onto the earth" (Luke 12.49), or for the Son of Man coming "to give his life" (Mark 10.45 par. Matt. 20.28). As a result, the movement "from A to B" makes best sense as from heaven to earth, as is the case in the angelic comings. At this point it will be useful to anticipate some objections which have perhaps already arisen in readers' minds.

Is the Argument Circular?

This objection runs as follows: Surely if one sets up angels as the parallels to be investigated, this simply smuggles in the desired conclusion of preexistence at the outset.[1] This is not the nature of the argument here, however.

It should be remembered that the other possible parallels — those of prophet, messiah, and the like — have been ruled out for lack of evidence. This chapter proposes, by contrast, that there are figures who do make use of the same "I have come" + purpose formula as is used by Jesus in the Synoptic Gospels. There are, furthermore, a great many instances of angels employing it: twenty-four are presented below. Hence the insistence here that the angelic parallels are far superior, both quantitatively and qualitatively, to any other body of parallel evidence that has hitherto been adduced by scholars. As a result, it is not simply a question here of conveniently picking angelic parallels from the range of options because they suit the purposes of the present argument.

Does This Argument Make Jesus an Angel?

By no means.[2] The point here is simply to draw an analogy between the respective "comings." Jesus sums up his life's work with the "I have come" +

---

1. I am grateful to Maurice Casey for noting this potential objection, and to Markus Bockmuehl for further alerting me to it.
2. I am grateful to Martin Hengel for encouraging me to clarify my position here.

THE ADVENT AND MISSION OF JESUS

purpose formula; similarly, angels also sum up the purpose of a particular earthly visit by using the formula. But the present argument does not intend to draw attention to any similarities of Jesus to the angels beyond the fact that they are sent by God from heaven. A common heavenly provenance and an analogous coming to the earthly realm do not imply any particular ontological similarity between Jesus and angels.

Irreconcilable Differences?

In the course of his argument for an idiomatic interpretation of the "I have come" formula (which has been criticized elsewhere) Eduardo Arens has questioned the relevance of the angelic sayings.[3] After discussing OT theophany references and the Danielic advents of angels, he concludes:

> The texts we have relevated (sic) could hardly have been in the background of the NT "I have come" sayings. In fact, they have found no echo in the NT. They are for the most part addressed to an individual and their content is of a different nature.[4]

As one might expect given the differences between Jesus and the angels, there are of course some discontinuities between the angelic statements and those of Jesus in the Synoptic Gospels. However, as we shall further see in the course of the chapter, Arens has greatly exaggerated these differences, which in any case would not affect the meaning of the "coming." His point about the content presumably relates to the fact that OT angelophanies are usually for the purpose of communicating a message from God. However, as we shall see, in a number of other texts, an angel comes not only to reveal something to an individual, but to save the whole nation (see, e.g., the discussions of the *Apocryphon of Jeremiah* and Midrash Tanḥuma below). Similarly, while visits from angels tend to be short by comparison with the life and ministry of Jesus, there are significant exceptions: Raphael's dealings with Tobit and Tobias, for example, are much more protracted and extend beyond revelation to Tobit's restoration. The angelic advents are therefore neither as homogeneous nor as different from the Gospels sayings as Arens implies; the problem is that

3. See my critique of Arens's whole approach in "On the Alleged Aramaic Idiom behind the Synoptic ἦλθον-Sayings," *JTS* 55 (2004), 84-91.

4. E. Arens, *The 'ΗΛΘΟΝ-Sayings in the Synoptic Tradition: A Historico-Critical Investigation* (Orbis Biblicus et Orientalis 10; Freiburg/Göttingen: Universitätsverlag Freiburg/ Vandenhoeck und Ruprecht, 1976), 275.

he reaches his conclusion on the basis of such a small selection of the early Jewish material.

Summary

To repeat, the analogy can be stated in two elements:

Angels announce their advents with the "I have come" + purpose formula. They can do this

(a) because they are summarizing *not* their whole *existence* (they visit on numerous occasions) but the purpose of a particular visit,
(b) because they have a preexistence in heaven.

Similarly, Jesus announces his advent with the "I have come" + purpose formula

(a) because he is summarizing the purpose of his whole earthly life and ministry. As with the angels, Jesus is not summarizing his whole *existence* (he will come again, with different purposes). However, he does — unlike other people in early Judaism — summarize his life's work with the "I have come" + purpose formula;
(b) therefore, it makes good sense to conclude that, as above, Jesus has come *from somewhere,* and therefore has a preexistence in heaven. The nature and duration of this preexistence, however, are not defined in any way by the "I have come" sayings per se.

We now move on from the abstract terms of the argument to examine the cases in which angels actually use the "I have come" + purpose formula.

II. Angels and the "I Have Come" + Purpose Formula

It is well known that "going" and "coming" language is frequently used of angels. From the perspective of the heavenly court, there are numerous cases where angels are described as "going forth" from there to earth: in 1 Kings 22, for example, the lying spirit says, "I will go forth (ἐξελεύσομαι), and will be a lying spirit" (1 Kgs. 22.22).[5] On the other hand, "coming" language is most

---

5. On this passage, see I. W. Provan, *1 and 2 Kings* (Peabody: Hendrickson, 1995), 165. For similar examples, note the language throughout Job 1–2; cf. Sir. 24.3.

commonly used where narratives recount angelic figures as already having entered the human realm.[6] To take one case from Josephus, an angel comes to Manoah to announce the birth of Samson.[7] The angel is described as "having come (ἐλθών) according to the will of God"; then later in the story, "he came (παραγίνεται) again by the grace of God." Similar language is also used extensively in the rabbinic literature.[8] To take one interesting case from the Talmud, we see a rabbinic exegetical solution to the puzzle of the identity of the three men who visited Abraham at the oaks of Mamre in Genesis 18. The men are interpreted as angels:

> Who were the three men? — Michael, Gabriel, and Raphael. *Michael came to bring the tidings to Sarah* (מיכאל שבא לבשר את שרה); *Raphael came to heal Abraham* (רפאל שבא לרפא את אברהם); and *Gabriel came to overturn Sodom* (גבריאל אזל למהפכיה לסדום). But is it not written, "And there came the two angels to Sodom in the evening"? — Michael came with him to rescue Lot (דאזל מיקאל בהדיה לשזביה ללוט). Scripture supports this too, for it is written, "And *he* overthrew those cities," not, "And *they* overthrew": this proves it. (*b. Baba Metzia* 86b).[9]

This passage offers a high density of references to "coming" + infinitive. As with the Josephus example above, there are two different words for "come" (Hebrew *bo'* and Aramaic *'azal*): the variation does not make any difference to the meaning, however. Here again, we see a wide diversity of functions assigned to the angels under discussion.

Our focus here, however, is not on general references to coming; we have already critiqued above the view that verbs meaning "come" can be treated as technical terms. Just as references to a figure "coming" do not immediately conjure up messianic or prophetic impressions, neither is the argument here that they necessarily have angelic nuances. Rather, the focus here is

---

6. For an early example, see Dan. 10.13.

7. The following examples come from *Antiquities* 5:278 and 280 respectively. See also *Antiquities* 1.200.

8. See H. Freedman and M. Simon, *Midrash Rabbah: Exodus* (London: Soncino, 1977), 29-30, 34. In Numbers Rabbah 1.11 (idem, *Midrash Rabbah: Numbers* [London: Soncino, 1977], 17-18), God reckons that "the Angel of Death, coming to slay Israel, . . . will find the tribe of Levi mixed up with them and will put them to death with the rest of Israel." Less frequently, the language of "coming *down*" is also used in connection with angels (as is the case with Jesus in John's Gospel). See, e.g., Exodus Rabbah 18.5 (Freedman and Simon, *Midrash Rabbah: Exodus*, 220): "Gabriel came down to deliver Hananiah, Mishael, and Azariah"; the angel says later on in the account, "I went down to save Abraham."

9. See the very similar account in Targum Pseudo-Jonathan to Gen. 18.2.

specifically on references to the *"I have come" + purpose formula* (usually, but not exclusively, involving a final clause).[10]

1-2. Daniel 9.22, 23

In the midst of Daniel's great prayer for restoration in accordance with Jeremiah's prophecy, Daniel reports that the angel Gabriel visited him at the time of the evening sacrifice (Dan. 9.20-21). The angel then speaks to the prophet in vv. 22-23:

> And he instructed me and conversed with me, and said, "Daniel, *I have come forth now to give you understanding* (ἐξῆλθον συμβιβάσαι σε σύνεσιν). As soon as you began to pray, a message went forth. And *I have come to announce to you* (ἐγὼ ἦλθον τοῦ ἀναγγεῖλαί σοι) that you are a man highly favored."[11]

The reference to the "message" going forth is probably to the revelation coming from God which Gabriel then goes forth to deliver.[12] Here, then, we have our first two examples — in quick succession — of "I have come" sayings referring to coming from heaven with prior intent and purpose. Gabriel's statements are interesting in that they attest usage of both simple and compound forms of the verb, "I have come" (ἦλθον: cf. Mark 2.17, etc.) and "I have come *forth*" (ἐξῆλθον: cf. Mark 1.38).

3-6. Daniel 10.12, 14, 20; 11.2

In the following chapter, Daniel sees a vision of a "man" who is nevertheless clearly a heavenly figure, as is deducible from his appearance (10.6) and the fact that the whole setting is visionary (vv. 1, 5, 7). The "man" tells him that he is highly favored and to stand up and listen, "because I have now been sent to you" (v. 11). But equally, having referred to his "sending," the heavenly figure can speak of his "coming," in this case, in response to Daniel's prayers:

---

10. Where relevant, Greek texts of OT passages will be cited because our purpose is comparison with the Synoptic Gospels. Of course in many other cases, there are only Hebrew or Aramaic texts available.

11. Thus Theodotion. Alternatively, the Old Greek text has ἐξῆλθον ὑποδεῖξαί σοι διάνοιαν ("I have come forth now to reveal understanding to you") and ἐγὼ ἦλθον ὑποδεῖξαί σοι ὅτι . . . ("I have come to reveal to you that . . .") in Dan. 9.22 and 23 respectively.

12. J. J. Collins, *Daniel* (Hermeneia; Minneapolis: Fortress, 1993), 352.

> And he said to me, "Do not fear, Daniel, because from the first day on which you gave your heart to understand and to be humbled, your words were heard before God. And *I have come on account of your words* (ἐγὼ ἦλθον ἐν τοῖς λόγοις σου)." (Dan. 10.12)[13]

This "I have come" saying is accompanied by a cause ("on account of your words") rather than, strictly speaking, a purpose. However, this is a distinction without a difference in this case, since it is clear that the figure comes precisely *in order to bring an answer to Daniel's prayers:* this purpose is implicit in the statement.

It is then interesting that this heavenly figure reports that while he was detained in Persia, he too received a divine envoy: "Michael, one of the chief princes, came to help me . . ." (Dan. 10.13).[14] The heavenly figure then speaks of his coming with the purpose of telling Daniel what is to take place in the future:

> And *I have come to reveal to you* (LXX: καὶ ἦλθον συνετίσαι σε; Old Greek: ὑποδεῖξαί σοι) what will happen to your people at the end of days, because your vision is for those days. (v. 14)

Immediately afterward, in vv. 16-17, it seems that another figure comes to Daniel. Finally, in v. 20 (perhaps) yet another figure touches Daniel and addresses him:

> *Do you know why I have come to you* (γινώσκεις τί ἦλθον πρός σε)? Now I am returning to fight the prince of Persia, and when I go, the prince of Greece will come. But first I will tell you what is written in the book of truth.

Here the heavenly being has come to Daniel specifically to inform him of some of the contents of the heavenly tablets. Interesting here is the implied purpose clause: the "why" clearly implies a purpose in the coming. The difference between this and the other examples is that the exact purpose is not stated — obviously, because the angel is asking a question precisely about it.

Finally, the angel gives the answer to the question above:

13. Again, this is following the text in Theodotion; OG has καὶ ἐγὼ εἰσῆλθον ἐν τῷ ῥήματί σου.

14. See also the interesting interpretation of this verse in *b. Berakoth* 4b, which we will discuss below.

> In the first year of Cyrus the King, he (the Lord) told me to strengthen him and give him courage. *But now I have come to reveal the truth to you* . . . (καὶ νῦν ἦλθον τὴν ἀλήθειαν ὑποδεῖξαί σοι). (11.2)[15]

The language here is very similar to the other instances from Daniel — the angel announces his coming for the purpose of revelation. More importantly for our purposes, the key point is that in the *"I have come" + purpose* statement, the angel is summarizing the reason for his visit to the human realm.

7. *Tobit 5.5*

An interesting possibility comes when Tobit is looking for a hired guide to accompany Tobias in his quest for the family fortune.[16] Azariah comes to interview for the job. In his self-introduction to Tobias, he says, *"I have come here to work"* (ἐλήλυθα ὧδε ἐργατεύεσθαι). As far as the characters in the story are concerned, this is all straightforward: the reference in the "I have come" in 5.5 is simply to Azariah's journey to Tobit's house to seek work. However, the reader knows that Azariah is not what he seems, having been told in the previous verse that he is in fact the angel Raphael. In the light of this, the "I have come here to work" can be read at a secondary level as a reference to the angel's coming from heaven.

This is further suggested by the degree to which it conforms not only to self-introductions of angels in other places but also to Raphael's statements later on in the book. Toward the end of the narrative, Raphael reveals his true identity to the other characters in the story. He has not been a merely human guide accompanying Tobias and guaranteeing the success of his mission. Rather, he is one of the great angels who stand in the presence of God. In 12.14 Raphael reveals to Tobias and Sarah that "God sent me." Since he is an angel, this "sending" is identical to a coming from heaven according to the will of God. He says in 12.18: "*I did not come* by my own grace, but by the will of our God" (οὐ τῇ ἐμαυτοῦ χάριτι ἀλλὰ τῇ θελήσει τοῦ θεοῦ ἡμῶν ἦλθον).[17] The "I have come" statement here makes explicit what was present at the ironic level in 5.5: the characters in the narrative now know what the reader has known all along.

---

15. Thus the Old Greek; Theodotion does not have an "I have come" saying here.

16. For the texts, see S. D. E. Weeks, S. J. Gathercole, and L. T. Stuckenbruck, eds. *The Book of Tobit: Texts from the Principal Ancient and Medieval Traditions. With Synopsis, Concordances, and Annotated Texts in Aramaic, Hebrew, Greek, Latin, and Syriac* (Berlin: de Gruyter, 2004), 160-61.

17. Cf., e.g., Gabriel's "I have been sent" in Luke 1.19, 26.

Where this instance in Tobit differs from the previous examples in Daniel is in the nature of the angelic visit. As we noted above, Arens stated that the theophanic and angelic self-introductions are inappropriate as parallels to the Synoptic "I have come" sayings, perhaps because he considered the Jewish parallels to refer merely to a very brief visit for the revelation of future events. However, Tobit 5.5 is the first example (we will see others below) of an angel visiting for a purpose other than the delivery of a divine message. The "work" which Raphael has come to do is to organize the marriage of Tobias and Sarah and to heal Tobit from his blindness. Again, in contrast to the examples from Daniel, the visit is more protracted: Raphael sums up in Tobit 5.5 (and 12.14) his long sojourn in the human sphere, though not, of course, his entire existence.

8. The Sode Raza (Book of Noah?)

A further example is spoken by the rare angel *Raziel.* The Hebrew text has been published in various editions; one of the more accessible is that of Jellinek.[18] Although Zunz considered this text composed (rather than simply copied) by Eleazar ben Judah of Worms (ca. 1176-1238), this late date was disproved by Jellinek, who saw the manuscript.[19] Jellinek further notes that Eleazar was a collator of ancient writings, so the text could well be very old. In fact, he believes that it has a close association with the *Book of Noah,* which was written as a sequel to what we know as *1 Enoch,* with which it has many parallels. As a result, he seems to imply that he considers the book to have originated in Essene circles.[20] Any such date around the turn of the era must remain tentative, however: it would be helpful to have a thorough reexamination of this document in the light of the new data and paradigms in the interpretation of early Judaism which have emerged since the mid-nineteenth century.

The work begins with a prayer of Adam after which the angel Raziel appears to him and addresses him:[21]

18. A. Jellinek, "Das Noah-Buch," in idem, *Beit ha-Midrash* (Jerusalem: Wahrmann, 1967 [1853]), 3:155-60 (Introduction at 3:xxx-xxxiii).

19. For Zunz's view, see L. Zunz, *Die gottesdienstlichen Vorträge der Juden, historisch entwickelt. Ein Beitrag zur Alterthumskunde und biblischen Kritik, zur Literatur- und Religionsgeschichte* (Frankfurt: Kauffmann, ²1892), 176-77 n. f: "Das Buch Rasiel gehört seiner Sprache und seinem Inhalt nach frühestens dem 11. Jahrhundert an."

20. Jellinek, "Das Noah-Buch," xxxii-xxxiii.

21. The "I have come" saying is registered by K. Berger, *Die Auferstehung des Propheten und die Erhöhung des Menschensohnes. Traditionsgeschichtliche Untersuchungen zur Deutung des Geschickes Jesu in frühchristlichen Texten* (SUNT 13; Göttingen: Vandenhoeck und Ruprecht, 1976), 527.

I have come to make known to you (באתי להבינך) pure words and great wisdom *and in order to make you wise* (ולהחכימך) by the words of this holy book. . . .[22]

Raziel thus announces his advent with a statement about his coming followed by two purpose clauses.[23] After his self-introduction, Raziel then gives Adam a book. The book is hidden by Adam, but later found by Enoch. It is then given again by Raphael to Noah, and thence passed on from generation to generation. This mysterious book is said to have taught Enoch the course of the stars, the names of the ministering angels, of the earth, of heaven, and of the sun and moon. Noah learned from it how to build the ark.

9. Apocalypse of Moses/*Greek* Life of Adam and Eve 16.2 *(3)*

In this section of the *Apocalypse of Moses,* probably from the first or second century CE, Eve tells her descendants how the fall came about. She recounts that the devil called the serpent, telling him, "*I have come to observe you* (ἐγὼ δὲ ἦλθον τοῦ κατανοῆσαί σε), having discovered that you were greater than all the animals."[24] Here again, we have a journey of the devil to earth, this time to lead an initially reluctant serpent to tempt Eve.

10-11. 4 Ezra 6.30; 7.2

4 Ezra is conventionally dated without much disagreement to the end of the first or beginning of the second century CE. At the end of the second vision, in 5.21–6.34, the angel Uriel concludes:

> *I have come to show you these things (haec ueni tibi ostendere)* tonight.[25] If therefore you will pray again and fast again for seven days, I will again declare to you greater things than these, for your voice has surely been heard before the Most High; for the Mighty One has seen your uprightness and

22. Jellinek, "Das Noah-Buch," 157.

23. Cf. the angel's later statement, "I have been sent (שולחתי) to you at the command of God to heal (לרפאות) the land, and to inform (להודיע) you of what will take place . . ." (Jellinek, "Das Noah-Buch," 158).

24. This is the reading preserved by ms. L. There is a great deal of variation in the textual tradition at this point.

25. The Peshitta of *4 Ezra* 6.30, similarly, has ܗܠܝܢ ܐܬܝܬ ܕܐܚܘܝܟ ܒܠܠܝܐ ("I have come to show you these things tonight").

has also observed the purity which you have maintained from your youth. Therefore he sent me to show you all these things *(et propter hoc misit me demonstrare tibi haec omnia).*

After 6.30-33 comes the famous speech by Ezra in which he asks why Israel has not possessed the nations when they are so far inferior to her and were indeed created for her. Then, in 7.1-2, the angel Uriel replies that in order to come into an inheritance, it is necessary first to pass through difficult trials. This speech of Uriel is introduced by the narrator, Ezra, as follows:

> When I had finished speaking these words, the angel who had been sent *(angelus qui missus fuerat)* to me on the former nights was sent to me again, and he said to me, "Rise, Ezra, and listen to the words *which I have come to speak to you (quos ueni loqui ad te).*"[26]

Again, there is a parallel between "being sent" and "coming," and we see the same construction of "I have come" + infinitive of purpose as in the Synoptic "I have come" sayings.

12. 2 Baruch 71.3 (2)

2 Baruch is by general consensus dated around the same time as *4 Ezra;* usually shortly after, as most consider it dependent on *4 Ezra.* The same parallelism of coming and being sent can be seen in the words of the angel Ramael, given to Baruch while he rests under the branches of a tree (55.1). Ramael is both *sent* to tell Baruch the words of God (56.1) and *comes* to recount them:

> This is the vision which you have seen, and this is its explanation. *For I have come to tell you these things* since your prayer has been heard by the Most High. (71.2/3).[27]

Here the advent of the angel takes place, as in Dan. 10.12, in response to the prayers of the prophet. The "I have come" saying again summarizes the purpose of the angel's visit from the heavenly to the human realm.

---

26. Cf. the very similar Peshitta: ܩܘܡ ܥܙܪܐ ܘܫܡܥ ܠܡܠ̈ܐ ܐܠܝܢ ܕܐܬܝܬ ܠܡ ("rise, Ezra, and listen to the words which I have come to speak to you").

27. Here, the Peshitta, again, also has a purpose clause: ܐܬܝܬ ܓܝܪ ܐܢܐ ܕܐܬܢܐ ܠܟ ܗܠܝܢ ("I have come to tell you these things").

13. Testament of Isaac 2

In a version of the *Testament of Isaac* preserved in the Ethiopic tradition, there is a similar example.[28] The origins of the *Testament* are shrouded in mystery: it may well have come from Alexandria, but attempts at dating have all been rather speculative. Stinespring guesses at the second century AD, but this is little more than a guess.[29] Kuhn gives up on trying to find a date, but does consider that although the final form is undoubtedly Christian, "the explicitly Christian elements may have been superimposed, for they appear to be easily detachable." This is in contrast to the *Testament of Jacob,* where "they form a more integral part of the whole."[30] Stinespring comes to the same verdict, apparently independently: "The Christianizing is not thoroughgoing, however, and it seems more likely that the original composition was a product of Egyptian Judaism."[31] However, whatever view one takes of the checkered history of the Isaac tradition here, the "coming" saying which is the focus here is clearly dependent on the Jewish angel-tradition, whether the particular statement was written by a Jew or a Christian.

In the *Testament,* it is stated that, shortly before Isaac died, he was visited by the archangel Michael. Isaac is delighted to see him and expresses his joy. Michael then gives a rather incongruous reply, however, one which would have been more suitable to a fearful and trembling Isaac:

> Be courageous in your spirit, for *I come* to you from the presence of God *in order to bring you up into heaven,* into the presence of your father Abraham and all the holy ones. (2)

Unfortunately, the Ethiopic is the only version which has not been translated into English; there is, however, a modern scholarly rendering into French, which the English above follows.[32] We see a "coming" statement — rendered

---

28. The Coptic and Arabic versions both read slightly differently. For details of the versions and publication of them, see K. H. Kuhn, "The Testament of Isaac," in H. F. D. Sparks, ed., *The Apocryphal Old Testament* (Oxford: Clarendon, 1984), 423-39 (425-27).

29. W. F. Stinespring, "Testament of Isaac," in J. H. Charlesworth, ed., *The Old Testament Pseudepigrapha* (New York: Doubleday, 1983), 1:903-18 (903).

30. Kuhn, "The Testament of Isaac," 425.

31. Stinespring, "Testament of Isaac," 904.

32. M. Chaîne's translation is as follows: "Sois fort en ton esprit, car je viens auprès de toi de chez le Dieu vivant, pour te faire monter dans les cieux, chez ton père Abraham et tous les saints." M. Delcor, *Le Testament d'Abraham. Suivi de la Traduction des Testaments d'Abraham, d'Isaac et de Jacob d'après les Versions Orientales* (SVTP; Leiden: Brill, 1973), 225. Berger supplies a very similar German translation, although he does not specify the version it comes from: "Sei

by Chaîne with a present tense — in the first person followed by a purpose clause: Michael announces his coming in order to effect the ascent of Isaac's soul to heaven.

14. Jeremiah Apocryphon 35

In his brief list of parallels to the "I have come" sayings of Jesus, J.-A. Bühner notes one further example.[33] This *Jeremiah Apocryphon* is cited by Bühner from a old translation which unfortunately provides rather inadequate discussion of the text; happily, a version of it has now been properly edited and translated into English by K. H. Kuhn.[34] Some other versions of the work have also been published.[35]

Although the *Jeremiah Apocryphon* has not attracted much scholarly attention beyond these editions, there has been some discussion of its provenance and date. In 1927, Harris argued that it is fundamentally a Christian text, and he is generally skeptical about the likelihood of direct Jewish influence.[36] The following year, however, Marmorstein provided a rebuttal and argued that it was Jewish in origin, "that only with reference to Talmud and Midrash can the work be explained."[37] The most recent detailed study by Kuhn takes a similar line: "On examination it would appear that the Christian elements can easily be detached and that the work is basically Jewish."[38] A fragment dating to the seventh century offers a *terminus ad quem,* and

stark in deinem Geiste, denn ich komme zu dir vom lebendigen Gott, um dich in den Himmel steigen zu lassen" (Berger, *Die Auferstehung des Propheten,* 532).

33. J.-A. Bühner, *Der Gesandte und sein Weg im vierten Evangelium. Die kultur- und religionsgeschichtlichen Grundlagen der johanneischen Sendungschristologie sowie ihre traditionsgeschichtliche Entwicklung* (WUNT 2; Tübingen: Mohr, 1977), 144. He cites the reference from E. Amélineau, *Contes et Romans de L'Égypte Chrêtienne* (Paris: Leroux, 1888). Amélineau's is a French translation of the Arabic. For a brief and rather insubstantial introduction to the text, see *Contes et Romans,* 1:lix-lxii. Volume 2 contains the translation. I am grateful to Richard Bauckham and Jim Davila for alerting me to the fact that the "History of the Babylonian Captivity" and the "Jeremiah Apocryphon" are one and the same.

34. K. H. Kuhn, "A Coptic Jeremiah Apocryphon," *Muséon* 83 (1970), 95-135, 291-350.

35. For the Garshuni version, see A. Mingana (with R. Harris), ed., "A Jeremiah Apocryphon," in idem, *Woodbrooke Studies* (Cambridge: Heffers, 1927), 1:125-38 (introduction by Harris), 148-49 (preface by Mingana), 149-91 (translation by Mingana), 192-233 (facsimiles).

36. Harris, "A Jeremiah Apocryphon," 137-38.

37. A. Marmorstein, "Die Quellen des neuen Jeremia-Apocryphons," *ZNW* 27 (1928), 327-37 (328).

38. Kuhn, "A Coptic Jeremiah Apocryphon," 103.

Marmorstein dates the work very tentatively to the third-fourth century CE.[39] Even if the work is basically a Christian product, it still, of course, attests the angelic "I have come . . ." tradition which we have been discussing. If, as Marmorstein and Kuhn maintain, it is Jewish, then this is a further non-Christian example of the motif.

The work is centered on Jeremiah's rebukes to Zedekiah, Israel's deportation into captivity by Nebuchadnezzar, and finally the return. Near this happy end, Michael delivers the good news to Jeremiah. The two versions with which we are concerned here are the Coptic (translated by Kuhn) and the Arabic (Amélineau):[40]

> Jeremiah, chosen one of God, behold I tell thee: *I have come to redeem this people and to take them to the land of their fathers* (Kuhn).[41]

> *I have come to you today to save your people,* for that is why God has sent me. This is what the Lord whom you serve says: "I have taken pity on this people and have decided to return them to their land so that they might glorify me . . ." (Amélineau).[42]

What is notable here is the scale of Michael's task: he comes not merely as an *angelus interpres,* but to rescue the nation of Israel from exile. Again, then, the distance between the angelic "I have come" sayings and the corresponding sayings in the Synoptics is considerably reduced.

15. Targums and Vulgate of Numbers 22.32

We turn in the next five examples to interpretations of preexisting scriptural angel texts. The context of the first is the well-known scene of Balaam's donkey in the OT. The angel of the Lord has appeared to prevent Balaam going to aid Balak, king of Moab. Balaam's donkey sees the angel holding a drawn sword, refuses to advance, and so incurs a beating from Balaam. Finally, Balaam sees that there is actually an angel standing before him: "The angel of the Lord said to him, 'Why have you struck your donkey these three times? I

---

39. Marmorstein, "Die Quellen des neuen Jeremia-Apocryphons," 337.

40. The Garshuni has "Here I am . . ." in place of "I have come" (Mingana, "A Jeremiah Apocryphon," 182 [ET], 211 [text]).

41. Kuhn, "A Coptic Jeremiah Apocryphon," 316-17.

42. Amélineau, *Contes et Romans,* 2:144. "Je suis aujourd'hui venu vers toi pour sauver ton peuple, car Dieu m'a envoyé pour cela. Voici ce que dit le Seigneur que tu sers: 'J'ai pris pitié de ce peuple et j'ai résolu de le faire retourner dans son pays afin qu'il me glorifie.'"

have come out as an opponent [or: 'to obstruct you'] (אנכי יצאתי לשטן), because your way is perverse before me.'" It is not quite clear here whether a literal rendering of the Hebrew would be "I have come forth *to oppose*" or "I
have come forth *as an opponent*." The three-letter Hebrew root *stn* can be either a verb ("oppose") or a noun ("an opponent").[43] The Septuagint and
some of the Latin versions translate it with a noun and the phrase as a whole
as "I have come forth as a hindrance." Even if this is a correct literal translation (as is likely), there is perhaps still a sense of the angel coming with a purpose. However, it may even be the case that we have the "I have come" with a
purpose clause, expressed by the infinitive.[44] This is certainly true in a number of the early versions of Num. 22.32.

Targum Onkelos probably received its final redaction in the third century CE. There appears to be variation in the manuscript tradition as to
whether at Num. 22.32 Onkelos simply has something very close to the Hebrew text or paraphrases it with "I have come" + final clause.[45] All the other
Targums are clearer, however. The form is changed slightly, and so there is a
purpose clause involving a verb ("I have come *to hinder . . .*").

In Targum Pseudo-Jonathan to Num. 22.32, the text clearly reads "I have
come" + infinitive: "I have come forth to oppose you." Clarke gives as a translation of the verse (which is a considerable expansion on the Hebrew):

> Then the angel of the Lord said to him: "Why did you strike your ass these
> three times? Behold, *I came out to oppose you* (הא אנא נפית למישמן לך).
> But the ass feared, saw, and turned from the way. It was revealed to me that
> you seek to go to curse the people, and the matter is not pleasing to me."[46]

Jastrow cites the present passage as an instance of the verb *stan,* "to be hostile
to; to hinder, accuse."[47]

Targum Neofiti does not expand the Hebrew text as much as Pseudo-
Jonathan, but there is a strong similarity in the texts in the portion with
which we are concerned.[48] Díez Macho in the Spanish translation and

---

43. Hence לשטן is either ל- + infinitive construct or ל- + noun.
44. Strictly, expressed by the preposition ל- + infinitive construct.
45. A. Sperber (*The Bible in Aramaic,* Volume 1: *The Pentateuch* [Leiden: Brill, 1992], 262)
gives a reading along the lines of the former, whereas the Davka Judaic Classics Library elec-
tronic text gives הא אנא נפקית למסטן.
46. M. McNamara and E. G. Clarke, *Targum Neofiti 1: Numbers. Targum Pseudo-Jonathan:
Numbers* (Edinburgh: Clark, 1995), 254.
47. M. Jastrow, *A Dictionary of the Targumim, the Talmud Babli and Yerushalmi, and the
Midrashic Literature* (London: Luzac, 1903), 973.
48. Targum Neofiti renders the phrase הא אנה נפקת למסטן לך.

McNamara in *The Aramaic Bible* agree that we have a verb rather than a noun. Díez Macho takes the sentence as a purpose clause in his translation,[49] and McNamara's English for the phrase in Targum Neofiti to Num. 22.32 is: "Behold I have come out to oppose you. . . ."[50] The Samaritan Targums run along the same lines.[51]

In a very different tradition of translation, the Vulgate unambiguously has in Num. 22.32: *"I have come to oppose you" (ego ueni ut aduersarer tibi).* This dates from the end of the fourth century CE, hence probably after Targum Onkelos but before Neofiti and Pseudo-Jonathan. In sum, whatever the intended syntax of the original Hebrew form of Numbers may have been, it was certainly paraphrased in later interpretation with the "I have come" + purpose formula.

16-18. Targum to Joshua 5.14

In Josh. 5.13-14, Joshua and the people are encamped at Gilgal, and the prince of the heavenly host appears. This figure is perhaps (as implied by 6.2) to be identified with Yahweh, although Boling and Wright identify him as "Joshua's heavenly counterpart," noting that the commander of the heavenly host is very reminiscent of the angel of the Lord in the OT.[52] From Joshua's perspective in 5.13, however, he simply sees "a man" standing before him carrying a drawn sword. Joshua asks him whose side he is on, to which the prince replies, in 5.14, "as the chief of the forces of the Lord I have come now" (אֲנִי שַׂר־צְבָא־יְהוָה עַתָּה בָאתִי/ἐγὼ ἀρχιστράτηγος δυνάμεως κυρίου νυνὶ παραγέγονα). In response, Joshua falls to the ground in worship.

Interestingly, in later Rabbinic interpretation, the chief of the Lord's hosts here becomes a more negative figure. The Talmud supplies a reason for the coming of the angel;[53] this is understandable, as the original account in Joshua is highly mysterious. In the interpretation, the figure begins by rebuking Joshua: "this evening you neglected the regular afternoon sacrifice, and

---

49. A. Díez Macho, *Neophyti 1. Targum Palestinense Ms de la Biblioteca Vaticana.* Volume 4: *Números* (Madrid: CSIC, 1974), 214-15, where the translation is "yo he salido a oponerme a ti" (214).

50. McNamara and Clarke, *Targum Neofiti 1: Numbers. Targum Pseudo-Jonathan: Numbers,* 128.

51. הא אנה אפקת להשדך (J); cf. הא אנא נפקת לסתנך (A).

52. R. G. Boling and G. E. Wright, *Joshua* (Anchor Bible; New York: Doubleday, 1982), 198-99.

53. See also *b. 'Erubin* 63b for a similar account again.

now you have neglected the study of the Torah" (*b. Megillah* 3a). Joshua asks the figure: "In regard to which of them have you come?" (עַל אֵיזֶה מֵהֶן בָּאתָ). He receives the reply, "I have come *now*," that is, on account of his neglect of Torah study (". . . and *now* you have neglected the study of the Torah"). Although there is no final clause here, the combination of question and answer corresponds loosely to the form of the question of the demons in Mark 1.24 ("have you come to destroy us?") and the indirect final clause in Mark 1.38 ("for this reason I have come").

One of the fragmentary Targums has language even closer to that of Jesus in the Synoptic Gospels. It exists in two different editions. The version which interests us here is a fragment found in the Cairo Genizah, covering Josh. 5.2–6.1; it was written in Palestinian Aramaic, and our manuscript of it was copied probably in the tenth century.[54] The later fragment (copied in around the fourteenth century) was discovered among manuscripts in the Jewish Theological Seminary and contains a Targum to Josh. 5.5–6.1 in Babylonian Aramaic.[55] This later manuscript will not be investigated in detail here, however.

Although even the earlier manuscript initially appears unpromisingly late, this is of course par for the course with much Jewish literature, especially the Targums. (Or for a similar case, it should be remembered that the most important manuscripts of the Ethiopic of *1 Enoch* all date from around the fifteenth century.) In fact, the editors of this earlier version note that the Targum has some very interesting theological tendencies, and they consequently date it to the intertestamental period, with a provenance in an eschatological group similar to the Qumran community.[56]

The main interest for our purposes is that in both editions of this Targum to Joshua we find more explicit statements of purpose on the part of the angel at this point in Josh. 5.14-15. In the original Hebrew text, when Joshua asks the figure whether he is on the side of Israel or her enemies, the angel simply replies "no." Joshua falls to the ground, whereupon he is told to take off his sandals, which he then does. In the Targum, however, this discussion is expanded somewhat, along the lines of *b. Megillah* 3a-b. I offer here a translation of the relevant part of the Targum to 5.14:

54. Ms. T.-S. B. 13,12 (in the Taylor-Schechter collection in the Cambridge University Library). For text, German translation, and discussion, see H. Fahr and U. Gleßmer, *Jordandurchzug und Beschneidung als Zurechtweisung in einem Targum zu Josua 5 (Edition des Ms. T.-S. B 13,12)* (Orienta Biblica et Christiana; Glückstadt: Augustin, 1991).
55. ENA 2576, f. 5 (Jewish Theological Seminary). For the *editio princeps*, see A. Díez Macho, "Un nuevo Targum a los Profetas," *Estudios Bíblicos* 15 (1956), 287-300.
56. Fahr and Gleßmer, *Jordandurchzug und Beschneidung als Zurechtweisung*, 109-10, 133.

fol. 4b: [7]Joshua fell before him [8]on the ground, and asked him and said to him, "Is it to support [9]us that you have come? Or do you belong to our enemies and [10]seek to kill?"

fol. 5a: [5]And he said to him: "*I have not come to support* (לא למסעאד אתתי), [6]and I am not an enemy. But as the angel who is sent from [7]Yahweh *I have come to complain* (אתתי למתפרע) because of the evening in which you [pl.] have neglected the sacrifice, and today have neglected [8]Torah-study." And he [Joshua] said, "For which of these two reasons have you come?" [9]And he said to him, "*I have not come to support* (לא למסעאד אתתי)." And Joshua fell on his face. . . .

Here we have, in quick succession, three instances of the "I have come" + purpose formula: "I have not come to support you," "I have come to complain," and then a reiteration of the first. The combination of the negative form ("I have not come to . . .") and the positive ("I have come to . . .") is of course particularly reminiscent of the way of speaking we find in the Synoptic Gospels.

19. Midrash Tanḥuma to Exodus 6 (Parashah Mishpatim)

In a discussion of Exod. 23.20 ("See, I send you an angel"), the fourth-century Midrash Tanḥuma offers several possible interpretations.[57] In one of these, the commander of the hosts of the Lord from Joshua 5 appears again:

[Another interpretation:] The Holy One said to Moses: "I am sending an angel before you but not before them." He (Moses) said: "If you send him out before me, I do not want him." But Joshua saw the angel and fell down before him. What did he say to him (in Josh. 5.13)? "Are you for us or for our adversaries?" When he (Joshua) said to him (the angel), "Are you for us?" he (the angel) began to cry in great anguish: "No, but I am the Captain of the Lord's host. Now I have come. *Here are two times I have come to give Israel an inheritance* (הרי ב' פעמים באתי להנחיל את ישראל). I am the one who came in the days of your master Moses, but he rejected me."[58]

57. Stemberger notes Böhl's argument for a completion by "400 at the latest," although recognizing the need to acknowledge later editing. See G. Stemberger, *Introduction to the Talmud and Midrash: Second Edition Translated and Edited by Markus Bockmuehl* (Edinburgh: Clark, 1995), 305.

58. The translation is from J. Townsend, *Midrash Tanḥuma*, Volume 2: *Exodus and Leviticus* (Hoboken: Ktav, 1989), 123-24, although I have adapted the punctuation to make it easier to understand.

The first part here, where Moses rejects the angel of the Lord, corresponds to the Rabbinic tradition that Moses is only interested in being accompanied by the Lord himself; he refuses any angel's assistance. Joshua on the other hand gives the angel a slightly more positive reception: "But Joshua saw the angel and fell down before him." Interestingly, the role of the angel here is seen in a much more positive light than in the previous instances we saw in the Targums. Here the angel claims, "I have come to give Israel an inheritance" (באתי להנחיל את ישראל). Again, then, the task is a considerable one: the angel mediates God's activity in taking the Israelites into the Promised Land.

20. Testament of Abraham (A) 16.15

With the next two examples, we come to instances of "I have come" + purpose sayings not from beneficial angels, but from the angel of death. In *Testament of Abraham* 16 we come to the dispute between the angel of death and Abraham. As Allison notes, "Chap. 16 is the major hinge in the narrative. Until now, the story has been about Michael's attempt to take Abraham's soul. But Michael has failed, so God now calls another to undertake his task."[59] The angel of death has been sent to collect Abraham's soul, but Abraham resolutely refuses to follow him. Eventually Death addresses Abraham as "father" and assures him that he is telling the truth about who he is. Then in 16.14-16:[60]

> Abraham said to him, "Why have you come here? (εἰς τί ἐλήλυθας ὧδε;)"
> And Death said, "I have come for your righteous soul (διὰ τῆς δικαίας σου ψυχῆς παραγέγονα)."
> (Abraham said to him,) "I know what you are saying, but I will not follow you." And Death was silent and did not reply.

Here we have purposes implied both in Abraham's question about Death's coming, and in Death's own statement of his advent. On the other hand, neither is expressed as clearly as has been the case in previous examples (i.e., with a purpose clause).

The form of Abraham's question corresponds closely to the question in *b. Megillah* 3a-b, in which Joshua asked the angel about his purpose in com-

---

59. D. Allison, *The Testament of Abraham* (CEJL; Berlin: de Gruyter, 2003), 322.

60. The text cited here, *Testament of Abraham* (A), is the long recension. For the text, see the critical edition: F. Schmidt, *Le Testament Grec d'Abraham. Introduction, Édition Critique des Deux Recensions Grecques, Traduction* (TSAJ; Tübingen: Mohr, 1986).

ing: "In regard to which [Joshua's neglect of sacrifice or of Torah study] have you come?" One could also draw parallels with the indirect question in Dan. 10.20 ("Do you know why I have come to you?") and the questions of the demons in Mark 1.24 and Matt. 8.29: "Have you come to destroy us?" Furthermore, the reference in Abraham's question to "coming for (εἰς)" + pronoun is common both to *Testament of Abraham* 16.16 and Mark 1.38. Death's response to Abraham's question, which is our major concern here, again uses a preposition rather than a verb to express the purpose ("I have come *for* your righteous soul").[61]

Interestingly, the same sequence of different Greek verbs for "come" is found, in the Josephus passage mentioned above, and in Luke 12.49-51:

Abraham said to him, "Why have you come (ἐλήλυθας) here?" And Death said, "I have come (παραγέγονα) for your righteous soul."

He spoke these things, and then departed, having come (ἐλθών) according to the will of God . . . [then] he came (παραγίνεται) again by the grace of God. (Josephus, *Antiquities* 5.278, 280)

I have come (ἦλθον) to cast fire onto the earth, and how I wish it were already kindled. . . . Do not think that I have come (παρεγενόμην) to bring peace on the earth; no, I tell you — not peace, but division. (Luke 12.49, 51)

The more usual *erchomai* is followed by *paraginomai* for the sake of variety. It is the particular statement of Death, "I have come for your righteous soul," however, which is our immediate interest here.

21. *Midrash Rabbah to Deuteronomy 11.10*

In a scene near the end of the Midrash Rabbah to Deuteronomy, we come to the heavenly scenes where God devises various means to orchestrate Moses' death. First, he asks Michael to carry it out, but Michael objects to the task on the grounds that he has been Moses' teacher. God then sends "Sammael the wicked," the angel of death. Sammael is terrified at the prospect when he comes face-to-face with Moses, but Moses speaks first and asks Sammael why he has come. (This is reminiscent of Abraham's question just mentioned above.) The angel replies, "I have come to bear away your breath"

---

61. While this is an unusual use of the preposition διά + genitive, there is no question of the meaning here.

(לטל נשמתך באתי).[62] This again, then, follows the same formula that we have seen thus far.

This form of words is also reused in later Hebrew storytelling in connection with the angel of death, and Bühner cites some examples. To take one case, there is the story in Gaster's compilation of *Exempla* of a "great and righteous man" called ben Sabar whose key action in the story is to help an orphan get married.[63] Afterward, however, he is confronted by the angel of death who makes a statement almost identical to that just seen above: "I am the angel of death, who has come to take your soul" (נפשך אני מלאך המות בא ליטול את).[64] Similarly, in one of the stories in Bin Gorion's compilation, the angel of death utters similar fateful words: "My son, I am an angel of God, *and behold I have come to take your soul*" (ובאתי הנה לקחת את נפשך).[65] These examples are obviously less clearly of value for our investigation because they come from a much later date even than Deuteronomy Rabbah.

22. Acts of Thomas 76

Although *Acts of Thomas* is a Christian text dating from the beginning of the third century, it nevertheless does in one place show familiarity with the OT/Jewish angelic formula which we have noted.[66] A. F. J. Klijn, in his translation and commentary on the work, considers it originally written in Syriac, but also (almost simultaneously) in Greek: according to him, the Greek is probably not a translation of the Syriac.[67] Others have commented that the Greek actually preserves the original better, as the Syriac has suffered some catholicizing corruption.[68] The "I have come" saying in question is spoken by

---

62. For the translation, see H. Freedman and M. Simon, *Midrash Rabbah: Deuteronomy* (London: Soncino, 1977), 185.

63. For the text, see M. Gaster, *The Exempla of the Rabbis* (New York: Ktav, 1968 [1924]), 94-96 (Hebrew pages); for a summary, see 84-85 (English pages).

64. Gaster, *Exempla*, 95 (Hebrew pages).

65. M. J. Bin Gorion, ed., *Mimeqor Yisrael* (Tel Aviv: Dvir, 1965-66), 354 (§621). See also E. Bin Gorion and M. Bin Gorion, *Der Born Judas*. Part 2: *Legenden, Märchen und Erzählungen* (Frankfurt: Insel, 1973), §14.

66. For this date, see H. J. W. Drijvers in "The Acts of Thomas," in W. Schneemelcher, ed., *New Testament Apocrypha* (Louisville: Westminster John Knox, 1991), 2:322-411 (323).

67. A. F. J. Klijn, *The Acts of Thomas: Introduction, Text and Commentary*, second revised edition (NovTSuppS; Leiden: Brill, 2003), 1, 3. (The title of the book is somewhat misleading: the volume contains a *translation*, rather than a *text*.)

68. See the comments of Drijvers, "The Acts of Thomas," in Schneemelcher, *New Testament Apocrypha*, 2:323.

a demon: "I have come to destroy" (ἀφανίσαι ἦλθον).[69] Interestingly, there is a strong parallel between the mission of the demon here and that of Thomas: "It turns out that he [the demon] is the Anti-apostle, for as the Anti-Christ counteracts Christ, so the demon counteracts the apostle, whose work he wants to destroy."[70] Thomas's location is supplied by the narrative: in *Acts of Thomas* 1, the disciples are each allotted places to go. "They divided the countries among them, in order that each one of them might preach in the region which fell to him and in the place to which his Lord sent him. And India fell by lot and division to Judas Thomas the Apostle."[71] While Thomas comes from Jerusalem at the commission of Jesus his Lord, the demon has come from the heavenly realms, having been sent by Satan. There is no need, however, to specify the demon's provenance explicitly, as the demon's statement taps into the traditional formula which we have been examining.

23. *Proclus,* Discourse 6

Proclus's discourse in praise of Mary is another example of a Christian text developing Jewish angelological motifs. Written some time before Proclus's death in 446-47 CE, it goes, in the Migne edition, under the title of *Praise for Holy Mary, Mother of God (Laudatio sanctae Dei genitricis Mariae).*[72] It consists of seventeen sections, and interestingly contains in the middle two imaginary dialogues, first between Mary and Joseph (section 9) and then between Mary and the archangel Gabriel (sections 11 and 12). This latter dialogue is a much expanded version of the exchange in Luke 1.34-38, which begins with Mary's question, "How will this be since I know not a man?" In the course of the rapid-fire exchange between the virgin and the angel, Gabriel offers a statement of the purpose of his visit to Mary:

> And the holy one (Mary) said: "I have never borne the yoke of a husband, so how can I become the mother of a child?"

---

69. The Greek text can be found in M. Bonnet, *Acta Thomae* (Leipzig: Mendelssohn, 1883), 51.

70. J. Bolyki, "Human Nature and Character as Moving Factors of Plot in the Acts of Thomas," in J. N. Bremmer, ed., *The Apocryphal Acts of Thomas* (Leuven: Peeters, 2001), 91-100 (99).

71. Translation from Klijn, *Acts of Thomas,* 17.

72. *Discourse 6* is printed in PG 65:721-58. It should not be confused with several other discourses on this theme such as *Discourse 1 (Laudatio in sanctissimam Dei genitricem Mariam),* and *Discourse 5 (Laudatio in S. Virginem ac Dei genitricem Mariam).*

> And the archangel said, "You are asking about a union (σύνοδος) of marital relations, but what of the descent (κάθοδος) of the power of the Lord?"
>
> And the holy one said, "I wish to have complete certainty, so that I may be strong enough to flee from all distress."
>
> And the archangel said, "*I have come to report to you* (ἦλθον ἀναγγεῖλαί σοι) the things which have been decreed by the creator of all, and — surely — *to interpret to you* (ἑρμηνεῦσαί σοι) what has been hidden from all."[73]

As in the *Acts of Thomas,* then, we have a Christian author making use of the angelic "I have come" + purpose formula.

24. *The* Vision of Daniel

Finally, a rather late example comes in the *Vision of Daniel,*[74] which because of its reference to particular Christian emperors can be fairly securely dated in the tenth century CE.[75] The text is preserved in a Hebrew manuscript found in the Cairo Genizah and has been published twice and translated into English.[76] Sharf translates the opening of the text as follows:

> I, Daniel, stood by the river Hebar, and the dread vision was heavy upon me, and I was amazed. And there came to me Gabriel, captain of the heavenly host, and said to me, "Know, beloved man, and hearken: *I have come to tell you* (באתי לך להגיד) that the Mighty Holy One commanded me, 'Go, Gabriel, and reveal to Daniel what is to be at the end of days.'"[77]

As Sharf notes, the text here is a conflation of Dan. 8.16 (where Gabriel appears to Daniel at the river Ulai) and Ezek. 1.3, which refers to the river Hebar.

---

73. PG 65:740.

74. Called by Berger the Hebrew *Apocalypse of Daniel* to distinguish it from the Christian Greek *Apocalypse of Daniel.* Berger, *Die Auferstehung des Propheten,* 528.

75. See the discussion in A. Sharf, *Byzantine Jewry from Justinian to the Fourth Crusade* (London: Routledge, 1971), 101-2.

76. The *editio princeps* was L. Ginzberg, *Geniza Studies in Memory of Dr. Solomon Schechter,* Volume 1: *Midrash and Haggadah* (New York: Jewish Theological Seminary of America, 1928), 313-23. It was reprinted with pointing in Y. Even-Shmuel, מדרשי גאלה (Jerusalem: Mosad Byalik ʻal yede Masadah, 1953-54), 249-52 (Introduction on 232-48). For the ET, see "Appendix I: The Vision of Daniel," in Sharf, *Byzantine Jewry,* 201-4.

77. Sharf, *Byzantine Jewry,* 201; for the text, see Ginzberg, *Geniza Studies,* 318; Even-Shmuel, מדרשי גאלה, 249.

However, it is also reminiscent of the angelic advents in Daniel 9 and 10, where Daniel is addressed as one beloved (Dan. 10.11) and where, as we have seen, Gabriel announces his own coming with a purpose (on which see the discussion above).

III. "Coming of Elijah" Traditions (especially *Midrash Mishle* 9)

Elijah's Eschatological Ministry

Language about the coming of Elijah abounds in the NT and other Jewish literature, as Elijah is of course envisaged as returning at the end of time, possibly as a precursor of the Messiah. This was a coming in order to exercise some form of eschatological ministry, largely on the basis of Mal. 3.1 and especially 4.5: "Behold, I will send you Elijah the prophet before the great and awesome day of the Lord comes." In later rabbinic interpretation, there is some debate on the details:

> Rabbi Joshua said, "I have received as tradition from Rabban Johanan ben Zakkai, who heard from his teacher, and his teacher from his teacher, as a *Halakah* given to Moses from Sinai, that Elijah will not come to declare unclean or clean (שאין אליהו בא לטמא ולטהר), to remove afar or bring nigh (לרחק ולקרב), but to remove afar those [families] that were brought nigh by violence and to bring nigh those [families] that were removed afar by violence. The family of Beth Zerepha was in the land beyond Jordan and Ben Zion removed it afar by force. And yet another [family] was there, and Ben Zion brought it nigh by force. The like of these Elijah will come to declare unclean or clean (לטמא ולטהר כגון אלו אליהו בא), to remove afar or to bring nigh." Rabbi Judah says, "To bring nigh but not to remove afar." Rabbi Simeon says, "To bring agreement where there is matter for dispute." And the sages say, "Neither to remove afar nor to bring nigh, but to make peace in the world, as it is written, *Behold I will send you Elijah the prophet* (הנביא הנני שולח לכם את אליה) . . . *and he shall turn the heart of the fathers to their children and the heart of the children to their fathers* (Mal. 4.5-6)." (*m. 'Eduyoth* 8:7)[78]

There is also a reference in the Bavli to this Mishnaic discussion. It is much shorter, and simply makes reference to Elijah as follows: "Elijah will come to

---

78. Translation follows H. Danby, *The Mishnah* (Oxford: Oxford University Press, 1985 [1933]), 436-37.

declare unclean or clean, to expel and admit" (*b. Kiddushin* 71a).[79] Here too the discussion concerns Elijah's eschatological role, particularly that of declaring which families are of pure Jewish blood and which are mixed. The key point is that here perhaps there is an interesting potential parallel with Jesus' statements in Luke 12.51 par. Matt. 10.34: Jesus says he has come *not* to bring peace on the earth. Elijah's coming from heaven on the other hand is, according to Rabbi Simeon, "neither to remove afar nor to bring nigh, but to make peace in the world." It is noteworthy that here again there is an eschatological ministry that is envisaged as having a cosmic scope, which, again, is difficult to imagine outside of a coming from *heaven*.[80]

Elijah's Ministry in the Present Age

Already before the end of the age, however, Elijah is pictured in early Judaism and the rabbinic literature as one who intervenes in human affairs, usually to help those in distress.[81] The earliest reference to a coming of Elijah of this kind comes in fact in the NT, in Mark 15.36. Here, misunderstanding Jesus' cry of dereliction, the bystanders assume he is calling to Elijah. One of their number asks the question, "let us see *if Elijah comes to take him down*" (εἰ ἔρχεται Ἡλίας καθελεῖν αὐτόν). Elijah could be imagined, then, to come in anticipation of his final advent to intervene in human affairs, and in this respect his activity resembles that of angels. This example is also interesting in that it has an explicit statement of purpose, using "come" + infinitive.

One interesting point that has not been discussed much is that Elijah's comings from heaven were already brought into association with angelic comings from heaven by the rabbis. This is evident from the discussion of their respective airspeeds:

> R. Eleazar b. Abina said furthermore: Greater is [the achievement] ascribed to Michael than that ascribed to Gabriel. For of Michael it is writ-

---

79. This passage is quoted again in H. Freedman and M. Simon, *Midrash Rabbah: Song of Songs* (London: Soncino, 1977), 224.

80. This is in fact one of the examples adduced by Jeremias for his Aramaic idiom, as I have discussed elsewhere: see S. J. Gathercole, "On the Alleged Aramaic Idiom behind the Synoptic ἦλθον-sayings," 86. Here it is fairly clear, however, that the statement is more than a reference to Elijah having a purpose, since a future coming from heaven is what is expected from Elijah. Elijah will come with the intention to remove or bring nigh, to declare clean or unclean, to bring agreement and make peace.

81. For examples, see H. Strack and P. Billerbeck, *Kommentar zum Neuen Testament aus Talmud und Midrash* (Munich: Beck, 1922-56), 4/2:769-98.

ten: "Then flew unto me one of the Seraphim," whereas of Gabriel it is written: "The man Gabriel whom I had seen in the vision at the beginning, being caused to fly in a flight etc." How do you know that this [word] "one" [of the Seraphim] means Michael? — R. Johanan says: By an analogy from [the words] "one," "one." Here it is written: Then flew unto me one of the Seraphim; and in another place it is written: But, lo, Michael, one of the chief princes, came to help me. A Tanna taught: Michael [reaches his goal] in one [flight], Gabriel in two, Elijah in four, and the Angel of Death in eight. In the time of plague, however, [the Angel of Death, too, reaches his goal] in one. (*b. Berakoth* 4b).

The Bavli here thus places Elijah alongside angels, without identifying him as one in any way.

25. Midrash Mishle 9

There are numerous other references to the coming of Elijah which we will not deal with in any detail.[82] Important for our purposes, however, is that we find the "I have come to . . ." formula used of Elijah in the Midrash to Proverbs.[83] The context is exegesis of Proverbs 9, where Wisdom has built her house, prepared the feast, "and also set the table" (Prov. 9.2). The clause "and also set the table" is apparently susceptible to two interpretations. In the first, it concerns "the Torah which furnishes a [rich] table for those who study it in this world and in the world to come." The alternative explanation is as follows:

> *"And also set the table"* — a story is told of R. Aqiba who was confined in prison and was cared for by Joshua of Gerasa. Once, on the eve of a holy day, Joshua took leave of his master and went home, whereupon Elijah the priest came by and stood at the door to his house, calling, "Come out,

---

82. In addition to those noted in Strack-Billerbeck, see also Genesis Rabbah 33.3 (Freedman and Simon, *Midrash Rabbah: Genesis*, 262); 71.9 (659-60); 96.5 (891); Numbers Rabbah 3.13 (Freedman and Simon, *Midrash Rabbah: Numbers*, 93); Deuteronomy Rabbah 2.17 (Freedman and Simon, *Midrash Rabbah: Deuteronomy*, 44); 3.17 (88); 6.7 (125); *b. Sanhedrin* 113b.

83. For the text, see B. L. Visotsky, *Midrash Mishle: A Critical Edition Based on Vatican MS. Ebr. 44, with Variant Readings from All Known Manuscripts and Early Editions, and with an Introduction, References and a Short Commentary* (New York: Jewish Theological Seminary of America, 1990). For English translation, see B. L. Visotsky, *Midrash on Proverbs: Translated from the Hebrew with an Introduction and Annotations* (Yale Judaica Series; New Haven: Yale University Press, 1992).

Joshua! Come out, Joshua!" Joshua asked, "Who are you?" Elijah replied, "*I am Elijah the priest, who has come to tell you* (אני אליהו הכהן שבאתי להגיד לך) that your master, R. Aqiba, has died in prison." (Midrash Mishle 9).

Thereafter, Joshua and Elijah rush off to get Rabbi Aqiba's body and find a bier. They find a bier with a table and a lamp next to it, and when they place Aqiba's body on it, the lamp lights of its own accord and the table is set all by itself. Hence, "and also set the table. . . ."

Rabbi Aqiba is known to have died around 135 CE, although the final composition of Midrash Proverbs is much later.[84] It is therefore difficult to date the tradition we have here with any precision. There are a number of noteworthy features in this passage, such as the growing rabbinic tradition of the *priestly* identity of Elijah: there was a long-standing debate over Elijah's genealogy and whether he was from the line of Levi or not.[85] Most important for our purposes is of course the portrayal of Elijah as someone who intervenes in human affairs even after his ascension into heaven. This passage is clearly tapping into the way of speaking in which heavenly figures announce their arrival in visits to earthly residents. In this respect, the statement attributed to Elijah here clearly resembles that of angels. There is also a similarity with the language used by Jesus: Elijah is a human figure who uses the "I have come" + purpose formula to summarize the reason for a particular visit to the human, earthly realm, though he is not, of course, summing up his entire existence.

Later Rabbinic Tales

Further references can be seen in the later tradition of Hebrew narrative, as we saw above in the case of the angel of death. Bühner cites an example in which Elijah warns a bridegroom that he will be approached by the angel of death: "My son, I am Elijah, and I have come to bring you news."[86] This combination of reference to coming with the angel's purpose "to bring good news" is an example which appears several times.[87]

---

84. See Visotsky, *Midrash on Proverbs*, 10, for a date in the ninth century.

85. See L. Ginzberg, *The Legends of the Jews* (Baltimore: Johns Hopkins, 1998 [1913]), 4:185, 210, and other references listed in 7:133 (index entry "Elijah, a Priest"). For an example, see Genesis Rabbah 71.9.

86. Bühner, *Der Gesandte und sein Weg*, 142. Bühner cites the source as Bin Gorion, *Mimeqor Jisrael*, 125, but I have not been able to find the reference he indicates.

87. In addition to this instance, we have seen *b. Baba Metzia* 86b; cf. Luke 2.10; Josephus, *Antiquities* 5.277.

In another case, there is a tale of three men who live in the same city, and each has an affliction.[88] The first is extremely rich, but suddenly loses all his wealth and property. The second studies the Torah day and night, and yet is very poor. The third is extremely pious, but has a terrible wife. Elijah, disguised as an old man, listens to the complaints of the three men, and then

> Elijah the prophet said to them, "Listen to me, my masters, and do not be anxious. Behold, I have come to rescue you (באתי להושיעכם) from your toil and your groaning, and you will return to your houses in great glory. . . .[89]

To the pious man with the bad wife, Elijah gives a magic ring: the wife has actually been possessed by a demon, and the ring will banish the demon. To the poor Torah scholar, he gives a magic book which multiplies into a whole stack of books. The man who was rich receives a magic coin which multiplies, but one condition of his restored wealth is that he must build a Torah school. Elijah comes again, however, and discovers that the man has a palace and a guard at the gate to keep out the poor. Elijah confronts him, saying that he helped him at a time of his great need:

> And moreover, I said to you, "Found a *bet midrash*" . . . But you have rejected my words. . . . Therefore I have come to you now so that you might return the coin to me (על כן באתי עתה אליך כי תחזיר לי את המטבע).[90]

Again, then, we can see the same formula applied to Elijah, even though in this case the text is very late. Because of the late date, these examples of course must be used (if at all) with extreme caution, but they attest to the strength of the tradition.

IV. Angelophanic (and Other) Appearances of God

Unsurprisingly perhaps, there are also a number of references in the OT and Jewish literature to the coming of *God*.[91] In Exod. 20.20 God comes to Moses

---

88. For German paraphrase, see Bin Gorion, *Der Born Judas*, 2:22-30.

89. For the Hebrew text, see Bin Gorion, *Mimeqor Yisrael*, 411 (§672). Cf. idem, *Der Born Judas*, 2:25.

90. Bin Gorion, *Mimeqor Yisrael*, 412 (Hebrew); cf. idem, *Der Born Judas*, 28-29.

91. Some of the examples below are taken from F. Schnutenhaus, "Das Kommen und Erscheinen Gottes im Alten Testament," *ZAW* 76 (1964), 1-22 (18). See further his comments, as well as E. Jenni, "'Kommen' im theologischen Sprachgebrauch des Alten Testaments," in H. J.

and Israel. In the Psalms there is the repeated formula "he comes to judge the earth" (Pss. 96.13; 98.9). In Isaiah, this is shown to be a coming both in punishment and salvation: "Say to those with anxious heart, 'Take courage, fear not. Behold, your God will come with vengeance; the recompense of God will come, but he will save you'" (Isa. 35.4).[92] In the first century CE, the *Assumption of Moses* uses similar language in the description of the inbreaking of the kingdom following Taxo's eschatological activity: "For the Most High God, the only eternal one, will arise and will manifestly come to punish the nations and to destroy all their idols *(et palam ueniet ut uindicet gentes et perdet omnia idola eorum)*" (10.7). To take a later example, from the rabbis:

> R. Hama son of R. Hanina said: "It was the third day from Abraham's circumcision, and the Holy One, blessed be He, came to enquire after Abraham's health; he drew the sun out of its sheath, so that that righteous man [sc. Abraham] should not be troubled with wayfarers." (*b. Baba Metzia* 86b)[93]

Another of the most common biblical references to God's coming, to Sinai, is explored in the Mekilta. In the course of the exegesis of Exod. 19.17, it is noted that according to Rabbi Jose, Rabbi Judah used to say: "'The Lord came from Sinai' (Deut. 33.2): Do not read it thus, but read: 'The Lord came to Sinai,' to give the Torah to Israel (יי לסיני בא ליתן תורה לישראל)."[94]

Angelophanic Theophany and the "I Have Come" + Purpose Formula

In a number of cases where God intervenes in human affairs before the eschaton, he is portrayed to some extent in angelomorphic terms (which is by no means to reduce God to an angel!). The most common occurrences of this in the OT and early Jewish literature are the references to the angel of the Lord, a figure almost indistinguishable from Yahweh himself. Stuckenbruck's language is helpfully nuanced here: in connection with Judges 6 where there is a transition from "the angel of the Lord" (vv. 20-22) to "the Lord" (v. 23), he writes:

Stocbc, J. J. Stamm, and E. Jenni, eds., *Wort, Gebot, Glaube. Beiträge zur Theologie des Alten Testaments. Walther Eichrodt zum 80. Geburtstag* (Zurich: Zwingli, 1970), 251-61.

92. On all these, see Schnutenhaus, "Das Kommen," 15-16.

93. One repeated example in the Bavli is where God "comes to see" the one worshiping; the worshiper correspondingly comes "to be seen" by God. See *b. Hagigah* 2a *(tris)*, 4b *(bis)*; *Sanhedrin* 4b *(bis)*. This is probably, however, an idiom of some kind.

94. J. Z. Lauterbach, *Mekilta de-Rabbi Ishmael* (Philadelphia: JPS, 1976), 2:219-20.

the "angel of the Lord" is difficult to distinguish from "the Lord," to whom the reassurance is attributed (v. 23). It is uncertain whether, at this stage, the angel is being referred to as an independent being or is intended as an angelomorphic theophany.[95]

Another example is in Exodus 3 and concerns God's announcement to Moses in the burning bush. At the beginning of the chapter, it is explicitly "the angel of the Lord" who appears to Moses in the burning bush (v. 2). Afterward, however, there is a shift similar to that discussed by Stuckenbruck in connection with Judges 6, such that "the Lord" is the speaker in vv. 4-10.[96] He reveals that he has heard the cries of his people, and so has resolved to rescue them:

> So I have come down to rescue them from the hand of the Egyptians (וָאֵרֵד לְהַצִּילוֹ מִיַּד מִצְרַיִם) and to bring them up out of that land into a good and spacious land (וּלְהַעֲלֹתוֹ מִן־הָאָרֶץ הַהִוא אֶל־אֶרֶץ טוֹבָה וּרְחָבָה), a land flowing with milk and honey. (Exod. 3.8)

This example is not so helpful, as it is explicitly a reference to "coming down," but the same phenomenon is also found in later texts with the simple form of the verb "to come."

A particularly close parallel to Exodus 3 comes in fragment 9 of the *Exagoge of Ezekiel,* a rewriting of God's speech to Moses in the burning bush. In this work there is an alternation similar to that which occurs in Exodus 3. God is portrayed straightforwardly, but also in terms which employ envoy language in such a way that the envoy is almost identified with Yahweh himself: first God speaks to Moses (*Exagoge* 98), and then later the "divine word" (*theios . . . logos*) shines forth (100). Immediately after this, we have an "I have come" saying. Holladay translates the key statement here:

> For you cannot see my face since you are mortal, but my words you are allowed to hear, *those which I have come to speak* (τῶν ἕκατ᾽ ἐλήλυθα). (101-3)[97]

In fact, there is no purpose *clause* in the Greek, though a purpose is implied: a literal translation would go something like ". . . those on account of which I

95. L. T. Stuckenbruck, *Angel Veneration and Christology: A Study in Early Judaism and in the Christology of the Apocalypse of John* (WUNT; Tübingen: Mohr, 1995), 89 n. 108.

96. J. Milgrom, *Numbers* (JPS Torah Commentary; Philadelphia: JPS, 1990), 192, gives some further examples.

97. For the text and translation, see C. R. Holladay, *Fragments from Hellenistic Jewish Authors,* Volume 2: *Poets* (Atlanta: Scholars, 1989), 370-71.

have come." Our aim here is not to say that Yahweh is particularly similar to the angels; merely that language more commonly applied to angels can also be used of him. There is, however, the additional factor here in the *Exagoge* of God's agency through "the divine word."

Later, in the first century, the "I have come" + purpose formula comes in Josephus's *Antiquities*. The context is Josephus's paraphrase of Jacob's vision at Beersheba where God promises that he will go with Jacob down to Egypt, and bring him safely back again (Gen. 46.1-4). In Josephus's version, Jacob is worried that either his descendants will be wiped out, or that he himself will die before seeing his son Joseph in Egypt. There is no explicit reference to an angelic figure, although the context of God's appearing (in a dream) and the initial purpose (as a guide on Jacob's journey) are loosely reminiscent of angelic advents:

> Your progeny has endured unto you by my providence, and the one from among your sons you thought you had lost, Joseph, him have I brought to an enjoyment of greater things, and made him lord of Egypt, only a little lower than the king. Now I have come to be a guide (ἧκω . . . ἡγεμὼν ἐσόμενος) on this way of yours, and to show (προδηλῶν) that the end of your life will be in the embrace of Joseph, to announce (καταγγέλλων) a long age of glorious rule for your descendants, and to establish (καταστήσων) them in the land which I have promised. (*Antiquities* 2.175)

Here the first purpose clause is expressed by the *future participle* in the Greek, and so the first goal of God's coming is clearly to be Jacob's guide. Thereafter the situation is grammatically a little more complicated. It seems likely, however, that all four participial clauses following the "I have come" are subordinate clauses expressing purpose, although their sequence is future-present-present-future. The second and third are probably simply in the present by way of variation. It is probable that God is announcing here his coming for the various purposes of revelation (the first three cases), and also of fulfillment of promise (the final participle).

In fact, in the rabbinic period, "coming" language in connection with Yahweh becomes a little more common. One very frequent example is the application of the Song of Songs verse, "I have come into my garden, my sister, my bride" (5.1), to God's coming to reside in the Tabernacle.[98] Similarly, there

---

. Song Rabbah 4.10.1 (Freedman and Simon, *Midrash Rabbah: Song of Songs*, 213). *Pesikta Rabbati* 5 (W. Braude, *Pesikta Rabbati: Discourses for Feasts, Fasts and Special Sabbaths* [New Haven: Yale University Press, 1968], 1:102).

are a few examples of the "I have come" + purpose formula applied to God in the rabbinic literature:

> When God revealed himself to Moses, Moses was a novice in prophecy; hence God thought, "If I reveal myself to him in a loud voice, I will terrify him, and if in a soft voice, he will think lightly of prophecy." So what did he do? He revealed himself in the voice of his father. Moses thereupon said, "Here am I; what does my father desire?" Then God said, "I am not thy father, but *'The God of thy father'* (Exod. 3.6). I have come to thee gently so that thou be not afraid." (Exod. Rabbah 3.1).[99]

> Said the Holy One, blessed be he, "First I came to heal the iniquities of Israel, and then *'is the iniquity of Ephraim uncovered, and the wickedness of Samaria'* (Hos. 7.1)." (Song Rabbah 4.5.1-2 [Freedman/Simon]).[100]

> Said the Holy One, blessed be he, "I came to bless you, but I found your palate hollow and unable to hold a blessing" (Song Rabbah 8.5.1 [Freedman/Simon]).[101]

In these Rabbinic examples, there is no hint of an association of theophany with angelophany. Nevertheless, these references are easily comprehensible as alluding to God's coming from his proper dwelling place of heaven.

Conclusion

We have seen above, then, a strong tradition which begins very early, in the numerous references in Daniel. This tradition is then appropriated repeatedly up to our *terminus ad quem* in the time of Midrash Mishle and the *Vision of Daniel*. There is a consistent use of the "I have come" + purpose formula *which is not conventionally used in early Judaism by human figures to describe the totality of their life's work.*[102] Instead, the formula refers *to the totality of the*

99. Freedman and Simon, *Midrash Rabbah: Exodus,* 58.
100. Freedman and Simon, *Midrash Rabbah: Song of Songs,* 199.
101. Freedman and Simon, *Midrash Rabbah: Song of Songs,* 305.
102. There are other uses of "I have come" language that might have been exceptions which on closer examination turn out to be rather different. The first comes in 2 *Baruch* 3.1, when, having been told of the disasters to come upon Jerusalem, Baruch asks: "O Lord, my lord, have I come into the world for no other purpose than to see the evils of my mother?" This, however, is an instance of the idiom "to come into the world" which is familiar from rabbinic literature as a way of talking about birth. See, e.g., *m. Rosh Ha-Shanah* 1.2; Sifre Deuteronomy §312

heavenly figure's earthly visit, and to the purpose of that visit. There is thus a strong comparison to be made between these Jewish traditions and the equivalent statements in the Gospels. These advents of angels constitute parallels considerably closer than any hypothetical prophetic or messianic tradition. Because of this, it makes sense to adopt a more literal, rather than idiomatic, interpretation of the sayings in the Synoptic Gospels as referring to a coming from "a" to "b," and thus implying a place of origin, namely heaven.

To mention again the most important example from our previous chapter, much scholarship has interpreted the "I have come" sayings in the light of the parallel with Josephus (*War* 3.400) discussed above; in fact, it is probably the most frequently drawn parallel and is used to support the idea that the "I have come" sayings potentially have a prophetic nuance.[103] However, the angelic parallels are much more suitable, in that they (as do the Synoptic sayings) summarize the purpose of the figure's whole visit to the human realm — whereas Josephus's statement merely refers to a single episode in his earthly life. It is not that the sayings sum up the purpose of the angel's whole existence, but they do sum up the purpose of the *particular visit.* (Similarly, the "I have come" sayings in the Synoptic Gospels do not sum up Jesus' whole existence: they sum up the purpose of his first coming — and do not include the purposes of the second coming, for example.) Furthermore, we have seen in this chapter that there is the important consideration of the *quantity* of parallels in favor of seeing the angelic statements in the background of those

---

(on Deut. 32.9); for further references, see Strack and Billerbeck, *Kommentar*, 2:358, who give a number of instances, describing the idiom as "besonders häufig." The second potential exception comes in the much later *Pesikta de-Rab Kahana:* according to Rabbi Hanina bar Papa, the nation asked Isaiah, "are we to suppose that you came to comfort only the generation in whose days the Temple was destroyed?" (16.10). To this Isaiah replies, "I came to comfort all the generations" (לכל הדורות באתי לנחם). Hanina uses this as proof that God's promise to comfort all generations is not something which "your God said," but that "your God will keep saying" (Isa. 40.1). This seems to be a variation on the rabbinic "the Scripture comes to teach" idiom but with "Isaiah" here a personification of Isa. 40.1. For discussion of this idiom, see Gathercole, "On the Alleged Aramaic Idiom behind the Synoptic ἦλθον-sayings," 88-89. For the translation of the passage, see W. G. Braude and I. J. Kapstein, eds., *Pesikta de-Rab Kahana: R. Kahana's Compilation of Discourses for Sabbaths and Festal Days* (Philadelphia: Jewish Publication Society of America, 2002 [1975]), 400. John 1.31 (cf. 1.7) diverges from the Synoptic passages discussed above not least in the very complicated nature of the syntax.

103. As noted above, see O. Michel, "Ich komme," *TZ* 24 (1968), 123-24; J. A. Bühner, "Zur Form, Tradition und Bedeutung der ἦλθον-Sprüche," *Das Institutum Judaicum der Universität Tübingen* (1971-72), 51 n. 1; Arens, *HΛΘON-Sayings*, 21 n. 9; J. D. G. Dunn, *Christology in the Making: An Inquiry into the Origins of the Doctrine of the Incarnation* (London: SCM, 1980), 89; J. Marcus, *Mark 1–8: A New Translation with Introduction and Commentary* (New York: Doubleday, 2000), 204.

in the Gospels. Arens's objections to the use of such angelic parallels are not compelling either.

Again, however, the point to be made here in relation to the Synoptic sayings under discussion is not that they depict Christ as an angel.[104] Rather, the implication is simply that the advents of Christ and the angels are of the same kind. Both angels and the Synoptic Jesus declare that they have come with a purpose. So the reference to the *decision and purpose* expressed in Jesus' statements of coming *with a prior intention* to save, teach, judge and so on points to a coming *from* somewhere.[105] The obvious conclusion is that this "somewhere" is heaven, which entails the corresponding idea of preexistence. This element of Jesus' own *prior intent* and *action* in coming has not been sufficiently recognized in analyses of the "I have come" sayings, and as a result, the implication of his existence *prior to* his coming has been missed. It is, then, not so much the reference to "coming" itself but the form in which this is expressed (coming *with a purpose*) which points to preexistence. The logic in the present argument is similar to that frequently used in the interpretation of Philippians 2. Scholars such as Caird see this passage as one of the clearest indications of personal preexistence in the NT because it identifies a voluntary act of Christ in the incarnation, attributing "to the pre-existent Jesus a personal act of *choice*."[106] We will see in the following chapter that this position is reinforced when we examine the sayings in the Synoptic Gospels themselves.

---

104. Knight's comment on the use of the category "angelomorphic" is useful here: "'angelomorphic Christology' denotes the portrayal of Christ in terms which were derived from angelology, but not the assertion that Christ was an angel." J. M. Knight, *Disciples of the Beloved One: The Christology, Social Setting and Theological Context of the Ascension of Isaiah* (JSPSupS 18; Sheffield: Sheffield Academic, 1996), 183.

105. D. Macleod, *The Person of Christ* (Contours of Christian Theology; Leicester: InterVarsity, 1998), 45-70, says of Mark 10.45 and Luke 19.10 that "[t]he point is not simply that the Son of Man is in the world because he came into it . . . but that these passages ascribe to him a deliberate intention in coming" (59-60). Hultgren notes the purpose issue and describes the coming as a coming into the world, but does not link the two (A. Hultgren, *Jesus and His Adversaries: The Form and Function of the Conflict Stories in the Synoptic Tradition* [Minneapolis: Augsburg, 1979], 110).

106. G. B. Caird (L. D. Hurst, ed.), *New Testament Theology* (Oxford: Clarendon, 1994), 343.

CHAPTER 6

A New Reading of the Synoptic "I Have Come" Sayings

To recap the arguments made thus far, then, we have seen:

- that the preexistence interpretation of the "I have come" sayings has *prima facie* plausibility on simple logical grounds (chapter 3),
- that none of the other scholarly options can be considered plausible (chapter 4), and
- that the "I have come" + purpose formula of the Gospels is most closely and most abundantly paralleled in the announcements by angels of their comings from heaven (chapter 5).

We have already been asking the question: How would the "I have come" sayings in the Gospels have been understood by the earliest Christians (including the Gospel-writers themselves)? We have noted that such sayings were not conventionally used by people to sum up their lives' work: there does not seem to be any well-established idiom which could explain the sense of the instances in Matthew, Mark and Luke. Of course, the "I have come" sayings *could* have a prophetic or messianic sense, or some other meaning altogether. But exegesis by conjecture is not a particularly sound way to proceed.

On the last "bullet point" above, the purpose of drawing the parallels with the angels lies in the fact that both Jesus and the angels use the "I have come" + purpose formula to summarize an entire earthly visit. It is not the whole *existence* of an angel which is summed up: angels such as Gabriel visit the human sphere many times. Similarly, it is not Jesus' whole existence (which would also include his *sessio ad dexteram* and second coming) which is in view, but it is the purpose of his whole earthly mission in that first advent.[1] Therefore, in using the "I have come" + purpose formula, both Jesus and the angels talk of a prior intent in their visitations from the heavenly sphere to the human realm. The purpose or intent points to an existence prior to the coming.

In the absence of a compelling idiomatic sense for the "I have come" + purpose formula, it makes better sense to understand the "coming" as a coming from "a" to "b." This essentially leaves two options for the "a," or the place of Jesus' origin. Does the "I have come" imply a coming from *heaven* (as with the angels), or can it be explained merely as a coming from *Nazareth?* We have already seen in chapter 4 the problems with the Nazareth view. The rest of the present chapter attempts to show how the heavenly view offers the best account of the "I have come" sayings in Matthew, Mark, and Luke. This should be particularly apparent from the two most important passages under discussion: Luke 12.49-51 and the partially overlapping Matt. 10.34-35. These, closely followed by the Son of Man sayings, represent the most important evidence in this chapter.

I. Exegesis of the "Coming" Sayings

The final aspect of the sayings that points to a background of preexistence, then, is the stated goals of Jesus in his coming. We have hitherto focused only on the form of the "I have come" sayings, where the key point is the reference to Jesus coming with prior intent from "a" to "b." We move now to questions of content. Particularly where that aim has a *cosmic scope* ("I have come to cast fire on the earth," "Do not think I have come to bring peace on the earth," etc.) there is perhaps a stronger indication than usual of a coming from heaven. Again, where there is further imagery which highlights the *dynamic movement* involved in the coming (e.g., "the Son of Man *came to seek* and to save the lost"), the sense of a coming from heaven is also strong. As noted earlier, this chapter will not only cover the "I" sayings, but also the third-person "Son of Man" sayings, as well as the two questions to Jesus about his coming. Because the first reference to appear in Mark's Gospel is the demon's question

---

1. Carter makes the point that the "I have come" sayings sum up Jesus' entire existence, but he is clearly (rightly) referring to the entirety of Jesus' *earthly ministry:* "By engaging with these seven sayings [Carter counts them in a different way from the present study] containing the expression 'I have come' the audience understands that all of Jesus' existence — *his words, actions, death, and resurrection* — carries out God's purposes. . . .'" W. Carter, "Jesus' 'I Have Come' Sayings in Matthew's Gospel," *CBQ* 60 (1998), 44-62 (62).

to Jesus, "have you come to destroy us?" the order will follow: the two questions asked by demons (1-2), the six "I have come" sayings proper (3-8), and finally the two "the Son of Man has come" sayings (9-10).

Mark 1.24 par. Luke 4.34

> The demon said, "What have we to do with you, Jesus of Nazareth? *Have you come to destroy us?* I know who you are: the holy one of God!"

In our discussion of the angelic sayings in chapter 5, we noted a pattern not just in the self-introductions, which were the main concern of the chapter, but also in what the heavenly figures were *asked*. Abraham asks Death: "Why have you come here?" (*Testament of Abraham* [A] 16.15). We saw further how in the later exegesis of Joshua 5, Joshua asks the angelic figure, "Because of which one (neglect of Torah-study or of evening sacrifice) have you come?" (*b. Megillah* 3a). Or again, "Is it to support us that you have come? Or do you belong to our enemies and seek to kill?" (Geniza Targum Josh. 5.14). This latter question particularly resonates with that of the demons in Matt. 8.29 and Mark 1.24.

The setting of Mark 1.24 is the first of Jesus' exorcisms in Mark (1.23-28), which takes place in a synagogue and is met with a reaction of astonishment by the crowd.[2] The key statement is uttered by the demon which is occupying a person in attendance at the synagogue. Grammatically, the person in the synagogue is the human speaker, but the demonic voice is clearly behind the utterance, in view of the supernatural knowledge in the "I know who you are — the holy one of God."

Jesus' Cosmic Coming and Threat to Demons En Masse

The demon begins by asking Jesus "what do you want with *us?*"[3] This plural is interesting. There is no indication from the context of a plurality of demons as with Legion in Mark 5.9; rather, the point of dispute here revolves around whether the demon here is identifying with those in attendance at the syna-

---

2. The major work on this pericope is J. C. Iwe, *Jesus in the Synagogue of Capernaum: The Pericope and Its Programmatic Character for the Gospel of Mark: An Exegetico-Theological Study of Mark 1:21-28* (Rome: Gregorian University Press, 1999). On the saying in Mark 1.24, see O. Bauernfeind's *Die Worte der Dämonen im Markusevangelium* (BWANT; Stuttgart: Kohlhammer, 1927), 3-18.

3. There is some debate on whether this is a question or a statement: for the various positions, see Iwe, *Jesus in the Synagogue,* 75.

gogue or with the whole demonic realm.[4] If the former, then there is an obvious local context for Jesus' coming: the demon is asking whether Jesus *has come to the synagogue* to destroy those present. But if the question refers to the destruction of demons *en masse*, then the sense is a more cosmic one: has Jesus come (in a more theologically weighty sense) to destroy demonic forces collectively? The latter sense seems more likely for three reasons. First, and principally, it is not immediately apparent why Jesus should want to destroy the entire congregation in attendance at the synagogue, demons and humans alike. Second, the assembled congregation seems to see the threat as to the *demonic* world, rather than to themselves:

> They were all astonished, and they asked one another, "What is this? A new teaching — with authority! He commands even the unclean spirits and they obey him." (Mark 1.27)

Their response to Jesus is described as "amazement," and Lane (who thinks that the threat is *not* specifically to the demons) emphasizes the fearful commotion among the congregation. But the astonishment in Mark 1.27 is not necessarily negative. In fact the congregation's reaction, "What is this? A new teaching with authority!" seems to be rather *positive*. Third, the other setting of an almost identical question asked by demons is explicitly and exclusively focused upon the *demons* as the object of Jesus' destructive work (Matt. 8.28-29).

So, if the question is asked by the demon in solidarity with the rest of the demonic realm, then a local sense which refers to Jesus coming to a specific geographical location is highly unlikely.[5] As Lohmeyer puts it, "The words are to be taken in their deep religious sense; they do not refer to that specific time and event, but to the entirety of Jesus' coming."[6] The reference is to Jesus' entry into a world which is in the grip of demonic forces.

---

4. According to W. F. Lane, *The Gospel according to Mark* (NICNT; Grand Rapids: Eerdmans, 1974), 73, the demon is hereby identifying himself with the whole *synagogue congregation*, such that "Jesus' presence entails the danger of judgment for all present." On the other hand, E. Klostermann, *Das Markusevangelium* (HNT; Tübingen: Mohr, 1950), 17, argues (with probably the majority of scholars) that the reference in the "us" is to "wir Dämonen überhaupt." So also P. Perkins, "The Gospel of Mark," in *The New Interpreter's Bible*, vol. VIII (Nashville: Abingdon Press, 1995), 541, and M. D. Hooker, *A Commentary on the Gospel according to St. Mark* (Black's New Testament Commentary; London: Black, 1991), 64.

5. As is generally agreed by commentators. See R. H. Gundry, *Mark: A Commentary on His Apology for the Cross* (Grand Rapids: Eerdmans, 1993), 76.

6. E. Lohmeyer, *Das Evangelium des Markus* (KEK; Göttingen: Vandenhoeck und Ruprecht, 1937), 37: "Die Worte sind in ihrem tiefen religiösen Sinne zu nehmen; sie gehen nicht auf diese Stunde und dieses Geschehen, sondern auf das Ganze von Jesu Gekommen-Sein."

Jesus the "Holy One of God"

It might be added that seeing an advent of a preexistent "holy one" is perhaps supported by the fact of this supernatural knowledge of Jesus that is possessed by the demon. We noted above in chapter 2 that the tendency for Jesus to be recognized fully in the Synoptics only by demons is a pointer to his heavenly identity. The demon simply knows who Jesus is either by sensing his power and goodness or by virtue of their common origin in the supernatural realm. Two pieces of evidence point to the latter, to a heavenly origin of both Jesus and the demon together. First, there is the *specific* knowledge of Jesus' identity as "the holy one of God." Second, the title "holy one" might well point to the identity of a heavenly messenger, an agent of judgment. "Holy ones" is a very common designation in the OT and early Judaism for heavenly beings.[7] Daniel refers to a (singular) "holy one from heaven" (Dan. 4.13) and "holy one coming down from heaven" (4.23).[8] Here, incidentally, the angels are announcing the destruction of the tree which is, symbolically, Nebuchadnezzar. There is also a reference to an angelic "holy one" in Dan. 8.13. Although the variety of references to a "holy one" or "holy ones" in the OT and early Judaism means that we cannot be certain of the implication here, the Danielic connotations would tie in with the demon's fear that Jesus has "come" to execute divine judgment upon the demonic forces.[9]

For these reasons, then, it is probable that Schlatter, Lagrange, Lohmeyer, Sevenster, Schreiber, and France are correct in their conclusion that the demons refer in their question to the advent of the preexistent holy one of God into the realm of human and demonic existence on earth.[10] As Klostermann puts it, Jesus' coming is "his coming into the world."[11]

---

7. See for example Deut. 33.2; Ps. 89.5, 7; Dan. 4.17; Zech. 14.5; Jude 14.

8. In the LXX, ἅγιος ἀπ' οὐρανοῦ in Dan. 4.13 and ἅγιον καταβαίνοντα ἀπὸ τοῦ οὐρανοῦ in 4.23.

9. Usually in the OT, the singular title "Holy One" refers to God himself, most frequently as the "Holy One of Israel." Plural "holy ones" are usually angels. Other references include David in Ps. 16.10 and Aaron elsewhere.

10. A. Schlatter, *Markus. Der Evangelist für die Griechen* (Stuttgart: Calwer, 1984 [1935]), 55: "bei Mr. kennzeichnet ἦλθες den Sohn Gottes als den, der in die Welt gekommen ist." M. Lagrange, *Évangile selon saint Marc* (Études Bibliques; Paris: Lecoffre, 1911), 23, talks of Jesus' "venue dans le monde sensible" here. See also Lohmeyer, *Evangelium des Markus,* 43; J. Sevenster, "Christologie," *RGG*³ I, col. 1753; J. Schreiber, *Die Markuspassion. Eine redaktionsgeschichtliche Untersuchung* (BZNW 68; Berlin: de Gruyter, 1993), 220, 374 n. 60; R. T. France, *The Gospel of Mark: A Commentary on the Greek Text* (NIGTC; Grand Rapids: Eerdmans, 2002), 113. France is, however, more hesitant than the others.

11. Klostermann, *Markusevangelium,* 17: "sein Kommen in die Welt."

Matthew 8.29

> And behold they screamed, saying, "What have we to do with you, Son of God? *Have you come here to destroy us* before our due time?"

While Mark's demons ask Jesus their question in a synagogue in Capernaum, in Matt. 8.29 it is a scene in the region of the Gadarenes that prompts the question (8.28-34).[12] However, for the reasons offered above, it is probably correct to conclude that preexistence is also assumed in the very similar demonic statement in Matthew, although it is not quite so clear. Lagrange, who in general does see Jesus' preexistence in the "I have come" sayings, actually demurs here on the grounds that there is a place specified in the reference to "here" (ὧδε).[13] However, the emphasis is probably not on the specific geographical location but on the presence of Jesus "here and now," the usual meaning of the word in connection with the arrival of Jesus as a fulfillment of expectation or promise.[14] It is not Jesus' arrival in that place that is the issue for the demons but rather that he has arrived before they expected. This, again, points very strongly to the advent of Jesus into the world which is in the grip of evil forces. Apparently, even the demons could not shake off the knowledge that Jesus would eventually come to destroy them. There is no escape for them, however hard they might try to persuade him that he is too early. In sum, Benoit is probably correct to see preexistence here again, although perhaps Mark 1.24 is clearer.[15]

---

12. This scene is paralleled in Mark 5.1-20 and Luke 8.26-39, but neither of these has the demons' question in the same form.

13. It is theoretically possible that in the ὧδε there is reference to Jesus' arrival in the land of the Gadarenes (Matt. 8.28). M. Lagrange (*Évangile selon saint Matthieu* [Études Bibliques; Paris: Lecoffre, 1923], 175) writes that ὧδε means "here in new territory" rather than "here on earth." He is perhaps led to this by the compounding of ἦλθον and ὧδε, since it is the *absolute* character of the ἦλθον sayings which impresses him elsewhere. However, the way in which ὧδε is used in other sayings strongly points away from Lagrange's reading.

14. Cf. Matt. 12.6; Matt. 12.41 par. Luke 11.32; Matt. 12.42 par. Luke 11.31.

15. P. Benoit, "The Divinity of Jesus in the Synoptic Gospels," in idem, *Jesus and the Gospel* (London: Dartman, Longman and Todd, 1973), 68. Even E. Arens (*The HΛΘON-Sayings in the Synoptic Tradition: A Historico-Critical Investigation* [Orbis Biblicus et Orientalis 10; Freiburg/Göttingen: Universitätsverlag Freiburg/Vandenhoeck und Ruprecht, 1976], 221) says, "It is not impossible that the awareness of Jesus' preexistence floats in the background of the demons' outcry."

Mark 1.38 (cf. Luke 4.43)

And he said to them, "Let us go elsewhere into the nearby villages, so that I may also preach there. *Because it is for this reason that I have come forth.*"

This statement is the conclusion to the scene in which, after an evening healing the sick and demon-possessed at the home of Simon and Andrew (Mark 1.33-34), Jesus rises early the next morning and goes out to a solitary place to pray. In response to the exasperation of Simon and the others, Jesus makes the pronouncement quoted above. The interpretation of this passage in terms of the preexistence of Christ has actually won quite a number of supporters. Hauck and Marcus raise it as a possibility, but Marcus leaves it in the realm of mere possibility on the grounds that "the idea remains largely undeveloped elsewhere in Mark."[16] Hamerton-Kelly and, it seems, Lindars refer to ideal preexistence, but we have seen already how unproductive this category is.[17] Others, however, are more definite about a real preexistence.[18] A still greater number, of course, continue to reject the interpretation.[19]

---

16. F. Hauck, *Das Evangelium des Markus* (Theologischer Handkommentar zum Neuen Testament; Leipzig: Scholl, 1931), 28; J. Marcus, *Mark 1–8: A New Translation with Introduction and Commentary* (Anchor; New York: Doubleday, 2000), 204.

17. See the guarded comments in B. Lindars, *New Testament Apologetic: The Doctrinal Significance of the Old Testament Quotations* (London: SCM, 1961), 211 n. 2. Lindars merely makes passing reference to Mark 1.38 and 10.45 in a section entitled "The Pre-existent Christ" (210-19), but there are also numerous references to "ideal preexistence" in the surrounding discussion. See also R. G. Hamerton-Kelly, *Preexistence, Wisdom, and the Son of Man: A Study of the Idea of Preexistence in the New Testament* (SNTSMS 21; Cambridge: Cambridge University Press, 1973), 48, 64.

18. H. B. Swete, *The Gospel according to St. Mark* (London: Macmillan, 1898), 240; Lagrange, *Marc*, 28, points to a mysterious parallel contrast between the departure from Capernaum in Mark 1.35 and the more significant departure in 1.38; B. B. Warfield, "Jesus' Mission, according to his own Testimony," *Princeton Theological Review* 13 (1915), 513-86 (586), who also mentions F. Godet, but without a reference; J. Knox, *Christ the Lord: The Meaning of Jesus in the Early Church* (Chicago: Willett, 1945), 96-97, who talks of a "casual allusion" to preexistence and brings Luke 4.43 as evidence to confirm this; Lohmeyer, *Evangelium des Markus,* 43; R. Earle, *The Gospel of Mark* (Grand Rapids: Baker, 1961), 39; R. H. Fuller, *A Critical Introduction to the New Testament* (London: Duckworth, 1966), 111; W. Grundmann, *Das Evangelium nach Markus* (Theologischer Handkommentar zum Neuen Testament; Berlin: Evangelische, 1968), 48-49; D. E. Nineham, *The Gospel of Saint Mark* (Harmondsworth: Penguin, 1969), 85; M. Wichelhaus, "Am ersten Tage der Woche. Mark 1.35-39 und die didaktischen Absichten des Markus-Evangelisten," *NovT* 11 (1969), 45-66 (57), who sees it strengthened by Luke 4.43; J. K. Elliott, "Is ὁ ἐξελθών a Title for Jesus in Mark 1.45?" *JTS* 27 (1976), 402-5; P. Benoit, "Préexistence et Incarnation," in idem, *Exégèse et Théologie* (Paris: Cerf, 1982), 4:11-61 (14); France, *Mark,* 113.

19. Representative here (in addition to the other scholars mentioned below) is J. Gnilka,

The distinctive element of this verse is that it does not follow exactly the same form as the other "I have come" sayings. First, the verb used is the compound verb "I have come *forth/out*" (ἐξῆλθον) rather than the simple "I have come." Second, the purpose is expressed not by an infinitive but by the phrase "for this reason" (εἰς τοῦτο). These two differences, however, are not differences of substance. Inclusion of this saying in our discussion is justified on the grounds that "I have come forth" and "I have come" are almost interchangeable in many contexts, as we have seen in the places where the verbs are used in connection with other heavenly figures in Jewish tradition: Dan. 9.22-23, for example, uses both synonymously in consecutive verses.[20] Similarly, the "reason" is "to preach." But since the verb "preach" has just been mentioned immediately before, it is smoother to use the pronoun (τοῦτο) in its place. This has been accepted by most scholars.

A further connection between the saying here and the material discussed in chapter 5 above lies in the fact that the ministry of Jesus is defined here in terms of *revelation,* of proclaiming the kingdom which has been prepared by God and is now breaking in with the coming of Jesus himself. There is of course no exact parallel in the material in chapter 5; there are no angels whose functions are described as so far-reaching as those of Jesus. But there are numerous angelic parallels to the function of "proclaiming" (κηρύσσειν). In the third person statements mentioned in the introduction to the previous chapter, we saw that Michael came "to proclaim good news" (לבשר) to Sarah (*b. Baba Metzia* 86b). But more specifically, the "I have come" sayings also had similar language: "to give understanding" (Dan. 9.22), "to announce" (Dan. 9.23; cf. Proclus, *Discourse* 6; *Vision of Daniel*), "to reveal" (Dan. 10.14), "to show" (Dan. 11.2; *4 Ezra* 6.30), and "to speak" (*4 Ezra* 7.2; *2 Baruch* 71.3). A further difference, of course, lies in the fact that it is usually individuals who are recipients of these oracles, in contrast to whole towns as in Mark 1.38. There is a strong emphasis in the Gospels on the public nature of Jesus' proclamation of the kingdom, in contrast to the secrecy of revelations in apocalyptic literature.[21] Over a third of the angelic statements examined in chapter 5 above, however, have this same revelatory character as the work of Jesus in Mark 1.38.

Das Evangelium nach Markus. Volume 1: *Mark 1–8,26* (Einsiedeln: Benziger, 1978), 89: "Die Formulierung klingt johanneisch, hat sich aber noch nicht zur Höhe des Präexistenzgedankens entwickelt." Cf. also V. Taylor, *The Gospel according to St. Mark* (London: Macmillan, 1952), 184: "it seems doubtful if so dogmatic an idea is intended."

20. Cf. also the versions of Num. 22.32 discussed in chapter 5 above: the Semitic versions all have a verb with a sense of "coming *forth,*" but the Vulgate simply uses *uenio.*

21. Cf. for example the fact that the revelations in Daniel are to him alone, and he is commanded to hide them away having received them (Dan. 12.4).

A Cosmic or Local Coming of Jesus?

The chief debate of interest to us here has again been over whether the reference to "coming forth" here relates to a geographical movement by Jesus or to his advent in a theological sense. The first possibility of a "local" understanding for the "coming forth" treats it as referring to Jesus' leaving the house, or perhaps Capernaum.[22] That is, "I have come forth" (ἐξῆλθον) in Mark 1.38 picks up on the "he went forth" (ἐξῆλθεν) in 1.35. As Warfield and Hooker note, however, the verb in 1.35 refers to Jesus leaving the house, and he clearly leaves the house at that time in order to pray, not to preach.[23] Hooker then suggests that "I have come forth" (ἐξῆλθον) in 1.38 refers to the departure from Nazareth for the wider area of Galilee; in other words, the reference is not back to 1.35 but to 1.9: "Jesus went from Nazareth in Galilee" (ἦλθεν Ἰησοῦς ἀπὸ Ναζαρὲτ τῆς Γαλιλαίας).[24] This is probably the strongest contender among the "local" options, although we have seen some of the problems with it in chapter 4 above.

Another possibility, perhaps stronger, would be to connect Mark 1.38 neither with 1.35 (leaving the house), nor with 1.9 (leaving Nazareth), but with what we have seen already in 1.24 in the question of the demons to Jesus: "have you come to destroy us?" There is not a very explicit correlation of the purposes: in 1.24 it is the destruction of demonic forces and now it is proclamation. These are, however, linked in the wider context of Mark's Gospel and this remains a strong possibility.

Are there, then, indications which clarify whether a theological or geographical sense should be attributed to "I have come forth" here? What is clear is that the earliest extant exegesis of this passage points in the direction of a theological advent here. This exegesis is found in Luke 4.43. Here, the wording makes reference to Jesus' proclamation of the kingdom of God as a divine necessity, because this is the purpose of his mission: "it is necessary for me to preach the kingdom of God in the other towns also, because for this reason *I was sent.*"[25] Marshall and Klostermann speak of Luke's correct interpretation of Mark here.[26]

22. See Taylor, *Mark*, 184, for scholars who take the "leaving Capernaum" view, which Taylor himself rejects. Hooker says that the Capernaum view "hardly fits the context, since we have been told that he came out to pray" (*Mark*, 77).

23. Hooker, *Mark*, 77. See further Warfield, "Jesus' Mission," 520-22, for criticism of Harnack's reference to Mark 1.38 as a local "coming forth."

24. Hooker, *Mark*, 77.

25. καὶ ταῖς ἑτέραις πόλεσιν εὐαγγελίσασθαί με δεῖ τὴν βασιλείαν τοῦ θεοῦ, ὅτι ἐπὶ τοῦτο ἀπεστάλην.

26. I. H. Marshall, *The Gospel of Luke: A Commentary on the Greek Text* (NIGTC; Grand Rapids: Eerdmans, 1978), 198; Klostermann, *Markusevangelium*, 19.

If this is right, then the use of the compound verb "I have come *forth*" rather than the simple form of the verb probably points to Mark's indication of an explicitly incarnational idea here.[27] While we should again resist the temptation to see the verb as a technical term, it is used commonly of coming from the heavenly court, as we saw above (1 Kgs. 22.22; Job 1–2). In terms of content, the task appointed for Jesus here (teaching) fits well with a prophetic ministry. However, the use of the verb "I have come forth" tells against it. The language here also contradicts very clearly Jeremias's minimalistic interpretation of the "I have come" sayings as meaning "I am here to. . . ." As Hamerton-Kelly points out, with the language of "came out" we are left to ask "came out from whence?"[28] While we cannot answer this question definitely, there is a very strong probability of a "coming forth" from heaven indicated here.

Mark 2.17 par. Matthew 9.13; Luke 5.32

> Jesus heard this and said to them, "It is not the healthy who need a doctor, but those who are sick. *I have not come to call the righteous, but sinners* [Luke adds 'to repentance']."

Following immediately after the healing and forgiveness of the paralytic in Mark's narrative are Jesus' call of Levi and a dinner at Levi's house, where Jesus dines with other tax-collectors and sinners (Mark 2.13-17). In his comment on this verse, Cranfield notes the general significance of the verb "to come" as a possible reference to preexistence: "The verb ἔρχεσθαι is often used of Jesus, particularly by himself, and expresses his consciousness of his mission. His use of it is perhaps a pointer to his consciousness of preexistence."[29] Others who have since followed this line of interpretation in-

27. Benoit ("Divinity of Jesus in the Synoptic Gospels," 68 n. 1) and France (*Mark,* 113) argue for preexistence here. See also Nineham, *Mark,* 85; Knox, *Christ the Lord,* 97 and n. 15: Knox points to the fact that "unquestionably" most of Mark's readers understood 1.38 to refer to preexistence, pointing to Luke 4.43. There is a certain amount of debate over whether preexistence is more explicit in the Lukan version or in the Markan. Lagrange (*Marc,* 28) takes the Markan version to be stronger than the Lukan here: "l'expression . . . ne marque pas seulement une mission, mais que Jésus est personellement sorti d'un autre monde, ou d'auprès de son père." We will discuss this point further in the next chapter.

28. Hamerton-Kelly, *Preexistence,* 48-49, although one should go further than Hamerton-Kelly, because of his restriction of preexistence here to protological, ideal preexistence.

29. C. E. B. Cranfield, *The Gospel according to St Mark* (CGTC; Cambridge: Cambridge University Press, 1959), 106. He also notes the similar interpretation in Lagrange, *Marc,* 45.

clude Benoit, Sevenster, Schürmann, and Schenke.[30] Arens makes explicit the distinction that a number of these others imply between the original saying of Jesus and the final setting of the logion in Mark. In its original setting, Arens argues, it carried no hint of preexistence, but it does perhaps acquire something of that sense in Markan redaction.[31] Our concern in this study, however, is simply with the Gospels as they stand.

In terms of the evidence for preexistence here, Lagrange is certainly correct to say that the ambiguity of Mark 1.38 is absent from 2.17.[32] While a local sense for Jesus' coming is conceivable in 1.24 and possible in 1.38, it becomes increasingly unlikely for 2.17. We have here, then, our first example of a straightforward "I have come" + infinitive that implies — as has already been argued — a deliberate action on the part of Jesus in "coming." The clear sense is *not* that Jesus is referring to a specific occurrence of "calling," but rather that this is the whole purpose of his mission. Again, as we have noted already, this is not a mode of speaking which is used by mere humans of their "coming on the scene": rather, the most appropriate parallel is that of the angel who comes to visit the human realm from heaven with a particular purpose. In conclusion, while the content of Jesus' mission in Mark 2.17 (calling sinners) fits prophetic categories, the form of the saying, which emphasizes Jesus' voluntary advent with the intent to call sinners, points away from a prophetic coming and toward a coming from heaven. If, as is at least possible, the "calling" is the invitation to the heavenly banquet, the implication of a coming from heaven might be stronger still.[33]

Luke's Version

It is not clear that there is any amplification or dilution of preexistence in the Matthean version (Matt. 9.13). Various opinions have been offered, however, as

30. Benoit, "Divinity of Jesus in the Synoptic Gospels," 68; idem, "Préexistence et Incarnation," 14; Sevenster, "Christologie," col. 1753; H. Schürmann, *Das Lukasevangelium*. Volume 1: *Kommentar zu Kap. 1,1–9,50* (HTK; Freiburg: Herder, 1969), 292; L. Schenke, "Gibt es im Markusevangelium eine Präexistenzchristologie?" *ZNW* 91 (2000), 45-71 (64). From among scholars who preceded Cranfield, Swete could be added to this list. See Swete, *Mark*, 240, as well as perhaps S. Légasse (*L'Évangile de Marc* [Paris: Cerf, 1997], 185), who is not explicit but compares the language here to Dan. 9.23; 10.14; 10.20; Tob. 12.18.

31. Arens, *The HΛΘON-Sayings*, 5.

32. Lagrange, *Marc*, 45: "Ἦλθον est encore plus mystérieux que ἐξῆλθον (I,38) parce qu'on ne peut pas dire que Jésus est venu spécialement à Capharnaüm pour appeler les pécheurs. Il s'agit donc au moins de sa mission divine."

33. Lohmeyer, *Evangelium des Markus*, 56. Gundry denies a hint of the heavenly banquet here (*Mark*, 130), however.

to the significance of Luke's redaction of Mark 2.17, in which "I have come to call not the righteous but sinners" becomes "I have not come to call the righteous, but sinners *to repentance*." Arens, for example, sees an ecclesiological interest here on Luke's part, a greater concern for the expansion and growth of the church.[34] Marcus remarks that Luke "lessens the radicality of the saying by adding 'to repentance,'" presumably on the grounds that in the Markan text the implication might be that Jesus simply has no interest in "the righteous."[35] As far as our interest in preexistence is concerned, understanding the "calling" as a call to *conversion* rather than as an invitation to the heavenly banquet might downplay that aspect of the Markan original. But this difference should not be pressed too far, since it is by no means clear that Mark has the heavenly banquet in mind anyway.[36] It would seem that all three Synoptic versions of the saying provide good evidence for preexistence in equal measure.

Matthew 5.17

> Do not think that I have come to abolish the Law or the prophets. *I have not come to abolish them, but to fulfill them.*

Matt. 5.17 is a notoriously difficult verse to interpret, and because of the wide variety of stances taken by interpreters with respect to early Christian understandings of Torah, it has attracted considerable controversy.[37] What is a shame, however, is that the verse has been largely ignored as an "I have come" saying; some commentators are so taken up with the issue of the Law that they actually ignore the reference to the coming of Jesus altogether. This is a problem, especially when one considers that it is the first "I have come" saying in Matthew's Gospel.

---

34. Arens, *The ΗΛΘΟΝ-Sayings*, 60-61.

35. Marcus, *Mark*, 228.

36. More important for some scholars is the change in the tense of the verb from the aorist (ἦλθον) to the perfect (ἐλήλυθα). Jülicher, Schürmann, and Arens draw attention to this as significant for preexistence. A. Jülicher, *Die Gleichnisreden Jesu* (Freiburg: Mohr, 1888), 2:175: "Wenn Lc das ἦλθον durch ἐλήλυθα ersetzt, so wird man darin, ohne anders zu übersetzen, gewähltere Ausdrucksweise finden." See also Arens, *The ΗΛΘΟΝ-Sayings*, 62, and Schürmann, *Lukasevangelium*, 1:292-93 (cf. also 19), for the whole discussion. However, with regard to Luke 5.32, it seems difficult to attribute a shift in Luke's attitude on the basis of the very superficial change from aorist to perfect. The Markan and Matthean versions of the saying surely also bring the entirety of the earthly existence of Jesus into focus.

37. For an overview of the issues involved in interpretation, see H. D. Betz, *The Sermon on the Mount* (Hermeneia; Minneapolis: Fortress, 1995), 166-97.

On the other hand, some do refer to the verse as a statement about Jesus' coming, but do not see its full significance. Hagner talks in general terms (following Arens) of the way in which the statement highlights Jesus' authority, but it is difficult to see how Jesus' coming and his authority relate specifically.[38] Trilling sees the statement about Jesus' coming as simply tantamount to him being sent, without paying attention to the focus on Jesus' own responsibility and intention.[39] We have seen above that "coming" and "being sent" cannot simply be collapsed together in this simplistic way, however.

Others still — both in older and more recent scholarship — see signs of preexistence undergirding the saying here. Plummer and Beare see preexistence implied both in the "coming" language and in the messianic associations it has. Plummer's comment has a more old-fashioned feel: "The 'I came' (ἦλθον) probably implies the preexistence of the Messiah."[40] Allen and Benoit follow the same tack.[41] But Beare is a good example of a modern commentator who takes a similar line: "The words 'I came' imply a claim of Messianic status."[42] He goes on to say that "I have come" has the sense of "heavenly origin," meaning "I came down to earth — I came from heaven."[43] Hare is similar again.[44]

With these commentators, we should see a gentle reference to preexistence here on Matthew's part. We can see Jesus' coming as a voluntary act, in the light of the intention which accompanies it: "Do not think I have come in order to. . . . I have not come in order to . . . but to. . . ." The focus is on the coming of Jesus in fulfillment of the Law and the prophets. As a result, Jesus' intent in coming is to act in submission to the plan of God expressed in the Old Testament.

---

38. D. A. Hagner, *Matthew 1–13* (WBC; Dallas: Word, 1993), 105, following Arens, *The ΗΛΘΟΝ-Sayings*, 114-16.

39. W. Trilling, *Das wahre Israel. Studien zur Theologie des Matthäus-Evangeliums* (SANT 10; Munich: Kösel, 1964), 171-72.

40. A. Plummer, *An Exegetical Commentary of the Gospel According to S. Matthew* (London: Scott, 1909), 75 n. 2.

41. W. C. Allen, *A Critical and Exegetical Commentary on the Gospel according to St. Matthew* (ICC; Edinburgh: Clark, 1907), 122; Benoit, "Divinity of Jesus in the Synoptic Gospels," 68.

42. F. W. Beare, *The Gospel according to Matthew* (Oxford: Blackwell, 1981), 141.

43. Beare, *Matthew*, 142. Contrast Davies and Allison, who argue that ἦλθον merely indicates "that his commissioning was of heavenly origin." W. D. Davies and D. C. Allison, *A Critical and Exegetical Commentary on the Gospel according to Saint Matthew*. Volume 1: *Introduction and Commentary on Matthew I–VII* (ICC; Edinburgh: Clark, 1988), 483. Similarly, Arens says that despite Jesus' surpassing of prophetic status (115), not even ideal preexistence (contra Hamerton-Kelly) is in view here (114-15).

44. D. R. A. Hare, *The Theme of Jewish Persecution of Christians in the Gospel according to St Matthew* (SNTSMS 6; Cambridge: Cambridge University Press, 1967), 133-34 n. 5.

Luke 12.49

I have come to cast fire onto the earth, and how I wish it were already kindled.

This saying from Luke 12.49 is one of those which is most clearly undergirded by a theology of preexistence. Not only does it share the features of the "I have come" sayings which we have discussed thus far, but it seems to provide even more explicit indication by making *casting fire upon the earth* the goal of Jesus' coming.[45] Benoit and Sevenster argue for preexistence in Luke 12.49-51, but they do not highlight the way in which the statements there indicate preexistence more clearly than the other "I have come" sayings.[46]

The "fire" is probably the fire of judgment.[47] The triad of sayings in Luke 12.49-51 has, as a whole, the character of an extended lament, and Jesus' saying in 12.49 has the sense of his wishing that a terrible time would pass. Fire from heaven to earth in the OT (and elsewhere in the NT) is almost invariably destructive rather than purifying: the most common verb associated with it is "devouring."[48] On the other hand, a reference to the Holy Spirit is not impossible; Jesus does after all long for the fire to be kindled.[49] The problem here, however, would be that in the Lukan scheme it is not Jesus' coming *per se* which is the occasion for his sending the Spirit; that will be enabled by his *ascension* (Acts 2.33). The majority of commentators are probably correct, then, in arguing that "the saying in its present context should be understood with reference to judgment."[50] The sense of the statement is that Jesus has

45. L. T. Johnson, *The Gospel of Luke* (Collegeville: Liturgical, 1991), raises the possibility of reference to "the land" here, rather than the earth, but he drops the idea later (207, then 209).

46. Benoit, "Divinity of Jesus in the Synoptic Gospels," 68; Sevenster, "Christologie," col. 1753. On the other hand, for Arens, there is no preexistence but merely Jesus' statement that "my intention is to . . ." (*The ΗΛΘΟΝ-Sayings*, 90), following Jeremias's understanding of ἦλθον as "I am here."

47. Thus, for example, C.-P. März, "'Feuer auf die Erde zu werfen, bin ich gekommen . . . ,'" in F. Refoulé, ed., *À cause de l'Évangile. Études sur les Synoptiques et les Actes Offertes au P. Jacques Dupont, O.S.B., à l'occasion de son 70ème Anniversaire* (Paris: Cerf, 1985), 479-511 (489); M. Black, "Not Peace but a Sword," in E. Bammel and C. F. D. Moule, eds., *Jesus and the Politics of His Day* (Cambridge: Cambridge University Press, 1984), 287-94 (294).

48. See in general on the destructive character of fire: Gen. 19.24; Exod. 9.23; Num. 26.10; Deut. 32.22; 2 Kgs 1.10-14; 1 Chr. 21.26; 2 Chr. 7.1; Ps. 46.9; Job 1.16; Ezek. 28.18; Zeph. 3.8; 2 Pet. 3.7; Rev. 8.5, 7; 20.9.

49. See Bultmann's statement, for example, that the fire is "the Christian church or the spirit which works in it." R. Bultmann, *History of the Synoptic Tradition* (Oxford: Blackwell, 1968), 154.

50. Marshall, *Luke*, 547; J. A. Nolland, *Luke 9:21–18:34* (WBC; Waco: Word, 1993), 708: "The closest parallels are Rev 8:5, 7, 8; 20:9 with their apocalyptic imagery of judgement."

come to bring with him the divine wrath. This he will also bear himself in his death, a prospect which — as the following verse makes clear — he dreads: "I have a baptism to undergo, and how I wish it were already accomplished!" (Luke 12.50). But it will also overflow to Jesus' followers and be the cause of division between them and their families (12.51-53). The specific connotations of the fire in 12.49, however, do not affect the argument that the verse alludes to preexistence.

The key point here for our argument is that the fire comes "from heaven,"[51] that is, it comes from the dwelling place of God. Although Elijah is able on one occasion to call down fire from heaven, he merely prays for it; he is not himself the bringer or the sender. As a result, the claim to be able to *bring* fire to the earth is an implicit claim, if anything, to divine rather than prophetic identity. In fact, the closest OT parallels to the action of Jesus described here are perhaps also the coming of the Lord with fire in Micah 1 or, more probably, the Lord's destruction of Sodom and Gomorrah in Genesis 19:

> Then the Lord rained brimstone and fire out of heaven from the Lord on Sodom and Gomorrah. (Gen. 19.24)[52]

By contrast, the claim of Grundmann and Marshall that the Qumran Teacher of Righteousness makes a comparable statement cannot be sustained. There are, as Grundmann says, striking self-representations in 1QH; but in fact there is nothing on the scale of Luke 12.49.[53] While Grundmann and Marshall are right to oppose Bultmann here, it is going too far to follow Jeremias's analysis of the "I have come" formula and to conclude that the saying is "an otherwise unexceptional statement."[54] If Jesus' intention in coming included bringing fire to the earth, then this more clearly than anything thus far identifies him as having come from heaven. Although "onto the earth" does not directly qualify "I have come," it is very probably implied in the fact that Jesus' coming means his bringing something to the world from the outside. (Would it make sense to talk of "casting" onto the earth *from* the earth?) In any case, the sheer *scale* of the claim to be bringing divine judgment of such a catastrophic kind also

---

51. As in Gen. 19.24; 2 Kgs 1.10-14; 1 Chr. 21.26; 2 Chr. 7.1; Job 1.16.

52. I am grateful to Dr. Nathan MacDonald for drawing my attention to this reference.

53. W. Grundmann, *Das Evangelium nach Lukas* (THKNT; Berlin: Evangelische, [5]1969), 269. The reference to 1QH 8.20 in Wiefel's revision of Grundmann is a possible reference to the fire of judgment, but there is no hint of an execution of this judgment by the Teacher of Righteousness himself. W. Wiefel, *Das Evangelium nach Lukas* (THKNT; Berlin: Evangelische, 1988), 247.

54. Marshall, *Luke*, 546.

points to an extremely exalted status for Jesus. He clearly stands, here, over against the rest of humanity. This saying, as well as some of the others we have looked at (such as Mark 1.24), also casts considerable doubt on the likelihood of Jesus simply referring here to coming from Nazareth or "coming on the scene." The exalted person of Christ and the cosmic nature of his task implied in the saying transcend such an interpretation of the "coming" here and point instead to a coming from heaven, implying preexistence.

Luke 12.51 par. Matthew 10.34

Do not think that I have come to bring peace on the earth; no, I tell you — not peace, but *division.* (Luke 12.51)

Do not think that I have come to bring peace on the earth; I have not come to bring peace but a sword. (Matt. 10.34)

For the same reasons, Luke 12.51 also indicates preexistence, even if not quite so forcefully as v. 49.[55] In continuity with vv. 49-50, judgment is still the dominant theme in v. 51. Various elements probably contribute to the sense of the saying. There is probably a kind of ironic reference here to the promise of peace for Israel in Leviticus 26.[56] Jesus is clearly contrasting his ministry with what might be expected from a "prince of peace."[57] Similarly, the expectation of Mal. 4.5 LXX and Sir. 48.10 that the hearts of fathers will be turned to their sons (actually anticipated as a blessing of the advent in Luke 1.17) is subverted by Luke 12.53. The visions of Leviticus 26 and Sirach 48, then, are replaced in Jesus' discourse by the picture of disruption and disharmony in Micah 7. As commentators have noticed, this is the strongest parallel to the idea which follows Luke 12.51 of family division, where according to Mic. 7.6b, "your enemies are the members of your own household." It is this situation which Jesus

---

55. As we saw in the previous chapter, παρεγενόμην in Luke 12.51 is simply a stylistic variation on ἦλθον: there is no difference in meaning. It could be argued, however, that δοῦναι does not conjure up such a transcendent picture as βαλεῖν and (even less significantly) perhaps that ἐπί + genitive is not quite so dynamic as ἐπί + accusative.

56. Here Israel is assured that on entering the land she will experience peace and prosperity, above all because God has destroyed both hostile beasts and Israel's human enemies: "And war will not come upon your land, and I will bring peace in your land (καὶ δώσω εἰρήνην ἐν τῇ γῇ ὑμῶν)" (Lev. 26.6).

57. "It is directed presumably against the expectation of a messianic prince of peace that was widespread in contemporary Judaism." U. Luz, *Matthew 8–20: A Commentary* (Hermeneia; Minneapolis: Fortress, 2001), 110.

comes into the world to bring, and the implication seems to be that this is a further aspect of his work of judgment which he brings from heaven, as in Luke 12.49.

Matthew's Version

The saying in Luke 12.51 is closely paralleled in Matt. 10.34,[58] where there is perhaps an even clearer reminiscence of Lev. 26.6-8 in that Matthew says Jesus comes to bring "a sword" rather than Luke's "division."[59] In Luke, the emphasis in the conjunction of Jesus bringing "division" with the subsequent account of divided families is on the fact that absolute loyalty to Jesus will mean the disruption of all earthly institutions. In Matthew on the other hand, the contrast is between peace and the simple fact of divine judgment which has been delegated to Jesus, just as elsewhere in the Gospel it is commonly associated with the Son of Man (Matt. 25.31-46).[60] These are of course not so very different: the judgment of the Son of Man itself involves division, in Matthew 25, of the sheep and the goats.

There is also an intriguing possibility of an echo of the angelic "I have come" sayings in which the angel of the Lord appears with a drawn sword. We noted in the previous chapter how both in opposition to Balaam in Numbers 22 and in the angel's neutral stance toward Joshua in Joshua 5 a sword is involved, and it is perhaps also important to note 1 Chronicles 21:

> Then the Lord opened the eyes of Balaam, and he saw the angel of the Lord standing in the road, with his drawn sword in his hand; and he bowed down, falling on his face. The angel of the Lord said to him, ". . . I have come forth as an adversary, because your way is perverse before me. . . ." (Num. 22.31-32)

> Once when Joshua was by Jericho, he looked up and saw a man standing before him with a drawn sword in his hand. . . . He said, ". . . As commander of the army of the LORD I have now come." (Josh. 5.13-14)

58. Instead of Luke's παρεγενόμην, Matthew has the more standard ἦλθον in Matt. 10.34.

59. '. . . and your enemies will fall before your sword (ἐναντίον ὑμῶν μαχαίρᾳ)' (Lev. 26.8). For references to "the sword" in eschatological expectations of affliction, see W. D. Davies and D. C. Allison, *A Critical and Exegetical Commentary on the Gospel according to Saint Matthew. Volume 2: Introduction and Commentary on Matthew VIII–XVIII* (ICC; Edinburgh: Clark, 1988), 218.

60. The question of whether "division" or "sword" is more original is ignored here as irrelevant for our purposes. For some discussion, see Davies and Allison, *Matthew VIII–XVIII*, 218.

> David looked up and saw the angel of the Lord standing between earth and heaven, and in his hand a drawn sword stretched out over Jerusalem. . . . (1 Chr. 21.16)

Jesus' coming with a sword might well reinforce the idea that he is portrayed in Matthew 10 as a heavenly figure, perhaps even — although the idea remains in the realm of mere possibility — that Matthew is portraying Jesus as the angel of the Lord.

Another aspect of the Matthean version which needs to be borne in mind is the immediately preceding context, which also places emphasis on Jesus' heavenly identity. 10.32-33 records the paired sayings:

> Therefore whoever confesses me before men, I will also confess him before my Father who is in heaven. But whoever denies me before men, I will also deny him before my Father who is in heaven.

Here, then, is a strong christological focus, and in particular a strong emphasis on Jesus as the one who will function in the future as the heavenly advocate (or accuser) before God. It is doubly interesting that immediately after this we meet another of Jesus' most immoderate statements, in which he claims to have come to bring a sword to the earth, standing over against humanity in his work of division. The destiny of Jesus as heavenly advocate mirrors his heavenly origin as the one who came with the intention of bringing future eschatological judgment into the present, in the course of his ministry.

Matthew 10.35

> *For I have come to divide* man against father and daughter against mother, and daughter-in-law against mother-in-law. . . .

In Matthew, the emphasis on Jesus' coming is pressed further with another "I have come" saying immediately afterward.[61] Here again, the logical approach to the saying would be to take the reference to the advent here in the same way as in 10.34. Relevant to our theme of preexistence is the way in which the image of Jesus continues (as in the last two sayings examined) to be of a figure

---

61. Luz rightly notes the prominence of christology: "For *Matthew* the christological aspect is initially important. 'I came' three times emphasizes that the disciples' suffering is a direct part of the sending of Jesus." Luz, *Matthew 8–20*, 111. The same point is also highlighted by Carter, "Jesus' 'I have come' Sayings in Matthew's Gospel," 57.

who stands over against the world (cf. Mark 9.19). While this implies his divine origin, too much should not be read into this motif in isolation.[62] However, in the context of a statement about Jesus' coming for a mission in the world, it reinforces the point nicely.

Luke 12.49-51 and Matthew 10.34-35: Summary

These three sayings are particularly relevant to the argument here for preexistence in the "I have come" sayings over against an interpretation which sees a *prophetic* understanding of Jesus or a reference simply to Jesus' "coming on the scene" (from Nazareth) or "having the intention" to do such-and-such. As we have said, casting fire upon the earth and bringing peace upon the earth go far beyond the *curriculum vitae* of any prophet in Israel's history.

Commentators often refer to an "Elijah-christology" in these exalted statements of Jesus in Luke 12.49-51; Matt. 10.34-36.[63] What should be noted, however, is that the *earthly* career of Elijah is not the model here. If there is any connection between the statements about Jesus and the Elijah traditions, it can only lie in the traditions about the *future, heavenly Elijah*. In Jewish statements about his eschatological advent, we do have an Elijah who (as noted above) will play an exalted role in the restoration of Israel, but who also, according to the sages, will bring peace to the world (*m. 'Eduyoth* 8.7). Although Jesus claims in Luke 12.49 a rather different role from the heavenly Elijah, there is at least some analogy in the scope of their functions.

In addition to the problems with seeing a prophetic christology in these verses, the usual difficulties arise with Jeremias's reductionistic interpretation of "I have come" + purpose as "my task is to. . . ." In addition, as in the case of the sayings of the demons ("have you come to destroy us?"), these logia in Luke 12.49-51 and Matt. 10.34-35 sit uneasily with the sense of "coming" as "coming on the scene." Since these roles are functions exercised in relation to, or over against, the *world*, the sense of coming from heaven is the most probable here.

---

62. Prophets, similarly, can make statements which set themselves against the vast majority of other people. See the references noted by Pesch on Mark 9.19. R. Pesch, *Das Markusevangelium* (HTK; Freiburg: Herder, 1976), 2:90.

63. See for example K. H. Rengstorf, *Das Evangelium nach Lukas* (NTD; Göttingen: Vandenhoeck und Ruprecht, 1978), 166.

Mark 10.45 par. Matthew 20.28

> For even *the Son of Man came not to be served, but to serve,* and to give his life as a ransom for many.

Mark 10.45 must rank high among the most hotly disputed verses in the NT. But none of the most frequently raised issues, such as the authenticity of the saying, the nature of the atonement propounded in it, or whether Jesus is here identified with the servant of Isaiah 52–53, will occupy us in depth here. Similarly, an attempt will be made to reserve discussion of the "Son of Man" issue until we examine the implications of that designation for our study of preexistence.

Our concern here, then, is exclusively with Mark 10.45 as a statement about Jesus' advent, and in fact a number of scholars have seen the concept of preexistence in the statement.[64] Without offering too many hostages to fortune, it can at least be said of the verse's basic content that again we have a clear indication of the purpose of Jesus' whole life in the human realm. His present earthly life is to be one of service, by contrast to what might otherwise be expected. In this respect, this statement is a good illustration of how the "I have come" + purpose formula is used only to sum up the present purpose of Jesus' *first* coming: in his second coming as forecast in all three Synoptic Gospels he *will* come with all his glory and impose his rule on the whole world. The second part of the purpose expressed in Mark 10.45 is that his death (the sense of "giving life") is to accomplish the release of many others who are in some kind of enslavement. We can therefore rule out any idea of local "coming" as irrelevant, since we have a clear indication of the purpose of Jesus' entire life and work.

It is also difficult to see a prophetic sense implied in the saying. One might want to connect the second part of the logion with the suffering servant of Isaiah 52–53 and thereby forge a link with a prophetic ministry. However, it is very difficult to see how one could make sense of Mark 10.45*a* in this

---

64. See, for example, Swete, *Mark,* 240; Knox, *Christ the Lord,* 97, who sees Mark 10.45 as "perhaps clearer" than Mark 1.38; A. W. Argyle, "The Evidence for the Belief That Our Lord Himself Claimed to Be Divine," *ExpT* 61 (1950), 228-32 (231); Benoit, "Divinity of Jesus in the Synoptic Gospels," 68; idem, "Préexistence et Incarnation," 14; Sevenster, "Christologie," col. 1753; O. Cullmann describes the reference as "at least implicit": *The Christology of the New Testament* (Philadelphia: Westminster, 1963), 163 = *Die Christologie des Neuen Testaments* (Tübingen: Mohr, ²1958), 166; Arens, (*The HAΘON-Sayings,* 345) says that there is a "possible implicit allusion," but later puts it more strongly (158-59); Schreiber, *Die Markuspassion,* 223; France, *Mark,* 113; Schenke, "Gibt es im Markusevangelium eine Präexistenzchristologie?" 64.

light; the antithesis would not have any value since there would be no expectation on anyone's part that a prophet ought to be served or worshiped. However, although the statement is in the third person with the subject as "the Son of Man," because it is still a self-reference on Jesus' part the standard features of reference to coming with a purpose are still present. The sense that Jesus comes *voluntarily*, with the intention to give his life for the many, points to preexistence.

Luke 19.10

For *the Son of Man came to seek and to save* what was lost.

Similar to the saying in Mark 10.45 is Luke 19.10, which has already been used as evidence for a preexistence christology by Benoit and Sevenster,[65] as well as more cautiously by Arens, Cullmann, and Fletcher-Louis.[66] The statement provides fairly strong evidence for preexistence, because it describes the dynamic movement of "seeking" and "saving" reminiscent of the parable of the prodigal son and of the metaphor of the shepherd who leaves his flock to go out to search for the one stray sheep. For this reason, Luke 19.10 appears to give an even stronger impression of preexistence than those sayings which talk merely in terms of the voluntary action of coming with a specified purpose, although these elements are also included in the sense of Luke 19.10 as well.

Nolland rightly observes the connection with the saying in Mark 2.17 par. Luke 5.32, as well as the OT motifs behind Luke 19.10: "This verse has obvious links with 5.32, but its particular imagery is inspired by Ezekiel 34, where God himself and David gather the scattered sheep of Israel."[67] But in the rest of his discussion, Nolland perhaps overplays the connection between Jesus' role and that of David.[68] Rather, Harnack and Warfield were right to argue that the action of Jesus here actually suggests the work of *God* in Ezekiel

---

65. Benoit, "Divinity of Jesus in the Synoptic Gospels," 68; Sevenster, "Christologie," col. 1753.

66. Arens, *The HΛΘΟΝ-Sayings*, 178-79, sees reference here to an epiphany, but also a "possible, implicit" allusion to preexistence (345 with n. 5); Cullmann, *Christology*, 163 (= *Christologie*, 166), says that preexistence is referred to "at least indirectly"; C. H. T. Fletcher-Louis, *Luke-Acts: Angels, Christology and Soteriology* (WUNT; Tübingen: Mohr, 1997), 238-39, raises it as a possibility, and later (*Luke-Acts*, 248) talks of Luke's "strong indication."

67. J. Nolland, *Luke 18:35–24:53* (WBC; Waco: Word, 1993), 906.

68. As does F. Bovon, who (in *Das Evangelium nach Lukas*. Volume 3: *Lk 15-19, 27* [Zurich: Benziger, 2001], 277-78) takes a similar line.

34.[69] The two elements in Luke 19.10 correspond to repeated declarations by God himself in the Ezekiel passage:

> I will rescue my sheep [from the mouths of the false shepherds]. . . . (Ezek. 34.10)

> I myself, I, will *search* for my sheep, and will *seek* them out. As shepherds *seek* out their flocks when they are among their scattered sheep, so I will *seek* out my sheep and I will *rescue* them. . . . (vv. 11-12)

> I will bring them out. . . . (v. 13)

> I will feed them. . . . (v. 14)

> I myself will be the shepherd of my sheep. . . . (v. 15)

> *I will seek the lost.* . . . (v. 16)

> Therefore will I *save* my flock, and they shall no longer be attacked. (v. 22)

After the extensive announcements by God about his own work in Ezek. 34.1-22, David is mentioned rather briefly in 34.23-24, whereupon the theme of the work of God is taken up again for the rest of the chapter. The role of David in Ezekiel 34 has thus been considerably overplayed by scholars, and so the association of the "coming" in Luke 19.10 with the advent of a Davidic Messiah described in Ezek. 34.23-24 is not necessarily the only interpretation. On the other hand, a messianic interpretation does not rule out preexistence, as we will see in our discussion of the "Messiah" idea in chapter 10. However, the goals of the advent in Luke 19.10 cannot be associated with a prophetic ministry: prophets do not save. And while one should not over-read the imagery, interpreting the coming here as "coming on the scene" or as "having a specific task" does not do justice to the dynamism expressed in the seeking. In conclusion, as a result of these considerations, it seems extremely likely that Luke has in mind the preexistence of Jesus, and a corresponding coming from heaven.[70]

---

69. A. Harnack, "'Ich bin gekommen.' Die ausdrücklichen Selbstzeugnisse Jesu über den Zweck seiner Sendung und seines Kommens," *ZTK* 22 (1912), 1-30 (14); Warfield, "Jesus' Mission," 566.

70. On the version of Luke 19.10 at Matt. 18.11 in some manuscripts, see the excursus at the end of chapter 3 above.

Conclusion to Exegesis

In conclusion, then, there is good reason to see evidence of preexistence in the ten statements examined. Specifically, we have found that they confirm the hypothesis established earlier that the grammatical form and the angelic parallels point toward preexistence. The grammatical form points toward a deliberate action in coming with a purpose, and the angelic parallels confirm that it is heavenly beings who make such statements in their references to coming into the world.

In terms of the specific content of the sayings of Jesus, we saw in particular that Jesus is represented as coming to cast fire and division onto the earth and as standing over against the rest of humanity. There is also a possible hint in Mark 2.17 of Jesus having come to invite sinners to the heavenly banquet. The statements in the mouths of demons echo this heavenly origin of Jesus in that they portray Jesus as one who has come into a world under the control of the servants of Satan.

We also saw that, supplementing the image of motion in the constant reference to "coming" is a further sense of dynamism in Jesus' coming "to seek and save the lost" in Luke 19.10. We turn briefly to some further evidence in the Synoptic Gospels that reinforces this picture of dynamic movement on the part of Jesus in his coming.

II. Supporting Evidence: Jesus' Coming Expressed in the Parables

There are of course significant problems with deducing theological propositions from parables, and such an approach has been rightly criticized in recent years. Nevertheless, as illustrative of points made elsewhere in more programmatic statements, the parables have a certain value. There are six references to a key figure in a parable "coming" or "going" on a journey, and we will examine them here in ascending order of significance for our theme.

First, there is the parable of the good Samaritan (Luke 10.25-37), which, as one of the longest parables, with a corresponding abundance of narrative elements, has been a particular victim of allegorimania.[71] In this light, it can only be mentioned very tentatively that the Samaritan "came" and encountered the wounded man (v. 33) — which may be significant if one adopts a christological interpretation of the parable, with the Samaritan occupying the

---

71. Augustine's interpretation has of course come under particularly heavy criticism.

role of Christ. This cannot be pressed very far at all, however, since the priest in v. 31 had "come down" (!) and the Levite also "came" (v. 32).

Second, Luke 13.6-9 has the owner of a fig tree going to look for figs over the course of three years and finding none. Unless the reference is more specifically to God, there is a probable self-reference here on the part of Jesus as one who "came (ἦλθεν) in search of fruit" (13.6), though again it is uncertain how much can be read into the details of the parable here.

Third, Matt. 18.12-14 par. Luke 15.3-7 has the shepherd who leaves behind ninety-nine sheep to go and look for the one who is lost. There is some emphasis here on the journey: the shepherd leaves the flock to go off in search (πορευθεὶς ζητεῖ) of the lost one (Matt. 18.12). Although the verb "seek" is not used by Luke, he does employ the phrase "going to find" (Luke 15.4). In reference to the sheep, while Matthew twice uses the verb "wander off" (the passive of πλανάω, Matt. 18.12), Luke refers to the fact that the shepherd has "lost" the sheep, and identifies the sheep as "what was lost" (τὸ ἀπολωλός, Luke 15.4, 6).

Fourth, in the statement about the binding of the strong man (Mark 3.27 par. Matt. 12.29), Stauffer states that there is a presupposition, though not an explicit assertion, of the coming of the preexistent, heavenly Son of Man.[72] While this is undoubtedly to read too much into the statement, there is nevertheless a reference to a "coming," specifically a breaking into and entering a house: "but no one can go into (εἰσελθών) the house of a strong man and seize his property, without first binding the strong man." Pesch notes the allegorical character of the metaphor here,[73] but to read too much into the "entering" would be dangerous.

Fifth, the beginning of the parable of the sower (Mark 4.3) has led some scholars to make reference to preexistence. The phrase "a sower went forth to sow," in the context of the parable as a whole, is certainly suggestive of the ministry of Jesus, as Marcus has strongly argued.[74] The sower's action of "going forth" has suggested to Lagrange an allegorical reference to Jesus' coming forth from heaven.[75]

Finally, there is the unusual expression in Mark 4.21, where Jesus asks

---

72. E. Stauffer, *New Testament Theology* (New York: Macmillan, 1955), 119: "in the apocalyptic tradition the Son of Man is a pre-existent heavenly being. The sayings about the Son of Man in the synoptic Gospels seem to presuppose that, but make no express reference to it (Matt. 12.29)."

73. Pesch, *Markusevangelium*, 1:215.

74. J. Marcus, *The Mystery of the Kingdom of God* (SBLDS; Atlanta: Scholars, 1987), 37-39, in part on the basis of the analogy between ἐξῆλθεν in 4.3 and the similar forms in 1.38, 2.17. He is followed here by B. Witherington, *The Gospel of Mark: A Socio-Rhetorical Commentary* (Grand Rapids: Eerdmans, 2001), 164-65.

75. Lagrange, *Marc*, 113.

whether "the lamp comes" (ἔρχεται ὁ λύχνος) in order to be placed under a bushel. While commentators have noted that such phraseology is known from classical texts (while Jeremias claims it is an Aramaism), the wording is still somewhat jarring. As a result, a number of scholars see a christological motif here.[76] Thus the question arises whether the awkward phrasing indicates an emphasis of some kind on the "coming," again on analogy with the coming of Jesus in Mark 1.38 and 2.17. Cranfield and Lagrange allude to Jesus' preexistence here, and Grundmann considers such a deduction "possible."[77]

How are we to assess the significance of all these references? A danger lies in both extremes: there is a risk of medieval-style hyper-allegory on the one hand, but also the lazy option of simply dismissing any possibility of correspondence.[78] Scholars today have to face the difficult task of assessing each case on its own merits rather than simply heavy-handedly applying a cure-all method.

It is necessary to reinforce the point made earlier that the evidence from the parables must be seen as supplementary to what we have deduced independently from the "I have come" sayings proper, but that they can have some confirmatory value in connection with these "I have come" sayings. The point which these parabolic metaphors, with the probable exception of the first (the good Samaritan), share, is that by and large the figure who "comes," comes with the specific intention of accomplishing something analogous to the purpose of Jesus' mission. This can be expressed as follows:

Luke 13.6-9: coming to seek fruit	Purpose of mission in Mark 12.2
Matt. 18.12-14: looking for lost sheep	Purpose of advent in Luke 19.10
Mark 3.27: binding the strong man	Purpose of advent in Mark 1.24
Mark 4.3: sowing the seed of the word	Purpose of advent in Mark 1.38
Mark 4.21: coming of the light	Purpose of "visit" in Luke 1.78-79

76. E. Schweizer, *Das Evangelium nach Markus* (NTD; Göttingen: Vandenhoeck und Ruprecht, 1967), 55; G. Schneider, "Das Bildwort von der Lampe," *ZNW* 61 (1970), 183-209 [188]; Pesch, *Markusevangelium*, 1:249 (following Schneider). But Pesch sees the "coming" reference here as to Jesus' "prophetisches Sendungsbewußtsein" (249-50 n. 13).

77. Cranfield, *Mark*, 164: "It seems likely then that for Mark the parable had reference to the ministry of Jesus . . . its [*sc.* that of ἔρχεται] use in connection with a lamp is odd, and this suggests the possibility that we should see in its use here an indication that Jesus was thinking of himself and his mission (cf. on ii. 17)." Thus Cranfield implies that this is an implicit reference to preexistence here, since (p. 206) that is how he takes Mark 2.17. Cf. Lagrange, *Marc*, 113: "Mc, comme dans l'explication du semeur, pense au sens métaphorique de la lampe qui vient dans le monde"; Grundmann, *Markus*, 96 ("möglich").

78. M. Wiles, "Early Exegesis of the Parables," *SJT* 11 (1958), 287-301, simply dismisses the enterprise of correlating elements in the parables in an allegorical fashion.

The parallels between the parables of the fig tree (Luke 13.6-9) and of the wicked tenants (Mark 12.1-12 par. Matt. 21.33-46; Luke 20.9-19) are clear enough. The vineyard owner goes looking for fruit in Luke 13.7, just as in the other parable the owner sends for "fruit/produce from the vineyard" (Mark 12.2 par.). The correlation is close. As we might expect from parables, the roles and the imagery are not exactly the same in each case, but the parallel is clear enough.[79]

In the second case, Matt. 18.12-14 par. Luke 15.3-7, it is clearer: there is a strong correlation between the parable of the lost sheep and the coming of the Son of Man in Luke 19.10. In the parable, there is a "going to seek/find" the sheep which is described as "what was lost" (τὸ ἀπολωλός). Similarly, Jesus in Luke 19.10 "came to seek and to save what was lost" (τὸ ἀπολωλός).

The "binding of the strong man" motif in Mark 3.27 deals with the precondition for being able to steal the strong man's possessions: "but no one is able, on entering the house of the strong man, to steal his property unless. . . ." This is reminiscent of the theme we noted earlier in Mark 1.24, where the demons comment on Jesus' entry into a world in the grip of demonic forces. The dynamic sense of Jesus' invasion of the world is further reinforced in Mark 3.27 by the imagery of the *stronger* man breaking into a house.

The reference to the sower "going forth" to sow the seed could easily line up beside the statement from Mark 1.38 which we discussed above. The sower "went forth to sow" (again, "coming [forth]" + infinitive), and the seed is the word (Mark 4.14). Interestingly, Mark 1.38 is the only statement where the verb "come/go forth" is used of Jesus in connection with his mission, and it is specifically in relation to preaching the word.

Finally, although there is no "I have come" saying explicitly in parallel with the "coming" of the lamp in Mark 4.21, the visitation of the Messianic light to shine on those in darkness (Luke 1.78-79) is still very closely related. The figure "from on high" may not "come," but he does "visit." (This will be discussed further in chapter 10 below.)

So the parables can be said to provide limited confirmation of the movement toward incarnation, albeit in a dependent and attenuated way. That is to say, they do not supply us with any new information but do reinforce the picture we already have from the "I have come" sayings. Principally, *the specific aspect that we can see reinforced in these parabolic statements is the dynamic movement involved in the coming of Jesus,* which is particularly problematic for any idiomatic interpretation of the "I have come" sayings as

---

79. In the parable of the fig tree, it seems to be God who is the figure who goes looking, whereas in the parable of the wicked tenants, the "God" figure sends the son to go for him.

merely referring to Jesus' presence to carry out a certain task. Similarly, the examples discussed here make trouble for any interpretation which would take "coming" as simply a "coming on the scene." There is a strong sense of dynamic movement implied here.

III. The Early Reception of the "I Have Come" Sayings

It is relevant here to discuss the question of the adaptation of the "I have come" sayings elsewhere in the NT. Again, while not constituting independent evidence, it is noteworthy how "coming" language is used in subsequent NT tradition.

One particularly interesting case is that of Heb. 10.9. Here an "I have come" + purpose saying is attributed to Jesus, having been constructed from the raw materials of Psalm 40 (LXX 39). In the Psalm, David says, "I have come (*sc.* to the Temple)[80] as it is written about me in the scroll of the book; to do your will, my God, I have purposed. . . ." Hebrews abbreviates this simply to "I have come to do your will" and applies it directly to Jesus' incarnation.

In addition to the numerous references to "coming *into the world*" in John's Gospel (John 1.9; 3.19; 6.14; 16.28; 18.37), in 1 Tim. 1.15 it seems to be an established "trustworthy saying" that "Christ Jesus came (ἦλθεν) into the world to save sinners," a clear indication of preexistence.[81] Similarly, 1 John 4.2 transmits, or creates, an incarnational formula as a test of orthodoxy: that Jesus Christ *has come in the flesh* (also 2 John 7). The incarnational dimension of Jesus' coming in the flesh from preexistence is unavoidable here. Hence, the clear language of preexistence in the later NT literature makes use of the earlier traditions in which Jesus talks about his coming. This shows that, at the very least, the "I have come" sayings in the Gospels lent themselves to such an interpretation.

The Synoptic Sayings and John's Gospel

This leads us back to the issue which we raised in Chapter 3: can it be argued that the Synoptic Gospels evince a more primitive sense for the "I have come"

80. A. Weiser, *The Psalms: A Commentary* (London: SCM, 1962), 338, quotes "Lo, I have come" and comments "add 'to the Temple.'"
81. See H. Stettler, *Die Christologie der Pastoralbriefe* (WUNT; Tübingen: Mohr, 1998), 54-55.

sayings than John's Gospel? This has been the standard way of explaining the difference between the Synoptics' plain reference to "coming" in contrast to the Johannine "coming into the world" or "coming down from heaven." Harnack, for example, argues that the frequent addition "into the world" indicates that a new horizon is in view which is foreign to Jesus himself (and thereby to the Synoptic Gospels).[82] The same point is made by Dunn in his discussion of the difference between the Johannine and Synoptic christologies, particularly on the preexistence question.[83]

However, it should be asked whether the absence of specific reference to coming "into the world" or "down from heaven" would have been noted as significant *by those who had not read John's Gospel.* In other words, it is easy for us to point to the apparent difference in form between the two sets of sayings, but would this have been meaningful for the original author of (say) Mark and his readers? If, as has been argued, the sayings of Jesus as they come in the Synoptic Gospels evoke the comings of angels, there would be no need to highlight the point by reference to heaven or the world. *Angelic* statements in early Judaism rarely make explicit reference to the angel "coming from heaven" or "coming into the world."[84] Similarly, as Schnutenhaus has observed, by far the most common way to refer to the coming of God from heaven in the OT is simply by reference to the word "come" without any further specification: "The verb *bo'* ['come'] is thus the most widespread and most general one used to denote the coming of God."[85] As such, the difference between the form in the Synoptic Gospels and John is somewhat exaggerated.

Conclusion

We have examined ten statements which have been adduced as evidence for the advent of Jesus from heaven in the Synoptic Gospels. To return to the question posed at the beginning of chapter 3, then, we can say that at least as far as these sayings are concerned, Matthew, Mark, and Luke can be seen to

82. Harnack, "Ich bin gekommen," 22.

83. J. D. G. Dunn, *Christology in the Making: An Inquiry into the Origins of the Doctrine of the Incarnation* (Grand Rapids: Eerdmans, 1996), 30.

84. As noted in chapter 5 above, references to, for example, Gabriel "coming down" are the exception rather than the rule.

85. F. Schnutenhaus, "Das Kommen und Erscheinen Gottes im Alten Testament," *ZNW* 76 (1964), 1-22 (19): "Das Verb *bo'* ist also das verbreiteste und allgemeinste, um Gottes Kommen zu nennen."

share with John the idea of preexistence. The first two statements discussed above (Mark 1.24; Matt. 8.29) were questions in the mouths of demons relating to the advent of Jesus, and these were deemed to be fairly strong evidence for preexistence. The next three (Mark 1.38 par. Luke 4.43; Mark 2.17; Matt. 5.17) probably counted as almost, though perhaps not quite, as firm confirmation. It was the next three statements (Luke 12.49; Luke 12.51 par. Matt. 10.34; Matt. 10.35) which gave the most striking indication, in that two of them describe the mission of Jesus in relation to "the earth," whether casting fire upon it or bringing peace to it. Our final two sayings, where Jesus uses the self-designation "Son of Man," and consequently the third-person form of the verb, were also deemed to be valuable evidence for our argument. Principally, the form used of Jesus in the Synoptic Gospels corresponds very closely to that used of angelic advents from heaven in the OT and early Jewish literature. The importance of the "coming" in all these statements is supported by the presence of the motif in a number of parables. While all ten of these Synoptic sayings have very different flavors and thus emphasize preexistence to different degrees, they all share (the exception being the slight modification in Mark 1.38) the basic pattern of coming + infinitive of purpose. Thus we have evidence of preexistence undergirding Jesus' statements that he came with prior intent and that that voluntary action was embarked on with a few closely interrelated purposes.

This is not to say that preexistence is the *main emphasis* here: the focus is of course on the *purposes* of Jesus' ministry. But preexistence is certainly still the presupposition of these purposes. We noted in the Introduction that we would flesh out the concept of preexistence in the course of the exegesis; the key point here is that this preexistence consists not least of a *will* which is the basis of Christ's coming to the human realm in accordance with the will of the Father.

CHAPTER 7

The Mission of Jesus in the Synoptic Gospels

In addition to the "coming" sayings of Jesus, we also have the similar statements referring to his having been "sent." The brief analysis here will focus on the references in the Synoptic Gospels to Jesus' mission under three headings:

I. the "sending" statements which are summaries of the goal of Jesus' ministry (Matt. 15.24; Luke 4.18, 43),
II. the references of Jesus to the Father as "the one who sent me" (Mark 9.37 par. Luke 9.48; Matt. 10.40; Luke 10.16), and
III. the more indirect references embedded in the parables (Luke 14.17; Mark 12.6).

The Ambiguity of "Sending"

That preexistence cannot be seen in statements about sending *per se* is clear from the fact that God also "sends" other non-heavenly figures, in particular, the prophets.[1] More specifically, this can be seen a number of times in reference to Moses,[2] and the same language is used in the OT in the cases of Sam-

---

1. General references to God "sending" the prophets come in, e.g., 2 Chr. 36.15; Jer. 14.14-15; Ezek. 13.6; Tob. 14.4.
2. Exod. 3.13-15; 5.22; 7.16; as well as Deut. 34.11, and the Lord's sending of both Moses and Aaron in 1 Sam. 12.8.

uel, Nathan, Elijah, Isaiah, and Jeremiah.[3] God also "sends" other deliverers, such as Joseph.[4] These sendings are obviously not sendings from heaven.[5]

On the other hand, there is also clear evidence of divine sendings as sendings from heaven in places such as Gen. 24.40, where the Lord sends an angel to Abraham's servant to give him success in his quest for Isaac's wife.[6] In Num. 20.16, God sends the angel who brought Israel out of Egypt, and there are numerous other examples throughout the OT and early Jewish literature of God sending angels from heaven.[7] In the Synoptic Gospels, one can point to Gabriel's statements "I have been sent" (Luke 1.19, 26). The OT also talks of God sending other heavenly figures, such as his word (Isa. 55.11) and Elijah in his second coming (Mal. 4.5). So, clearly, "sending" language in itself neither points toward nor tells against preexistence.

Hypothesis: The "Coming"-"Sent" Correspondence Revisited

The position taken in this chapter on the question of preexistence is essentially that the sending statements do not in themselves indicate preexistence, but that they should be interpreted in this way in the light of the strong evidence for preexistence in the "coming" sayings, to which they are very closely related. Indeed, some of the "sending" sayings strongly invite an interpretation along the lines of preexistence christology, as we shall see.

A number of scholars argue, however, that it is merely the sending of Jesus as a *prophetic* figure that is in view in the Synoptic Gospels. Dunn, for example, presumes that the language of the sending of the Son both in Gal. 4.4 and in its background in the statements of Jesus (he refers to Mark 9.37 and 12.6) cannot safely be assumed to refer to more than "divine commissioning."[8]

3. See 1 Sam. 15.1; 2 Sam. 12.1; 2 Kgs 2.2-6; Isa. 37.21; and Jer. 19.14 respectively.

4. Gen. 45.8; cf. 1 Sam. 12.11; Isa. 19.20.

5. Campbell describes the sending of prophets as "the *immanent* reading of 'send,'" in which it is basically synonymous with "commanding." D. A. Campbell, "The Story of Jesus in Romans and Galatians," in B. W. Longenecker, ed., *Narrative Dynamics in Paul: A Critical Assessment* (Louisville: Westminster/John Knox, 2002), 97-124 (119). J. D. G. Dunn, *Christology in the Making: An Inquiry into the Origins of the Doctrine of the Incarnation* (London: SCM, 1980), 38-39, also identified "two broad groups that he (God) 'sends forth,'" referring to *heavenly beings* (principally angels, but also the Spirit/a spirit, and wisdom), and "most often, the prophets."

6. See also Gen. 19.13, cf. 19.1.

7. See, e.g., 1 Chr. 21.15; 2 Chr. 32.21; Zech. 2.12-13 (8-9); 6.15; LXX Dan. 3.96; Dan. 6.23 (22); Tob. 12.14.

8. Dunn, *Christology in the Making*, 39-40.

Thus the references in the Synoptic Gospels most closely reflect the OT and early Jewish language of God sending the prophets.

The problem with this approach, however, is that it simply observes the ambiguity and draws the lowest-common-denominator conclusion. We have seen, however, the strong indication of preexistence in the "I have come" sayings discussed in the previous chapter, and it is clear that there is a close formal correspondence between the "coming" and the "sending" sayings. This is obvious from the frequent parallelism between the two kinds of sayings, a point on which all are agreed. To repeat two examples from those cited in Chapter 5:

> He said, "Daniel, you who are highly esteemed, consider carefully the words I am about to speak to you, and stand up, for *I have now been sent to you.*" And when he said this to me, I stood up trembling. Then he continued, "Do not be afraid, Daniel. Since the first day that you set your mind to gain understanding and to humble yourself before your God, your words were heard, and *I have come in response to them.*" (Dan. 10.11-12)

> When I had finished speaking these words, *the angel who had been sent to me* on the former nights *was sent to me again,* and he said to me, "Rise, Ezra, and listen to the words which *I have come to speak to you.*" (*4 Ezra* 7.2)

This same correspondence was noted in the several other examples from chapter 5, such as *4 Ezra* 6.30-33; Midrash Tanhuma to Exodus 6, and the Geniza Targum to Josh. 5.14.[9] Clearly, then, if the "I have come" statements in the Synoptic Gospels refer to a *heavenly* coming, then the "being sent" should be taken the same way.

In each of these Jewish examples above, when the language of "sending" is used, it is clearly to focus on the fact that the envoy stands under the authority of God. We noted above in chapter 4 that "coming" and "being sent" are not identical; the former focuses much more on the action of the subject and the latter on the subordination of the one sent to the sender. In the case of the sayings in the Synoptic Gospels, then, the accent will not be on Jesus' own coming, but on the fact that his mission is the result of the action of the Father.

---

9. See also the discussion in W. Grimm, *Weil Ich Dich Liebe. Die Verkundigung Jesu und Deuterojesaja* (Bern: Lang, 1976), 83, and in a less extreme form, J.-A. Bühner, *Der Gesandte und sein Weg im vierten Evangelium. Die kultur- und religionsgeschichtlichen Grundlagen der johanneischen Sendungschristologie sowie ihre traditionsgeschichtliche Entwicklung* (WUNT 2; Tübingen: Mohr, 1977), 147-52. For further discussion of this point, see chapter 4 above.

To return to the earlier point, the close correspondence between "coming" and "sending" is still clear. As a result, it makes good sense to interpret the ambiguous "sending" sayings of Jesus in the light of the clearer "I have come" sayings. Due to the clear implication of the "I have come" sayings, we should understand the sending sayings in the Synoptic Gospels in the "heavenly" sense, rather than as merely referring to commissioning. However, we will also see that the motif of sending from a preexistence in heaven is not *in competition with* Jesus' messiahship.

I. Summaries of Jesus' Mission in the "Sending" Sayings

The most obvious point about the "I have come" sayings of Jesus is that they all sum up the purpose of his ministry. In this respect, the first three "sending" sayings which we will examine correspond particularly closely in form to the "coming" sayings. On the other hand, the focus is less on Jesus' initiative, and more on his divinely ordained mission, a mission which certainly includes prophetic and messianic functions.

Matthew 15.24

> A Canaanite woman from that vicinity came to him, crying out, "Lord, Son of David, have mercy on me! My daughter is suffering terribly from demon possession." Jesus did not answer a word. So his disciples came to him and urged him, "Send her away, for she keeps crying out after us." And he replied, "I was only sent to the lost sheep of the house of Israel."

The statement of Jesus in question comes, then, in response to the plea of a Canaanite woman who begs Jesus to heal her daughter, whom he does in fact subsequently help (15.21-28).[10] What is noteworthy in the imagery here is that this saying picks up on the "shepherd" motif common elsewhere in Jesus' statements about his self-understanding. We saw above how the references in the Synoptics to the coming of the shepherd involve dynamic movement: coming "to seek and to save what was lost" (Luke 19.10) and "going and seeking (the sheep) that had wandered off" (Matt. 18.12-14 par. Luke 15.3-7). This fits well with the combination of the sending and the shepherd imagery here in Matt. 15.24, though the focus — as ever in the sending sayings — is not so

---

10. For bibliography on this pericope, see U. Luz, *Matthew 8–20: A Commentary* (Hermeneia; Minneapolis: Fortress, 2001), 336.

much on the action of Jesus, but on the authority of the Father over him.[11] Furthermore, there is almost certainly a combination here of preexistence as the presupposition of the dynamic sending language, and the Davidic-messianic resonances of the shepherd motif.

Luke 4.18

> And the scroll of the prophet Isaiah was given to him, and he unrolled the scroll, and found the place where it was written: "The Spirit of the Lord is upon me, because he has anointed me to proclaim good news to the poor. And he has sent me to proclaim release for the captives and sight for the blind, to grant liberty to the oppressed, and to proclaim the year of the Lord's favor."

Luke's first mention of Jesus being "sent" is an indirect reference, coming in the course of Jesus' reading from Isaiah in the Nazareth synagogue.[12] Although this example is different from Matt. 15.24 in that it is not explicitly a statement of Jesus about himself, it is relevant because he does draw it very clearly into connection with himself through his subsequent statement, "Today this Scripture has been fulfilled in your hearing" (Luke 4.21). Here, the most obvious point is Jesus' messianic identity, but as we have seen, this need not be considered incompatible with preexistence.

Luke 4.43

> He said to them that, "It is necessary for me to proclaim the kingdom of God in the other towns also, because it is for this I have been sent (ἀπεστάλην)."

Although the correspondence between "coming" and "sending" is already clear from the OT and other Jewish texts, it is particularly obvious in the Synoptic Gospels from the parallel statement to Luke 4.43 in Mark 1.38:

11. Lohmeyer's comment that the saying places Jesus in the line of the prophets and says nothing to mark him out from them is especially strange considering Lohmeyer's comments about the "shepherd" theme in the OT and his statement that Jesus is seeing here with "the eyes of God." E. Lohmeyer (W. Schmauch, ed.), *Das Evangelium des Matthäus* (Göttingen: Vandenhoeck und Ruprecht, ³1962), 254.

12. For bibliography on the passage, see F. Bovon, *Luke 1: A Commentary on the Gospel of Luke 1:1–9:50* (Hermeneia; Minneapolis: Fortress, 2002), 148-49.

> And he said to them, "Let us go elsewhere into the nearby villages, so that I may also preach there. For this is why I have come forth (ἐξῆλθον)." (Mark 1.38)

The setting of this saying is after a day at Peter's house, which ended with an evening of intensive miracle-working by Jesus, as in the Markan parallel passage. We saw in the previous chapter that the parallel sayings about Jesus' coming/sending here indicated that the coming was understood at least by Luke in *theological* rather than geographical terms. There is no particular indication of preexistence in Luke's paraphrase here, although since Luke saw preexistence in the Markan *Vorlage,* it seems unlikely that his paraphrase is intended to remove such a connotation. In any case, it is clearly a summary of Jesus' ministry in the same way in which Luke's "I have come" sayings are. As such, it should be interpreted in the light of them.

II. "The One Who Sent Me"

Mark 9.37 par. Luke 9.48

> Whoever receives one of these children in my name, receives me; and whoever receives me, does not receive me but the one who sent me.

A preexistent sense is seen in this statement by Hofius, Mohr, and L. Schenke.[13] The setting of the saying (although the geographical reference is omitted in Luke) is the arrival of Jesus and the disciples in Capernaum (Mark 9.33), and the embarrassed silence of the disciples in response to Jesus' question as to what they were arguing about (Mark 9.34; cf. Luke 9.46-47).[14] Knowing that they were discussing who was "the greatest" among them, he takes a child and expresses his divine origin in the course of two *a minore ad maius* statements: whoever receives a child, receives me, and whoever receives me, receives the one who sent me.

The Markan version in its wider context has associations with Mark

---

13. O. Hofius, "Jesu Zuspruch der Sündenvergebung. Exegetische Erwägungen zu Mk 2,5b," in idem, *Neutestamentliche Studien* (WUNT; Tübingen: Mohr, 2000), 38-56 (55); T. A. Mohr, *Markus- und Johannespassion. Redaktions- und traditionsgeschichtliche Untersuchung der markinischen und johanneischen Passionstradition* (Zurich: Theologischer Verlag, 1982), 423; L. Schenke, "Gibt es im Markusevangelium eine Präexistenzchristologie?" *ZNW* 91 (2000), 45-71 (65).

14. For bibliography on the literary contexts in each of the Gospels, see C. A. Evans, *Mark 8:27–16:20* (WBC; Nashville: Nelson, 2001), 58-59, and Bovon, *Luke I,* 389.

10.45, as Evans and France have already noted.[15] Jesus' response to the disputes of the disciples about who was the greatest (Mark 9.34) consists in (a) an aphorism, (b) an action, and then (c) an explanation of the action. The aphorism, in Mark 9.35, is: "If anyone wants to be first, let him be last of all and a servant of all" — very probably intended by Jesus as a reference to himself. He then places a child in their midst (Mark 9.36), and remarks that receiving the child is tantamount to receiving Jesus, and receiving Jesus tantamount to receiving the Father (v. 37). The whole discussion in Mark 9.33-37 is strikingly similar to 10.35-45: both consist of a desire for greatness by the disciples, which is rebuked by Jesus with reference to his own personal status as the servant. In this respect, the concluding statements in Mark 9.37 about Jesus being sent by the Father and in 10.45 about the Son of Man coming to serve have a clear relation to one another. Here, then, Mark and Luke bring the motif of "the servant" into association with divine sending.

Matthew 10.40

> Whoever receives you, receives me, and whoever receives me, receives the one who sent me.

Luke 10.16

> Whoever listens to you listens to me, and whoever rejects you rejects me. And whoever rejects me rejects the one who sent me.

These next two sayings are similar to Mark 9.37, but ground the representative character of the disciples in their status as Jesus' *envoys*.[16] In both these Matthean and Lukan sayings, the undergirding presupposition is that the envoy is representative of the sender such that rejection of the embassy is tantamount to rejection of the party represented.[17] However, there is little here ei-

---

15. Evans, *Mark 8:27–16:20*, 62; R. T. France, *The Gospel of Mark: A Commentary on the Greek Text* (NIGTC; Grand Rapids: Eerdmans, 2002), 375.

16. For bibliography on these, see Luz, *Matthew 8–20*, 119; F. Bovon, *Das Evangelium nach Lukas (Lk 9,51–14,35)* (Zurich: Benziger, 1996), 42-43.

17. This recalls the envoy christology often discussed in connection with John's Gospel. Hagner notes it in connection with Matt. 10.40, citing the well-known rabbinic parallel: "To receive one is to receive the other. The Jewish background of the *shaliach* may underlie these statements (cf. 'a man's emissary or agent [*shaliach*] is like the man himself' [*m. Ber.* 5.5, cf. *Mek. Exod.* 14:31; 18.12])." D. A. Hagner, *Matthew 1–13* (WBC; Dallas: Word, 1993), 295.

ther to shed further light on, or to call into question, what we have said about the "sending" motif thus far.

As a result, W. C. Allen's suggestion of preexistence in Matt. 10.40 seems rather old-fashioned.[18] On closer inspection, however, there is evidence from the context that points in this direction. Matthew has just included three references to Jesus' "coming" in quick succession, which culminate in the divisive impact on families of following Jesus (10.34-39). Then comes the saying in question: "whoever receives you receives me, and whoever receives me receives the one who sent me." The "you" in question here is explained in v. 41 as referring to Christian "prophets" and "righteous."[19] As such, Jesus is depicted in the exalted terms of one who sends prophets — just as he is later on in 23.34-36. Thus the heavenly advent of Jesus preceding 10.40 and the divine status of Jesus immediately after it encourage one to see an exalted christology in 10.40 itself. Certainly on these terms, Jesus cannot easily be described as a mere prophet, and there may well be a further implication of preexistence.[20]

III. Jesus' Sending Expressed in Parables

Despite the fact that scholars are instinctively wary of drawing theological implications from allegorical interpretations of parables, it is actually Mark 12.6 (and parallels) which has attracted most attention of all the "sending" statements in previous discussions of preexistence. First, however, we will look briefly at the sending in the parable of the great banquet.

Luke 14.17

> He said to him, "A certain man was holding a great banquet, and he invited many people, and sent his servant at the time of the banquet to say to those invited, 'Come, because it is now ready!'"

We noted in the previous chapter that there is a possibility of reference to heavenly banquet imagery in two "I have come" sayings (Mark 2.17; 10.45). Here, however, this possibility becomes a certainty: Jesus is dining at the

18. W. C. Allen, *A Critical and Exegetical Commentary on the Gospel according to St. Matthew* (ICC; Edinburgh: Clark, 1907), 122.

19. So, rightly, Hagner, *Matthew 1–13*, 295-96.

20. By contrast, the reference to "sending" in the negative form of the saying in Luke 10.16 is not illuminated to any great degree by its immediate context.

house of a leading Pharisee (Luke 14.1-14), and one of the guests comments, "Blessed is the man who will eat at the feast in the kingdom of God" (Luke 14.15). Jesus then tells the parable introduced with the words cited above.[21] The parable thus identifies Jesus as the servant going to summon guests to the heavenly banquet: "The action corresponds to Jesus' invitation of his contemporaries into the Kingdom of God."[22] The sending of the servant in Luke 14.17 here corresponds to the master's instruction "go forth!" (ἔξελθε) at two further points in the parable (14.21, 23). Here, then, there is another correspondence between "sending" and "coming/going," and the image of the heavenly banquet reflected in the parable may well reinforce the christology of preexistence in the "I have come" sayings.[23]

Mark 12.6 par. Matthew 21.37; Luke 20.13

He still had one — a beloved son. He sent him last to them, saying to himself, "They will respect my son."

The possible preexistence of the Son here in the parable of the wicked tenants was already mooted in Jülicher's great work on the parables in 1899.[24] More recently, Merklein, Schreiber, Kümmel, Hofius, and L. Schenke have offered arguments in favor of the preexistence interpretation — arguments which we will examine below. Mohr, Frenschkowski, and H.-M. Schenke, and Fischer also mention their support for such a reading.[25] Clearly, then, it is predominantly a few German scholars who have espoused this view, although Talbert and Fuller are exceptions.[26]

---

21. For extensive bibliography on the parable, see J. Nolland, *Luke 9:21–18:34* (WBC; Waco: Word, 1993), 752-53.

22. Nolland, *Luke 9:21–18:34*, 755.

23. The imperative "go forth" (ἔξελθε) here also occurs elsewhere in the context of the heavenly court (e.g., 1 Kgs. 22.22).

24. A. Jülicher, *Die Gleichnisreden Jesu* (Freiburg: Mohr, 1888), 2:392.

25. Mohr, *Markus- und Johannespassion*, 423; M. Frenschkowski, *Offenbarung und Epiphanie* (WUNT; Tübingen: Mohr, 1995), 197-98; H.-M. Schenke and K. M. Fischer, *Einleitung in die Schriften des Neuen Testaments* (Gutersloh: Mohn, 1978), 2:72.

26. C. H. Talbert, *What Is a Gospel? The Genre of the Canonical Gospels* (London: SPCK, 1978), 39; R. H. Fuller, *The Foundations of New Testament Christology* (New York: Scribner, 1965), 194; idem, *A Critical Introduction to the New Testament* (London: Duckworth, 1966), 111, points to Mark 12.6. However, he changes his mind later in "The Conception/Birth of Jesus as a Christological Moment," *JSNT* 1 (1978), 37-52 (43): "Here the sending of the Son is the last in a series of sendings, and the Son is no more preexistent than were the Old Testament prophets before him."

There has also, however, been strong reaction against suggestions of such a christology. Snodgrass, Best, and Dunn, for example, point to the obvious parallelism between the sending of the son and the sending of the servants, who clearly represent the prophets, and ask the question-expecting-the-answer-"no": "Must preexistence also be assumed for the prophets?"[27] L. Schenke, on the other hand, maintains that there is a reference to preexistence.[28] The arguments for preexistence in Mark 12.6, then, should be examined. They can be categorized under four questions, two concerned with the various "backgrounds" to the parable and two dealing more directly with its language.

Does the use of Psalm 118 after the parable color the parable in such a way as to imply or reinforce a sense of preexistence? It is difficult to see how the citation of Ps. 118.22-23 in Mark 12.10-11 helps the case, as Schreiber thinks it does.[29] The text certainly envisages an eschatological installation of the Son as the center or summit of God's work, but is thereby much more strongly suggestive of the resurrection than of preexistence. The former does not necessitate the latter. Schreiber's presupposition that it does — and that both elements tap into the Gnostic redeemer myth — is now widely, and rightly, recognized to be erroneous.

Is there an association with the Wisdom tradition which would suggest an aspect of preexistence? Similarly, the way in which Merklein and L. Schenke bring the parable into consideration alongside the Wisdom tradition is also questionable.[30] Although the theme of the rejection of prophets can occur in a wisdom setting, it does not necessarily evoke that context strongly. There do not

27. E. Best, *The Temptation and the Passion: The Markan Soteriology* (SNTSMS; Cambridge: Cambridge University Press, 1965), 129. Best asks this question in his critique of Schreiber, who would in fact answer "yes," however! See also K. Snodgrass, *The Parable of the Wicked Tenants: An Inquiry into Parable Interpretation* (WUNT; Tübingen: Mohr, 1983), 87; Dunn, *Christology in the Making*, 280 n. 106; S. Légasse, *L'Evangile de Marc* (Paris: Cerf, 1997), 714.

28. Schenke, "Gibt es im Markusevangelium eine Präexistenzchristologie?" 65.

29. J. Schreiber, "Die Christologie des Markusevangeliums," *ZTK* 58 (1961), 154-83 (167 n. 5). Schreiber sees Mark 12.10-12 as confirming the preexistence reading of 12.6; see also idem, *Die Markuspassion. Eine redaktionsgeschichtliche Untersuchung* (BZNW 68; Berlin: de Gruyter, 1993), 225 and 374, where it is clear that Schreiber sees in the reference to resurrection an implicit reference to the whole Christ-myth.

30. H. Merklein, "Zur Entstehung der urchristlichen Aussage vom präexistenten Sohn Gottes," in G. Dautzenberg, H. Merklein, and K. Müller, eds., *Zur Geschichte des Urchristentums* (Freiburg: Herder, 1979), 33-62 (61-62); L. Schenke, *Die Urgemeinde. Geschichtliche und theologische Entwicklung* (Stuttgart: Kohlhammer, 1990), 153.

seem to be any particular pointers here which give the impression of an allusion to the wisdom tradition.[31] As we will argue again below, the title "Son" is
in any case rather ill-suited to an association with lady Wisdom.

Does the "had" (εἶχεν) have any significance? This point is pressed by Kümmel
and Fuller: "For the first time, the Son's preexistence is broached: God "had"
yet one, a beloved Son (Mark 12:6) even before he 'sent' him."[32] More recently,
this has been strongly argued by Schenke, who raises the interesting point
that reference to the fact that the father "still had one, a beloved son" is super-
fluous and even awkward.[33] As a result, he argues that we should see an emphasis on the preexisting relationship.

However, it would seem to be an over-reading of the parable to take the
phrase "he still had one" as referring to a preincarnate dwelling of the Son "in
the bosom of the Father" as per John 1.18. In fact, the phrase probably has
quite the opposite meaning: that the vineyard owner had "had" the servants,
but after sending them, "he still had one" left, the son. Grammatically, the
"one" (ἕνα) does not really emphasize the uniqueness of the son and the father's special concern for him but simply that after all the servants were gone
there was only one other left in the household whom the father could send.

*Is the "sending" qualitatively different in view of the facts that it is the son who is
being sent, and that this is an eschatological sending?* Merklein argues the position that the idea of preexistence cannot simply be dismissed, as it is by Blank
and the other scholars noted above, on the basis of the parallel between both
servants and son alike being "sent."[34] The envoy after all is a "beloved son"
who is sent "last." Merklein is certainly right to point out that because the son
is sent last, he can thereby be seen to stand in special relation to the owner of

---

31. For example, the similarity to Wis. 9.10 is of a very loose, general kind.

32. Fuller, *Foundations of New Testament Christology,* 194. The same reasoning is found in
W. G. Kümmel, *The Theology of the New Testament according to Its Major Witnesses: Jesus-Paul-
John* (London: SCM, 1974), 119-20: "In the parable of the wicked tenants of the vineyard (Mark
12:1ff. par.), which in the text as handed down cannot go back to Jesus . . . , we hear of the owner
of the vineyard who 'had one, a beloved son,' whom he sends to the tenants when his efforts
with the sending of slaves comes to naught. It is undisputed that the vineyard owner of the parable stands for God, and therefore here, in the language of the parable the theme is the sending
of the Son of God, who accordingly exists before he is sent."

33. Schenke, "Gibt es im Markusevangelium eine Präexistenzchristologie?" 65.

34. Merklein, "Zur Entstehung der urchristlichen Aussage," 46-47. Cf. also H. B. Swete,
The Gospel according to St. Mark (London: Macmillan, 1898), 268: "the one and only Son . . . is
contrasted sharply with the many servants." V. Taylor, *The Gospel according to St. Mark* (London: Macmillan, 1952), 474, also contrasts the one son with the many servants.

the vineyard. Yet it is difficult to see how being sent last can have significance for the discussion of preexistence.

More to the point, Schenke notes that the "son" is emphasized as qualitatively different from the line of the servants who have preceded him. The statement "they will respect my son" makes sense only if the son is superior to the servants.[35] The son is also the only, beloved son ("he had yet *one*, a *beloved* son").[36] Schenke's point here is surely correct, that the son is not presented as one in the line of the servants. Clearly, then, it is not the case in Mark 12.6 that "Jesus comes as the last in the prophetic line."[37]

One of the problems with some previous interpretations is that this parable has been treated atomistically, in isolation from the Gospels in which it stands. At least within the narratives of Matthew, Mark, and Luke, the "son" in the parable is clearly to be identified with the subject of those narratives, "the Son," Jesus. As a result, the heavenly nuance of the "Son" title also needs to be borne in mind. In all three of the Synoptic Gospels, it is the title by which Jesus is addressed by God, both in the baptism at which his elect status is announced, but also — more importantly — at the transfiguration, where his heavenly status is revealed before Peter, James, and John. (See the discussion in chapter 2 above.) In this respect, the reader comes to the parable of the wicked tenants in Mark 12/Matthew 21/Luke 20 having already encountered the heavenly identity of the Son. After the parable, this heavenly identity is then reaffirmed a chapter later, in Mark 13.32 par.

Within the parable there is the obvious point that the word "send" is the same in the case of the servants and in the case of the son. But the parables are intended to be read with imaginative attention to the reality which they are depicting. In this connection, the sendings of the servants would have been heard as the commissions of the prophets, but the "sending" motif in connection with the "son" would have brought the heavenly resonances of that title into association with the sending.

Conclusion

Our initial question began with the analogy of the "coming" and "sending" and the fact that we have already seen such a strong indication of preexistence

---

35. Schenke, "Gibt es im Markusevangelium eine Präexistenzchristologie?" 64.

36. Schenke, "Gibt es im Markusevangelium eine Präexistenzchristologie?" 65.

37. N. T. Wright, *Jesus and the Victory of God* (London: SPCK, 1996), 185, citing Mark 12.6 here.

in the "I have come" sayings in the previous chapter. Since the "coming" sayings are considerably clearer than the sending sayings (which on their own are ambiguous), the latter can reasonably be interpreted in the light of the former. As such, the "sending" sayings do not on their own indicate preexistence; this sense is *contingent* upon our interpretation of the "coming" sayings above.

However, it is not the intention here to emphasize preexistence to the detriment of Jesus' prophetic or messianic identity. Clearly, if the "sending" motif should be understood as closely related to the "I have come" sayings, it also needs to be seen as highlighting *God's* role in the mission of Jesus, and as emphasizing Jesus' subordinate function as his servant.

There are elements in these sayings which fit well with a presupposition of preexistence: the coming-and-seeking imagery in Matt. 15.24 ("I was only sent to the lost sheep of the house of Israel") as well as the portrait of Jesus as the servant of the heavenly banquet in Luke 14.15-23, for example. Mark 9.37 brings Jesus the servant into association with Jesus the Son of Man in Mark 10.45. Finally, the parable of the wicked tenants makes it clear Jesus cannot adequately be described in prophetic categories, and that his sending is not simply the sending of a prophet. The character of the "son" points to the identity of Jesus as "the Son," a central aspect of which is his heavenly identity. As we said above, the sending (and indeed the accompanying imagery) does not on its own entail preexistence. But when these statements are placed within the framework of Jesus' coming from God and his heavenly identity expressed in the "I have come" sayings, the sending sayings also make best sense in that framework. To repeat, however, the idea of preexistence in this context does not exclude the elements of Jesus' messianic (or prophetic) identity.

PART THREE

Jesus, the Incarnation of Preexistent Wisdom?

CHAPTER 8

A Critique of the Wisdom
Christology Hypothesis

Lady Wisdom in the OT and Jewish tradition is a very richly characterized figure with a long *curriculum vitae.* Some of the main features of her identity and functions are as follows: she (a) has a unique relation to God himself and remains unknown and mysterious to human beings, (b) is a figure who, on God's behalf, comes to the human realm from heaven and (c) appeals to humanity to turn to her and God, often by sending prophets. However, since (d) she is a figure of impenetrable mystery, in the course of her visitation of the human realm, she (e) is rejected by the great majority, and, having experienced this general rejection, (f) returns to God in heaven.

To tell the story in this way is to invite comparison with the portrait of Jesus in the Gospels. Jesus is depicted as a figure in a uniquely close relationship to God whom God has sent to announce the kingdom of heaven and to summon people to enter it. However, the vast majority of Israel reject his invitation, and this rejection is instantiated in particular in his execution. After this, however, he is raised from the dead and ascends to heaven. Where the controversy arises for our purposes, however, is in whether the use of Wisdom motifs by Matthew, Mark, and Luke leads to the conclusion that Jesus, like Wisdom, has *come from a preexistence in heaven.*

Precisely this line of argument has been proposed fairly recently by Suggs, Christ, and Hamerton-Kelly.[1] They all suggest that because numerous

---

1. M. J. Suggs, *Wisdom, Christology and Law in Matthew's Gospel* (Cambridge: Harvard University Press, 1970); F. Christ, *Jesus Sophia: Die Sophia-Christologie bei den Synoptikern* (ATANT; Zurich: Zwingli, 1970); R. G. Hamerton-Kelly, *Preexistence, Wisdom, and the Son of*

elements of the Wisdom tradition are attributed to Jesus in the Synoptic Gospels (and in particular, in *Matthew's* Gospel) he is thereby being portrayed there as *Wisdom incarnate.* Having come from God's side in heaven, he has come to the human realm as the human manifestation of God's firstborn companion in creation. While these three scholars propose a strong form of this theory, a number of others express it in more moderate terms.[2]

This chapter, then, will explore the hypothesis that Wisdom christology is a promising route toward preexistence. In the first section, we will examine Jesus' and Wisdom's appeals on behalf of God (Matt. 11.28-30; 23.34), as in function (c) above. Secondly, we will explore the analogy drawn between Jesus' and Wisdom's unique relationships to God and their mysterious unknowability, with special reference to Matt. 11.27 par. Luke 10.22, as in (a) above. Thirdly, the motif of Wisdom's rejection and its relation to the rejection of Jesus will be explored through exegesis of Matt. 11.19; Mark 9.19 par.; and Luke 12.50. The ultimate concern of our discussion will remain centered on whether these elements imply that element (b) of Wisdom's activity above (coming from a preexistence in heaven) is attributed to Jesus by the Evangelists.

I. Jesus' and Wisdom's Appeals on Behalf of God

Jesus and Wisdom's "Easy Yoke" (Matthew 11.28-30)

> Come to me all who labor and are burdened, and I will give you rest. Take my yoke upon you, and learn from me, because I am meek and humble in heart. Then you will find rest for your souls. For my burden is pleasant, and my yoke a light one.

The Strong Wisdom Christology Interpretation

The first passage to be discussed here has probably been the most important in discussions of Wisdom christology. The wisdom-based approach to the so-called "Heilandsruf" in Matt. 11.28-30 appears to have flourished when the

---

Man: A Study of the Idea of Preexistence in the New Testament (SNTSMS 21; Cambridge: Cambridge University Press, 1973). There was, as we shall see, also an older tradition of scholarship which took this line.

2. See for example C. Deutsch, *Hidden Wisdom and the Easy Yoke: Wisdom, Torah and Discipleship in Matthew 11:25-30* (JSNTSS; Sheffield: JSOT, 1987).

star of the *religionsgeschichtliche Schule* was in the ascendant.[3] More recently, Stauffer, Christ, and Merklein have advocated a direct identification with Wisdom which also entails Jesus' preexistence,[4] and this has been echoed in English-language scholarship by Hamerton-Kelly.[5] Felix Christ has made one of the most sustained arguments for preexistence here, taking the *Heilandsruf* to be associated principally with the wisdom mythology contained in Ben Sira and the Similitudes of Enoch.[6] In particular, he argues for a strong connection with the call/promise pattern in Sirach 24, where Lady Wisdom calls out:

> Come to me, you who desire me, and be filled with my fruits. For my memorial is better than sweet honey, and my inheritance is better than the honeycomb. Those who eat from me will still be hungry, and those who drink from me will still be thirsty. The one who obeys me will not be put to shame, and those who work for me will not sin. (Sir. 24.19-22)

Even more important is Sirach 51, where the sage's speech contains the themes of the call, the yoke, and rest. These common elements thus cement the connection, so that this chapter becomes the key background to Matt. 11.28-30:

> *Draw near to me, you who are untaught,* and lodge in my school. Why do you say you are lacking in these things, and why are your souls thirsty? I opened my mouth and said, Get these things for yourselves without money. *Put your neck under the yoke, and let your souls receive instruction;* it is to be found nearby. See with your eyes that I have labored little, yet found for myself great *rest.* (Sir. 51.23-27)

These parallels would seem to imply some kind of dependence of Jesus on the wisdom tradition, and seeing a strong connection here leads the scholars noted above to the conclusion of preexistence.

---

3. See for example E. Norden, *Agnostos Theos. Untersuchungen zur Formengeschichte religioser Rede* (Berlin: Teubner, 1913), 280-85; H. Windisch, "Die göttliche Weisheit der Juden und die paulinische Christologie," in A. Deissmann, ed., *Neutestamentliche Studien. Georg Heinrici zu seinem 70. Geburtstag* (Leipzig: Hinrichs, 1914), 220-34 (231).

4. E. Stauffer, *Theologie des Neuen Testaments* (Gütersloh: Mohn, [4]1948), 106-9; H. Merklein, "Zur Entstehung der urchristlichen Aussage vom präexistenten Sohn Gottes," in G. Dautzenberg, H. Merklein, and K. Müller, eds., *Zur Geschichte des Urchristentums* (Freiburg: Herder, 1979), 33-62 (35); Christ, *Jesus Sophia,* 119. See also U. Wilckens, *Weisheit und Torheit. Eine exegetisch-religionsgeschichtliche Untersuchung zu 1. Kor. 1 und 2* (Tübingen: Mohr, 1959), 198-200: ". . . hier die Person Jesu mit der Gestalt von Weisheit verschmolzen ist."

5. Hamerton-Kelly, *Preexistence, Wisdom, and the Son of Man,* 68.

6. Christ, *Jesus Sophia,* 100-119.

Criticisms of the Wisdom Hypothesis

However, other scholars have argued, more cautiously, that the Matthean Jesus is doing little more than making use of several wisdom motifs here, rather than *identifying himself with Wisdom*. Stanton draws attention to three problems with the strong Wisdom-christology reading, some of which were already identified by M. D. Johnson. First, he notes that "the verbal links between Mt 11.28-30 are in fact quite slender." Secondly, "there is nothing in Sirach quite comparable with *two* of the most important clauses in Mt 11.28-29."[7] Another objection from Johnson and Stanton is one of gender: Wisdom is portrayed in strongly feminine terms, and so it is unlikely that this imagery would be regarded as important, after Jesus has very strongly identified himself as the Son.[8] However, perhaps more pertinent is a fundamental difficulty with the way Sirach is used by scholars here.

An Alternative Proposal

One possible solution to the problem of how the language of Matt. 11.28-30 should be construed lies in an analysis of the way in which wisdom typology functions in Sirach itself.

The portrait of Wisdom in Sirach 24 is well known, and needs no detailed exposition here. In brief, she is depicted as an exalted figure who proceeds from the mouth of God and has circumnavigated both the heavens and the earth (Sir. 24.1-6), but has taken up special residence in Israel (24.7-8). She is also depicted in cultic terms, as one who has served before God in the tabernacle (24.10). But the dominant aspect of the portrayal in the chapter uses tree and plant imagery to praise her exalted status, refreshing fruit, and pleasant aroma (24.12-21). In conclusion, we see that all this has actually been in praise of the Law of Moses, with which Wisdom is identified (24.23).

There has also recently been scholarly examination of the way in which Simon ben Onias is depicted in Sirach 50 as the embodiment of this Wisdom.[9] Simon may already lie behind the portrait of Wisdom in Sirach 24, in-

---

7. G. N. Stanton, "Salvation Proclaimed X: Matthew 11:28-30: Comfortable Words?" *ExpT* 94 (1982-83), 3-9 (5).

8. Stanton, "Salvation Proclaimed," 6; cf. M. D. Johnson, "Reflections on a Wisdom Approach to Matthew's Christology," *CBQ* 36 (1974), 44-64 (61-62).

9. C. T. R. Hayward, "Sacrifice and World Order: Some Observations on Ben Sira's Attitude to the Temple Service," in S. W. Sykes, ed., *Sacrifice and Redemption: Durham Essays in Theology* (Cambridge: Cambridge University Press, 1991), 22-34; C. H. T. Fletcher-Louis, "Wisdom Christology and the Partings of the Ways between Judaism and Christianity," in S. E. Porter and

asmuch as Wisdom is depicted there as like a priest in the tabernacle (Sir. 24.10, noted above). Chapter 50 begins with the commendation of Simon for his repair and fortification of the sanctuary (vv. 1-4). While this is clearly his greatest achievement according to the author, there is still much more to be said about his priestly identity and about his similarity to Lady Wisdom. This portrait of Simon draws on a number of features from Sirach 24 which have already been noted by Hayward and Fletcher-Louis. We have seen already (1) the common motif of priestly service, and to this can be added the numerous common natural images: (2) the depiction of both as like a "cedar of Lebanon" (24.13; 50.12; cf. 50.8), and as (3) "like a cypress" (24.13; 50.10). The list continues with both alike being compared with (4) "roses" (24.14; 50.8), (5) "olive trees" (24.14; 50.10) and (6) as growing "beside water" (24.14; 50.8). Finally, (7) the priests who surround Simon in 50.12 are like palm trees, as Wisdom is depicted as like a tall palm tree (24.14). These additional six elements all occur together in the two short, concentrated sections, 24.10-15 and 50.8-12. Presumably the author is emphasizing a degree of identity between Simon and Wisdom rather than simply referring to the plants in his back garden on both occasions. Even though there is no suggestion that preexistence is attributed to him, the clear sense is that Simon in some sense embodies Wisdom/Torah here.

What has not been observed in most studies of Matthew, however, is a second (considerably looser) typology at work in Sirach. This concerns the similarity between the presentations of Wisdom in Sirach 24 and the sage in the conclusion to the book (Sirach 51). Here again, although the textual links are certainly not as strong as those between Wisdom and Simon ben Onias, there are parallels which suggest a characterization of the sage in terms of motifs associated with Wisdom. First, just as Wisdom utters a call to the uninitiated to come to her to learn (24.19), so also the sage who has been instructed by wisdom thereby has the authority to do the same, and to pass on the teaching he has received, saying: "Draw near to me you unlearned, and dwell in the house of learning" (51.23). Second, Wisdom and the sage are both depicted as "opening their mouths" (24.2; 51.25), which implies deliberate speech for the impartation of special knowledge. Finally, the learning which the sage acquired from Wisdom is similar in value to that which he himself is offering.[10]

B. W. R. Pearson, eds., *Christian-Jewish Relations through the Centuries* (JSNTSS; Sheffield: JSOT, 2000), 52-68 (especially 55).

10. This is clear from the fact that the benefits of the teaching of Wisdom and of the sage are both disproportionate to the effort expended: just as the sage inclined his ear a *little* but learned *much* (Sir. 51.27), so also what he offers is an abundance of *gold*, whereas to study in his house of learning may only cost a large amount of *silver* (51.28)!

Clearly, the sage takes on some of the characteristics of Wisdom insofar as he has already learned from her, and thus is in possession of knowledge which he can then teach to others.

Thereafter, one can speak further of a still more distant typology. In Sirach 39, the sage addresses his "holy children," and calls upon them to exhibit the characteristics of wisdom by budding "as a rose growing by the brook of the field," giving a sweet savor like frankincense, and flourishing like a lily, and so on (39.13-14).

It is within this framework of typology that Matt. 11.28-30 can best be situated. But where on the spectrum of connections with Wisdom does Jesus belong? Some scholars, such as Deutsch, have advocated that Matthew is speaking of Jesus as absolutely identified with Wisdom here, such that Jesus assumes in Matthew the place which is occupied in Sirach by the Torah.[11] Others, as noted above, see the embodiment of Wisdom in Simon ben Onias as a helpful analogy. The complexity here lies in the fact that while Jesus is no doubt presented as an extremely exalted figure in Matt. 11.28-30, this effect is not achieved by extremely close correlation of Jesus with Wisdom. Rather, as Stanton has put it, "In short, it is not at all clear that Matthew identifies Jesus as Sophia. The use of some Wisdom themes in 11.28-30 is not being disputed, but they do not seem to be the key to the passage as it now stands in Matthew's Gospel."[12]

We have, then, a loose characterization of Jesus by motifs associated with Wisdom (just as we saw between Wisdom and the sage above). This by no means detracts from the stature of Christ in Matthew 11, however, as the preceding statement in Matt. 11.27 makes clear.[13] It simply appears that it is

11. Deutsch, *Hidden Wisdom and the Easy Yoke,* 130: "The presence of these motifs (invitation, yoke, promise of rest) in our passage, indicates that Matthew is presenting Jesus as Wisdom incarnate, thus making explicit the Wisdom tendencies already present in the Q saying of 11.25-27." Or again, "we believe the presentation of 11.28-30 is analogous to the way in which Wisdom is represented in Sirach 24. There Wisdom comes to reside in Torah, thus becoming 'incarnated' in and identified with Torah. So in Matthew, Wisdom is identified with Jesus as its incarnation" (134). Jesus is both incarnation and teacher of Wisdom. Alternatively, Jesus is "Wisdom personified," and Matthew "uses the notions of mystery and the revelation of hidden things so prevalent in apocalyptic literature and describes the function of Jesus through the myth of personified Wisdom" (142).

12. Stanton, "Salvation Proclaimed," 6.

13. The "hand-over" Christ has received far exceeds what the sage has learned: this can be observed by comparing the relative claims of Sirach and Matthew. In Sirach's depiction of Wisdom, "the first man did not have perfect knowledge of her, nor will the last search her out" (Sir. 24.28). In Matthew 11, by contrast, God has handed over *all things* to the Son, and the Son has exclusive knowledge of the Father.

not the concern of Matthew to present Jesus as identified with preexistent Wisdom in any strong sense.

Jesus' and Wisdom's Appeals through the Prophets (Luke 11.49-51 par. Matthew 23.34)

> Therefore also the Wisdom of God said, "I will send them prophets and apostles, some of whom they will kill and persecute. . . ." (Luke 11.49)

> Therefore I [Jesus] am sending prophets and sages and scribes to you. Some of these you will kill and crucify, and others you will flog in your synagogues and persecute from city to city. . . ." (Matt. 23.34)

We noted at the beginning of this chapter that Wisdom in Jewish tradition does not always make her appeal directly, but is also depicted as the sender of prophets. This is picked up on in Luke 11.49, where the preexistent figure of (personified) Wisdom pronounces that she will send envoys to the Israel of Jesus' generation. There is no sense of the preexistence of Christ here in Luke's statement, however: it is not *Jesus* who is portrayed as the sender of the prophets but Wisdom.[14] In the light of this, despite attempts by some to argue for an identification of Jesus with Wisdom in Luke at this point, such a view is extremely difficult to sustain.

As far as the Matthean version is concerned, the case is often made for Wisdom christology on the basis of Matthew's alleged redaction of the original form of the saying.[15] Matthew thus takes what was originally an utterance of Lady Wisdom and puts it into the mouth of Jesus. In so doing, he identifies Wisdom with Jesus. As a consequence, Matthew appropriates for Jesus the attributes of Wisdom, including preexistence: this is helped by the fact that Wisdom's utterance in Luke 11.49 takes place before the creation of the world, as the reference to Abel implies. Felix Christ, for example, concludes that with the identification of Jesus and Wisdom, the doctrine of the preexistence of Christ is taken on board: "Jesus speaks as Wisdom. Wisdom sends envoys, and Jesus also sends envoys. He appears as identified with her. Thus the following are attributed to Jesus: (a) preexistence; (b) the summons, through the sending of envoys; (c) rejection, in the murder of his envoys; (d) the threat of

---

14. For some of the interpretive options on this passage, see Suggs, *Wisdom, Christology and Law in Matthew's Gospel*, 17-20.

15. Most commentators regard the Lukan version as representing the original form of the hypothetical Q logion.

judgment."[16] In short, "like Wisdom, Jesus is also preexistent."[17] Jesus speaks not only like Wisdom, but *as* Wisdom.[18] Suggs also concludes that in Matthew's Gospel, Wisdom has become incarnate in Jesus.[19] Hamerton-Kelly is equally convinced that both the change of tense from the future to the present, and the change of speaker from Wisdom to Jesus himself "clearly identifies Jesus and preexistent Wisdom."[20] Other scholars arguing for preexistence here include Windisch, Merklein, Feuillet, Wilckens, and Burnett.[21]

However, there are some serious problems with this. Principally, although it is possible that Matthew himself thought of an identification of Jesus and Wisdom, it is scarcely possible that he could expect his readers to pick up on this unless they were somehow privy to his sources and aware of the original content of the saying.[22] It is only by combining the Lukan and Matthean versions that any identification of Jesus with Wisdom could be made.

Secondly, there is an important difference between the Lukan and Matthean versions. Luke personifies Wisdom as speaking *in primeval time* and declaring that she will send prophets and apostles in the future. It is for this reason that she can be described as a preexistent personification. On the other hand, in Matthew, Jesus is speaking *in the time of his earthly ministry* of what he will do. As a result, there is clearly no implication of a preexistent action or utterance of Jesus.[23] As in Matt. 11.28-30, we have some of the features

16. Christ, *Jesus Sophia,* 130: "[Jesus] spricht als die Weisheit. Die Weisheit sendet Boten, und auch Jesus sendet Boten. Er erscheint *identisch* mit ihr. Damit ist nun auf Jesus übertragen worden (a) die Präexistenz, (b) der Ruf (Botensendung), (c) die Ablehnung (Botenmord), (d) die Androhung des Gerichts."

17. Christ, *Jesus Sophia,* 130: "So wie die Weisheit ist auch Jesus präexistent."

18. Christ, *Jesus Sophia,* 133.

19. Suggs, *Wisdom, Christology and Law,* 57.

20. Hamerton-Kelly, *Preexistence, Wisdom and the Son of Man,* 32.

21. Windisch, "Göttliche Weisheit," 231; Merklein, "Zur Entstehung der urchristlichen Aussage vom präexistenten Sohn Gottes," 35-37, 47; A. Feuillet, "Jésus et la Sagesse Divine d'après les Évangiles Synoptiques. Le 'logion johannique' et l'Ancien Testament," *RevB* 62 (1955) 161-96 (196); Wilckens, *Weisheit und Torheit,* 163-64, 197; F. W. Burnett, *The Testament of Jesus-Sophia: A Redaction-Critical Study of the Eschatological Discourse in Matthew* (Washington: University Press of America, 1979), 170-71.

22. As Pregeant wonders, "Can we reasonably imagine that readers not privy to the author's sources would in fact make the identification of Jesus with Wisdom that the redaction seems to intend?" R. Pregeant, "The Wisdom Passages in Matthew's Story," *SBLSP* (1990), 469-93 (470).

23. This would be a problem for Hamerton-Kelly's reading of Matthew's statement here (*Preexistence, Wisdom and the Son of Man,* 33). In this passage, Matthew does not identify Jesus with the Wisdom who sent the prophets in the past; rather, just as Wisdom sent prophets in the past, so Jesus will send prophets, wise men, and scribes in the future. Von Lips notes in this con-

of Wisdom drawn in to contribute to the characterization of Jesus, but not an identification of the two figures.

II. Jesus and Wisdom's Mysterious Unknowability (Luke 10.21-22 par. Matthew 11.25-27)

> At that time, Jesus replied, "I thank you, Father, lord of heaven and earth, because you have concealed these things from the wise and clever, and revealed them to little children. Yes, Father, for such was your gracious will. All things have been handed over to me by my Father, and no one knows the Son except the Father, neither does anyone know the Father except the Son [Luke 10.22: 'no one knows who the Son is except the Father, or who the Father is except the Son'], and those to whom the Son chooses to reveal him." (Matt. 11.25-27)[24]

The second principal argument made for preexistence via Wisdom christology is through the portrayal of Jesus in Matt. 11.27. The most extensive arguments for this position are made by Celia Deutsch and Felix Christ, though it is the latter who emphasizes that the presence of Wisdom motifs implies Jesus' preexistence: "the idea of preexistence is not explicitly expressed in Matthew 11.25-27, but is included in the fact that the Son appears as divine Wisdom in person."[25] In this passage, Jesus and Wisdom share an important and rare characteristic — that of mysterious unknowability and secrecy.[26] This is a widely assumed personality trait of Lady Wisdom in Jewish tradition; Agur

---

nection, "Der bei Q (Lk 11,50) implizierte Gedanke der Präexistenz der Weisheit entfällt bei Mt durch die Streichung des Hinweises auf den Beginn der Welt sowie durch die präsentische Formulierung der Sendungsaussage." H. von Lips, *Weisheitliche Traditionen im NT* (WMANT 64; Neukirchen: Neukirchener, 1990), 281.

24. On the text-critical issues, see A. Harnack, *The Sayings of Jesus: The Second Source of St. Matthew and St. Luke* (London: Williams and Norgate, 1908), 272-301; J. Chapman, "Dr Harnack on Luke x 22: No Man Knoweth the Son," *JTS* 10 (1908-9), 552-66; P. Winter, "Mt XI 27 and Lk X 22 from the First to the Fifth Century: Reflections on the Development of the Text," *NovT* 1 (1956), 112-48. Winter's analysis, though comprehensive, has not persuaded many.

25. Christ, *Jesus Sophia*, 91: "Der Präexistenzgedanke ist im Jubelruf nicht explizit ausgesprochen, aber darin enthalten, daß der Sohn als die göttliche Weisheit in Person erscheint."

26. Feuillet, "Jésus et la Sagesse Divine," 189, for whom it has more to do with Jesus' divine being (190 n. 3). Feuillet offers two grounds: first, the mutuality of the knowing, and secondly, that the unknowability of the Son points to his divinity. Jesus is both divine wisdom and the heavenly Danielic Messiah (194). On the Son and Wisdom as "secret," see Windisch, "Göttliche Weisheit," 231: "Daß der Sohn ein Geheimnis sei, in das kein Mensch eindringt, nur Gott allein, ist eine Anschauung, die erstmalig der Weisheit zugeschrieben worden ist."

says of the divine arrangement of the world in Prov. 30.18-19: "Three things are too wonderful for me; four I do not understand: the way of an eagle in the sky, the way of a serpent on a rock, the way of a ship on the high seas, and the way of a man with a maiden." Earlier in the chapter, Agur asks who has managed to gain Wisdom: "I have not learned Wisdom, nor have I knowledge of the Holy One. Who has ascended to heaven and come down? Who has gathered the wind in his fists? Who has wrapped up the waters in a garment . . . ?" (Prov. 30.3-4). Similarly, in Matthew 11 the Son is unknown to anyone except the Father and those to whom he chooses to reveal himself.[27] But the similarities are rather limited. Again, the problem of the very masculine definition of Jesus as "Son" in Matthew 11 and Luke 10 makes it doubtful that hearers or readers would pick up on the association with Wisdom. Similarly, she is not really depicted as one who stands in the same relationship to God as the Son here, or as one who has the power of election. As a result, Matt. 11.27 does not offer much help to the case for Wisdom christology in the Synoptics. The same also applies to Luke's version.

III. Jesus and Wisdom's Discomfort in the World

We addressed above the question of whether Sirach 51 formed part of the background to the christology of Matthew 11. Here we move to the other key passage in Jewish tradition which is often discussed at this point:

> Wisdom found no place in which she could dwell, and her dwelling was in heaven. Wisdom went out in order to dwell among the sons of men, but did not find a dwelling; Wisdom returned to her place and took her seat in the midst of the angels. (1 Enoch 42.1-2, tr. Knibb)

Here, then, we come to examine a group of passages in which Jesus' rejection and discomfort in this world is alleged to resemble that of Lady Wisdom.

Wisdom and Her Deeds/Children
(Matthew 11.18-19 par. Luke 7.33-35)

> For John came neither eating nor drinking, and they say, "He has a demon." The Son of Man came eating and drinking, and they say, "Look

27. Christ, *Jesus Sophia*, 99: "Wie die präexistente Weisheit ist Jesus Sophia der Masse (Weisen und Verständigen) verborgen, einzelnen Erwählten (Unmündigen) aber offenbar."

— a glutton and a drunkard, a friend of tax collectors and sinners!" And wisdom is absolved of her actions (Luke: "children").

First, we come to the parable of the children who play in the street and complain that other people (or perhaps other children) are not joining in. Jesus draws a parallel with his contemporaries in "this generation" who wanted John the Baptist to be rather less of a spoilsport. Jesus on the other hand was far too worldly for their comfort.[28] Jesus next describes the behavior of both himself and John in Matt. 11.18-19a par. Luke 7.33-34. Following this description of John the Baptist, Jesus then says, according to most translators and commentators: "But Wisdom will be justified by her deeds/children" (Matt. 11.19b par. Luke 7.35). That is, despite the disapproval of this generation, it is inevitable that God in his wisdom will be shown to be right after all.

Wisdom Christology in Matthew 11.19b?

In scholarly discussion of Matt. 11.19b par. Luke 7.35, scholars vary in their assessment of its contribution to christology. Schenke seems prompted simply by the mention of wisdom to talk of the preexistence of Jesus,[29] and Breech makes the connection with the marketplace in Matthew 11.16 and the marketplace as the location of Wisdom's call in Proverbs 8, concluding: "The appended saying interprets Jesus as the heavenly Wisdom who comes down to earth and calls men in the marketplace but they do not heed (Proverbs 8)."[30]

The standard way, however, in which a strong Wisdom christology is argued for here is as follows. The original Q saying read as we have it in Luke: not "wisdom is justified by her deeds" but "wisdom is justified by (all) her children."[31] Matthew, then, takes this saying and raises the christological stakes by altering "children" to "deeds." Some have attributed this to two separate renderings of an Aramaic original, but this interpretation has fallen

---

28. In contrast to the view of D. Verseput, *The Rejection of the Humble Messianic King: A Study of the Composition of Matthew 11–12* (Europäische Hochschulschriften; New York: Lang, 1986), 114, here, the preservation of the sequence in each case seems more probable than a chiasm. Verseput also exaggerates the difference between the goals of John's and Jesus' ministries.

29. L. Schenke, *Die Urgemeinde. Geschichtliche und theologische Entwicklung* (Stuttgart: Kohlhammer, 1990), 339: "Jesus spricht hier als die präexistente göttliche Weisheit."

30. J. Breech, *The Silence of Jesus: The Authentic Voice of the Historical Man* (Philadelphia: Augsburg, 1987), 25 (on Matt. 11.19).

31. A number of scholars think that the "all" is not original to the hypothetical Q saying. See for example W. J. Cotter, "The Parable of the Children in the Market-Place, Q (Lk) 7:31-35: An Examination of the Parable's Image and Significance," *NovT* 29 (1987), 289-304 (292-93).

from favor.[32] The significance, it is alleged, lies in the fact that in Matt. 11.2 John the Baptist has heard about "the deeds of the Christ," which forms an *inclusio* with the deeds of Wisdom in v. 19. As a result, the conclusion is drawn that Matthew has identified the deeds of Wisdom with the deeds of Jesus and therefore has identified Jesus with Wisdom. This reading has been taken up by many, although not all who argue for wisdom christology talk in terms of preexistence.[33] However, a number of scholars such as Suggs, Hamerton-Kelly, and Christ do deduce the preexistence of Christ here.[34] Merklein and Schweizer also imply sympathy for such a reading.[35]

Objections to the Wisdom Christology Hypothesis

Since the key point here has been argued at length elsewhere, we will confine the discussion here to some brief observations.[36] The principal problem with this interpretation lies in the strained connection between the deeds of Christ in Matt. 11.2 and the deeds of Wisdom here in 11.19b. Rather, the previous reference to *the ministries of John and Jesus* provides a much stronger and more immediate context for these deeds of Wisdom. Wisdom's works are in fact manifest in *both* John *and* Jesus, as they announce the kingdom. The difference between their lifestyles is not simply a matter of how these two basically similar prophets happened to turn out, but is a function of God's deliberate strategy to convict this last generation of sin. The deeds of Wisdom, then, are the ministries of both John and Jesus, and there is no identification of Wisdom with Jesus.[37]

32. P. M. Casey, *An Aramaic Approach to Q: Sources for the Gospels of Matthew and Luke* (SNTSMS; Cambridge: Cambridge University Press, 2002), 142.

33. Schweizer, for example, talks about the incarnation of Wisdom in Jesus in Matt. 11.19 par. Luke 7.35 and Matt. 23.34 par. Luke 11.49. E. Schweizer, "Aufnahme und Korrektur jüdischer Sophiatheologie im Neuen Testament," in idem, *Neotestamentica. Deutsche und Englische Aufsätze, 1951-1963/German and English Essays, 1951-1963* (Zurich: Zwingli, 1963), 110-21 (110). But his commentaries show that he is not thinking in terms of preexistence.

34. Suggs, *Wisdom, Christology and Law*, 100-108; Hamerton-Kelly, *Preexistence, Wisdom, and the Son of Man*, 42; Christ, *Jesus Sophia*, 80.

35. Schweizer, "Aufnahme und Korrektur," 110; Merklein, "Zur Entstehung der urchristlichen Aussage vom präexistenten Sohn Gottes," 35; cf. also "Im Kontext von Q ist durch V.35b aber eindeutig, daß jetzt Jesus der Sprecher ist und damit die Attribute der Weisheit auf sich gezogen hat" (Merklein, "Zur Entstehung," 36).

36. S. J. Gathercole, "The Justification of Wisdom (Matt 11.19b/Luke 7.35)," *NTS* 49 (2003), 476-88.

37. Thus F. Mussner, "Der nicht erkannte Kairos (Mt 11,16-19 = Lk 7,31-35)," *Biblica* 40 (1959), 599-612 (611): "Aber in der Schlußsentenz sind nicht mehr bloß die 'Taten' des Messias Jesus gemeint, sondern auch die 'Taten' des Täufers."

Jesus and This Unfaithful Generation

> Jesus said to them in reply, "O faithless generation, how long will I be with you? How long must I endure you? Bring him to me." (Mark 9.19 par. Matt. 17.17; Luke 9.41)

We have seen in the course of this chapter that it is generally Matthew's Gospel which is mined for a Wisdom christology; this saying, however, is common to all three Synoptics. In it, Jesus laments the lack of faith on the part of "this generation," most likely on the grounds that it is this unbelief which has prevented the disciples from driving out an evil spirit.[38] It is probably true to say that the majority of commentators do not see any suspicious signs of preexistence or wisdom christology in this saying. Hooker, for example, does not even mention the possibility.[39] Pesch sees Jesus' statement merely as that of an eschatological *prophet,* pointing to the numerous OT parallels to the phrase "how long. . . ."[40] On the other hand, a number of scholars see Jesus here cast as a heavenly figure,[41] or at least as speaking from a heavenly perspective.[42] Moreover, a number go further and talk of Jesus in divine terms.

A Preexistent Divine Figure?

The classic interpretation of this saying in terms of preexistence came from M. Dibelius, who commenting on Mark 9.19 writes: "Thus speaks the god

38. As M. D. Hooker (*A Commentary on the Gospel according to St. Mark* [Black's New Testament Commentary; London: Black, 1991], 223) and R. H. Gundry (*Mark: A Commentary on His Apology for the Cross* [Grand Rapids: Eerdmans, 1993], 497) argue, Jesus himself is prevented from working miracles by the unbelief of others in Mark 6.1-6. It is unnecessary, then, to argue that the reference is to the unbelief of the disciples. It would, in any case, be strange to refer to the disciples as "this generation."

39. Hooker, *Mark,* 223.

40. R. Pesch, *Das Markusevangelium* (HTK; Freiburg: Herder, 1976), 2:90. However, Pesch has also come under heavy fire from Gundry and Frenschkowski. Both note that Pesch's parallels work for the question "How long will I put up with you?" but not for "How long will I *be with you?*" M. Frenschkowski, *Offenbarung und Epiphanie* (WUNT; Tübingen: Mohr, 1995), 173; Gundry, *Mark,* 497. In fact, Frenschkowski criticizes Pesch for simply dragging his parallels out of a concordance without any attention to real parallels of content or context.

41. E. Schweizer, *The Good News according to Mark* (London: SPCK, 1971), 188: "He does not belong to this 'unbelieving generation' but stands diametrically opposed to it. He stands at God's side, grieving with God at the distress caused by such unbelief."

42. C. A. Evans, *Mark 8:27–16:20* (WBC; Nashville: Nelson, 2001), 51: "Jesus has adopted God's viewpoint."

who appeared only temporarily in human form quickly to return to heaven."[43] This is largely on the basis of the statement "how long shall I be with you?"[44] Around the same time, Windisch argued on the basis of the close connection of Mark 9.19 with the transfiguration. Since the transfiguration was not merely a revelation of Jesus' *future* glory, but of his true nature, the question "how long will I be with you?" soon after evinces this same divine man christology, with Jesus longing to return whence he came.[45] A number of German scholars such as Klostermann, Kertelge, and L. Schenke reflect the view of Dibelius here.[46] This line is not taken nearly so frequently in English-language scholarship, although Nineham remarks similarly: "Jesus speaks here as an incarnate deity whose human form and earthly existence are only temporary and who already has one foot in the next world."[47] The majority of commentators would furthermore view this epiphanic language as a later product of Hellenistic communities, although Grundmann seems to be an exception here.[48] H.-M. Schenke and Fischer support the overall exegesis, but see preexistence as having become redundant for Mark.[49] Most re-

43. M. Dibelius, *From Tradition to Gospel* (London: Nicholson and Watson, 1934), 278. For some of the numerous references to the influence of Dibelius in later scholarship on this point, see Frenschkowski, *Offenbarung und Epiphanie,* 172 n. 114.

44. Frenschkowski, *Offenbarung und Epiphanie,* 171-76, 198.

45. H. Windisch, "Urchristentum und Hermesmystik," *Theologisch Tijdschrift* 52 (1918), 186-240 (217-18); see also now O. Hofius, "Die Allmacht des Sohnes Gottes und das Gebet des Glaubens," *ZTK* 101 (2004), 117-37, who argues for a similar relation between the two pericopes.

46. E. Klostermann, *Das Markusevangelium* (HNT; Tübingen: Mohr, [5]1971), 91: ". . . nicht aus der gegenwärtigen Situation, dem Gegensatz gegen die Zeichen verlangenden Juden zu verstehn *(sic)* sondern als Wort eines Gottes" (following Dibelius); K. Kertelge, *Die Wunder Jesu im Markusevangelium. Eine redaktionsgeschichtliche Untersuchung* (Munich: Kösel, 1970), 179; L. Schenke, "Gibt es im Markusevangelium eine Präexistenzchristologie?" *ZNW* 91 (2000), 45-71 (64).

47. D. E. Nineham, *The Gospel of Saint Mark* (Harmondsworth: Penguin, 1969), 243: "Jesus speaks here as an incarnate deity whose human form and earthly existence are only temporary and who already has one foot in the next world." For another example, see A. D. Nock, "Early Gentile Christianity and Its Hellenistic Background," in idem, *Essays on Religion and the Ancient World* (Oxford: Clarendon, 1972), 1:89 n. 167.

48. W. Grundmann, *Das Evangelium nach Markus* (THKNT; Berlin: Evangelische, [3]1968), 190: "In einer fast johanneischen Weise zeigt diese Klage Jesu als den, der aus einer anderen Welt kommt und in eine andere Welt geht und auf eine bestimmte Zeit als Fremder bei Menschen weilen muß, deren Ursprung ein anderer ist als seine."

49. H.-M. Schenke and K. M. Fischer, *Einleitung in die Schriften des Neuen Testaments II. Die Evangelien und die anderen neutestamentlichen Schriften* (Gütersloh: Mohn, 1978), 72. Schenke and Fischer identify a number of characteristics of the christology of Mark, for example: "Jesus wird im Markus-Evangelium gezeigt zugleich also θεῖος ἀνήρ, als präexistentes göttliches Wesen, als Prophet," etc. However, the dimension of preexistence, while presupposed

cently, Frenschkowski has articulated a view which seems similar: "The divinity is tired of interaction with humanity: he longs for a return to the heavenly existence which is free of trouble."[50] However, Frenschkowski is very skeptical about whether there is any association with Wisdom here.[51] Others, however, do take this step.

Jesus as Wisdom Incarnate?

It is Feuillet who most explicitly refers to Jesus in terms of preexistent divine Wisdom. Feuillet sees Mark 9.19 as one of a number of places at which the Synoptic Gospels talk in these terms: "he often behaves as a divine being whose true home is in heaven, or more precisely, as the divine Wisdom who has come down from heaven to earth to deliver her message to the world."[52] He understands Mark's statement here as echoing precisely the sentiments of the *1 Enoch* passage quoted above. However, we ought to be cautious here in view of the fact there is very little verbal resemblance between Mark 9.19 and *1 Enoch* 42. There is a certain conceptual parallelism, but it is rather weak.

Despite Pesch's failure to make the saying simply a prophetic lament, we should be still cautious before attributing preexistence to Jesus as a result. The logic of Mark 9.19 does not require a theology of preexistence: to ask how long one *will* be somewhere does not necessarily imply a previous existence elsewhere. What it does require, however, is a theology of *post*-existence. Gundry also notes that there is a motif within Jesus' own teaching that provides a better context for his temporary stay with "this generation": that of his approaching death and resurrection (Mark 8.31; 9.12, etc.).[53] Within this framework, then, it makes more sense to focus attention on the fact that Jesus' mind is directed toward his destiny rather than toward his origin in heaven.

---

and appearing occasionally, has lost its significance: "für das Markus-Evangelium keine Bedeutung (mehr) hat."

50. Frenschkowski, *Offenbarung und Epiphanie,* 174-75: "Die Gottheit ist des Umganges mit den Menschen müde; sie sehnt sich zurück in die Unbeschwertheit der himmlischen Existenz."

51. Frenschkowski, *Offenbarung und Epiphanie,* 174.

52. Feuillet, "Jésus et la Sagesse Divine," 196: "il se comporte souvent comme un être divin dont la véritable patrie est au ciel, ou plus précisément encore comme la Sagesse divine descendue du ciel sur la terre pour délivrer au monde son message."

53. Gundry, *Mark,* 497.

"I Have a Baptism to Undergo, and How I Lament Until It Is Accomplished" (Luke 12.50)

Very similar to Mark 9.19 is the saying unique to Luke in Luke 12.50. Here, Bultmann sees a possible fragment of the Gnostic myth of salvation, where it is the words "how I lament until it is accomplished" which depend on an understanding of preexistence.[54] He implies that it refers to the "frequently depicted anxiety of the one who has been sent, which he feels because he is a stranger in this world," noting the parallel in John 12.27 ("Now is my soul troubled; and what shall I say? Father, save me from this hour. But for this cause came I unto this hour."). As such, "there would be no genuine dominical saying as the source of Lk 12.49f., but a section (a quotation?) of the Wisdom myth would have been transferred to his lips."[55] However, the same applies here as with Mark 9.19. The focus of Jesus' lament is on his future destiny rather than being retrospective. He does not express a desire to return to where he has come from, but simply for his work to be finished.

Conclusion to Matthew 11.19 par. Luke 7.35; Mark 9.19 par.; Luke 12.50

As a result, there is no clear indication in these sayings of either wisdom christology or preexistence christology. In Matt. 11.19, the reference to Wisdom is in connection with Jesus and John alike. If the laments of Mark 9.19 and Luke 12.50 are oriented toward Jesus' death and resurrection (or even ascension?), then they are merely forward-looking and do not say anything about where Jesus has come from. They do not tap into the Jewish tradition of Wisdom longing to return to her heavenly home. In conclusion, then, for these verses the question of preexistence must remain an open one. In conjunction with other motifs such as the "I have come" sayings, the statements here fit well into a framework of preexistence, but do not themselves give evidence for it.

---

54. R. Bultmann, *History of the Synoptic Tradition* (Oxford: Blackwell, 1968), 153-54, also offers other possible readings and it is rather difficult to see which he is espousing. At this point he is more interested in what the passage cannot mean if attributed to Jesus himself.

55. Bultmann, *History of the Synoptic Tradition*, 154.

Conclusion

We have seen, then, that rumors of a full-blown Wisdom christology in the Synoptics have in some circles been greatly exaggerated, even in the case of Matthew's Gospel. There is little sense of the Evangelists tapping into the kind of descent-ascent schema implied in texts from the Wisdom tradition such as *1 Enoch* 42. Nevertheless, it is certainly the case that *some* Wisdom motifs are drawn in for the portrayal of Jesus in the Synoptic Gospels — most explicitly in Matt. 11.28-30 and 23.34. But, as Pregeant notes, attributing some aspects of wisdom to Jesus does not a doctrine of preexistence make.[56]

Another important consideration is that, in fact, even if there was such strong use of Wisdom motifs that an identification with Wisdom seemed inevitable, this would still not necessarily entail preexistence. The key factor here is that Wisdom was, by and large, not regarded in Judaism as a preexistent *entity* distinct from or independent of God, but rather as an attribute of God and a way of speaking about his purpose: in short, a personification rather than a person. And as G. B. Caird has observed, "there is all the difference in the world between a preexistent personification and a preexistent person."[57] As a result, identification of Jesus with Wisdom would — if one were convinced of the exegetical case — still only mean that he was in some sense the *embodiment* of God's creative activity and redemptive purpose, rather than the *incarnation* of an actually preexistent person or being.

We have thus far omitted mention of one passage which has played a key role in discussions of Wisdom christology. We have done so because the passage in question deserves special treatment, to which we now turn.

---

56. R. Pregeant, "The Wisdom Passages in Matthew's Story," 476, following E. Schweizer, *Matthäus und seine Gemeinde* (Stuttgart: Katholisches Bibelwerk, 1974), 56-57.

57. G. B. Caird (L. D. Hurst, ed.), *New Testament Theology* (Oxford: Clarendon, 1994), 340.

CHAPTER 9

The Preexistent Christ and the History of Israel
(Matthew 23.37)

> "Jerusalem, Jerusalem, who kills the prophets and stones those sent to
> her — *how often have I desired to gather your children* (ποσάκις ἠθέλησα
> ἐπισυναγαγεῖν τὰ τέκνα σου), as a bird gathers her nestlings under her
> wings. But you have not been willing. Behold, your house is left to you
> desolate, for I say to you, you will not see me from now until you say,
> 'Blessed is he who comes in the name of the Lord.'" And Jesus went
> forth from the temple and set off, and his disciples came to him to point
> out the temple buildings to him. (Matt. 23:37-24:1)

We noted in chapter 2 above that of all the Synoptic Gospels, Matthew tends
to emphasize the most exalted features of Jesus and the most honorific responses to him. The focus of this chapter will be to show that Matthew alone
portrays Christ as having been intimately involved in the entire duration of
Israel's history. There was an explosion of this kind of christology in the second century, and it can be seen in particular in the writings of Justin.[1] But
even in the first century, the preexistent Christ's involvement in history before
his incarnation was presumed: for example, in the "rock" incident of Numbers 20 (1 Cor. 10.4), and in the vision of Yhwh in Isaiah 6 (John 12.41). More
controversially, we also argued the same point for Jude 5 in chapter 1 above.

---

1. See, e.g., D. C. Trakatellis, *The Preexistence of Christ in the Writings of Justin Martyr*
(Chico: Scholars, 1976); L. W. Hurtado, *Lord Jesus Christ: Devotion to Jesus in Earliest Christianity* (Grand Rapids: Eerdmans, 2003), 564-78.

Matthew also reasons in the same way, portraying Jesus as one who has historically been calling Israel — albeit unsuccessfully — to repentance: "how often have I desired to gather your children as a bird gathers her nestlings under her wings. But you have not been willing."

I. Wisdom Christology in Matthew 23.37-39: Recent Approaches

As was discussed in the previous chapter, one way in which scholars have argued for this kind of preexistence in the past has been via Wisdom christology.[2] Matt. 23.37-39 in general and the saying in v. 37 in particular have been seen by many as identifying Jesus in a strong sense with Wisdom. First, some have argued that v. 37 has its origin in a pre-Christian source. Bultmann and Hamerton-Kelly take the view that a Jewish Wisdom saying has been attributed to Jesus here.[3] Even if that is the case, however, it would not be sufficient to identify Jesus with Wisdom.

Second, Suggs sees the exalted imagery of the statement as sure-fire evidence that it reflects far too high a christology to be authentic: "The saying cannot be attributed to Jesus. The sentence, 'How often would I have gathered your children together as a hen gathers her brood under her wings' is in itself sufficient proof of that. The metaphor requires a heavenly, indeed a divine being."[4] As such, Suggs concludes that "Matthew intends the saying to be understood as a word of incarnate Wisdom whom he sees in Jesus."[5] Third, Wilckens draws on the aspect of Wisdom's *rejection:* "The wisdom myth stands even more plainly behind the threat against Jerusalem: as the wisdom which has come down from heaven, which seeks a home (Eth. En. 42) and which preaches (Prov. 1:20-33), Jesus wanted to gather the inhabitants of Jerusalem around him, but they 'would not,' so that judgment now hangs over them."[6]

---

2. The interpretation of Matt. 23.37-39 along the lines of Wisdom christology seems to have been pioneered by D. F. Strauss, "Jesu Weheruf über Jerusalem und die σοφία τοῦ θεοῦ," *Zeitschrift für die Wissenschaftliche Theologie* 6 (1863), 84-93.

3. R. Bultmann, *History of the Synoptic Tradition* (Oxford: Blackwell, 1968), 114; R. G. Hamerton-Kelly, *Preexistence, Wisdom, and the Son of Man: A Study of the Idea of Preexistence in the New Testament* (SNTSMS 21; Cambridge: Cambridge University Press, 1973), 32.

4. M. J. Suggs, *Wisdom, Christology and Law in Matthew's Gospel* (Cambridge: Harvard University Press, 1970), 66.

5. Suggs, *Wisdom, Christology and Law*, 67.

6. U. Wilckens, "σοφία," *TDNT,* 7:465-526 (515). See also idem, *Weisheit und Torheit. Eine exegetisch-religionsgeschichtliche Untersuchung zu 1. Kor. 1 und 2* (Tübingen: Mohr, 1959), 164.

Fourth, Burnett takes this even further and notes intriguingly that Matt. 23.38 and 24.1 also point in the direction of a *sophia* christology. Here he argues that it is significant that Jesus pronounces, "Behold, your house is left to you desolate," and then leaves the Temple. For Burnett, this represents "Jesus-Sophia's definitive withdrawal from Israel."[7] So when the Evangelist reports in 24.1 that "Jesus went out and set off from the temple" (ἐξελθὼν ὁ Ἰησοῦς ἀπὸ τοῦ ἱεροῦ ἐπορεύετο), we are witnessing the fact that "when his presence leaves the temple in 24.1, the judgment of 23.38 is fulfilled."[8] Here, Burnett sees a clear reference to a christology which taps into ideas about the relationship between Wisdom and Israel. As he puts it, "The judgment comes to Israel also because they have rejected Jesus, the Sophia-Shekinah of God. Consequently, Israel will not have the presence of Jesus-Sophia again until he returns as Son of Man."[9]

On the basis of the preexistence of Wisdom and her descent to earth and subsequent rejection, a number conclude that Matthew presupposes the identification of Jesus with *preexistent* Wisdom in Matt. 23.37-39. Christ sees an *implicit* reference to preexistence here.[10] Hamerton-Kelly again sees ideal preexistence in the frame.[11] Bultmann sees the speaker as "a supra-historical entity namely, Wisdom."[12] Other scholars who also explicitly articulate a robust sense of preexistence on the basis of Jesus' identification with Wisdom here include Feuillet, Suggs, Burnett, Merklein, and Riesner,[13] as well as, as we have seen, Wilckens.[14]

---

7. F. W. Burnett, *The Testament of Jesus-Sophia: A Redaction-Critical Study of the Eschatological Discourse in Matthew* (Washington: University Press of America, 1979), 112, following, e.g., E. Schweizer, *The Good News according to Matthew* (London: SPCK, 1976), 448.

8. Burnett, *Testament of Jesus-Sophia*, 116.

9. Burnett, *Testament of Jesus-Sophia*, 80. Here he is following Christ closely.

10. F. Christ, *Jesus Sophia. Die Sophia-Christologie bei den Synoptikern* (ATANT 57; Zurich: Zwingli, 1970), 152.

11. Hamerton-Kelly, *Preexistence, Wisdom, and the Son of Man*, 32-33.

12. Bultmann, *History of the Synoptic Tradition*, 114.

13. A. Feuillet, "Jésus et la Sagesse Divine d'après les Évangiles Synoptiques. Le 'logion johannique' et l'Ancien Testament," *RevB* 62 (1955), 161-96 (196); Suggs, *Wisdom, Christology and Law*, 66-67; Burnett, *Testament of Jesus-Sophia*, 170-71; H. Merklein, "Zur Entstehung der urchristlichen Aussage vom präexistenten Sohn Gottes," in G. Dautzenberg, H. Merklein, and K. Müller, eds., *Zur Geschichte des Urchristentums* (Freiburg: Herder, 1979), 33-62 (35 and especially 55-57); R. Riesner, "Präexistenz und Jungfrauengeburt," *Theologische Beiträge* 12 (1981), 177-87 (180-81). Riesner also argues strongly for the authenticity of these statements, arguing (following M. Plath, "Der neutestamentliche Weheruf über Jerusalem [Luk 13,34-35 = Matth. 23,37-39]," *TSK* 78 [1905], 455-60) that it would be impossible for an absent, *risen* Jesus to say the words in Matt. 23.39. This would counter R. J. Miller's contention (in "The Rejection of the Prophets in Q," *JBL* 107 [1988], 225-40 [238]) that it is the risen Jesus speaking in Matt. 23.37.

14. Wilckens, "σοφία," 515.

However, as we saw with the other passages discussed in the previous chapter, there are several problems with this Wisdom christology reading of Matt. 23.37-39. First, it is often part of an argument that finds Wisdom christology throughout Matthew: this we have already questioned. Second, the approach which reads 23.34-39 in particular as a seamless robe in which Jesus speaks in the person of Wisdom is problematic. Although there are Wisdom motifs employed in 23.34-36, the perspective of v. 37 is very different: Jesus moves from prophecy in the earlier verses to a comment on the *past* in v. 37. A number of scholars have already noted the way in which 23.37-39 cannot simply be regarded as a continuation of 23.34-36 because of this very different temporal perspective.[15]

Third, even if those scholars who argue for the presence of Wisdom motifs in Matt. 23.37-39 are correct, it is clearly not a dominant theme. Of the three motifs of Wisdom, the glory of God, and Jesus' divine identity in longing to gather Israel, the Wisdom aspect is the weakest. Nevertheless, Suggs is indeed correct to talk in terms of a heavenly, indeed divine, speaker here, pointing to the frequency of the "gathering" image in connection with God (on which more below). As we saw in connection with 23.34, the simplest solution is again to see the primary substructure of Jesus' teaching and activity as a christology of divine identity. Similarly, the depiction of Jesus as the glorious presence of God in the temple seems implied in the connection between verses 38 and 39: "Behold, your house is left to you desolate, *for* I say to you, you will not see me again until. . . ."[16] It seems the "ichabod" of v. 38 is pronounced precisely because Jesus is abandoning the temple. There are, then, several divine images used in v. 37, and "Wisdom" does not by any means seem especially prominent among them.

15. D. Zeller, "Entrückung zur Ankunft als Menschensohn (Lk 13, 34f.; 11, 29f.)," in F. Refoulé, ed., *À cause de l'Évangile. Études sur les Synoptiques et les Actes Offertes au P. Jacques Dupont, O.S.B., à l'occasion de son 70ème Anniversaire* (Paris: Cerf, 1985), 513-30 (514 n. 5), refers to "die unterschiedliche Zeitperspektive," following J. Dupont, *Les Béatitudes* (Paris: Gabalda, 1969-73), 2:305-8, and E. Haenchen, "Matthäus 23," in J. Lange, ed., *Das Matthäus-Evangelium* (Darmstadt: Wissenschaftliche Buchgesellschaft, 1980), 134-63 (151). Plath, "Der neutestamentliche Weheruf über Jerusalem," 457, had already made this point in 1905. She talks of "keine organische Einheit" in the two statements. Her argument, however, that Matt. 23.37-39 is a quotation of a saying of a prophet from a lost apocryphon is somewhat speculative, however (see 456-59).

16. On v. 39, see D. C. Allison, "Matt. 23:39–Luke 13:35b as a Conditional Prophecy," *JSNT* 18 (1983), 75-84.

II. Preexistence in Jesus' "How Often Have I Longed . . ." (Matthew 23.37)

Even though there is no identification of Jesus with preexistent Wisdom in Matthew 23 at this point, it will nevertheless be argued here that the reference to "how often" in connection with Jesus' attitude to Jerusalem portrays Jesus in Matthew's Gospel as a transcendent figure who has been summoning Israel to repentance throughout her history. Although we have disagreed with Burnett's emphasis on Wisdom christology in the interpretation of Matt. 23.37-39, we can to a large extent agree with his statement that "for Matthew, Jesus is a trans-historical figure."[17] The only qualification which should be issued at this point is that terms such as "trans-historical" and certainly "supra-historical" should be used with care.[18] This is because they may imply the transcendence of history altogether, whereas the depiction of Jesus here is clearly as one longing for Israel's repentance through successive generations *within* history.

There are four key elements which point to preexistence in the statement in Matt. 23.37: first, there is the narrative framework of Matthew's Gospel as a whole, in which this particular saying is striking because Jesus has not yet been to Jerusalem; second, there is the context in ch. 23, in which Jesus pronounces his verdict on both present and past generations of Israel alike; third, there is the content of the saying itself; and fourth, there is the inadequacy of the alternative explanations.

The Narrative Framework of Matthew's Gospel

The first reason, then, why it is striking that Jesus should address Jerusalem with the words "how often have I longed to gather you" is that *within the narrative of Matthew's Gospel, Jesus has neither been to Jerusalem, nor expressed any feeling about the city in his ministry up to this point.* There are frequent references to others coming from Jerusalem to Jesus (3.5; 4.25; 15.1), and Jesus refers in the Sermon on the Mount to "swearing by Jerusalem" (5.35), and talks (in 16.21) of his need ultimately to go to Jerusalem. But there is no sense of his

17. Burnett, *Testament of Jesus-Sophia*, 171.
18. Both adjectives seem to be derived from Bultmann's reference to Wisdom as "übergeschichtlich." See R. Bultmann, *Die Geschichte der Synoptischen Tradition* (Göttingen: Vandenhoeck und Ruprecht, 1921), 69, where he describes the speaker of Matt. 23.39 as "ein übergeschichtliches Subjekt." As we have seen, it is rendered "suprahistorical" in Bultmann, *History of the Synoptic Tradition*, 114.

spiritual burden for the city during his ministry: Jerusalem is somewhat distant until right at the end.[19] Hence Beare refers to the incongruity of Jesus' statement in 23.37: "'How often' — strange enough here, stranger still in Luke, where it is spoken before Jesus has even reached Jerusalem (Lk. 13:34). As the story is told in the Synoptic Gospels, Jesus has never once been in Jerusalem since his ministry began."[20] Of course, one might presume that the reader would take it as understood that Jesus had regularly been to Jerusalem to celebrate festivals, but Matthew draws no attention to this point.

The Context in Matthew 23

In Matt. 23.1-28, the focus is exclusively on Jesus' contemporaries as he pronounces his condemnation on their outward righteousness in contrast to the inner corruption of their lives. The speech as a whole is addressed not to the scribes and Pharisees themselves, however, but to the crowds and to the disciples (v. 1) and begins with the instruction to do as the teachers of the Law say but not as they do (vv. 2-3). The criticism that they burden people with loads but offer no help (v. 4) gives way to the indictment that their deeds are for show, as is their adornment (v. 5). They seek status through prime seats and the title "rabbi" (v. 6). This leads to Jesus' instruction not to use such titles as rabbi, father, and judge, which should be reserved for God (and Jesus) alone (vv. 7-11). There then follow seven woes, repeatedly attacking the hypocrisy of the scribes and the Pharisees (vv. 13-36).

The final woe is the longest, although it is difficult to determine where it ends (vv. 29ff.).[21] Wherever it ends, it flows almost seamlessly into Jesus' prophecy in vv. 34-36 that he will send a final generation of prophets to their deaths:

> Woe to you Scribes and Pharisees, you hypocrites — because you build graves for the prophets and adorn the tombs of the righteous, yet you say,

19. The exception would be Matt. 4.5, where Jesus is taken by Satan to the pinnacle of the temple, but this would hardly provide an opportunity for Jesus to desire Jerusalem's acceptance of him; the setting may, in any case, be visionary.

20. F. W. Beare, *The Gospel according to Matthew* (Oxford: Blackwell, 1981), 460.

21. Carson gives vv. 29-32 as the seventh woe (D. A. Carson, *Matthew* [Grand Rapids: Zondervan, 1995], 2:483). Beare, *The Gospel according to Matthew*, 446, and D. A. Hagner, *Matthew 14–28* (WBC; Waco: Word, 1995), 666, include v. 33. Another possibility is that it spans the whole of vv. 29-36 (E. Lohmeyer [W. Schmauch, ed.], *Das Evangelium nach Matthäus* [KEK; Göttingen: Vandenhoeck und Ruprecht, 1962], 345.)

"If we had lived in the days of our fathers, we would not have been party to the blood of the prophets." So you bear witness against yourselves that you are sons of those who murdered the prophets, and you will fill up the measure of your fathers. Snakes! Brood of vipers! How will you escape from the judgment of Gehenna? Therefore, behold, I send to you prophets and wise men and scribes: some of them you will kill and crucify, and some of them you will scourge in your synagogues, and pursue from city to city. This is in order that all the righteous blood poured out on the earth — from the blood of Abel the righteous to the blood of Zechariah the son of Barakiah, whom you killed between the sanctuary and the altar, might come upon you. Truly I say to you, all this will come upon this generation. (vv. 29-36)

The substance of this final woe and Jesus' prophecy, then, is his attack on the Pharisees because they build graves for the prophets and yet protest their innocence of prophetic blood. To demonstrate that the Pharisees would in fact have done the same in their fathers' time, Jesus promises (vv. 34-36) to send more prophets, whom, he predicts, the current generation of Pharisees will in fact kill. The purpose of this will be to bring the wrath of God on that generation in a decisive way, as a culmination of divine wrath on (in some sense) the totality of human sin (from Abel to Zechariah) inasmuch as it has manifested itself in the killing of the righteous.

The attention in Matt. 23.1-28 was, as we noted above, focused exclusively on the current generation of leaders and teachers and their corruption. Vv. 29-36 see a shift in defining Jesus' contemporaries in relation to previous generations. First, Jesus sneers at the assumption that the current scribes and Pharisees are innocent by comparison with their fathers. He notes their attempt to dissociate themselves from the actions of their murderous forebears — they even (falsely) honor those whom their ancestors killed (vv. 29-30). But Jesus confirms that just as they are children of murderers, so also they will follow in their fathers' footsteps in being murderers themselves. Thus Jesus prophesies that they will kill *Christian prophets* in their role in the eschatological drama to be played out in the near future. Crucially, then, Matthew knits together the present generation in a continuum with every previous generation in Israel.

Exegesis of Matthew 23.37

It is this solidarity that Jesus has created between the current generation and the previous generations of Israel which provides the context for v. 37: "Jerusalem, Jerusalem, who kills the prophets and stones those sent to her — how often have I desired to gather your children as a hen gathers her chicks under her wings. But you have not been willing." We will now examine this statement in detail.

"Jerusalem, Jerusalem . . ."[22] The "apostrophe to Zion," in which a speaker personifies the city of Jerusalem and addresses it, is a conventional mode of speaking common in Jewish literature. It has various functions: sometimes it is little different from an address to God (11QPs 22), but sometimes it is also concerned with the actual bricks and mortar of the city, as in Tobit's prayer about the city's reconstruction (Tob. 13.10-18). Here in Matthew 23, however, the focus is very clearly on the *inhabitants,* as is clear from the reference to the children shortly afterward. It is likely that the children of the city represent the nation of Israel as a whole; certainly the scope of the group is now extending well beyond the "scribes and Pharisees" who have been the main concern in Matthew 23.

"who kills the prophets and stones those sent to her." In the context of the preceding woes and prophecy of Jesus, this designation of Jerusalem as murderous points both backward to past history, but also into the next generation, the final generation of Christian prophets.

"How often have I desired to gather your children. . . ." Striking here is the point we noted earlier, that Jesus moves from prophecy about the *future* in 23.34-36 to a comment on the *past* in v. 37. The Jerusalem which Jesus is addressing here spans generations and thus includes the population of the city (and beyond) throughout Israel's history. Against this background, it is thus this transgenerational sin of Jerusalem (and by extension that of the nation as a whole) which Jesus laments here. It is this city, in its historic rejection of the prophets, which is the addressee of Jesus' lament. As a result, it is clear that both Jesus' longing to embrace Jerusalem's children and their rejection of him

---

22. There are probably no christological implications in the "doubled" address of "Jerusalem, Jerusalem." Berger argues that it has some kind of epiphanic sense (e.g., the use of the double-vocative by God in Gen. 46.2). See K. Berger, *Die Auferstehung des Propheten und die Erhöhung des Menschensohnes. Traditionsgeschichtliche Untersuchungen zur Deutung des Geschickes Jesu in frühchristlichen Texten* (SUNT 13; Göttingen: Vandenhoeck und Ruprecht, 1976), 436 n. 31 for further references. On Luke 13.34, J. A. Nolland, *Luke 9:21–18:34* (WBC; Waco: Word, 1993), 741-42, takes a similar line: "The double form of address may align here with a pattern of divine revelations." See also his references at this point. There are, however, also counterexamples, such as Matt. 7.21.

are also depicted as transgenerational. Again, against the backdrop of the nonexistent relation of Jesus to Jerusalem thus far in the Gospel, it is much more likely to be the whole history of Israel which is in focus here, over against which Jesus depicts himself as having stood.

"as a bird gathers her nestlings under her wings." What we have seen so far fits very well with the exalted claim implicit in the bird simile: although translations often make it a specifically hen-and-chicks image, the language is actually of birds more generally. This feminine image picks up on language which is used of Yahweh in the OT, in particular:

> Like an eagle that stirs up its nest, that flutters over its young, spreading out its wings, catching them, bearing them on its pinions, the Lord alone guided him (Jacob); no foreign God was with him. (Deut. 32.11)

Here we have the motif very specifically applied to Yahweh's relationship with Israel. Again, the image of the righteous sheltering under the shadow of the Lord's wings occurs three times in the Psalms (Pss. 17.8; 36.7; 91.4; cf. *2 Baruch* 41.4). Thus again, as with the emphasis of chapter 2 above, we see some kind of identification of Jesus with the Lord of Israel in the OT. This, again, fits very well with a christology of preexistence.

Objections to Preexistence

Having examined the evidence for preexistence from the broader literary context, and from the specifics of Matthew 23.37 itself, we turn now to the adequacy of the alternative explanations. The principal objections go along two lines.[23]

First, for some scholars, this saying does not require much substantial contact with Jerusalem at all. Zeller raises the possibility that this can be at-

---

23. Gench also notes Pregeant's objection to the preexistence interpretation of Matt. 23.37 in the course of his argument that, though Jesus can speak transhistorically, this does not necessarily entail preexistence. See F. T. Gench, *Wisdom in the Christology of Matthew* (Lanham: University Press of America, 1997), 69, and R. Pregeant, "The Wisdom Passages in Matthew's Story," *SBLSP* (1990), 469-93 (476). Although Pregeant is slightly slippery on the issue, it seems that in the end he does not seem to endorse a transhistorical persona for Jesus. Initially, he states, "The fact remains, however, that 23:34-39 — at least when read in light of redaction criticism — seems clearly to present Jesus as a trans-historical being" (476). Later, however, his "preferred reading" is one which "avoids an understanding of Jesus as a trans-historical being altogether" (489).

tributed to Jesus' "hyperbolic manner of speaking" ("übertreibender Rede-weise").[24] This is of course a possibility, though it should of course remain a last resort. Manson also argues that Jerusalem is not necessarily to be taken literally and that Jesus says not "how often I have *tried*," but "how often have I wished."[25] This is rather weak, however. There is no reason why Jerusalem is not to be taken literally, or more probably metonymically: Jesus is after all *in* Jerusalem. A dichotomy between "wishing" and "trying" is also hairsplitting: Matthew's Jesus is highlighting the fact that he has wished to bring Jerusalem to repentance but that she has been unwilling. This implies a call on Jesus' part and a negative response on the part of the inhabitants of the city.

Second, and more commonly, scholars simply see in the claim of Jesus in Matt. 23.37 reference to several visits to Jerusalem.[26] The main difficulty with this line, however, is that — as we have seen — this does not fit well with Matthew's or Luke's presentations of the course of Jesus' ministry, which has not yet been focused on Jerusalem in any way.[27]

Conclusion

In conclusion, then, four principal points indicate Jesus' preincarnate longing for Israel's repentance in continuity with his present desire. First, there is the wider framework of Matthew's Gospel, as we have seen. Second, there is the immediate context of Jesus' statement of his desire and Israel's unwillingness: it is the lament over Jerusalem as the city which has historically rejected and killed the prophets which is the addressee of Jesus' statement in 23.37. Third, we have seen that the first phrase of Jesus' statement is accompanied by an ex-

---

24. Zeller, "Entrückung zur Ankunft," 514.

25. T. W. Manson, *The Sayings of Jesus: As Recorded in the Gospels according to St. Matthew and St. Luke* (London: SCM, 1949), 127, here opposing postulating numerous more visits to Jerusalem, rather than against preexistence. He is followed on this point by J. D. G. Dunn, *Christology in the Making: An Inquiry into the Origins of the Doctrine of the Incarnation* (Philadelphia: Westminster, 1980), 203, and Gench, *Wisdom in the Christology of Matthew*, 69.

26. D. Hill, *The Gospel of Matthew* (Grand Rapids: Eerdmans, 1972), 315, offers a longer ministry (as per John's Gospel) as a possibility, as does H. von Lips, *Weisheitliche Traditionen im NT* (WMANT 64; Neukirchen: Neukirchener, 1990), 275, in disagreement with Bultmann. Zeller also raises this as a possibility, but then his two objections here cancel each other out: if Jesus made numerous journeys to Jerusalem, his speech is hardly hyperbole. The result is that one gets the impression that Zeller is more interested in avoiding the preexistence interpretation at any cost than in working out what the saying means.

27. Zeller, "Entrückung zur Ankunft," 514.

tremely exalted christological claim. Fourth, probably the only other serious alternative to the preexistence interpretation would be to understand Jesus' repeated desires as coinciding with repeated visits to Jerusalem. However, as we have seen, the wider narrative context of Matthew's Gospel makes this interpretation unlikely. In addition to the positive evidence for Jesus' preincarnate identity being highlighted in 23.37, then, there are no significant arguments against it.

III. The Lukan Version (Luke 13.34)

We should also consider the Lukan version of the saying, which in the key part of the phrase is virtually identical.[28] The context is somewhat different, however. Here, the Pharisees have warned Jesus of Herod's intention to kill Jesus, but he insists on pursuing his journey to Jerusalem, because it would be wrong for a prophet to die outside Jerusalem (Luke 13.31-33). The Lukan version is perhaps harder to judge for our theme, because Jesus presents himself more as one in a line of prophets.[29] On the other hand, the wording is precisely the same as in Matthew. Furthermore, as we saw mentioned by Beare, "how often have I longed . . ." is even more strange in Luke because in Luke 13 Jesus has not yet been to Jerusalem. In fact, Caird offers a further argument which might imply that preexistence is even stronger in Luke than in Matthew, noting that the lament cannot refer to repeated visits to Jerusalem because in Luke the statement is "you will not see me until. . . ."[30] This implies, then, that Jesus has not yet embarked on any ministry in Jerusalem.[31] Nevertheless, part of what is so striking about Matthew's version of the saying is the context of the generations of Israel in the foregoing discus-

28. For the minor disagreements, see F. D. Weinert, "Luke, the Temple and Jesus' Saying about Jerusalem's Abandoned House (Luke 13:34-35)," *CBQ* 44 (1982), 68-76.

29. As Zeller puts it, "Der Sprecher ist auch nicht der Sendende wie die Weisheit von Lk 11,49, sondern stellt sich in einer Reihe mit den bereits Gesandten" ("Entrückung zur Ankunft," 514 n. 7).

30. See G. B. Caird, *Saint Luke* (Harmondsworth: Penguin, 1963), 173-74. Caird and Robinson argue that God is the speaker here. However, it would be odd to describe Jesus simply as acting as a mouthpiece for God but not speaking his own words. In view of the evidence we have seen for the divine identity of Jesus as portrayed in the Gospels, it makes better sense to see the words as genuinely those of *Jesus*. On this, see also G. B. Caird (L. D. Hurst, ed.), *New Testament Theology* (Oxford: Clarendon, 1994), 364-65, and J. A. T. Robinson, *Jesus and His Coming* (London: SCM, 1957), 61-62, citing *4 Ezra* 1.28-33 as an interesting reception of Matthew 23.

31. Within the Lukan scheme, however, Jesus is present in Jerusalem at the temple both in the presentation after his birth and when he is twelve years old.

sion (Matt. 23.29-36). Similarly, our interpretation of Matt. 23.37 sits happily in the immediate vicinity of a very exalted portrait of Jesus as one who *sends* prophets (v. 34). The immediately preceding discussion in Luke, on the other hand, highlights Jesus' own prophetic identity. As a result, despite Luke's portrayal of Jesus as still on the way to Jerusalem, we should probably be more cautious about finding a reference here to the preincarnate Son.

Conclusion

We have seen, then, that there are no serious obstacles to the portrayal of Jesus as a figure who transcends the particular generation of Israel into which he was born: Matthew has, throughout his Gospel, portrayed Jesus in strikingly exalted terms. Moreover, Matthew 23 offers a good deal of evidence for understanding Jesus' words in v. 37 as referring to his preincarnate experience. Although the context of the Lukan version points in a different direction, the various ingredients of Matthew's setting of the saying indicate that the saying should be interpreted as relating the preexistent Jesus to previous generations of Israel. In this respect, the statement is unique in the Synoptic tradition in that it clearly describes *continual activity on the part of Christ* prior to his incarnation. It is, on the other hand, only a single reference and so should not be overemphasized.

EXCURSUS: AN INCIPIENT LOGOS CHRISTOLOGY IN LUKE-ACTS? (LUKE 1.2; ACTS 10.36; 13.26; CF. 20.32)

We have seen already that André Feuillet has shown considerable enthusiasm for preexistence in the Synoptic Gospels, especially in the sphere of Wisdom christology. However, his most intriguing suggestion in this area comes in his contention that there is a "movement toward the hypostatization of the Word in the third Gospel and in the Acts of the Apostles."[1] Or again, he thinks in terms of:

---

1. A. Feuillet, "Témoins oculaires et serviteurs de la Parole (Luc 1.2b)," *NovT* 15 (1973), 241-59 (246), commenting on the "marche vers l'hypostase de la Parole dans le troisième Évangile et les Actes des Apôtres."

the Word conceived as a sort of mediatorial living power between God and human beings, distributing grace, and endowed with an energy whereby it is made to participate in the sovereign working of divine action.[2]

Feuillet's point that, by comparison with Mark and Matthew, Luke's Gospel was further along the way toward the christology of the Johannine prologue had been made in a similar way by G. Frost in 1963.[3] As does Feuillet, Frost notes that this aspect of the christology of the Synoptics has not been sufficiently recognized.[4] Again, his conclusions resemble those of Feuillet: "The evangelists are hesitant to name Jesus explicitly the Word of God, but the tensions are found; to all intents and purposes Jesus is ὁ λόγος τοῦ θεοῦ."[5] Nevertheless, this "to all intents and purposes" is a necessary qualification: both Feuillet and Frost stop short of attributing a logos christology to Matthew, Mark, and Luke.

This step was taken, however, by E. C. Hoskyns.[6] He does not have the same scruples as Frost and Feuillet, and talks of the hypostatization of the "Word." For Hoskyns, when Luke writes in 1.2 of the "eyewitnesses and servants of the word," he clearly means more than just Jesus' teaching: he is talking about "the eyewitnesses and servants of the Son of God," as the word of God is "drawn into the orbit of his person."[7] This interpretation of Luke 1.2 can also be seen in a number of the early fathers such as Origen, Ambrose, Cyril, and Euthymius.[8] We will examine briefly the evidence for this position, without coming to any definite conclusions. Similarly, two similar references in Acts mentioned by Feuillet will also be discussed briefly below.

I. Luke 1.2

... just as those who were eyewitnesses and servants of the word handed down to us ...

In his gloss on this verse, Feuillet deems it appropriate to capitalize the "p" of "Parole," hence: "eyewitnesses and servants of the Word." He thus views Luke

---

2. Feuillet, "Témoins oculaires," 252: "la Parole conçue comme une sorte de puissance médiatrice vivante entre Dieu et les hommes, distributrice de la grâce et dotée d'une énergie qui la fait participer à la souveraine efficacité de l'action divine."

3. Compare G. Frost, "The Word of God in the Synoptic Gospels," *SJT* 16 (1963), 186-94 (194), and Feuillet, "Témoins oculaires," 246.

4. Frost, "The Word of God," 193.

5. Frost, "The Word of God," 194.

6. E. C. Hoskyns, *The Fourth Gospel* (London: Faber and Faber, 1954), 160.

7. Hoskyns, *Fourth Gospel,* 160.

8. See Feuillet, "Témoins oculaires," 246.

as thinking in terms of a logos which is on the way to being a hypostasis, and which has a very close relation to, or even an identity with Jesus.[9] In fact, this is, according to Feuillet, a function of the influence of Johannine tradition upon the Third Evangelist; not the full-blooded logos christology of the Johannine prologue, but rather the motifs of the introduction to 1 John.

Feuillet sees considerable common ground between Luke's prologue and that of 1 John:

> concerning the things fulfilled among us . . . just as those who were from the beginning eyewitnesses and became servants of the word (Luke 1.1-2)

> That which was from the beginning, which we have heard, which we have seen with our eyes, which we have looked upon and which our hands have touched concerning the word of life: this life has been made manifest. We have seen it, and borne witness to it. . . . (1 John 1.1-2a)

On this similarity, he writes, "It is staggering that up until this point the resemblance between 'eyewitnesses and servants of the word' (Luke 1.2b) and the Johannine tradition has scarcely been taken into account."[10] In line with most modern scholarship, however, Nolland's reaction is typical: Luke's other uses of *logos* cannot sustain a christologically loaded meaning for the term.[11] However, some of the usages in Acts might bear out this meaning.

II. Acts 10.34-38

> Peter opened his mouth and said, "Truly I understand that God shows no partiality, but in every nation anyone who fears him and does what is right is acceptable to him. The word that he sent to Israel (τὸν λόγον [ὃν] ἀπέστειλεν τοῖς υἱοῖς Ἰσραήλ), preaching good news of peace through Jesus Christ, he is Lord of all. You yourselves know of the event that took place (τὸ γενόμενον ῥῆμα) throughout all Judea: he began from Galilee after the baptism that John proclaimed, Jesus of Nazareth, whom God

---

9. See the tension between Feuillet's statements: "Enfin l'expérience apostolique a porté dans les deux cas sur un message qui est indissolublement lié à la personne de Jésus et, en fin de compte, s'identifie avec lui. . . . [He then cites Luke 1.2 and 1 John 1.1-2.] Cependant, ni dans un cas ni dans l'autre, la réflexion théologique n'a encore abouti à l'hypostase de la Parole" (Feuillet, "Témoins oculaires," 255).

10. Feuillet, "Témoins oculaires," 252: "Il est étonnant que jusqu'ici l'on n'ait guère pris en considération la ressemblance entre 'témoins oculaires et serviteurs de la Parole' de Lc i 2^b et la tradition johannique."

11. J. Nolland, *Luke 1–9:20* (WBC; Waco: Word, 1989), 8.

anointed with the Holy Spirit and with power. He went about doing good and healing all who were oppressed by the devil, for God was with him."

In addition to Luke 1.2, Feuillet also mentions Acts 10.36 in passing.[12] Rehkopf's revision of Blass and Debrunner's grammar also mentions this verse as a possible example of *attractio inversa*.[13] The result is that "the word" is grammatically identified with Jesus the Lord. Karl Barth also interprets the statement in a Johannine manner.[14] According to this view, Acts 10.36 can be glossed as "the Word is Lord over all." "He is Lord of all" (οὗτός ἐστιν πάντων κύριος) has often been explained as a parenthesis,[15] but it makes much better sense understood as the climax of the kerygmatic statement, as balancing "the word which God sent to the sons of Israel."

This argument can be further strengthened when one considers the importance of relative clauses in the kerygmatic statements of Acts.[16] These statements follow a pattern whereby the preacher, in order to place additional focus on Christ, announces "Jesus, whom . . ." and then makes a balancing statement that "he is. . . ." Or, alternatively, the order can be reversed. The following examples illustrate this "kerygmatic statement" form:

Jesus of Nazareth . . . the one (τοῦτον) handed over by the fixed plan and foreknowledge of God, him you put to death through the power of the

---

12. Feuillet, "Témoins oculaires," 247, 250, though not to advocate a logos christology. For some of the key studies on this verse see U. Wilckens, "Kerygma und Evangelium bei Lukas (zu Act 10 34-43)," *ZNW* 49 (1958), 223-37; J. Corell, "Actos 10,36," *Estudios Franciscanos* 76 (1975), 101-13 (which has a very useful history of research and argues that ON is a corruption of OC); M. Dömer, *Das Heil Gottes. Studien zur Theologie des lukanischen Doppelwerkes* (Bonner Biblische Beiträge 51; Colgne/Bonn: Hanstein, 1978), 63-68; H. Riesenfeld, "The Text of Acts 10.36," in E. Best and R. M. Wilson, eds., *Text and Interpretation: Studies Presented to Matthew Black* (Cambridge: Cambridge University Press, 1979), 191-94; F. Neirynck, "Ac 10,36-43 et l'Évangile," *ETL* 60 (1984), 109-16; idem, "Acts 10,36a τὸν λόγον ὄν," *ETL* 60 (1984), 118-23: Neirynck's two articles focus on the history of research on the pericope as a whole and then on 10.36 in particular; C. Burchard, "A Note on Ῥῆμα in JosAs 17:1f.; Luke 2:15, 17; Acts 10:37," *NovT* 27 (1985), 281-95.

13. That is to say, τὸν λόγον in Acts 10.36 is said to be in the accusative because of the influence of the relative pronoun ὄν. F. Blass and A. Debrunner (F. Rehkopf, ed.), *Grammatik des neutestamentlichen Griechisch* (Göttingen: Vandenhoeck und Ruprecht, [14]1976), 245 (§295). This also occurs in 1 Cor. 10.16, and Blass/Debrunner also supply a number of LXX occurrences.

14. K. Barth, *Church Dogmatics* IV: *The Doctrine of Reconciliation*, Part 2 (Edinburgh: Clark, 1958), 196.

15. E. Haenchen, *The Acts of the Apostles: A Commentary* (Oxford: Blackwell, 1971), 352; F. F. Bruce, *The Book of the Acts* (Grand Rapids: Eerdmans, 1965), 261.

16. See H. Conzelmann, *A Commentary on the Acts of the Apostles* (Hermeneia; Minneapolis: Fortress, 1987), 20.

lawless by crucifixion, whom (ὅν) God raised up, having freed him from the pangs of death, as it was not strong enough to hold him. (Acts 2.23-24)

God has made both Lord and Christ this (τοῦτον) Jesus whom (ὅν) you crucified. (2.36)

Let it be known to all of you and to all the people of Israel that it is in the name of Jesus Christ of Nazareth, whom (ὅν) you crucified, whom (ὅν) God raised from the dead, in him (ἐν τούτῳ) this man has been healed before you. (4.10)

A similar, though more abstract, example is found in Paul's address to the Athenians:

What (ὅ) you are worshiping in ignorance, this (τοῦτο) I declare to you. (17.23b)

If this is a reasonably well established pattern, then a likely rendering of Acts 10.36 would be:

The Word whom (ὅν) he sent to the sons of Israel to preach peace through Jesus Christ, he (οὗτος) is Lord of all.

This is obviously slightly awkward, but any interpretation of the verse suffers from awkwardness, as the commentaries invariably note — grammatically the sentence is extremely tortuous.[17] In fact, however, it is a feature of these kerygmatic statements that they are often convoluted because of the amount of information about Jesus which Luke frequently wants to pack into single sentences (as in Acts 2.22-24; 4.10; and 10.36-38).

Further, the parallel between "word" and "Lord" in 10.36 might be strengthened by the parallel between the *rhēma* ("word," "thing," "event") and Jesus in vv. 37-38.[18] V. 36 is most likely to be a kerygmatic statement, a

---

17. See, for example, Conzelmann, who describes Acts 10.36-38 as "not a properly constructed sentence" (*Acts*, 83), and B. Witherington, *The Acts of the Apostles: A Socio-Rhetorical Commentary* (Grand Rapids: Eerdmans, 1998), 356: "enormously convoluted"; likewise, L. T. Johnson, *The Acts of the Apostles* (Collegeville: Liturgical, 1992), 191: "The Greek text of 10.36-38 is very difficult, with awkward transitions and obscure syntactical connections; textual variants make it even more confusing."

18. λόγος and ῥῆμα are virtual synonyms in the NT. Both are translations in the LXX of דבר. See Burchard, "Note on 'Ῥῆμα"; Feuillet, "Témoins oculaires," 246: "Plus que les deux autres Synoptiques, le troisième évangile met en évidence le caractère privilégié et l'efficacité souveraine de la Parole de Dieu ou de Jésus, qu'il appelle tantôt *logos,* tantôt *rhēma.*"

sentence in itself. Immediately after, in vv. 37-38, "the event that took place" (τὸ γενόμενον ῥῆμα) is followed by "he began from Galilee" and "Jesus who came from Nazareth," which are both in apposition to it. Thus, on the surface at least, the "word-event" is explained as the one who began from Galilee, Jesus of Nazareth. The grammatical problems are no greater for this interpretation than with any other reading.[19] However, this interpretation must remain in the realms of possibility rather than certainty; it can perhaps claim, nevertheless, to be a good possibility.

III. Acts 13.26-28

> Men, brothers, sons of the family of Abraham, and those among you who fear God, to us *the word of this salvation* has been sent. For those who live in Jerusalem and their rulers did not recognize *him* or the voices of the prophets, which are read every Sabbath, and fulfilled them by condemning *him*. And though they found in him no guilt worthy of death, they asked Pilate to have him executed.

Much the same could be said for Acts 13.26.[20] Commentators often refer to the close similarity of 13.26 to 10.36-38, and it is very likely that, however one takes "word"/"Word" (λόγος), the meaning is the same in both passages. There are, however, also internal reasons why a christological understanding of the "word" here is a good possibility. Principally, it is notable that in both places Paul/Luke immediately follows up the reference to "the word of this salvation" with the masculine pronoun "him" (τοῦτον in 13.27, αὐτόν in 13.28), which would normally refer to the aforementioned noun, in this case "the word of salvation."[21] However, the ensuing discussion in 13.27-28 is clearly focused on Jesus, though without mentioning his name. He is, nevertheless, obviously the one referred to in both instances of "him" (τοῦτον and αὐτόν).[22] As a result, then, the syntax connects Jesus, via these pronouns, to the "word" (λόγος) of v. 26.

---

19. The main difficulty would be the strangeness of the Word being sent to preach "through Jesus Christ."

20. Again, mentioned by Feuillet, "Témoins oculaires," 250, though not to advocate a logos christology.

21. Though this is not, of course, a hard and fast rule.

22. This is not disputed in the commentaries. See for example Johnson, *Acts,* 228; Haenchen, *Acts,* 405; Bruce, *Acts,* 307-8; G. Schneider, *Apostelgeschichte* (Freiburg: Herder, 1980, 1982), 2:135; A. Weiser, *Apostelgeschichte* (Gütersloh: Mohn, 1981), 2:333; R. Pesch, *Die Apostelgeschichte* (EKK; Zurich: Benziger, 1986), 2:37.

Conclusion

As a result, then, a christological interpretation of the "word" in Luke should perhaps not be so quickly ruled out.[23] On the other hand, if it is the case that *logos* should be understood this way, then it is still probably not in the fully Johannine sense. It is interesting however that in both cases in Acts, the *logos* is the object of divine sending, which most closely recalls the word which came to the prophets in the OT. There may also be some interesting correspondences between Luke's usage and that of the *memra* in the Targums. In conclusion, it is quite possible that Luke regards Jesus as the embodiment (not necessarily *incarnation* in the full sense) of the Word of God which came upon the prophets in the OT (e.g., Jer. 1.2; 2.1; 7.1; 11.1, etc.). This perhaps merits further exploration.

---

23. Less clear evidence comes in Acts 20.32, the final passage mentioned by Feuillet in this regard: "And now I commit you to God, and to the word of his grace, which is able to build up and give the inheritance to all those who have been sanctified." There is on the face of it here a reference to "the word" as an agent or instrument involved in the construction of the church. See Feuillet, "Témoins Oculaires," 252. Note also Schneider's comment that "Er (*sc.* Paul) vermacht ihnen den λόγος nicht wie einen verfügbaren Besitz, sondern empfiehlt sie dem Wort Gottes als einer geheimnisvollen Macht" (*Apostelgeschichte*, 2:298). This is a peculiar expression, and commentators have offered various ways of alleviating the situation. For example, Zmijewski ties δυναμένῳ οἰκοδομῆσαι κτλ. to God: J. Zmijewski, *Die Apostelgeschichte* (Regensburg: Pustet, 1994), 745-46 (or at least "nicht nur" to the word, "sondern auch" to God). Whatever is the case here, it seems difficult to attribute any binitarian sense to Acts 20.32. The majority of scholars see "the word of his grace" as essentially equivalent to the Gospel. "Die beiden Ausdrücke sind synonym, wie Lk 4,22 und Apg 14,3 zeigen": H. J. Michel, *Die Abschiedsrede des Paulus an die Kirche (Apg. 20,17-38). Motivgeschichte und theologische Bedeutung* (Munich: Kösel, 1973), 85. See also Pesch, *Apostelgeschichte*, 2:205, and T. Budesheim, "Paul's *Abschiedsrede* in the Acts of the Apostles," *HTR* 69 (1976), 9-30: "This 'word' is a characterisation of the Christian proclamation" (23). Michel is typical in offering Luke 4.22 and Acts 14.3 as parallels. Luke 4.22 is something of a red herring — the plural λόγοι and the context point more to a sense of "words full of grace." The Acts parallel, however, is closer and clearly evidences the meaning of "the Gospel," which also makes good sense of Acts 20.32. As a result, there is no clear indication of any kind of personification.

The Titles of Jesus in Matthew, Mark, and Luke

CHAPTER 10

"Messiah" and *Anatolē* (Luke 1.78)

It has been increasingly appreciated in the past generation that investigation of titles is not determinative for, or even central in, the study of earliest christology. But it is, of course, still a necessary element. We turn, then, here in Part Four to examine the extent to which the various titles and other designations of Jesus in the Synoptic Gospels lend support to the argument that has been made thus far. The focus here will be on what R. T. France has called the "big four": "Christ," "Lord," "Son of Man," and "Son of God."[1]

The present chapter focuses on the title "Christ" or "Messiah." In a sense, of course, to divide up the following chapters among "Christ," "Son of Man," and so on is somewhat artificial: the interpenetration of the various titles must be taken into account. Despite the distinctive emphases of the titles attributed to Jesus in the Synoptics,[2] a number of scholars have pointed out the way in which different images of expected figures are already intertwined in early Judaism.[3] For example, Hengel comments, "In at least two places [*sc.*

---

1. R. T. France, *The Gospel of Mark: A Commentary on the Greek Text* (NIGTC; Grand Rapids: Eerdmans, 2002), 23.

2. Wenham's statement is a nice summary of some of the differences: "Whereas 'Son of God' suggests Jesus' relationship to the Father and 'Lord' his relationship to the world and individuals, 'Christ' suggests his relationship to Israel and to the Church." D. Wenham, *Paul: Follower of Jesus or Founder of Christianity?* (Grand Rapids: Eerdmans, 1995), 121. Wenham is talking about Paul, but his statements apply equally well to the Synoptic Gospels.

3. See the comments on this point in W. D. Davies, "The Jewish Sources of Matthew's Messianism," in J. H. Charlesworth, ed., *The Messiah: Developments in Earliest Judaism and Christianity. The First Princeton Symposium on Judaism and Christian Origins* (Minneapolis: Fortress, 1992), 494-511.

in *Similitudes*] 'the Son of Man' is identified with the Messiah."[4] Even more strikingly, Horbury shows how Ps. 110.1 was combined with Daniel 7 already in early Jewish exegesis.[5] But whatever the precise extent to which such strands as these had already been woven together, they are even more closely bound together for the Evangelists because they have been fixed on Jesus, the single historical concretization of all these expectations. As a result, "Messiah" is often supplemented with another title: Mark links it to "King of Israel" (Mark 15.32), "Son of the Blessed One," and "Son of Man" (14.61-62); Matthew has a further reference to "the Christ, the Son of the Living God" (Matt. 26.63); Luke has "Christ, the Lord" in Luke 2.11. Breytenbach rightly notes that "For Mark, the titles 'Son of God' and 'Christ' are already tied together because of their common attribution to Jesus. This interchangeability between 'Son of God' and 'Christ' was further developed in Matthew and Luke."[6] He goes on further to comment that the same is true of "Christ" and "King of Israel."[7] As a result, then, it must be remembered that "Messiah" is also shaped by the other titles which we will examine in subsequent chapters.

The extent of the expectation in early Judaism of a preexistent Messiah is much disputed by scholars.[8] As far as Qumran is concerned, the majority view is that there probably was no such expectation.[9] Beyond Qumran, it ap-

---

4. M. Hengel, "Christological Titles in Early Christianity," in Charlesworth, ed., *Messiah*, 425-48 (446).

5. W. Horbury, *Messianism among Jews and Christians: Biblical and Historical Studies* (New York: Continuum, 2003), 137-42.

6. C. Breytenbach, "Grundzüge markinischer Gottessohn-Christologie," in C. Breytenbach and H. Paulsen, eds., *Anfänge der Christologie. FS F. Hahn* (Göttingen: Vandenhoeck und Ruprecht, 1991), 169-84 (174-75): "Für Markus sind die Titel Gottessohn und Christus bereits wegen ihrer gemeinsamen Anwendung auf Jesus miteinander verklammert. Diese Wechselbeziehung zwischen Sohn Gottes und Christus wurde in den Großevangelien [i.e., Matthew and Luke] weiter ausgebaut."

7. Breytenbach, "Grundzüge markinischer Gottessohn-Christologie," 179.

8. The comments here on the Jewish literature are, of course, woefully brief. For recent discussions of Messianism in early Judaism, see in particular J. Day, *King and Messiah in Israel and the Ancient Near East: Proceedings of the Oxford Old Testament Seminar* (JSOTSup 270; Sheffield: JSOT, 1998); Charlesworth, ed., *Messiah*; Horbury, *Messianism among Jews and Christians*, especially the helpful bibliography of recent work (25-31). Issue 8 of the *Jahrbuch für Biblische Theologie* (1993) offers a particularly useful overview of recent German scholarly opinion. For studies more focused on Qumran, see n. 9 below.

9. This is probably the majority view, though see P. Sigal, "Further Reflections on the 'Begotten' Messiah," *Hebrew Annual Review* 7 (1983), 221-33, and W. Horbury, *Jewish Messianism and the Cult of Christ* (London: SCM, 1998), 98-99, on 1QSa 2.11-22. On Qumran messianism generally, see J. J. Collins, *The Scepter and the Star: The Messiahs of the Dead Sea Scrolls and Other Ancient Literature* (New York: Doubleday, 1995); J. Zimmermann, *Messianische Texte aus*

pears that, while the majority of references to the Messiah focus on his Davidic identity, there are also numerous (though, relatively speaking, fewer) cases in which messianic figures are portrayed in superhuman terms, as preexistent.[10] The best known examples of this are of course the "Son of Man" figure in the *Similitudes of Enoch,* and the one "like a man" in *4 Ezra* 13.[11] But there are also more fleeting, but still important, references elsewhere, not least in the Septuagint. On the other hand, Trypho (at least as far as he is portrayed by Justin) is unambiguous on the point: "For we all expect that Christ will be *a man born of men,* and that Elijah when he comes will anoint him. If this man appear to be Christ, he must certainly be known as *man born of men*" (*Dialogue* 49).[12]

The evidence below shows that the Synoptic Gospels in some sense mirror this distribution with the majority of references not alluding to preexistence in any way, while a small number of places constitute the exceptions. It will be argued here that while the references specifically to Jesus' messiahship do not *en masse* suggest preexistence, there are two places which do (section I below). In section II, we will discuss neglected evidence for preexistence in the controversy over the origins of the Christ in Mark 12.35-37 par. Finally, section III will examine one designation of Jesus which, while being a kind of messianic designation, also has a strong flavor of preexistence. The present chapter will end, then, with a treatment of the *anatolē* figure in Luke 1.78 because of its special significance for our study of preexistence.

Qumran. Königliche, priesterliche und prophetische Messiasvorstellungen in den Schriftfunden von Qumran (WUNT; Tübingen: Mohr, 1998); J. H. Charlesworth, H. Lichtenberger, and G. Oegema, eds., *Qumran-Messianism: Studies on the Messianic Expectations in the Dead Sea Scrolls* (Tübingen: Mohr, 1998). For a more extensive bibliography of works up to 2000, see M. G. Abegg and C. A. Evans, "Bibliography of Messianism and the Dead Sea Scrolls" (completed by G. Oegema) in *Qumran-Messianism,* 204-14.

10. Horbury, *Jewish Messianism and the Cult of Christ,* 86-87: "spiritual and superhuman portrayals were more customary than has been commonly allowed; they take up the exalted characteristics of many messianic passages in the Hebrew scriptures, are widely attested in biblical interpretation from the time of LXX Pentateuch onwards, and continue to be influential in rabbinic tradition." Cf. also Sigal, who talks of "the long-continuing tradition of a preexistent Messiah beginning from pre-Christian Judaism into the Rabbinic period" ("Further Reflections on the 'Begotten' Messiah," 231).

11. The preexistence of the Messiah or at least of the Messiah's *name* is common also in rabbinic literature (*b. Pesaḥim* 54a; *b. Nedarim* 39b). For preexistence in a stronger sense, see *Pesikta Rabbati* 33.6; 36.1.

12. Trypho's "we all" here is certainly an exaggeration; there was clearly no consensus on whether the Messiah had preexisted.

I. "Messiah" in Matthew, Mark, and Luke: The Basic Data

It is not the intention of this section to provide anything like a systematic overview of the sense of "Messiah." We will merely sketch the evidence from the Synoptic Gospels: as only a small proportion of the NT's 531 uses occur in Matthew, Mark, and Luke, this is relatively simple.[13]

Eight are found in Mark: in the opening verse (Mark 1.1),[14] in Peter's confession (8.29), in the high priest's question "Are you the Christ?" at the trial (14.61),[15] and in the chief priests' taunts of Jesus on the cross (15.32), and three in sayings of Jesus, twice implicitly in relation to himself (9.41; 12.35), and the other of a false Messiah (13.21).[16] Much of the scholarly discussion of these passages has of course focused on the famous "messianic secret."

Matthew has seventeen uses of the term. It again appears in the opening verse, and on four more occasions in the genealogy (Matt. 1.16-18) and birth narrative (2.4). John the Baptist hears from prison about "the deeds of the Christ" (11.2). In addition to a number of parallels with Mark, Matthew supplements Peter's confession with an injunction from Jesus that the disciples not tell anyone that he is the Christ (16.20). There is also the saying in the woes about there being only "one Christ" (23.10), an extra reference to a false Christ in the eschatological discourse (24.5), and two references by Pilate on Good Friday to "Jesus, called 'Christ'" (27.17, 22).[17]

---

13. This figure is taken from C. Blomberg, "Messiah in the New Testament," in R. S. Hess and M. D. Carroll R., eds., *Israel's Messiah in the Bible and the Dead Sea Scrolls* (Grand Rapids: Baker, 2003), 111-41 (141). The references to follow come from W. F. Moulton and A. S. Geden, *Concordance to the Greek New Testament,* ed. I. H. Marshall (London: Clark, 2002), 1098-99.

14. According to some texts, the demons know that Jesus is the Christ in Mark 1.34. The Nestle-Aland committee appear to have no doubt that this is secondary, however. See B. M. Metzger, *A Textual Commentary on the Greek New Testament* (Stuttgart: UBS, 1975), 75.

15. Joel Marcus has made the intriguing suggestion that the high priest is specifically asking Jesus whether he is the "Messiah-Son-of-God," as opposed to the Messiah in a lower sense (e.g., "Messiah-Son-of-David"). J. Marcus, "Mark 14:61: 'Are You the "Messiah-Son-of-God"?'" *NovT* 31 (1989), 125-41. However, as Marcus himself suggests, the Gospel envisages anyone in the narrative expecting only a single Messiah (as per 12.35: "*the* Messiah . . . the son of David"), and there seems no reason to attribute a different view to the high priest (137 n. 47). The blasphemous nature of Jesus' confession in 14.61, which Marcus's argument here aims to explain, can be seen in the claim to a place on a/the throne at God's right hand.

16. On the "Messiah"/"Christ" title in Mark, see most recently D. H. Juel, "The Messiah in Mark's Christology," in Charlesworth, ed., *Messiah*, 449-60; E. K. Broadhead, *Naming Jesus: Titular Christology in the Gospel of Mark* (JSNTSS; Sheffield: Sheffield Academic, 1999), 145-54.

17. For discussion of the Matthean "Christ" in recent scholarship, see, e.g., W. D. Davies, "The Jewish Sources of Matthew's Messianism," in Charlesworth, ed., *Messiah*, 494-511; B. Gerhardsson, "The Christology of Matthew," in M. A. Powell and D. R. Bauer, eds.,

Luke (twelve instances in total) also refers to the birth of the Messiah in 2.11, 26, although the first reference thereafter is to the question over whether John the Baptist is Messiah (3.15). The demons, however, know that the Messiah is Jesus (4.41). Again, a number of the other references have parallels in Mark and Matthew, but distinctive are the two references in Luke 24 to the necessity that the Messiah suffer before resurrection (24.26, 46).[18]

Preexistence?

As a preliminary conclusion, it can be said that in none of these is there any clear-cut reference to preexistence, and this is certainly the general consensus as far as the Synoptic Gospels are concerned.[19] Even if Horbury and others are correct that there is a considerable body of evidence pointing to a superhuman, preexistent Messiah in early Judaism, there is little evidence to suggest that the Synoptic "Christ" references *as a whole* explicitly aim to evoke this portrayal.

On the other hand, there is an emphasis in some of these passages on Jesus' identity as "Messiah"/"Christ" as a heavenly secret. In the first instance — that is, before the resurrection — it is known only by demons (Luke 4.41), and it is "not flesh and blood but my Father in heaven" who revealed Jesus' messianic identity to Simon Peter (Matt. 16.17). It is not, then, an empirically observable fact, but a heavenly secret.[20] We argued above in chapter 2 that this motif is related to Jesus' heavenly identity.

The next two sections aim to make the case that Jesus' messianic identity is not merely as a "man born of men" but as a figure who has come from a preexistence in heaven. Before turning at the end to the designation of Jesus in the Benedictus as the *anatolē,* we will first examine some of the evidence that Matthew, Mark, and Luke tap into some of the messianic traditions of a transcendent origin of the Messiah. This will require investigation of the Son of David controversy in Mark 12.35-37 par.

Who Do You Say that I Am? Essays on Christology (Louisville: Westminster John Knox, 1999), 14-32.

18. On Luke's use of "Christ," see J. A. Fitzmyer, *The Gospel according to Luke: Introduction, Translation, and Notes* (New York: Doubleday, 1981), 1:197-200 and the bibliography he supplies.

19. In a recent example, the preexistence of the Messiah is only mentioned very briefly in connection with the *Johannine* literature in Blomberg's "Messiah in the New Testament," 138. Hofius is in the minority in seeing preexistence as strongly evident in the Synoptics. O. Hofius, "Ist Jesus der Messias? Thesen," *JBT* 8 (1993), 103-29 (124-25).

20. Gerhardsson, "The Christology of Matthew," 20.

II. The Divine Origin of Jesus in Mark 12.35-37
par. Matthew 22.41-45; Luke 20.41-44

Since, for the purposes of this section, the substance of the three Synoptic versions is the same, we will simply cite the Markan passage:

> While Jesus was teaching in the temple courts, he asked, "How is it that the teachers of the Law say that the Christ is the son of David? David himself, speaking by the Holy Spirit, declared: 'The Lord said to my lord: "Sit at my right hand until I put your enemies under your feet."' David himself calls him 'Lord.' How then can he be his son?" And the crowd listened to him with delight. (Mark 12.35-37)

The argument of this passage is simple: since David hails the Messiah as Lord, the former cannot be regarded as the forefather of the latter. The clear implication here is that Jesus is not so much son of David as Son of God. This in itself could have a number of different implications — that Jesus was born of the virgin, for example. It is suggested here that the *preexistence* of the Christ is one possible resonance of the argument here. The principal reason for this is that just as the Jesus of the Gospels supplies Ps. 110.1 as support for the idea that the Messiah cannot be David's son — and therefore can lay claim to being Son of God — so also Ps. 110.3 *and* 4 would have been understood by the readers of the Gospels in much the same way and would have been taken to imply the preexistence of the Messiah.

First, then, Ps. 110.3 (LXX Ps. 109.3). The meaning of the Hebrew text is extremely opaque, as is widely recognized by scholars. The Hebrew and Greek talk of the same figure in vv. 1-2, that is, David's lord, who will ultimately rule over his enemies from Zion. The Greek translation, however, clears up the difficulties in the Hebrew as follows:

> With you is the rule on the day of your power,
> In the radiance of your holy ones;
> From the womb, before the morning star, I gave you birth.

Schaper rightly recognizes this as a reference to the preexistence of the Messiah; he notes that the last line quoted above can only be understood as such.[21] The savior's birth in primeval time is the mirror image of his supremacy in the events of the *end*.[22] This birth of the Messiah prior to creation has a

---

21. J. Schaper, *Eschatology in the Greek Psalter* (WUNT; Tübingen: Mohr, 1995), 104.

22. This is in line with the early Jewish idea (also held more widely in the Ancient Near East) of *Endzeit gleich Urzeit*.

parallel in the *Similitudes of Enoch,* where before the creation of the sun, "his name was named" (*1 Enoch* 48.3) and, though less clearly, in LXX Ps. 71.17: "before the sun his name remains."[23] While for some scholars a primeval *naming* (as in *1 Enoch*) is less radical a position than a primeval birth (as in Psalm 110/109), in fact "birth" and "naming" are more naturally understood as two closely connected events.[24] In any case, LXX Ps. 109.3 is clearly a reference to preexistence in a strong sense.

Second, LXX Ps. 109.4:

> The Lord has sworn and will not change his mind:
> "You are a priest forever, according to the order of Melchizedek."

This is clearly understood in early Christianity as implicit evidence for the preexistence of Christ. The transition from Hebrews 6 to Hebrews 7 is the key passage here. Heb. 6.20b applies the Psalm reference directly to Christ: "He has become a high priest forever according to the order of Melchizedek." Immediately the figure of Melchizedek is explained in a brief biography (7.1-2a) and in an interpretation of his name and the title "king of Salem" (7.2b). The comparison between Jesus and Melchizedek comes in the following statement in 7.3: "without father, without mother, without genealogy, having neither beginning of days nor end of life, but made like (or 'portrayed like') the Son of God, he remains a priest forever."[25] 7.15-16 also draws an analogy between Melchizedek and Jesus on the basis of their "indestructible life." Their common features, then, are clearly their mysterious origins, their immortality, and their everlasting priesthoods. LXX Ps. 109.4 is the means of forging these links between the two figures.

To synthesize the conclusions, then, LXX Ps. 109.1 is the basis in Mark 12 par. for saying that since the Christ is David's lord, he cannot be David's son. As a result, the Christ's lineage is more exalted than that of David. LXX Ps. 109.3 talks of the birth of this savior figure (David's lord) as having been born of God before even the morning star was created. The following verse likens him to Melchizedek, who is understood in earliest Christianity (and perhaps more widely) as a heavenly figure without father and mother. The meanings

---

23. The Targum to Ps. 71.17 is clearer on preexistence at this point than its Septuagintal counterpart (Schaper, *Eschatology in the Greek Psalter,* 94-95).

24. In Jewish literature, one frequently encounters the pattern of "she gave birth to (for example) a son" followed by "and they called his name . . ."; e.g., 1 Sam. 1.20; Matt. 1.21. The conjunction of the two events is not particularly specific to Judaism either!

25. Cf. the heavenly identity of Melchizedek in 11Q13, on which see most recently, Zimmermann, *Messianische Texte aus Qumran,* 389-412.

of these three verses can certainly not all be collapsed together. Nevertheless, for the authors and readers of the Synoptic Gospels there would be a curious coherence in them: the Christ's lineage must be more exalted than merely Davidic; the figure is actually born primevally of God; like Melchizedek, his origins are shrouded in mystery.

This interpretation does not necessarily depend on the view of some scholars that quotation of any OT verse necessarily evokes the wider context. However, since the Psalms were sung as part of Jewish worship, they would most likely be known as wholes: the first line cited in the Gospels would be very likely to suggest the rest of this short Psalm. The author of Hebrews clearly viewed vv. 1 and 4 as related.[26] Moreover, vv. 1 and 4 function in the arguments of the Gospels and Hebrews respectively in astonishingly similar ways. It is not often that christological points are made in the NT by explicitly *undermining* a particular connection with the OT. But this is the case here. Just as Ps. 110.4 becomes the means by which the Christ is decoupled from Levi, so Ps. 110.1 is the vehicle for severing the connection with David.

Returning to Mark 12.35-37 par., then, we can conclude that the reference to LXX Ps. 109.1 would be likely to evoke the whole Psalm. Hence, both authors and readers of the Synoptic Gospels (especially if they were familiar with the LXX) may well have been prompted by the "David's son controversy" to understand Jesus Christ to be portrayed in the Psalm as transcending Davidic lineage, born primevally of God, and timeless like Melchizedek.[27]

III. The *Anatolē* Who Visits from On High

> on account of the clement mercies of our God, by which the *anatolē* will visit us from on high, to shine on those who are in darkness and in the shadow of death. (Luke 1.78-79)

Finally, we come to a strong indication of Jesus as a preexistent Messiah in the *Benedictus* in Luke 1.[28] Here, (1) the heavenly-messianic designation of

26. Hebrews 7 is completely occupied with Melchizedek and his priesthood, and centers around the interpretation of Ps. 110.4, particularly in the second half of the chapter. This discussion is then followed by the reference in Heb. 8.1 to such a high priest "who sits at the right hand of the great throne in heaven" (cf. Ps. 110.1).

27. The thought of preexistence may well be particularly associated with the Greek version of the Psalm. It is very difficult to know how those more familiar with the Hebrew and Aramaic versions of the Psalter would have understood Psalm 110 at this time.

28. For the important literature on this, see A. Jacoby, "ΑΝΑΤΟΛΗ ΕΞ ΥΨΟΥΣ," *ZNW* 20 (1921), 205-14; P. Winter, "Two Notes on Luke I, II with Regard to the Theory of 'Imitation

anatolē is combined with (2) a statement of his origin in heaven, (3) from where he visits with a divine-like coming (4) specifically to carry out the task prophesied of the angelic ruler figure in LXX Isaiah 9. As such, those scholars who have interpreted the figure here in merely Davidic terms have missed a key aspect of the exegesis. This argument has been presented in greater detail elsewhere, so here the discussion will be restricted to a summary.[29]

The Anatolē

First, then, the designation *anatolē* itself. The meaning of this term has occasioned endless debate, and I have left it in transliterated form because it has two main connotations which cannot easily be captured by a single English word.

Its first connotation is that of the dawn, a motif which is clearly present here in Luke 1 because the very next verse goes on to talk of how the figure provides illumination for those in darkness (v. 79). The literal sense of *anatolē* is "rising," and even on its own its default meaning both in classical and Jewish Greek was the rising of the *sun,* whether in the sense of "dawn" or — by extension — "east."

In addition, however, in Judaism the term was in some contexts almost synonymous with, or a name of, the Messiah. Luke's readers would clearly have had this in mind as well, since Jesus has already been identified in the Gospel as the Messiah.[30] The messianic sense of the word comes from the much rarer classical sense "growth" and is seen in the LXX particularly where *anatolē* translates the Hebrew *ṣemaḥ*.[31] The word is the name of a redeemer figure in Zechariah, and then explicitly of the Messiah in Rabbinic tradition:[32]

> Behold, I am bringing my servant *Ṣemaḥ/Anatolē*. (Zech. 3.8)

> Behold the man, *Ṣemaḥ/Anatolē* is his name. (Zech. 6.12)

Hebraisms' (1) ἀνατολὴ ἐξ ὕψους," *Studia Theologica* 7 (1953), 158-64; W. D. Davies, "Appendix IV: Isaiah XLI.2 and the Preexistent Messiah," in idem, *The Setting of the Sermon on the Mount* (Cambridge: Cambridge University Press, 1963), 445; U. Mittmann-Richert, *Magnifikat und Benediktus* (WUNT; Tübingen: Mohr, 1996), especially 121-27; P. Vielhauer, "Das Benedictus des Zacharias," *ZTK* 49 (1952), 255-72; J. Gnilka, "Der Hymnus des Zacharias," *BZ* 6 (1962), 215-38, and see also n. 29 below.

29. For more detail, see S. J. Gathercole, "The Heavenly ἀνατολή," *JTS* 56 (2005), 471-88.

30. The term "Christ" is not actually used, but the idea is implied throughout the chapter.

31. On the meaning of the latter, see W. H. Rose, *Zemah and Zerubbabel: Messianic Expectations in the Early Postexilic Period* (JSOTSup; Sheffield: Sheffield Academic, 2000), especially 91-120.

32. See also Jer. 23.5.

> The Rabbis say, "This King Messiah, if he is from the living, his name is David. If he is from the dead, his name is David. . . ." Rabbi Joshua ben Levi said, "His name is *Ṣemaḥ*." (*y. Berakoth* 2.4)

In some contexts, the term has a strongly Davidic association; in others strongly heavenly resonances. (It needs to be remembered, however, that in early Judaism the two are by no means mutually exclusive.)[33] As an example of the latter, in Philo the figure has the nature of a kind of emanation from God:

> I have also heard of one of the companions of Moses having uttered such an oracle as this: "Behold, a man whose name is *Anatolē!*" A very novel appellation indeed, if you consider the one mentioned as consisting of body and soul. But if it is that incorporeal being no different from the divine image, then you will agree that his name *Anatolē* is attributed to him most appropriately. For the father of all things has caused him to spring up (ἀνέτειλε) as his eldest son — the one elsewhere he calls his firstborn. And this one thus begotten imitates the ways of his father: paying attention to this father's archetypal patterns, he has formed the kinds. (*De Confusione Linguarum* 62)

Later, in fact, Philo identifies the figure with the divine *Logos* (*Conf.* 146). Clearly, the likelihood of direct influence from this work to Luke is small, but at the very least, Philo states that the name lends itself very strongly to an incorporeal, spiritual interpretation.[34] This is another factor which points to the *anatolē* in Luke 1 contrasting sharply with the more human, Davidic emphasis.

An Anatolē *Coming "from On High"*

In one passage in the LXX, it is specifically said of the man *Anatolē* that he "will arise from beneath" (ὑποκάτωθεν αὐτοῦ ἀνατελεῖ in Zech. 6.12 LXX). By a striking contrast, however, Luke's figure comes not "from beneath" but "from on high" (ἐξ ὕψους), the very opposite of the figure's place of origin in LXX Zechariah. The usage of "from on high" in the LXX indicates unambiguously that this phrase means "from heaven": all six occurrences in the Septuagint have this sense.[35] Ps. 101.19 LXX illustrates the point particularly well:

---

33. See for example the discussion of *4 Ezra* in chapter 14 below.

34. Luke probably does not understand the word here as a proper name.

35. 2 Sam. 22.17 (par. Ps. 17.17 LXX); Pss. 101.19; 143.7 LXX; Sir. 16.17; Lam. 1.13.

he (God) peeped out *from his holy height* (ἐξ ὕψους ἁγίου αὐτοῦ), the Lord looked *from heaven* (ἐξ οὐρανοῦ) to earth.

The other occurrence in Luke points in the same direction: "but you, remain in the city until the time when you will be clothed with power *from on high*" (Luke 24.49). One implication of this is that the phrase does not mean simply "from God" but rather from God's dwelling place, heaven. A small modification of the standard translations of Luke 1.78 is probably in order, however: "on high" probably modifies the verb ("will visit") rather the noun *anatolē*. (The end result is of course much the same either way.) This verb in question further supports the high christology which undergirds the two elements which we have already examined.

"Will Visit"

Thirdly, then, the language used for the coming of this *anatolē* is significant.[36] In particular, the verb "visit" (ἐπισκέπτομαι) is most commonly used in the LXX in connection with God, where salvation and judgment are concerned.[37] As with "from on high," the Lukan usage reproduces this tendency in the Septuagint.[38] Clearly, then, Luke's portrayal of the advent of the *anatolē* from heaven attributes to the figure divine-like qualities.

The Purpose of the Anatolē

Finally, the function of Jesus on which Luke elaborates in the subsequent verse (Luke 1.79) perhaps sheds further light on the *anatolē* motif. Specifically, the background to this function lies in the messianic oracle in Isaiah 9 LXX:

> You people walking *in darkness,* behold — a great light! You who dwell *in the land and the shadow of death* — *a light will shine* upon you. . . . Because a child has been born to you and a son has been given to you, whose rule has come on his shoulder. And his name will be called, "Angel of

36. As the commentaries note, the evidence marginally favors reading a future tense (ἐπισκέψεται) rather than an aorist (ἐπεσκέψατο). Again, however, the difference is of little significance. If the future is read, the statement anticipates the *birth* of Jesus; if the aorist, the statement reports the *conception,* which has already happened.

37. Gathercole, "The Heavenly ἀνατολή," and H. W. Beyer, "ἐπισκέπτομαι κτλ.," *TDNT* 2:599-622 (especially 602, 605).

38. See Luke 1.68; 7.16.

great counsel" (μεγάλης βουλῆς ἄγγελος), for I will bring peace over those who rule, peace and health to him. (Isa. 9.1, 5-6)

Here, the "wonderful counselor, mighty God" of the Hebrew text has become the "angel of great counsel," as Horbury probably correctly renders it.[39] Although less explicit than the other elements discussed above, this probably further highlights the exalted, heavenly characteristics of the figure in Zechariah's prophecy.

Conclusion

In sum, these four elements together create a strong impression of Jesus as a preexistent Messiah figure who has come from heaven. Attempts to reduce the sense to a merely human, Davidic Messiah fail particularly to explain away "from on high" in Luke 1.78.[40] In forecasting the *anatolē* who will visit with a purpose, Luke 1.78-79 here has certain formal resemblances to the "I have come" sayings, and — as will be discussed in chapter 14 — it is particularly interesting that such a reference to preexistence crops up in the Lukan birth narrative.

Conclusion

All in all, the references to Jesus as "Messiah" do not in themselves give evidence for or contribute to our understanding of preexistence. However, like the "Son" references (from which they cannot be detached) they do have connotations of heavenly secrecy. More promising for our purposes is a passage where the nature of messiahship is actually thematized, Mark 12.35-37 par. Here we noted a strong emphasis on the mysterious, divine origin of the Messiah, and the use of Psalm 110 in this context may well point to preexistence, although this is not certain. More important still, however, is the reference to Jesus as the *anatolē* who will visit from heaven. Here in Luke 1.78-79 we have the strongest impression in the Synoptic Gospels of messiahship specifically associated with heavenly preexistence.

---

39. Horbury, *Jewish Messianism and the Cult of Christ*, 90.
40. See, e.g., Mittmann-Richert, *Magnifikat und Benediktus*, 121-27.

CHAPTER 11

"Lord"

As with the study of "Messiah," this chapter is not concerned to map out the meaning of the title "Lord" (κύριος) systematically. The major concern here is whether the term sheds any light on our theme of preexistence, with some preliminary remarks on general issues sufficing. It is certainly not *a priori* impossible, or even unlikely, that "Lord" might have resonances of preexistence. It is a very exalted title which more than any other brings the identity of Jesus into close correlation with that of Yahweh in the OT. Here, we are not concerned with the question of the origin of the title — whether it was used by Aramaic speakers in Palestine or whether it was first used in Hellenistic communities. Our concern here is strictly with the meaning within the Greek Gospels as they stand.

Often, discussion of "Lord" in the NT is concerned with whether the reference is to Yahweh or is merely a polite address, like "sir." Unfortunately, the situation is more complicated. The old study by Wainwright is helpful here in categorizing four different senses.[1] First, there is the sense of "owner," which Wainwright labels the possessive sense (Mark 11.3). Second, he refers to the "polite" sense, such as one might use addressing a stranger, "conveying respect without special reverence" (John 12.21). Third, Wainwright makes the helpful distinction between those usages and the "courtly" sense, which does presuppose the superior status of the addressee. Finally, there is of course the religious usage, which in Greek-speaking Judaism meant that *kyrios* ("Lord") became a divine title used as an equivalent for the untranslatable tetragram-

1. A. W. Wainwright, *The Trinity in the New Testament* (London: SPCK, 1969), 76-77.

maton. We begin with an overview of the usage of the title in Matthew, Mark, and Luke and then proceed to explore an area which has been used as evidence for preexistence christology.

I. General Considerations

Mark

The title "Lord" is used sparingly but tellingly in Mark's Gospel. It can by no means be confined to the realm of "polite address" or even of courtly usage. Furthermore, Broadhead's description of Jesus as "kyrios-designate," who only becomes Lord at the parousia, is also inappropriate.[2] Already in Mark 2.28, Jesus presents himself as Lord of an extremely exalted sphere, that of the Sabbath. In Mark 5, it is the author's editorial comment which is instructive. Jesus heals the demon-possessed man living in the land of the Gerasenes and tells him:

> "Go to your home, to your relatives, and tell them what the Lord has done for you (ὅσα ὁ κύριός σοι πεποίηκεν), and how he has had mercy on you." And he went away and began to proclaim in the Decapolis what Jesus had done for him (ὅσα ἐποίησεν αὐτῷ ὁ Ἰησοῦς). (Mark 5.19-20)

Thus, it is probable that Mark understands Jesus' statement as a self-reference to himself as Lord, although the reference may simply be to Jesus doing the work of the Lord God.[3] The designation of Jesus as "Lord" in Mark 1.2-3 points quite clearly to an identification between himself and Yahweh. In Mark 1.2, God makes the promise to his Son to send John "to prepare your way," which is then rephrased in the next verse as "to prepare the way of the Lord" (Mark 1.3).[4] This is obviously of particular importance for christology since the original reference in Isa. 40.3 is to preparing "the way of Yahweh." This is to be distinguished from the reference by David to Jesus as "my lord" in Mark 12.35-37, where Jesus cites Ps. 110.1: "The Lord said to my lord. . . ." Here, Jesus is the second "lord" in the phrase, and the reference is merely (!) to the fact

---

2. E. Broadhead, *Naming Jesus: Titular Christology in the Gospel of Mark* (JSNTSS; Sheffield: Sheffield Academic, 1999), 143.

3. R. A. Guelich, *Mark 1–8:26* (WBC; Dallas: Word, 1989), 286.

4. *Pace* R. T. France, *The Gospel of Mark: A Commentary on the Greek Text* (Grand Rapids: Eerdmans, 2002), 232, this is probably an instance of the titular usage of "Lord" in connection with Jesus in Mark. Mark 5.19-20 could merely be functional, but 1.2-3 really cannot be.

that Jesus is David's lord, rather than to his being Yahweh. We will return to these two key passages later.

Matthew

Matthew uses the title "Lord" rather more frequently than Mark. As is generally the case in Matthew, much of the Markan material is taken over, most notably, the "Lord of the Sabbath" saying (Matt. 12.8) and the David's son/David's lord controversy (22.41-45). But there are many additional non-Markan references. Especially common is the use in Matthew's parables, where "lord" is found in opposition to "slave" (δοῦλος) in the master-servant relationship. This is by far the dominant use of *kyrios* in the words of Jesus in Matthew. There is, however, one occasion when Jesus does refer to himself as *kyrios* outside a parabolic context: "Therefore keep watch, because you do not know on what day your lord will come" (24.42). The future coming of the Lord in judgment is a frequent motif in the OT, particularly — as here in Matthew — in connection with a certain "day." The associations with the coming of Yahweh and the day of Yahweh mean, then, that there is a blurring here of the lordly identity of Jesus and of Yahweh in the OT.[5]

Immediately striking is the sheer extent of Jesus' authority in Matthew's Gospel. This is no surprise, as Matthew has thematized the fact that the Father has handed over *all* things to the Son (Matt. 11.27). At various points it is said that Jesus heals *all* the ailments of *all* who came to him (4.23-24; 9.35); he even raises a girl from the dead (9.18-26). Jesus is frequently addressed as "lord" in contexts when these speakers express not only Jesus' superiority to themselves, but also his power over their *circumstances* (8.2, 8, 25; 14.28).[6] The general way in which he sets himself over against both his contemporaries (17.17 par. Mark 9.19) and indeed humanity as a whole (Matt. 10.34-37) should also be noted.

There are two other areas in particular where Matthew's usage echoes

---

5. W. D. Davies and D. C. Allison, *A Critical and Exegetical Commentary on the Gospel according to Saint Matthew*, Volume 3: *Introduction and Commentary on Matthew XIX–XXVIII* (ICC; Edinburgh: Clark, 1997), 384, point out that it "recalls the Aramaic *Maranatha*."

6. On Matt. 8.2, the commentaries draw attention (following John Chrysostom) to the fact that the address of the leper locates the authority *simpliciter* in Jesus. W. D. Davies and D. C. Allison, *A Critical and Exegetical Commentary on the Gospel according to Saint Matthew*, Volume 2: *Introduction and Commentary on Matthew VIII–XVIII* (ICC; Edinburgh: Clark, 1991), 12: "The sovereign authority and divine power of Jesus are presupposed by the leper, a man obviously full of faith." See also the references in connection with the Psalms below.

OT Yahweh language.[7] We have already discussed in chapter 2 above the way in which "the name of Jesus" stands in for "the name of Yahweh" in the OT. Equally striking is the application of other OT "Lord" formulas to Jesus in the Gospels. Matthew includes a number of sayings which tap into the invocations "Lord, save," and "Lord, have mercy," which are found most commonly in LXX Psalms:[8]

Ps. 11.2	Save me, Lord.
Ps. 105.47	Save us, Lord our God.
Ps. 117.25	O Lord, save.
Matt. 8.25	Lord, save.[9]
Matt. 14.30	Lord, save me.
Ps. 6.3	Have mercy on me, Lord.
Ps. 30.10	Have mercy on me, Lord.
Ps. 40.5	Lord, have mercy on me.
Ps. 40.11	You, Lord, have mercy on me.
Ps. 85.3	Have mercy on me, Lord.
Ps. 122.3	Have mercy on us, Lord, have mercy on us.
Matt. 15.22	Have mercy on me, Lord.
Matt. 17.15	Lord, have mercy on my son.
Matt. 20.30	Have mercy on us, Lord.
Matt. 20.31	Have mercy on us, Lord.

Similar to these appeals to Jesus are the instances — envisaged by Jesus for the future — in which people call on Jesus as "Lord" in judgment scenes (Matt. 7.21; 25.37, 44). Again, this is a distinctively Matthean phenomenon.

If the naming of Jesus as Lord is determined on one side by the Father's

---

7. *Pace* B. Gerhardsson, "The Christology of Matthew," in M. A. Powell and D. R. Bauer, eds., *Who Do You Say That I Am? Essays on Christology* (Louisville: Westminster/John Knox, 1999), 14-32 (19): "In Matthew (as well as in Mark) the flexible term *kyrios* is applied to Jesus only as a form of address, only in vocative form. That ought to mean that this word had not yet received any proper Christological connotation for Mark and Matthew in their congregations. It meant 'sir' (certainly very respectfully)."

8. U. Luz, *Das Evangelium nach Matthäus* (EKK; Neukirchen-Vluyn: Neukirchener Verlag, ¹1985), 1:60. In the second edition, the point is made in a slightly more complicated table.

9. Luz comments that "The disciples address him as 'Lord,' the Old Testament designation of God." U. Luz, *Matthew 8–20* (Hermeneia; Minneapolis: Fortress, 2001), 20.

gift of all things to the Son (Matt. 11.27), on the other it receives the human response of reverence. (We come back to the problem we faced in chapter 2 of the meaning of the ambiguous *proskynein* in Matthew.) In Matt. 15.25, the two ideas are brought together: "She (the Canaanite woman) came and worshiped (προσεκύνει) him, saying: 'Lord, help me!'"

Luke

Luke has the largest number of references to Jesus as *kyrios*.[10] Unlike Mark and Matthew, Luke frequently refers to Jesus as "the Lord" in the course of his own narration: "the Lord felt pity" (Luke 7.13), "the Lord said . . ." (10.41; 11.39; 12.42; 18.6; cf. 13.15), "the Lord appointed seventy-two . . ." (10.1), "the Lord turned and looked at Peter . . ." (22.61), and the like.[11] Also distinctively Lukan are 2.11 and 24.3, where we find the combinations of "Christ the Lord" and "the Lord Jesus" respectively. In addition to the more common *kyrios*, Luke also uses the Greek term *epistatēs*, always in the vocative in the context of an address.[12] As in Matthew 7, the name of Jesus is the means by which the disciples cast out demons (Luke 10.17), thus suggesting that the name of Jesus is, as argued in chapter 2, an extension of the name of Yahweh. It is not quite as clear as in Mark that Jesus is equated with the Lord of Isa. 40.3 (referred to in Luke 1.17, 76; 3.4), but it is still probable in the latter two cases.[13]

A good number of the instances of *kyrios* are also used in the context of disciples addressing Jesus and so could simply be a form of polite address, or better, an address from the servant in the servant-master relationship.[14] However, just as we saw Mark's slide from the address "Lord!" to "the Lord" as a title (Mark 5.19-20), Luke makes a similar move in Luke 10.39-41:

> Martha had a sister called Mary, who was sitting *at the Lord's feet*, listening to what he said. Martha . . . said, "*Lord*, do you not care that my sister

10. J. A. Fitzmyer, *The Gospel according to Luke: Introduction, Translation and Notes* (Anchor; New York: Doubleday, 1981), 1:200-204.

11. See also Luke 7.19; 10.39; 17.5. J. A. Nolland, *Luke 1–9.20* (WBC; Waco: Word, 1989), 322-23.

12. Luke 5.5; 8.24; 9.33, 49; 17.13. All instances are spoken by disciples, except the last (the ten lepers who are healed).

13. On Luke 1.76, Nolland talks of "a happy ambiguity" as to the object of the reference (*Luke 1–9.20*, 89) and sees the reference as more clearly christological in 3.4 (143).

14. Luke 6.46; 10.40; 11.1; 12.41; 13.23; 17.37; 18.41; 19.8; 22.33, 38, 49.

has left me alone to wait on you? Tell her to help me!" But *the Lord* said to her in reply, "Martha, Martha. . . ."

This implies a lack of distinction on Luke's part between the authorial "the Lord" and the address "O, lord" of the participants.

One of the most intriguing of Luke's accounts is that of Jesus' sending the disciples to obtain the donkey at the town gate (Luke 19.29-35). As the commentators note, the account is odd because of the space devoted to an apparently minor incident.[15] The interesting point for our purposes, however, is the way in which the word *kyrios* is used. After telling the disciples to go and get the donkey, Jesus prepares them:

> And if anyone asks you, "Why are you releasing this donkey?" then tell them, "Because its owner/the Lord needs it." (19.31)

This is exactly what happened:

> As they were releasing the donkey, *its owners* said to them, "Why are you releasing this donkey?" So they said, "Because its owner/the Lord needs it." (19.33-34)

The point of peculiarity here is that both Jesus and the new characters in v. 33 are described as "masters"/"owners" of the donkey. However, Jesus' ownership takes precedence over that of the others. It seems likely, then, that Luke is offering this as an illustration of Jesus' mastery over all things (cf. 10.22). As such, for Luke and his readers, *kyrios* in the statements in 19.31, 34 would probably have the sense of "the full Christian affirmation."[16]

Conclusion

In general, then, the "lordly" portrait of Jesus in the Synoptic Gospels is an extremely exalted one. In addition to depicting Jesus as Lord of the Sabbath (Mark 2.28) and of David (12.37), Mark's Gospel begins with probably the closest identification of Jesus with Yahweh that is to be found in the Synoptic Gospels. On the other hand, Matthew and Luke more than compensate for this with their inclusion of the saying about Jesus' lordship over all things,

---

15. I. H. Marshall, *The Gospel of Luke* (NIGTC; Grand Rapids: Eerdmans, 1978), 713-14; J. A. Nolland, *Luke 18:35–24:53* (WBC; Waco: Word, 1993), 924.

16. Nolland, *Luke 18:35–24:53*, 925.

which has been given him by the Father (Matt. 11.27 par. Luke 10.22). Furthermore, their special use of the "name" of Jesus brings it into close association with the "name of Yahweh" in the OT, and Matthew's application of appeals to Yahweh in the Psalms to Jesus again presupposes an extremely high christology. In none of the elements which we have discussed so far, however, is there any clear indication of preexistence.

II. A Preexistent Heavenly Lord in the Synoptics?

We noted above in the excursus at the end of chapter 1 ("'Prophetic Dialogue' in Hebrews") the way in which several scholars have seen in Hebrews the phenomenon of speech between Father and Son in heaven being captured in the OT. Most scholars see this exegetical device first in Philo, but only influencing Christian texts in the second century. The classic case is the interpretation of Gen. 1.26 ("And God said, 'Let us make man according to our image and likeness'") as such a divine address: Philo sees this as God speaking to the angels in heaven, whereas the *Epistle of Barnabas* takes it as address from the Father to the Son.[17]

This kind of "heavenly conversation" or "prophetic dialogue" has also been seen in Mark 1 and 12 by scholars of very different stripes. The vast majority of these are German commentators, and both conservative and radical scholars alike have attempted to argue for preexistence: conservatives open to the possibility of an early high christology (Schlatter, Hofius) and Bultmannians who see Mark's Gospel as a product of the later Hellenistic communities which had been influenced by the Gnostic redeemer myth or wisdom speculation (Schreiber). What is striking is almost a total absence of discussion of this idea (either with approval or disapproval) in English-speaking scholarship: Dunn's *Christology in the Making,* for example, makes no reference to any of the debate on the subject.[18]

In favor of the application of this theory to Mark 1 and 12 is that the Markan texts (as well as Matthew 22 par. Luke 20) could be seen as heavenly court utterances. There is a well-established form of divine discourse in the OT where God is pictured as engaging in conversation with members of his heavenly entourage. The first of these are obviously in Genesis, where God

17. Philo, *De Opificio Mundi* 72-75; *Barnabas* 5.5.
18. Dunn does refer to Hanson's attempts to find "prophetic dialogue" in Paul and Hebrews, but not to any of the German discussion of the Synoptic Gospels on this point. J. D. G. Dunn, *Christology in the Making: An Inquiry into the Origins of the Doctrine of the Incarnation* (London: SCM, 1980), 157.

confers (in all probability) with the divine council, first in the creation account (Gen. 1.26), then after the fall (3.22), then in the Babel story (11.7). More
elaborate conversations are pictured as taking place between God and the
wicked angels (Psalm 82), between God and the lying prophetic spirits (1 Kgs.
22.19-23), and between God and Satan in particular (Job 1–2). Dialogue takes
place between God and both Satan and a holy angel in Zech. 3.1-7. There are
numerous other examples.[19] Furthermore, it is widely recognized by OT
scholars that Isaiah 40 is a heavenly court passage.[20]

Mark 1.2-3 and 12.35-37

Mark 1.2-3 announces the ministry of John the Baptist as the one who will
prepare the way for the Lord, and the two verses consist of two OT citations,
the first of which is a promise from God that he will send a messenger ahead
of Jesus: "Behold, I send my messenger before you, who will prepare your
way" (Mark 1.2). Kampling gives a good description of the interpretation of
this statement along the lines of preexistence christology:

> Mark 1.2-3 stands outside the narrated time of the Gospel. God speaks of
> the future, of what will be fulfilled in the time which Mark is reporting.
> Far from the time of Mark and of the earthly Jesus, God speaks in conver-
> sation with his Son about that which Mark knows already to have taken
> place. . . . This happens in a "Prologue in Heaven." . . . According to this
> understanding, this divine discourse is to be understood as an address to
> the Christ who is always already at God's side. Hence it is an indication
> that Mark is aware of the concept of pre-existence.[21]

19. See E. T. Mullen, *The Assembly of the Gods: The Divine Council in Canaanite and Early
Hebrew Literature* (HSM 24; Chico: Scholars, 1980), 226-44. Scholars also point to the fact that
prophets can be described as entering the heavenly council (Jer. 23.18-22; cf. Isaiah 6), on which
see Mullen, *Assembly of the Gods,* 209-26.

20. See for example, J. A. Motyer, *The Prophecy of Isaiah* (Leicester: Inter-Varsity, 1993),
299.

21. R. Kampling, *Israel unter dem Anspruch des Messias* (Stuttgart: Katholisches Bibelwerk, 1992), 39-40: "Mark 1,2-3 steht außerhalb der erzählten Zeit des Evangeliums. Gott spricht
vom zukünftigen, was in der Zeit, von der Markus berichtet, erfüllt. Fern der Zeit des Markus
und der des irdischen Jesu legt Gott im Gespräch mit seinem Sohn das, was Markus als schon
Stattgehabtes weiß, als sich zu Ereignendes fest. Es geschieht dies gleichsam in einem 'Prolog im
Himmel.' . . . Nach diesem Verständnis ist diese Gottesrede als Anrede an den immer schon bei
Gott seienden Christus zu verstehen und daher ein Indiz dafür, daß Markus den
Präexistenzgedanken kannte."

On this reading, then, Mark's prologue describes a prehistoric scene which stands outside of the narrated time of his Gospel. Schlatter is one of the first modern scholars to have taken this line, and he is followed by Schniewind and Hofius.[22]

It has also been argued that the address to the preexistent Son seen by some in Mark 1.2-3 is also found in 12.35-37:

> While Jesus was teaching in the temple courts, he asked, "How is it that the teachers of the law say that the Christ is the son of David? David himself, speaking by the Holy Spirit, declared: 'The Lord said to my lord: "Sit at my right hand until I put your enemies under your feet."' David himself calls him 'Lord.' How then can he be his son?" And the crowd listened to him with delight.

There are two possible ways to seeing a preexistent Christ here. "The Lord said to my lord" might imply a heavenly address from Father to Son in eternity, a snapshot of which is captured in the Psalm here by the inspired author. Schreiber's description sums up this line of interpretation nicely: "the reader hears . . . by virtue of David's possession of the Spirit, the one Kyrios speaking in heaven to the other."[23]

Alternatively, since David appears to be speaking to the Messiah and addressing him reverently as "my lord," it could be argued that this must mean that the Messiah already existed in the time of David. Knox gives an account of this pericope as including a statement made by David to Christ: "Certainly this passage can be most naturally interpreted on the assumption that Mark thinks of Jesus as a pre-existent supernatural being, to whom David could address himself."[24]

---

22. A. Schlatter, *Markus. Der Evangelist für die Griechen* (Stuttgart: Calver, 1984 [1935]), 15: "Mal. 3,1 ist mit Exod. 23,20 verbunden, wodurch aus dem Spruch eine Anrede Gottes an den Christus wird, der als der Präexistente von jeher bei Gott war"; cf. also J. Schniewind, *Das Evangelium nach Markus* (NTD; Göttingen: Vandenhoeck und Ruprecht, 1956), 44; O. Hofius, "Jesu Zuspruch der Sündenvergebung: Exegetische Erwägungen zu Mark 2,5b," in idem, *Neutestamentliche Studien* (WUNT; Tübingen: Mohr, 2000), 38-56 (55 n. 66).

23. J. Schreiber, *Die Markuspassion. Eine redaktionsgeschichtliche Untersuchung* (BZNW 68; Berlin: de Gruyter, 1993), 238: "der Leser . . . hört kraft der Geistbegabung des David den einen Kyrios zum anderen im Himmel sprechen." A similar line is taken by T. A. Mohr, *Markus- und Johannespassion. Redaktions- und traditionsgeschichtliche Untersuchung der markinischen und johanneischen Passionstradition* (ATANT 70; Zurich: Theologischer Verlag, 1982), 423.

24. J. Knox, *Christ the Lord: The Meaning of Jesus in the Early Church* (Chicago: Willett, 1945), 97. Cf. also P. E. Davies: "Jesus points out that David, author supposedly of the Psalm, in his time called Jesus Lord," in Davies, "The Projection of Pre-existence," *Biblical Research* 12 (1967), 28-36 (33).

On the other hand, however, there are reasons to be wary of accepting these readings of Mark 1 and 12. Clearly, since this line of interpretation has not even occurred to a number of commentators, it is possible that it simply involves reading too much into this use of the OT. Additionally, it is possible that the divine speech in Mark 1.2-3 and 12.35-37 has an *eschatological* focus, rather than requiring preexistence: that is, it may be that the divine testimony in the OT is regarded as speaking into the future in which Jesus comes (Isa. 40.3; Mal. 3.1) and is vindicated (Ps. 110.1). In short, it is very difficult to decide whether the line of interpretation which advocates a preexistence christology should be adopted or not.

Conclusion: A Question for English-Language Scholarship

As noted above, this question has been debated in German scholarship, but in my view without a satisfactory answer on either side.[25] With the exception of the brief comments by Boobyer (1939-40), Knox (1945) and Davies (1967), scarcely anything has been said in Anglo-American scholarship on this line of interpretation.[26] More attention could certainly be devoted to what is potentially a fascinating exegetical device. Alternatively, it would also be useful if the interpretation could be given a decent burial should the evidence point in a more negative direction.

---

25. Hofius continues to pursue the line of interpretation, whereas it is dismissed in H.-J. Klauck, *Vorspiel im Himmel? Erzähltechnik und Theologie im Markusprolog* (Neukirchen-Vluyn: Neukirchener, 1997).

26. G. H. Boobyer, "Mark xii.35-37 and the Pre-Existence of Jesus in Mark," *ExpT* 51 (1939-40), 393-94; J. Knox, *Christ the Lord*, 97; Davies, "The Projection of Pre-existence," 33.

CHAPTER 12

"Son of Man"

Most recently, much of the discussion of the Son of Man in Britain in particular has focused on the Aramaic background to the title and to the sayings in which it occurs.[1] However, in line with the emphasis throughout this book, we are focusing here on the final form of the Gospels rather than on the historical Jesus. In any case, as Tuckett is right to emphasize, "methodologically, one's first question should be about the meaning and intentions of those who recorded the words that now appear in the Gospels."[2] The particular focus in this chapter will again be to explore the "Son of Man" references for the light they shed on preexistence christology in the Gospels.[3]

1. See in particular G. Vermes, "Appendix E: The Use of נשא בר/בר נש in Jewish Aramaic," in M. Black, *An Aramaic Approach to the Gospels and Acts* (Oxford: Oxford University Press, 1967), 310-28, and his *Jesus the Jew* (London: SCM, [2]1983). Most prominent in the discussion has probably been P. M. Casey in such articles as "The Jackals and the Son of Man (Matt. 8.20//Luke 9.58)," *JSNT* 23 (1985), 3-22; "General, Generic and Indefinite: The Use of the Term 'Son of Man' in Aramaic Sources and the Teaching of Jesus," *JSNT* 29 (1987), 21-56; "Method in Our Madness, and Madness in their Methods: Some Approaches to the Son of Man Problem in Recent Scholarship," *JSNT* 42 (1991), 17-43; "The Use of the Term (א)שנ(א) בר in the Aramaic Translations of the Hebrew Bible," *JSNT* 54 (1994), 87-118; and "Aramaic Idiom and the Son of Man Problem," *JSNT* 25 (2002), 3-32. There is, however, quite a lot on the other side, on which see J. A. Fitzmyer, "The New Testament Title 'Son of Man' Philologically Considered," in idem, *A Wandering Aramaean* (Atlanta: Scholars, 1979), 143-60; and P. Owen and D. Shepherd, "Speaking Up for Qumran, Dalman and the Son of Man: Was *Bar Enasha* a Common Term for 'Man' in the Time of Jesus?" *JSNT* 81 (2001), 81-122.

2. C. Tuckett, "The Present Son of Man," *JSNT* 14 (1982), 58-81 (58).

3. This chapter will refer to "Son of Man" as a *title,* since it is highly probable that this is how it functions in the Gospels.

I. The Preexistent Son of Man in Previous Research

In the Gospels, the questions "Who is this Son of Man?" (John 12.34) and "Who do men say that the Son of Man is?" (Matt. 16.13) receive equally complicated answers. Sorting out the various scholarly positions on the Son of Man question has evidently always been almost as difficult as solving the so-called "Son of Man problem" itself. Fortunately, there are a number of articles which attempt to bring order into the chaos of the scholarly discussion, and now there is an entire (albeit extremely brief) monograph devoted to the subject.[4] We will focus to a much greater degree on previous research in this chapter because, by comparison with the other titles, there has been a much longer history of "Son of Man" attracting particular interest as far as preexistence is concerned.

Brief mention of Burkett's reference to some Fathers will have to suffice as representative of the period before the rise of the historical-critical method. According to him, theologians examining Dan. 7.13 in the patristic period "often identified the figure in Daniel as the pre-existent Logos or Christ."[5] Examples he cites can be found in Eusebius (*Historia Ecclesiastica* 1.2.26) and Epiphanius (*Adversus Haereses* 2.1; 57.8). Eusebius, for example, quotes Dan. 7.13-14 and comments immediately afterward: "Clearly this would apply to none but our Savior, the God-logos who was in the beginning with God, called 'son of man' because of his ultimate incarnation." The vision in Daniel 7, then, is a vision of the one who in Daniel's time is the preexistent Christ.

To move quickly on to the nineteenth century: R. Laurence indicated in his preface to the first English translation of *1 Enoch* (1821) two references (in chs. 48 and 61) where the Son of Man was identified, he argued, as a preexistent divine being.[6] As a result, scholars such as Ewald in Germany and R. H. Charles in Britain understood the title — in accordance with what was seen in *1 Enoch* — to refer to Jesus' supernatural, heavenly origin. Thereafter, according to Burkett, this became established as the consensus view for some time: "The idea that 'Son of Man' meant a pre-existent heavenly Messiah became the prevailing view through the first six decades of the twentieth century."[7]

This view was bolstered in some quarters where the designation was

---

4. D. R. Burkett, *The Son of Man Debate: A History and Evaluation* (Cambridge: Cambridge University Press, 1999).

5. Burkett, *Son of Man Debate*, 23.

6. R. Laurence, *The Book of Enoch the Prophet, Translated from an Ethiopic MS. in the Bodleian Library* (Oxford, 1821). See Burkett, *Son of Man Debate*, 27.

7. Burkett, *Son of Man Debate*, 29, and see 27-28 more generally. He notes that there were, however, some exceptions.

understood as having its origin in an Iranian "primal man myth."[8] Myths such as these presupposed a heavenly form of a Man of cosmic and divine proportions and nature (in Jewish contexts, usually Adam). The scholars most commonly associated with this position are Gunkel, Bousset, and Reitzenstein, who flourished in the hey-day of the *religionsgeschichtliche Schule,* and the idea was also maintained later by Borsch.[9]

This line, however, was soon destined to become a minority position. Burkett charts nicely the dissolution of the apocalyptic understanding of the Son of Man in the 1950s and 60s and cites the most memorable expression of this, from Paul Winter: "the place of origin of the Son of Man myth must be sought neither in Iran, nor in Judea, not even in Ugarit, but in German universities."[10] This is not to say, however, that there was a thoroughgoing abandonment of the heavenly Son of Man. Some scholars, for very different reasons, have continued to see preexistence implicit in the image. The German Bultmannian Schreiber (who sees strong Gnostic influence on the christology of the Synoptics) and conservative French Roman Catholic Benoit are in superficial agreement on this issue.[11]

Another argument which has continued to persist through this controversy is the view that the Son of Man is the human incarnation of Wisdom. In addition to the association of the Son of Man with wisdom in *1 Enoch* 48.7; 49.3; and 51.3, he also features in this connection in scholarly discussions of Matt. 8.20 par. Luke 9.58 and Matt. 11.19 par. Luke 7.34-35:

Foxes have holes, and birds of the air have nests,
But the Son of Man has nowhere to lay his head. (Matt. 8.20)

The Son of Man goes about eating and drinking, and they say, "Behold the glutton and drunkard." But Wisdom is justified by her deeds. (Matt. 11.19)

---

8. Burkett, *Son of Man Debate,* 28, also refers to other sources seized upon: the Babylonian myths about Adapa or Ea-Oannes, and Canaanite plenipotentiaries.

9. F. H. Borsch, *The Son of Man in Myth and History* (London: SCM, 1967), and idem, *The Christian and Gnostic Son of Man* (London: SCM, 1970). See the discussion in Burkett, *Son of Man Debate,* 61-62, as well as I. H. Marshall, "The Synoptic Son of Man Sayings in Recent Discussion," *NTS* 12 (1966), 326-51 (328). Now, from a different angle, there is Walter Wink's Jungian archetype theory in his *The Human Being* (Minneapolis: Fortress, 2002), but Wink's whole reconstruction of early Christian views of God and Jesus is so bizarre that his conclusions are ultimately worthless.

10. Burkett, *Son of Man Debate,* 76.

11. P. Benoit, "The Divinity of Jesus in the Synoptic Gospels," in idem, *Jesus and the Gospel* (London: Dartman, Longman and Todd, 1973), 67-68, argues that the title refers not only to an eschatological role but also to heavenly origin; cf. J. Schreiber, *Die Markuspassion. Eine redaktionsgeschichtliche Untersuchung* (BZNW 68; Berlin: de Gruyter, 1993), 221-24.

In the former, Jesus is allegedly portrayed in similar terms to Wisdom in *1 Enoch* 42: she comes down from heaven, but finds no place to dwell. As Grundmann puts it: "Perhaps the relationship between this saying and the Son of Man, who is Jesus, should be determined by the fact that it refers to 'Wisdom,' who wanders homeless on the earth and has her home in heaven?"[12] In Matt. 11.19, the argument often goes that the deeds of Wisdom in the concluding aphorism are in fact identical to the deeds of Christ mentioned in Matt. 11.2.[13]

Various scholars in the 1980s and 90s saw the reference to the Son of Man as implying a specific reference to a preexisting figure of whom Jesus is the incarnation or reincarnation.[14] Gerleman, for example, takes Jesus to be David *redivivus*, although this requires the combination of two unlikely theses: First, the *bar* in *bar (e)nash(a)* refers not to the root for "son" but to *bar* meaning "separated" so that *bar enash* means "separated from men,"[15] which Collins sees as "fanciful" and without a good linguistic basis.[16] It would furthermore mean that the LXX translators and the early Christian translators of the Gospels among others all misunderstood it. Secondly, the "separated man," the "outsider," is David. Therefore, "David has returned to the earth in person" as Jesus.[17] This is somewhat unlikely. Even so, Gerleman's argument is not directly relevant to our concerns, since it deals with the Aramaic *Vorlage* rather than with the text of the Gospels.

By far the most substantial recent exposition of the Son of Man as preexistent comes in C. Caragounis's *The Son of Man*, which argues that the Son of Man in Daniel 7 is El Elyon ("God Most High") himself.[18] The tradition of the Son of Man as "a pre-existent, heavenly Being, who appears as the leader of the saints"[19] influences the Synoptic Gospels most explicitly in Mark 12.35-37 and 14.62. The latter, for example ("I am, and you will see the Son of

---

12. W. Grundmann, *Das Evangelium nach Lukas* (THKNT; Berlin: Evangelische, 1969), 204: "Oder sollte die Beziehung zwischen diesem Wort und dem Menschensohn, der Jesus ist, dadurch hergestellt sein, daß es sich auf die 'Weisheit' bezogen hat, die unbehaust auf der Erde umherirrte und ihre Heimat in Himmel hat . . . ?"

13. We have examined the problems with this hypothesis in Part III above. See also my alternative interpretation of this verse in S. J. Gathercole, "The Justification of Wisdom (Mt. 11.19b/Lk 7.35)," *NTS* 49 (2003), 476-88.

14. See Burkett, *Son of Man Debate*, 65.

15. G. Gerleman, *Der Menschensohn* (Leiden: Brill, 1983). See also the discussion of Gerleman in P. M. Casey, "Method in Our Madness," 24-26.

16. J. J. Collins, *Daniel* (Hermeneia; Minneapolis: Fortress, 1993), 304 n. 242.

17. Gerleman, *Menschensohn*, 63: ". . . David in Person zur Erde zurückgekehrt ist."

18. C. C. Caragounis, *The Son of Man* (Tübingen: Mohr, 1986).

19. Caragounis, *Son of Man*, 188-89, 189-90.

Man seated at the right hand of power, and coming with the clouds of heaven") "implies that in Jesus' view the Messiah is David's Lord, not so much on account of his resurrection or exaltation, but because he was conceived from the outset in Danielic fashion as a heavenly pre-existent agent of God's kingdom."[20]

Also heavily dependent on Daniel 7, though with more emphasis on the angelic character of the Son of Man, are the arguments of Barker and Fletcher-Louis.[21] Barker's interpretation is heavily reliant on her broader reconstruction of the history of OT theology, in which Israel's earliest worship was essentially ditheist, with the God El having a divine son called Yahweh. With the advent of the Deuteronomic school, this ditheism was suppressed and the two figures were identified. The distinction between the God Most High and his son/angel was not wholly blotted out, however, and persists according to Barker in particular in Jewish apocalyptic literature, Philo, and the NT. For our purposes, her key point is that "Son of Man meant the manifested second God, the Man."[22] Fletcher-Louis's version of Barker's theory (in particular its application to Luke's Gospel) will be discussed later in the present chapter.

A fascinating challenge to almost every existing hypothesis on the Son of Man sayings has recently been voiced by Michael Goulder.[23] This very original theory argues for preexistence inherent in the "Son of Man" title in Mark under the influence of Paulinism and Psalm 8. Before being "crowned with glory and honor," the Son of Man was "made for a little while lower than the angels": this latter phrase implies preexistence and incarnation, and this is read by Goulder back into the Gospel of Mark.[24] However, as has been argued elsewhere, I remain unconvinced that this is a legitimate move.[25]

This brings us up to the present: we need now to delve into the individ-

---

20. Caragounis, *Son of Man,* 225.

21. Sahlin adopts a "soft" angelic interpretation of the Son of Man sayings, arguing that the Son of Man was widely understood in early Judaism and Christianity to be the archangel Michael. The evidence for an angelic figure in Dan. 7.13-14 is strong, Sahlin argues, and in addition to the widely held tradition of Michael as Israel's defender, Dan. 10.21 and 12.1 also point toward Michael. H. Sahlin, "Wie würde ursprunglich die Benennung 'Der Menschensohn' verstanden?" *ST* 37 (1983), 147-79 (149). When it comes to early Christianity, however, *Shepherd of Hermas,* Revelation, and Hebrews have a strong Michael-christology, but in the Gospels the identification of Jesus and Michael is more one of functional equivalence (174).

22. M. Barker, *The Great Angel: A Study of Israel's Second God* (London: SPCK, 1992), 225.

23. M. Goulder, "Psalm 8 and the Son of Man," *NTS* 48 (2002), 18-29.

24. Goulder, "Psalm 8 and the Son of Man," 24-25.

25. See my criticisms in Gathercole, "The Son of Man in Mark's Gospel," *ExpT* 115 (2004), 366-72 (367).

ual Gospels. The famous "Son of Man problem" will certainly not be solved here, and we will not answer the question of what led Jesus to use such language. Our focus here will be restricted to the implications for preexistence christology (if any) of Matthew's, Mark's, and Luke's uses of "Son of Man."

II. Mark's Gospel

The treatment of Mark's Gospel here will be brief; I have discussed the issue elsewhere and will merely summarize the main lines of argument.[26] As Hooker and Moule have argued, Daniel 7 remains fundamental to the interpretation of the Son of Man sayings, even in Mark 2.10 and 2.28. There is no problem with the difference between the Danielic "one like a son of man" and "the Son of Man" of Mark's Gospel, because, as the observations of Moule and Collins suggest, the definite reference to *the* Son of Man is a way of referring to *that* Son of Man whom the audience knows from Daniel.[27] In the light of this, the sayings in Mark follow a strikingly consistent pattern. We encounter a narrative in which the Son of Man initially *displays* or *reveals* his power and authority (Mark 2.10; 2.28). However, second he does not *impose* his authority on all, since (in contrast to the expectation of Daniel 7) the Son of Man has come in the first instance not to be served but to serve by dying for his people (Mark 10.45; cf. 8.31; 9.9, etc.). As a result, his present ministry in the Gospel is one of suffering, in the course of which he actually dies as the representative of the saints of the Most High. On the other hand (thirdly), he promises his vindication in the resurrection (8.38) and in his final parousia, at which all will see his glory and power manifested in its fullness, and when he will in fact impose his authority on all (13.26; 14.62).

A Preexistent Son of Man in Mark?

The maximalist proposals of Caragounis and Goulder for preexistence in Mark cannot really stand up to close scrutiny.[28] Nevertheless, there is cer-

---

26. See Gathercole, "The Son of Man in Mark's Gospel."

27. C. F. D. Moule, "'The Son of Man': Some of the Facts," *NTS* 41 (1995), 277-79 (278); J. J. Collins, *The Scepter and the Star: The Messiahs of the Dead Sea Scrolls and Other Ancient Literature* (New York: Doubleday, 1995), 177, notes the way in which the *Similitudes* makes the same moves.

28. In addition to my observations on Goulder's theory, see the fairly devastating critique of Caragounis in Casey, "Method in Our Madness," 34-42.

tainly still mileage in a more moderate proposal for understanding the Son of Man as a figure from heaven. We have already seen above that the "I have come" + purpose formula used regularly of Jesus in the Synoptic Gospels presupposes an understanding of preexistence on the part of the Evangelists. We also noted that almost synonymous with the "I have come" formula is the "the Son of Man has come" formula, which appears in Mark 10.45. In the light of this, the Son of Man *in Mark's Gospel* is brought into association with a coming from heaven. This is not necessarily to say that the "Son of Man" designation itself had connotations of preexistence for Mark and his readers independently of that reference to the advent. But then, we do not have in Mark the figure independently of reference to his advent: so as far as Mark is concerned, it is part of the Son of Man's history that he *has come.*

The key point about this coming is that its purpose is contrary to expectation: while one might expect the Son of man to be a *recipient* of service, he has actually come to serve and, despite his exalted status, to die on behalf of his people. The demonstration of the Son of Man's authority in the opening episodes of the Gospel (Mark 2.1–3.6), and especially the Danielic elements in 2.10, 28,[29] means that there is a good possibility that Mark envisages this first coming of the Son of Man as a *partial, and paradoxical,* fulfillment of Daniel 7.[30]

III. Matthew's Gospel

Unlike the ordered pattern of references to the "Son of Man" designation in Mark, searches for a method in Matthew's usage have not proven nearly so successful. Kingsbury argues that "Son of Man" in Matthew is "public" in nature, by contrast to the "Son of God" title, which is "confessional."[31] Pamment, by contrast, concludes that the phrase functions to define Jesus' destiny "and to call the disciples to participate in it."[32] Luz criticizes both these approaches, but his own conclusion is very vague and general: "Matthew's Jesus speaks about 'the son of the man' when he speaks about his history and his way."[33] It may be that the long-sought order may be so elusive

---

29. See Gathercole, "The Son of Man in Mark's Gospel," 369.

30. *Pace* Maurice Casey, who comments that no early Christian until Cyprian identified the coming of the Son of Man with the first advent. P. M. Casey, *Son of Man: The Interpretation and Influence of Daniel 7* (London: SPCK, 1979), 161; idem, "Method in Our Madness," 29-30.

31. J. D. Kingsbury, "The Title 'Son of Man' in Matthew's Gospel," *CBQ* 37 (1975), 193-202.

32. M. Pamment, "The Son of Man in the First Gospel," *NTS* 29 (1983), 116-29 (126).

33. U. Luz, "The Son of Man in Matthew: Heavenly Judge or Human Christ," *JSNT* 48 (1992), 3-21 (17). He follows Hoffmann, however, in the useful observation that the "Son of

precisely because there is no particular plan, or Son of Man "concept," in Matthew's use of the title. We shall concern ourselves here simply with the question of whether preexistence is part of the general characterization of the Matthean Son of Man.

A Preexistent Son of Man in Matthew?

The observation made above in connection with Mark also applies to Matthew, who also brings the Son of Man into relation with the coming of Jesus: "even as the Son of Man came not to be served but to serve and to give his life as a ransom for many" (Matt. 20.28). The theory of radical redaction critics that because a statement comes from a source it does not *really* constitute part of the author's thought-world is untenable, and so this statement should not be regarded as in any way un-Matthean.[34] We should observe, then, that Matthew also regards the first coming of the Son of Man as a coming from heaven. The idea of the Son of Man's having already come with authority is in some ways stronger in Matthew and Luke, in that they reinforce the point that there is no time in Jesus' ministry when he is not invested with all authority from the Father (Matt. 11.27; cf. Luke 10.22).

We saw above in our account of previous research that the saying about the foxes, birds, and the Son of Man (Matt. 8.20 par. Luke 9.58) has suggested preexistence to some scholars.[35] This inference is probably not correct, however. The main way in which this line has, nevertheless, been justified is through the argument that Jesus is tapping into the myth in which Wisdom descends to earth to call people back to God, but on her rejection returns to her home in heaven:

Man" designation is a way of ensuring that the reader, when coming across reference to the suffering of Jesus, also bears in mind his glorious place in the judgment, and vice versa.

34. *Pace,* e.g., G. Strecker, *Theology of the New Testament* (Louisville: Westminster/John Knox, 2000), 386 (in connection with the comments on Mark 10.45 on 362), 388.

35. For some of the most important bibliography on the verse, see S. Luria, "Zur Quelle von Mt 8.19," *ZNW* 25 (1926), 282-86; Casey, "The Jackals and the Son of Man"; K. Löning, "Die Füchse, die Vögel, und der Menschensohn (Mt 8,19f. par Lk 9,57f.)," in H. Frankemöller and K. Kertelge, eds., *Vom Urchristentum zu Jesus. Festschrift J. Gnilka* (Freiburg: Herder, 1989), 82-102; M. H. Smith, "No Place for a Son of Man," *Forum* 4 (1988), 83-107; J. D. Kingsbury, "On Following Jesus: The Eager Scribe and the Reluctant Disciple (Matthew 8.18-22)," *NTS* 34 (1988), 45-59; V. K. Robbins, "Foxes, Birds, Burials & Furrows," in B. L. Mack and V. K. Robbins, *Patterns of Persuasion in the Gospels* (Sonoma: Polebridge, 1989), 69-84. The version of the saying in *Thomas* is analyzed in detail in A. Strobel, "Textgeschichtliches zum Thomas-Logion 86 (Mt 8,20/Lk 9,58)," *Vigiliae Christianae* 17 (1963), 211-24.

Wisdom found no place in which she could dwell, and her dwelling was in heaven. Wisdom went out in order to dwell among the sons of men, but did not find a dwelling; wisdom returned to her place and took her seat in the midst of the angels. (*1 Enoch* 42.1-2)

Thus Grundmann (as noted above) strongly implies a connection between this passage and Matt. 8.20, as does Keener: "his [*sc.* Jesus'] depiction of his ministry might also allude to rejected divine Wisdom without a dwelling place on earth."[36] The generic view of a statement about people in general does not fit well in the Matthean or Lukan context, where "Son of Man" is used in exclusive reference to Jesus. Even so, having no place in the world for the Son of Man does not automatically imply his preexistence. If in Matt. 8.20 Jesus taps into the myth of the unsuccessful descent of Wisdom to find a dwelling place, it is very fleeting indeed and not really detectable.

However, there is another way in which the preexistence of the Son of Man perhaps does emerge in Matthew, although it is more complicated, and — admittedly — somewhat speculative. In brief, the key point is that there is a close relationship between Matthew's view of the kingdom and the Son of Man on the one hand, and the view of the preexistent kingdom in the *Similitudes* on the other. In particular, this comes to the surface in Matt. 13.35, where the preexistent Son of Man is viewed by Matthew as the speaker of Ps. 78.2.

Son of Man, Kingdom, and Parables in the Similitudes

We will perhaps appreciate the relation of these ideas more clearly in Matthew if we see first how they are laid out in the *Similitudes*.[37]

First, in the *Similitudes* the Son of Man is depicted as preexistent: "he was chosen and hidden before Him [the Lord of Spirits] before the world was created, and forever" (*1 Enoch* 48.6), or again, "from the beginning, the Son of Man was hidden, and the Most High kept him in the presence of his power" (62.7).[38] Second, he is depicted as ruling over a kingdom which is kept secret,

---

36. C. S. Keener, *A Commentary on the Gospel of Matthew* (Grand Rapids: Eerdmans, 1999), 275. Keener makes reference also to B. Witherington, *The Christology of Jesus* (Minneapolis: Fortress, 1990), 52-53.

37. For a comprehensive assessment of the relationship between the *Similitudes* and Matthew's Gospel, see J. Theisohn, *Der auserwählte Richter. Untersuchungen zum traditionsgeschichtlichem Ort der Menschensohngestalt der Bilderreden des Äthiopischen Henoch* (Göttingen: Vandenhoeck und Ruprecht, 1975).

38. As Collins has noted, it does not make much sense for someone to be hidden if he does not exist (*The Scepter and the Star*, 179).

as one "who rules everything which is hidden." *1 Enoch* 71.15 highlights the preexistence of the kingdom, which has been the source of peace in the earthly world since the world was created. So both Son of Man and his kingdom are preexistent. Third, it is interesting to consider the way in which the *Similitudes* are framed, that is, how *1 Enoch* 37 (the first chapter of the *Similitudes*) describes the revelation of the secrets of the kingdom:

> The second vision which he saw, the vision of wisdom which Enoch, the son of Jared, the son of Malalel, the son of Cainan, the son of Enosh, the son of Seth, the son of Adam saw.
>
> And this is the beginning of the words of wisdom which I raised my voice to speak and say to those who dwell on dry ground. Hear, you men of old, and see, you who come after, the words of the Holy One which I speak before the Lord of Spirits. It would have been better to have said these things before, but from those who come after we will not withhold the beginning of wisdom. Until now, there has not been given by the Lord of Spirits such wisdom as I have received in accordance with my insight, in accordance with the wish of the Lord of Spirits by whom the lot of eternal life has been given to me. And three parables were imparted to me, and I raised my voice to those who dwell on dry ground.

In addition, then, to a preexistent Son of Man and kingdom, a key feature of *1 Enoch* 37–71 is the "words of wisdom" which are "the beginning of wisdom." No one has ever received them before the Son of Man, so he now "raises his voice" to enunciate these "parables" he has received.[39]

Connecting Matthew to the Kingdom Traditions of Similitudes

Before comparing the elements above with similar features in Matthew, we will note some other aspects which *1 Enoch* and Matthew share. The argument here is not that there is some kind of literary dependence; rather, Matthew is probably dependent on traditional material which has been shaped by traditions close to those of the *Similitudes*. Catchpole has produced a list of twelve correspondences, but we will restrict ourselves to three relevant observations specifically about the kingdom.[40] The first connection consists in the relation

---

39. I am presupposing here the — admittedly contested — identification of Enoch with the Son of Man.

40. See D. Catchpole, "The Poor on Earth and the Son of Man in Heaven: A Reappraisal of Matthew xxv.31-46," *BJRL* 61 (1979), 355-97 (380).

between the Son of Man and "the throne of glory." Luz and others have protested that "throne of glory" is a standard way of referring to the divine throne, and so one should not infer a direct relationship between Matthew and *1 Enoch* as a result.[41] However, the phrase is not *very* frequently used in this period, and the commonality is the reference not only to the throne of glory but to the fact that at the judgment, the Son of Man will be seated on it. References to the "throne of glory" appear throughout the *Similitudes*, invariably in judgment scenes. In the first instance, it is the throne of God (*1 Enoch* 47.3; 60.2; 62.2 *bis*), but the Ancient of Days also installs the Son of Man on the same throne (45.3; 55.4; 61.8; 62.5; 69.29).[42] Matthew uses very similar language in 19.28 and 25.31. Second, it is also noteworthy that the kingdom has been "prepared." Again, although this language is not exclusive to *1 Enoch* and Matthew, it is quite distinctive (*1 Enoch* 53–54, 60; cf. Matt. 25.34). Third, the kingdom has been prepared "since the foundation of the world." This phrase occurs twice in Matthew (Matt. 13.35; 25.34) and is ubiquitous in the *Similitudes*.

Son of Man, Kingdom, and Parables in Matthew

As far as the kingdom in Matthew is concerned, it is clearer in Matthew than in Mark or Luke that the kingdom is a preexisting reality in heaven, understood as the sphere where God reigns absolutely and where his will is done perfectly: "May your kingdom come; may your will come to pass on earth as it does in heaven" (Matt. 6.10).[43] This, and the fact that the kingdom has been prepared from before the foundation of the world (25.34), are Matthean emphases.[44]

Second, it is important to see the relation of the Son of Man to this kingdom. In Matthew's Gospel, the kingdom is even more closely associated with the Son of Man than is the case in Mark. This is perhaps clearest in Mat-

---

41. Luz, "Son of Man in Matthew," 8; R. J. Bauckham, "The Throne of God and the Worship of Jesus," in J. R. Davila, G. S. Lewis, and C. C. Newman, eds., *The Jewish Roots of Christological Monotheism: Papers from the St. Andrews Conference on the Historical Origins of the Worship of Jesus* (Leiden: Brill, 1999), 43-69 (60 n. 32). On this theme, see now D. D. Hannah, "The Throne of His Glory: The Divine Throne and Heavenly Mediators in Revelation and the Similitudes of Enoch," *ZNW* 95 (2003), 68-96.

42. In two cases there is some ambiguity as to whether the reference is to the Ancient of Days or the Son of Man (*1 Enoch* 69.27; 71.7).

43. Cf. Luke 11.2, which has simply "your kingdom come."

44. On the other hand, references to the kingdom "coming," being "entered," and in some sense having places prepared in it can be seen more widely in the Gospels.

thew 16, where some of those present will not die before seeing "the Son of Man coming in *his* kingdom" (Matt. 16.28). Similarly, the disciples elsewhere acknowledge the kingdom as belonging to Jesus (20.21). Again, in 25.31-46, the Son of Man is the king in the parable (vv. 34, 40). The preexistent kingdom, then, belongs to the Son of Man.

Third, we should see the place of the parables in this scheme. As in *1 Enoch* 37, the parables explicate the kingdom of heaven. The series of parables in Matthew 13 begins with the introductory formula "the kingdom of heaven is like . . ." (Matt. 13.24, 31, 33, 44, 45, 47). In the parable of the weeds, the sower is the Son of Man (v. 37) and the good seed is the "sons of the kingdom" (v. 38).[45]

As in the *Similitudes,* then, we have in Matthew a mysterious preexistent kingdom which is revealed by the Son of Man in parables that explicate the long-hidden mystery. As a result, the possibility must also be entertained that Matthew thinks (like the author of the *Similitudes*) of a preexistent Son of Man who has been hidden in the presence of God since before the foundation of the world — a preexistent Son of Man associated with the preexistent kingdom. The reference in Matt. 20.28 to preexistence in the coming of the Son of Man might well point in that direction, but there is a further aspect of the parables in Matthew which should also be explored.

Matthew 13.35 as Speech by the Pre-Incarnate Son of Man

The key statement comes in Matt. 13.34-35:

> All these things Jesus spoke to them in parables, and he did not say anything to them except in parables, in order to fullfill what was said through the prophet, "I will open my mouth in parables, I will shout forth things hidden since the foundation of the world."

Here Matthew summarizes Jesus' teaching in parables thus far in the chapter and cites a scriptural statement which is peculiarly well-suited to his own conception of the kingdom. As van Segbroeck has shown, the references in v. 35 to the "things hidden" and the mystery being a secret "from the foundation of the world" tap into the picture of the kingdom in Matthew more broadly.[46]

---

45. In the earlier parable of the sower, these are identified as those who have heard "the word of the kingdom" (Matt. 13.19).

46. F. van Segbroeck, "Le Scandale de l'incroyance. La signification de Mt 13,35," *ETL* 41 (1965), 344-72 (especially 357-60).

They also, as we have seen, have a great deal in common with the picture in the *Similitudes.*

In terms of the function of the scriptural quotation, it is a climactic summary of the previous statements such as "He spoke another parable to them . . ." (13.33; cf. also vv. 3, 24, 31). As a result, the parabolic teaching of Jesus in Matthew 13 is seen as the direct fulfillment of the promise in the Psalm. This "I" in Ps. 78.2, then, makes best logical sense as the preexistent Son of Man, according to the way in which Matthew cites it. A figure prophesies "I will shout forth things hidden," and then the same figure comes to do that very thing. This line of argument, or something like it, was in fact already alluded to by Johannes Weiss when he wrote on Matt. 13.35 in 1907: "in fact, here the pre-cosmic Christ is speaking."[47]

It might be objected that there are no other similar examples of such christological speech in Matthew. However, such an objection does not carry weight, because the form of this saying is unique among Matthean scriptural citations. The key feature lies in the fact that in other similar Matthean fulfillment citations, if a prophesying figure says "I will do such-and-such," it is the same "I" who fulfills it. This pattern is straightforward enough when God is the speaker and actor (e.g., 12.18; cf. 2.15; 22.32).[48] Here, however, the speaker is not God but Christ. In saying "I will open my mouth in parables, I will shout forth things hidden since the foundation of the world," the preexistent Son of Man prophesies that he will fulfill a function very similar to that of the Enochic Son of Man who was to "raise his voice to speak" in "parables" the wisdom never before revealed by God about the kingdom (*1 Enoch* 37).

The formula used here in Matthew 13 ("in order that what was said through the prophet would be fulfilled . . .") designates the Psalm reference as a prophetic oracle. Although this oracle comes "*through* the prophet," the ultimate origin is the Son of Man himself. This should not be dismissed too quickly; the same phenomenon of Christ speaking through the Psalmist is also found in *1 Clement* 16.15 and 22.1.

---

47. J. Weiss, *Die Schriften des Neuen Testaments* (Göttingen: Vandenhoeck und Ruprecht, 1907), 1:335: ". . . eigentlich redet hier der vorweltliche Christus."

48. Matt. 12.18 provides a parallel example of God speaking in the first person singular future (ἰδοὺ ὁ παῖς μου ὃν ᾑρέτισα, ὁ ἀγαπητός μου εἰς ὃν εὐδόκησεν ἡ ψυχή μου· θήσω τὸ πνεῦμά μου ἐπ᾽ αὐτόν . . .). Similarly, Matt. 2.15; 22.32 provide further examples of God as the first person speaker, although in reality all the oracles in Matthew refer to God as the speaker, even if they do not contain first person verbs.

Conclusion

In conclusion, then, we have the primary point of the Son of Man's coming expressed in Matt. 20.28. We then have the interesting combination of the association of this preexistent Son of Man with the preexistent kingdom. Within this framework, the Son of Man speaks in the OT of his future coming to reveal the kingdom in parables, and in this complex of ideas Matthew's thought-world is very similar to that of the *Similitudes*. Although the latter elements are rather more speculative, the reference in Matt. 20.28 nevertheless establishes the point that integral to Matthew's characterization of the Son of Man is his coming from heaven, again — counter-intuitively — his coming from heaven to die.

IV. Luke's Gospel

Relative to the mountainous literature on the Son of Man in general, comparatively little is focused particularly on the Lukan understanding of the title.[49] Part of the reason for this is perhaps, as Fitzmyer notes, that "Luke's use of it is scarcely distinctive."[50] As in Matthew and Mark, the title is used in connection with Jesus' earthly ministry, his passion, and his future coming in glory. Again, as in the other Gospels, there is no question of Luke's identification of the Son of Man with a figure other than Jesus.[51] On the other hand, the principal distinctive feature of Lukan usage is Acts 7.56, where Stephen says he sees "the Son of Man seated at the right hand of God."[52] This, as has widely been recognized, is notable as (probably) the only place where Matthew, Mark, or Luke has a person other than Jesus talking of him as the Son of Man.[53]

49. For one such study, see G. Schneider, "'Der Menschensohn' in der lukanischen Christologie," in idem, *Lukas, Theologe der Heilsgeschichte. Aufsätze zum Lukanischen Doppelwerk* (Bonner biblische Beiträge; Bonn: Hanstein, 1985), 98-113. There are also numerous studies of individual passages: see, for example, in addition to those mentioned below D. R. Catchpole, "The Son of Man's Search for Faith (Luke xviii 8b)," *NovT* 19 (1977), 81-104; idem, "The Angelic Son of Man in Luke 12:8," *NovT* 24 (1982), 255-65.

50. J. A. Fitzmyer, *The Gospel according to Luke: Introduction, Translation, and Notes* (New York: Doubleday, 1981), 1:211. For an attempt to press a distinctive Lukan portrait, see H. E. Tödt, *The Son of Man in the Synoptic Tradition* (London: SCM, 1965), 94-112.

51. Fitzmyer, *Luke*, 211, notes Luke 17.25 as particularly clear in this regard.

52. On this, see, e.g., C. Focant, "Du fils de l'homme assis (Lc 22,69) au fils de l'homme debout (Ac 7,56)," in J. Verheyden, ed., *The Unity of Luke-Acts* (Leuven: Leuven University Press), 563-76, and the other bibliography there.

53. However, Fitzmyer, *Luke,* 210, regards the reference in Mark 2.10 par. as the narrator's statement.

A Preexistent Son of Man in Luke?

As with Mark 10.45 and Matt. 20.28, the clearest way in which Luke's Gospel implies that preexistence is part of the characterization of the "Son of Man" is by including the saying in Luke 19.10: "For the Son of Man came to seek and to save what was lost." Here, then, the self-reference by Jesus to coming with a purpose points in the direction of his coming from a preexistence in heaven. The dynamic imagery of the shepherd going out to find the lost sheep further strengthens this reading.

Second, it has been argued that the Son of Man is a heavenly figure who is the counterpart to the earthly Jesus, particularly on the basis of Luke 12.8-9:

> I say to you, whoever confesses me before men, the Son of Man will also confess him before the angels of God. But whoever denies me before men will be denied before the angels of God.

Scholars such as Bultmann saw Jesus and this Son of Man figure as entirely distinct. Some have agreed with this position, but others have attempted to push the two more closely together.[54] Chilton has argued that Jesus does refer in Luke 12 to the Son of Man figure from Daniel 7 and thinks of himself as "intimate with" this heavenly Son of Man without being identified with him.[55] Catchpole took the line that just as Matt. 18.10 envisages "the little ones" having angelic sponsors, so also the Son of Man is described in Luke 12 as the heavenly sponsor of Jesus.[56]

Fletcher-Louis agrees to a substantial degree with the interpretations of Catchpole and Chilton that the Son of Man is the heavenly guarantor of the earthly Jesus but differs from their view in an important way. The separation of the two persons is a false dichotomy, resting on "too rigid a distinction between Jesus and his angelic counterpart."[57] Identifying the two figures as one is not a conceptual problem: the analogous situation in the *Similitudes* means that there we have an earthly Enoch who has a heavenly counterpart in the Son of Man figure, but a counterpart who is not a figure distinct from Enoch

---

54. Thus for example Fletcher-Louis on Luke: "A Lukan separation between two distinct individuals is impossible since they have already been securely identified with each other." C. H. T. Fletcher-Louis, *Luke-Acts: Angels, Christology and Soteriology* (Tübingen: Mohr, 1997), 235.

55. B. Chilton, "(The) Son of (the) Man, and Jesus," in B. Chilton and C. A. Evans, eds., *Authenticating the Words of Jesus* (Leiden: Brill, 1999), 259-88 (285).

56. Catchpole, "The Angelic Son of Man in Luke 12:8," 260: "the Son of Man is the heavenly guarantor of the earthly Jesus."

57. Fletcher-Louis, *Luke-Acts,* 235.

himself. In any case, all agree that in the Gospels as we have them Jesus and the Son of Man are one and the same. For Fletcher-Louis, the *contrast* between the *Similitudes* and Luke's Gospel lies in the fact that "In the Gospel Jesus, not Enoch, is the earthly manifestation of the heavenly Son of Man."[58] His conclusion is relevant to our theme: "The very close analogy with the *Similitudes* would suggest that as such Jesus the Son of Man is both preexistent, present and future."[59]

While this interpretation is in some ways attractive, particularly in relation to Luke 12.8-9, there are nevertheless weaknesses. One principal problem lies in the fact that for Luke it is the Son of Man himself who is "on earth" (Luke 5.24; 12.49, 51), who eats and drinks (7.34), and who also *suffers and dies* (9.22, 44). As such, it is hard to see how the "Son of Man" title particularly picks out the heavenly identity of the earthly Jesus. The case for the Son of Man as an angelic sponsor figure of the human Jesus, then, should probably be regarded as not proven. Luke 19.10 is the only clear case of the Son of Man motif being brought into relation with preexistence.

V. The "One Like a Son of Man" and the Interpretation of Daniel 7.13 in Early Judaism

The characteristics of the Son of Man in early Judaism can only support an understanding of a preexistent Son of Man in the Synoptic Gospels. Whatever is the case as regards the proper interpretation of the "one like a son of man" in Dan. 7.13, it is clear that there is a good deal of agreement between the two most substantial Jewish interpretations of this passage.[60] Furthermore, they (*1 Enoch* and *4 Ezra)* seem to be independent from each other and are roughly contemporary with the Synoptic Gospels.[61]

Collins and Slater summarize four common features of the Son of Man in *1 Enoch* and *4 Ezra* which are not clearly evident in Daniel 7. The Son of Man is[62]

---

58. Fletcher-Louis, *Luke-Acts,* 236.

59. Fletcher-Louis, *Luke-Acts,* 237. Pp. 235-37 constitute a section entitled "Jesus as the Son of Man, Pre-existent, Present and Future."

60. This is not to say that these are the only interpretations, but merely that they are the most substantial. For more of the *Wirkungsgeschichte* of Dan. 7.13-14 in early Judaism, see W. Horbury, *Messianism among Jews and Christians: Biblical and Historical Studies* (New York: Continuum, 2003), 125-56.

61. For some comment on the consensus, see Burkett, *Son of Man Debate,* 72.

62. Collins, *The Scepter and the Star,* 175, 187; T. B. Slater, "One Like a Son of Man in First-Century CE Judaism," *NTS* 41 (1995), 183-98 (183).

(a) an individual figure,
(b) Messiah,
(c) preexistent, and
(d) instrumental in the judgment and destruction of the wicked.

While two witnesses are not really enough to talk about a consensus, as Collins perhaps seems to imply, the attempts to undermine the points of commonality between *1 Enoch* and *4 Ezra* have not been successful. We will focus here simply on preexistence.

4 Ezra 13 (to take just one section of the apocalypse) follows a traditional pattern. Ezra has a mysterious dream (13.1-13), he prays to God to show him the meaning of it (13.13-20), and God replies to Ezra (13.21-24) and gives the interpretation of the dream (13.25-58). At the beginning of the chapter, Ezra sees in the dream "something like the figure of a man come up out of the heart of the sea" (13.3). In the interpretation, the Most High explains this figure:

> The Most High said, "As for your seeing a man come up from the heart of the sea, this is he whom the Most High has been keeping for many ages, who will himself deliver his creation; and he will direct those who are left." (13.25-26)

There are several indications of preexistence here. First, the one like a man is a figure whom "the Most High has been keeping for many ages" (13.25). Second, the implication of the Latin is that creation belongs to him: "he will by himself set free his creation *(per semetipsum liberabit creaturam suam).*" Hence, although this has not been recognized by scholars to my knowledge, it is probable here that there is an allusion to the figure as a co-agent of creation. Finally, there is the origin of the man in the heart of the sea. This is a point which the Most High explains last of all in the interpretation: "Just as no one can explore or know what is in the depths of the sea, so no one on earth can see my Son or those who are with him, except in the time of his day" (13.51-52). So the fact that the figure comes out of the sea is not really a divergence from the traditional picture of the Son of Man who comes from heaven. The "heart of the sea," recalling the place of origin of the beasts in Daniel 7, is a symbol of unexplored, inscrutable mystery. So the origins of the Son of Man and the identity of his people must remain a mystery until his "day."

As we noted above, Enoch is luckier. Unlike Ezra, who is permitted to know only a certain amount about the Son of Man and then is denied further access, Enoch learns everything: "And I asked one of the holy angels who went with me, and he showed me all the secrets, about that Son of Man, who he was, and whence he was, and why he went with the Head of Days" (*1 Enoch* 46.2). The "whence he was" is explored: "he was chosen and hidden before Him (the Lord of Spirits) before the world was created, and forever" (48.6).[63] As scholars note, it does not make much sense for someone to be hidden if he does not exist.[64] This is more explicit later: "For from the beginning the Son of Man was hidden, and the Most High kept him in the presence of his power" (62.7).

While the imagery differs, it can safely be concluded that *1 Enoch* and *4 Ezra* alike identify the Son of Man as preexistent. They do not refer to "the Son of Man" as a well-established title, but they are referring to the figure mentioned in Daniel's vision and are engaging in creative interpretation of Dan. 7.13. In this respect, we can see in the *Similitudes* and *4 Ezra* parallel cases which can only lend support to our suggestion of preexistence in the Synoptics.

Conclusion

While our study has not reached a maximalist conclusion like some of the studies noted in the introduction to this chapter, there are important implications for the theme of preexistence in the Synoptic Gospels. In sum: (a) the association in each of the three Synoptic Gospels of "the Son of Man" with a purposive coming means that there is an association (which is nevertheless not emphasized) of the Son of Man with coming from heaven and consequent preexistence; (b) there is something of a stronger emphasis in Matthew on the preexistence of the Son of Man by virtue of his association with the preexistent kingdom. Finally, the interpretation of the one like a Son of Man figure in *1 Enoch* and in *4 Ezra* probably strengthens this interpretation of the Synoptic Gospels. It should also be noted, however, that in order to avoid the atomistic approach of viewing "Son of Man" in isolation, the motif must also be viewed in conjunction with the other designations, especially "Messiah" and "Son."[65] One of the key aspects of the "Son of Man"

63. Sahlin ("Wie würde ursprunglich die Benennung 'Der Menschensohn' verstanden?" 157) refers to preexistence in *1 Enoch* 48.2-3, 6; 49.2; 62.7, 14(?).

64. Collins, *The Scepter and the Star*, 179.

65. For the close relationship between the "one like a son of man" and messiahship even in pre-Christian Judaism, see above all Horbury, *Messianism among Jews and Christians*, 125-56. Similarly, the explanation of the "something like a figure of a man" (*4 Ezra* 13.3) as God's son (13.51-52) resembles the use of Dan. 7.13-14 to talk about the "Son of God" who is the "Son of the Most High" in 4Q246. On this latter text, see J. J. Collins, "The *Son of God* Text from Qumran," in M. C. De Boer, ed., *From Jesus to John: Essays on Jesus and New Testament Christology in Honour of Marinus de Jonge* (Sheffield: Sheffield Academic, 1993), 65-82.

title is that it is employed both in contexts of the exalted heavenly identity of the preexistent Christ, and also — paradoxically — where Jesus is the one who came to die. This is seen further in the depiction of Jesus as "Son" in Matthew, Mark, and Luke.

CHAPTER 13

"Son of God"

Finally, we come to focus attention on the "Son of God" title, although here again it needs to be remembered that this title cannot be treated in isolation from the other designations which we have already discussed.[1] In the case of "Son of God" it is especially necessary to examine the usage of the title within the narrative frameworks of the individual Gospels: in fact, much of the literature even since 1980 (which will be the principal focus of interaction here) still concentrates on the extent to which use of the title goes back to Jesus or on whether the Son material is traditional or redactional.[2] The attempt here, then, will be to determine the sense of the title within the narrative frameworks of the Gospels as literary wholes.[3] Nevertheless, as ever, attention in this chapter will examine in particular the extent to which the "Son" title contributes to a preexistence christology.

---

1. C. Breytenbach, "Grundzüge markinischer Gottessohn-Christologie," in C. Breytenbach and H. Paulsen, eds., *Anfänge der Christologie. Festschrift F. Hahn* (Göttingen: Vandenhoeck und Ruprecht, 1991), 169-84 (174-75). Theobald's article on Markan christology is a good example of an integration of the various titles without collapsing them into one another. M. Theobald, "Gottessohn und Menschensohn. Zur polaren Struktur der Christologie im Markusevangelium," *SNTU* 13 (1988), 37-79.

2. D. Verseput, "The Role and Meaning of the 'Son of God' Title in Matthew's Gospel," *NTS* 33 (1987), 532-56, notes the lack of attention in other studies to the *content* of the title (532).

3. See, e.g., J. D. Kingsbury, *Matthew: Structure, Christology, Kingdom* (London: SPCK, 1975), 40-83, who uses the "Son of God" title as a lens through which to read the Gospel as a whole; however, it will not be assumed here, *pace* Kingsbury, that the Son of God title is the primary aspect of Matthew's presentation.

I. Mark's Gospel

The Gospel of Mark has only six explicit references to Jesus as "Son" or "Son of God." In the first place, there is doubt over whether the text of Mark 1.1 should include "the Son of God"; there has been an enormous amount of debate on this, and we will not go into the question here.[4] On a different note, we have also examined in chapter 7 above the extent to which the vineyard owner's "son" in 12.6 should be seen as mirroring the relationship between Jesus and the Father and therefore worthy of inclusion with the more explicit references to Jesus as "Son of God."

The first undisputed reference to Jesus as "Son" comes at his baptism, where the voice of the Father declares him as such (Mark 1.11). The next two acclamations of Jesus as "Son" come from demons; this is accompanied in the first case by them bowing down to Jesus and crying out (3.11), and in the second they fear destruction by him, hailing him as "Son of the Most High" (5.7). There follows another declaration by God, this time at the Son's transfiguration, which we discussed above in chapter 2 (9.7).[5] The next two instances are spoken by Jesus, in the parable of the wicked tenants (12.6) and in the ignorance logion (13.32). This last case is significant because it is the only absolute use of "*the* Son" in Mark.[6]

So far, then, Jesus' identity as Son of God has been revealed only by spiritual figures (God, demons) and by himself. In the passion narrative, this changes. First, Jesus is confronted by the High Priest as to whether he is the Christ, the Son of the Blessed (Mark 14.61). Finally, it is clearly a function of Mark's theology of the cross that the first human confession of Jesus as Son of God immediately follows Jesus' death: "When the centurion who stood opposite him saw that he died in this way, he said, 'Surely this man was the Son of God'" (15.39).

One final aspect of the presentation in Mark (and indeed in all the Syn-

4. For one of the best recent treatments, see P. M. Head, "A Text-Critical Study of Mark 1.1: 'The Beginning of the Gospel of Jesus Christ,'" *NTS* 37 (1991), 621-29, the title of which gives a clue to the conclusion!

5. J. Zmijewski, "Die Sohn-Gottes-Prädikation im Markusevangelium. Zur Frage einer eigenständigen markinischen Titelchristologie," *SNTU* 12 (1987), 5-34 (31), rightly argues that the transfiguration is the revelation of Jesus as God's Son; similarly E. Lohmeyer, *Das Evangelium nach Markus* (KEK; Göttingen: Vandenhoeck und Ruprecht, [17]1967), 24, on the issue of revelation.

6. On this point, see Lohmeyer, *Das Evangelium nach Markus,* 283. R. T. France, *The Gospel of Mark: A Commentary on the Greek Text* (NIGTC; Grand Rapids: Eerdmans, 2002), 543-44, rightly notes: "It is ironic that a saying which has such far-reaching christological implications has in fact become more familiar in theological discussion as a christological embarrassment."

optic Gospels) is the dispute over the Davidic sonship of the Messiah (Mark 12.35-37 par.). Although the divine sonship of the Messiah (and therefore of Jesus) is not explicitly mentioned, a number of commentators agree that it is strongly implied. This is important for our purposes since it points beyond a merely functional sonship possessed by someone with otherwise entirely natural origins. This passage by contrast points to a supernatural, transcendent origin and sonship for Jesus. However, the nature of this sonship is not spelled out any further.

One of the principal recent attempts to argue for preexistence in the "Son of God" title has come from J. Schreiber. In a section entitled "Pre-existence, Redeemer and Redeemed," he maintains that it is "clear" that the parable of the wicked tenants shows that Mark thinks in terms of the preexistence of the "beloved son," a point which extends to the baptism and to the transfiguration because they use this same phrase.[7] The problem with Schreiber's approach, however, is that he sees allusions to the whole of the redeemer myth in numerous different places throughout the Gospel. This line of interpretation, however, is not likely to persuade anyone who is not a hard-line Bultmannian.

On the other hand, a more powerful explanation has been offered by Joel Marcus. The "son" title, finding at least some of its background (especially as far as Mark 1.11 is concerned) in Psalm 2, is most obviously a *royal* title.[8] However, in view in the early chapters of Mark is "not just the king's task but also the superhuman power necessary to accomplish that task."[9] The task of rule in the Gospel involves the subduing of cosmic, spiritual forces of evil. As such, in the baptismal pronouncement, "Jesus is the Son of God because he is granted substantial participation in God's holiness, God's effective opposition to the powers of evil (see 1:21-28, in which Jesus' exorcism of the demon is linked with the title 'Holy One of God')."[10] So for Marcus, Jesus' sonship must be understood not only in royal terms but also as stressing "Jesus' participation in God's power and being."[11]

7. For the whole section, see J. Schreiber, *Die Markuspassion. Eine redaktionsgeschichtliche Untersuchung* (BZNW 68; Berlin: de Gruyter, 1993), 374-77. For further discussion see also the section "Die Präexistenz des Gekreuzigten," in *Markuspassion*, 210-59.

8. Scholars such as France are surely right to see both Psalm 2 and Isaiah 42 as behind the voice from heaven. France, *Mark*, 81.

9. J. Marcus, *The Way of the Lord: Christological Exegesis of the Old Testament in the Gospel of Mark* (Louisville: Westminster/John Knox, 1992), 71. Lohmeyer, *Das Evangelium nach Markus*, 25-26, points out a possible reference to creation here in the statement about the Spirit resting on the Messiah, which perhaps echoes Genesis 1.

10. Marcus, *Way of the Lord*, 71.

11. Marcus, *Way of the Lord*, 72. Cf. also Lohmeyer, *Das Evangelium nach Markus*, 4-5, who stresses the recognition by demons and not by disciples and other humans.

Confirming Marcus's interpretation of Mark 1.11 here is the next reference, in which Mark highlights the fact that it is not just the human realm which is the sphere of Jesus' rule, but the spiritual sphere as well. In 3.11, when the unclean spirits see Jesus, they *acknowledge him as Son of God,* and *bow down before him.* So Marcus is right about the rule which Jesus exercises as Son, but is also probably correct that there is no explicit idea of preexistence intrinsic to the title.[12]

Nevertheless, even if there is no explicit evidence for preexistence here, there are strong indications of the heavenly contours of Jesus' identity as "Son of God." We noted in chapter 2 that this category of heavenly identity aims to explain how Jesus, while firmly planted on earth, is also depicted in the Gospels as part of the heavenly realms as well. In particular, in Mark 9.7 Jesus' (a) ascent to the mountain top, (b) shining garments, and (c) heavenly company point to the fact that he is a heavenly person on earth. Moreover, the "voice from the cloud" confirms that it is precisely this figure who is the "Son."

The heaven-earth divide in Mark is epistemological as well as ontological: there is a clearly defined set of characters in the Gospel who know Jesus' identity as Son of God (God and the evil spirits, the devil as well in Matthew and Luke), and, on the other hand, all the human participants are ignorant of it.[13] This is true at least until Mark 15.39 and the centurion's confession: even here, however, it must be remembered that the centurion's confession follows immediately after the tearing of the temple curtain, which is a clear indication of the breaking of the epistemological divide between heaven and earth.

In addition to the role which Jesus carries out as king, the "Son" title clearly identifies him as in the closest possible relation to God, his Father. The transfiguration, as argued in chapter 2, emphasizes that the Son's nature is not simply human but radiantly heavenly. Jesus' questioning of the Davidic sonship of the Messiah (Mark 12.35-37) also strongly implies that his *origins* are not merely human either. Similarly, Mark 13.32 not only places Jesus alongside the angels, but does so by placing "Father and Son" in conjunction with the angels.[14] This points strongly away from any kind of *functional* son-

---

12. This is in contrast to O. Hofius, who argues that the correct tradition-historical background to the "Son" title is not 2 Samuel 7 and Psalm 2, but early Jewish wisdom theology. See O. Hofius, "Ist Jesus der Messias? Thesen," *JBT* 8 (1993), 103-29 (especially 117-18). It is difficult to see, however, how this background is preferable as far as the Synoptic Gospels are concerned.

13. On this point, see, e.g., O. Cullmann, *The Christology of the New Testament* (Philadelphia: Westminster, 1963), 279.

14. On the juxtaposition of Jesus with the angels here, see E. Schweizer, *Das Evangelium nach Markus* (NTD; Göttingen: Vandenhoeck und Ruprecht, [13]1973), 162.

ship or a sonship which is of the same kind as that of Israel or the king in the OT. Rather, it is assumed here that the Son participates in the same reality as the angels and the Father.

Finally, we can recall that this same Son is the one "sent": the *"beloved son"* in Mark 12.6 would recall the baptism and the transfiguration.[15] Within Mark's story, this language would at the same time evoke the picture immediately narrated of a pitiful figure being sent to the vineyard to die at the hands of the tenants, but would also be particularly jarring because of the previous characterization of the "beloved son" as the unique object of God's election (εὐδόκησα in 1.11 and 9.7) and as the one on the mount of transfiguration shining with heavenly glory. The Son of Man — a glorious figure one would expect *to be served* — came from heaven with the prior goal to serve and give his life as a ransom for many. A similar reversal of expectations comes into play with "Son *of God*" in Mark: the glorious companion of Moses and Elijah, the Son whose proper dwelling place is heaven[16] in shining glory, is the one whom God *sends* into the world only for him to be rejected and killed. As such, although there may be no strong tradition-historical evidence for the preexistence of the Son,[17] this is the strong implication of the Gospel narrative on the basis of the sending motif in 12.6.

II. Matthew's Gospel

In the first half of Matthew's Gospel, the pattern of Jesus being recognized only by spiritual figures is very similar to that in Mark. The first reference to Jesus as God's son comes in the statement of his being called "out of Egypt" (Matt. 2.15), as prophesied in Hos. 11.1, although in general Matthew (surprisingly, and in contrast to Luke) does not relate the virginal conception to Jesus' divine sonship.[18] The following chapter then has the baptismal declaration in — as is well known — more public form (Matt. 3.17: *"this is* my son"). The characteristics of the Son here as "beloved" and "chosen" are the same as in Mark 1.11 and also identical to those of the Son in the transfiguration (Matt.

15. So, rightly, France, *Mark*, 460.

16. To repeat again in this chapter the comment of Pesch: "Daß Elija und Mose mit Jesus reden . . . zeigt an, daß Jesus ihrer Welt zugehört." R. Pesch, *Das Markusevangelium 2. Kommentar zu Kapitel 8,27–16,20* (HTK; Freiburg: Herder, 1977), 74.

17. It remains possible, as we indicated in chapter 10, that Ps. 109.3 LXX influenced the christology of the Gospels more widely, though it remains in the realms of speculation how much this may have shaped the Evangelists' understanding of the "Son" title.

18. This is pointed out by Verseput, "Role and Meaning of the 'Son of God' Title," 532.

17.5). The key difference between Matthew's account of the baptism and that of Mark is that the former is sandwiched between two emphatic references to Jesus' obedience: the fulfilling of all righteousness (Matt. 3.15) on one side and the longer version of the temptation narrative in Matthew 4. So Luz is right to note that obedience is an important aspect of Jesus' baptism and sonship in Matthew.[19]

After the declarations by Scripture and God of Jesus' identity, the next two instances of "Son of God" are spoken by the devil in the temptation narrative. The devil's assumption, or temptation, is that as Son, Jesus could turn stones into bread (Matt. 4.3) and rely on angelic protection if he would jump off the pinnacle of the temple (4.6). The next reference, in ch. 8 (paralleled in Mark), is rather more timid: demons are fearful of this Son of God, in particular that they will be *destroyed* by him (Matt. 8.29). In ch. 11, we eventually come to a *self*-declaration by Jesus as Son, in which he claims to have received all things from the Father (including the power of election to salvation) as well as exclusive knowledge of the Father. 11.27 is also the first absolute usage of "the Son" in the Gospel, a self-designation which is repeated in the ignorance-logion in 24.36. So far, in the first half of the Gospel, then, the title "Son of God" is confined to heavenly speakers: in this respect, Jesus is counted with God, the devil, and the unclean spirits as one who has supernatural knowledge of his identity. Again, the contexts of the usages also highlight the heavenly identity of Jesus as one who is known by the devil to have supernatural power and who was to come to destroy the demonic realm, having been given all things by the Father. This is in addition to the points which were already made in chapter 2 in connection with the transfiguration and the Son's position in the "heavenly hierarchy" in 24.36.

In the second half of the Gospel, the emphasis shifts to human beings reckoning with Jesus as Son of God. The first case is the incident where Jesus walks on the sea, an episode which is clearly intended by the Evangelist to be revelatory of Jesus' identity (Matt. 14.22-33). The disciples' actions and words in response confirm this (14.33). Even more explicit is the realization by Simon of Jesus' identity as Son of God at Caesarea Philippi (16.16). To maintain the fact that Jesus' true identity as Son of God is spiritual and supernatural, Matthew wants to clarify that Simon only knew this by divine revelation, and emphatically not by "flesh and blood" (16.17).

Three references in the passion narrative have a rather different focus

19. U. Luz, *Matthew 1–7* (Continental Commentary; Minneapolis: Fortress, [1]1989), 180. See also Verseput, "Role and Meaning of the 'Son of God' Title," 538 and *passim* on this emphasis.

and appear to represent the unbelieving world in its skepticism of Jesus' identity as Son. First is the high priest's demand: "tell us if you are the Christ, the Son of God" (Matt. 26.63). In the course of the actual crucifixion, similar demands are made in the form of taunts first by passers-by and then by the chief-priests, scribes, and elders:

> If you are the Son of God, come down from the cross. (27.40)

> He trusted in God: let Him deliver him if He wants. For he said, "I am the Son of God." (v. 43)

Commentators typically refer to the interesting parallel with Wisdom 2 here.[20] In the narrative of the passion, however, these skeptical questionings and taunts only highlight more clearly the climactic confession of the centurion: "Surely this man was the Son of God" (v. 54). This is prompted by the destruction of the temple curtain, the earthquake, and the resurrection of the saints (vv. 51-53): like the walking on the water, these events reveal the identity of Jesus and lead to the confession. As Mowery rightly notes, the confessions in ch. 14 and here in ch. 27 emphasize Jesus' *divine* sonship by the word order.[21] Finally, the Gospel concludes with another self-reference of Jesus to his identity as Son, sandwiched between "Father" and "Holy Spirit" in the great commission (28.19).

Preexistence in Matthew 11.27?

Traditionally, perhaps the most important evidence for preexistence in the Synoptic Gospels has been Matthew 11.27 par. Luke 10.22. This is even taken by Schweitzer and Cullmann as evidence for a possible self-consciousness of preexistence in Jesus himself.[22] The traditional view of Matt. 11.27 was that

---

20. See also J. M. McDermott, "Jesus and the Son of God Title," *Gregorianum* 62 (1981), 277-317 (281). Davies and Allison rightly comment that Matt. 27.40 recalls in particular the temptations in 4.3 and 6. W. D. Davies and D. C. Allison, *A Critical and Exegetical Commentary on the Gospel according to Saint Matthew,* Volume 3: *Introduction and Commentary on Matthew XIX–XXVIII* (ICC; Edinburgh: Clark, 1997), 618.

21. Cf. also Matt. 27.43. In these three places, Matthew alone uses the order θεοῦ υἱός. Mowery rightly notes that this is to emphasize the θεοῦ element. R. J. Mowery, "Subtle Differences: The Matthean 'Son of God' References," *NovT* 32 (1990), 193-200 (197).

22. A. Schweitzer, *The Quest of the Historical Jesus: First Complete Edition* (London: SCM, 2000), 255; Cullmann, *Christology of the New Testament,* 288.

the handing over of all things to the Son was a pre-temporal event. This line was still taken in the commentaries of Allen and Plummer:[23]

> The idea involved is of a pre-temporal act, and carries with it the conception of the pre-existence of the Messiah. . . . Whether the words as originally uttered involved consciousness of pre-existence is, no doubt, open to question. But it is difficult not to suppose that the editor of this Gospel interpreted them in this sense.[24]

Allen then refers to the virgin birth and Christ's election from all eternity evidenced in the voice from heaven and thus comments that the handing over refers to a "pre-temporal" act in eternity or in the "pre-historic" beginning.[25] Similarly, Plummer: ". . . the aorist points back to a moment in eternity, and implies the pre-existence of the Messiah."[26] The problem, however, lies in the fact that those scholars who argue for a gift from the Father to the preexistent Son do not offer any substantial argument: the aorist clearly cannot bear the weight which Plummer gives it here.

The main factor which might point toward a pre-temporal transfer would be evidence from a *heavenly council* setting. Some scholars such as Schlatter and Feuillet have argued that Matt. 11.25-27 par. Luke 10.21-22 situate Christ in the divine throne room among the hosts of heaven.[27] Feuillet remarks on the "borrowing in the style of the ancient Eastern court, which evokes an assembly of heavenly beings in discussion before the divine throne."[28] The single statement in Matt. 11.27 par. Luke 10.22 on its own is difficult to assess in this regard: as we have said, the verb (παρεδόθη, "was handed over") would not automatically require a heavenly court setting. But the previous statement does: "Yes, Father, because this is your decree" (Matt. 11.26). Important here is the surrounding context of the acceptance of the kingdom by

---

23. See also W. F. Albright and C. Mann, *Matthew* (Anchor; New York: Doubleday, 1971), 145; B. W. Bacon, *The Gospel of Mark: Its Composition and Date* (New Haven: Yale University Press, 1925), 251. Bacon also sees it in Luke 10.21.

24. W. C. Allen, *A Critical and Exegetical Commentary on the Gospel according to St. Matthew* (ICC; Edinburgh: Clark, 1907), 122.

25. Allen, *Gospel according to St. Matthew*, 123.

26. A. Plummer, *An Exegetical Commentary on the Gospel According to S. Matthew* (London: Scott, 1909), 168-69.

27. A. Schlatter, *Der Evangelist Matthäus. Seine Sprache, sein Ziel, seine Selbständigkeit* (Stuttgart: Calver, 1948), 383; A. Feuillet, "Jésus et la Sagesse Divine d'après les Évangiles Synoptiques. Le 'logion johannique' et l'Ancien Testament," *RevB* 62 (1955), 161-96 (177-78).

28. Feuillet, "Jésus et la Sagesse Divine," 177-78: "un emprunt au style de cour de l'Ancien Orient évoquant une assemblée délibérative des êtres célestes devant le trône divin."

those who welcome it and the corresponding rejection by the proud. The point here is that this is *no surprise to Jesus:* he is aware that this was what was decided as the predestined divine will (εὐδοκία) in God's presence (ἔμπροσθέν σου), both of these phrases evoking images of the heavenly court. In the light of Jesus' knowledge of this divine decree, Matt. 11.27 par. Luke 10.22 can be interpreted in a similar setting. The imagery of Jesus' presence in the heavenly council at the deliberation of the predestined divine purpose (Matt. 11.26) might perhaps point in the direction of preexistence. Again, the statement immediately after about the Father's commission of all things to the Son (Matt. 11.27) could then be interpreted as involving the preexistent Christ in a similar heavenly court setting, but this really only remains in the realm of possibility.

Heavenly Origin

Although the evidence for preexistence *per se* is somewhat ambiguous here, the overall portrait in Matthew (11.27 included) gives a very strong sense of the Son as both a heavenly and earthly figure. As Hurtado has rightly observed, "In Matthew, not only is Jesus the ultimately authoritative spokesman for God, whose teachings supervene any other relative authority, he is also the Son of God who combines full messianic significance and transcendent divine-like status as well."[29] As well as highlighting Jesus' rule over all things, Matthew also emphasizes how Jesus stands in the closest possible relation to the Father.[30] Much of the Markan material is also adopted by Matthew, however. As well as taking over the transfiguration material and the ignorance logion (Matt. 24.36) from Mark, the sending of the son also features in Matthew's version of the parable of the wicked tenants. In fact, in Matthew, the parable does not refer to the son as "beloved," and so in this sense the linguistic cues might not point back so readily to the baptism and the transfiguration. But Matthew drives the point home in his own way by the repetition of "the son": "Last he sent *his son* (τὸν υἱὸν αὐτοῦ) to them, saying, 'They will respect *my son* (τὸν υἱόν μου)." The farmers, seeing *the son* (τὸν υἱόν), said to themselves . . ." (21.37-38). So there is no mistaking where Matthew wants to direct the hearers' attention. Again, then, we have the paradox of God handing over all things to the heavenly Son, but also handing him over to be rejected and crucified.

29. L. W. Hurtado, "Pre–70 CE Jewish Opposition to Christ-Devotion," *JTS* 50 (1999), 35-58 (40).

30. See Verseput, "Role and Meaning of the 'Son of God' Title," 539, who lists numerous distinctively Matthean references in which Jesus addresses God as Father.

III. Luke's Gospel

The basic elements of the Lukan usage of the "Son of God" title can be sketched very briefly since it is very similar to that of Matthew and Mark. In fact, the general pattern seen in the first half of Matthew and in Mark's account up to the cross is even carried through the entirety of Luke's narrative: there is no human confession of Jesus as Son of God in the whole Gospel. The six references to Jesus as Son by God (Luke 3.22; 9.35),[31] Satan (4.3, 9), and the unclean spirits (4.41; 8.28) are all reasonably closely paralleled in either Mark or Matthew or both.

But there is one important section which is distinctively Lukan. In Luke 1, Mary receives the visit from the angel who relates two points about her child which are relevant for our purposes:

> He will be great and will be called "Son of the Most High," and the Lord God will give him the throne of his father David, and he will reign over the house of Jacob forever, and of his kingdom there will be no end. (Luke 1.32-33)

> And the angel said to her, "The Holy Spirit will come upon you and the power of the Most High will overshadow you. Therefore the holy one born will be called 'Son of God.'" (1.35)

Discussion of the "Son" titles here has been renewed particularly recently since the publication of the "Aramaic Apocalypse" from Qumran, where the titles also appear closely together: "He will be called son of God, and they will call him son of the Most High" (4Q246 2.1). In addition, the figure's "kingdom will be an everlasting kingdom . . . his rule will be an everlasting rule . . ." (2.5, 9). The similarities here are startling, but in fact — largely because of the fragmentary nature of the text — Luke 1 has actually shed more light on 4Q246 than vice versa.[32]

Perhaps the most striking element of the Son's identity here is his apparently everlasting life. The Davidic promise in the OT generally envisaged an everlasting throne for David and his descendants, but the only really ex-

---

31. In fact, Bovon sees preexistence underlying the "Son" title in Luke 9.35. F. Bovon, *Luke 1* (Hermeneia; Minneapolis: Fortress, 2002), 379.

32. For example, the parallel in Luke 1 clarifies that the "Son of God" in 4Q246 is not an antichrist but a positive and probably messianic figure (perhaps like the "Son of Man"), as is now generally agreed. See, e.g., J. J. Collins, *Apocalypticism in the Dead Sea Scrolls* (New York: Routledge, 1997), 84, who notes Luke 1.32, 35 in this connection.

plicit statement of a kind of "immortal" Messiah is Ezek. 37.25: "David my servant shall be their prince forever." This is also the clear sense of Luke 1.33: not only will Jesus guarantee the everlasting endurance of the Davidic throne, but *he himself* will be its sole occupant: "he will reign over the house of Jacob forever." This cannot simply be understood as a reign that will be extremely long, as is made explicit by the final clarification: "of his kingdom there will be *no end*." Clearly in Luke 1.33, the *indestructibility* of Jesus is a crucial part of his identity as Son.

Furthermore, the reference to the child as one who is "holy" highlights the fact that the child belongs at the outset to God's sphere.[33] As in Mark and Matthew, the disputation initiated by Jesus over the Davidic origins of the Messiah (Luke 20.41-44) also emphasizes this point implying Jesus' divine sonship. Some scholars argue that in Mark's Gospel, it is the baptism and the gift of the Spirit that really constitutes Jesus' identity as Son;[34] even if this is conceivable for Mark, it is impossible in the Lukan scheme, in which Jesus is "the holy one" at his birth.[35] On its own, this should not be pressed, although in combination with Luke's emphasis on Jesus' indestructibility and other material in Luke (the parallels with Matthew 11.25-27 and the like), the total picture is striking. Jesus is again portrayed as one who is superhuman and belongs in the divine sphere of reality.

With Luke's narrative of Jesus the Son of God depicted as an indestructible king, the degree of paradox in the Gospel as a whole is even more difficult to bear than it is in Mark and Matthew. It is this immortal Son of God who is sent to be executed. The parable of the wicked tenants thus makes very disturbing reading in Luke's Gospel, since the "beloved son" of the vineyard owner recalls not only the baptism and (to some degree) the transfiguration, but also the handing over of all things and the promise at the beginning of the Gospel that this figure will be the one to rule everlastingly from David's throne.[36] Again,

33. See the astute discussion of the relationship between "Son" and "holy one" in Cullmann, *Christology of the New Testament*, 285.

34. Breytenbach, "Gottessohn-Christologie," 175 (although he sees this as only one aspect of Jesus' sonship). Breytenbach probably falls for the *post hoc ergo propter hoc* fallacy here, however, in arguing that Jesus is essentially Son in Mark 1.11 *because of* the coming of the Spirit upon him in 1.10. France, *Mark*, 82-83, is more careful.

35. See, e.g., Bovon, *Luke 1*, 129: "In view of 1:31-32, the readers are not learning something completely new. What is new is only that Jesus is here now, receives the Spirit, and hears the voice himself. Luke thus does not understand the words in the sense of an adoption, but as the revelation of a truth, of a mystery."

36. In fact, in Luke's version of the transfiguration Jesus is not proclaimed by the voice to be the "beloved son" strictly speaking, but the "chosen (ἐκλελεγμένος) son."

then, the beloved Son acclaimed by God is the very one sent (from heaven) to the human realm to suffer an unjust death.

Conclusion

All the Synoptic Evangelists, then, present their readers with a startling paradox. On the one hand, there is the clear sense of the "Son of God title as a super-human revelation," as a secret known to humanity only by divine revelation.[37] This identity of Jesus as Son of God is revealed in the Gospel narrative in the transfiguration, where Jesus is seen by the three disciples in all his heavenly glory. By contrast, however, the identity of Jesus is fully and finally seen in the Gospel narrative in his death, and in Matthew's and Mark's Gospels, Jesus is proclaimed as Son of God by the centurion when the latter sees Jesus' death and the events surrounding it.

As we argued in chapter 7, the sending of Jesus should be interpreted in the light of the "I have come" sayings and so should be seen as implying that Jesus was sent from heaven by the Father. Although a parable, Mark 12.1-12 par. has very strong linguistic connections with the language about Jesus elsewhere in the Synoptics, especially in the key statement in Mark 12.6 about the father having "sent" the figure of "the beloved son." As Schweizer comments: "Finally [after the servants], the 'beloved son' is of course a direct reference to Jesus as the Son of God (cf. 1.11)."[38] As such, the parable here should not be regarded as incidental to christology.[39] Rather, it is a crucial part of the characterization of the "Son" in the Synoptic Gospels and contributes the vitally important element of the sending of the Son by the Father. This "sending" — as was seen in chapter 7 — should not be taken merely in terms of a prophetic commission, but refers rather to the mission of Jesus from a preexistence in heaven, into the earthly realm to his death.[40]

---

37. McDermott, "Jesus and the Son of God Title," 282.

38. Schweizer, *Markus*, 136: "Endlich ist der 'geliebte Sohn' natürlich direkter Hinweis auf Jesus als Gottessohn (1,11!)." (See also the comment on 138.) In fact, Schweizer entitles the parable "The Parable of the Passion of Jesus."

39. Unfortunately, what often seems to happen in scholarly discussions is that in talking of Mark 12.6 par., the other "Son" passages are brought in, but when the "Son" texts are discussed, Mark 12.6 tends to get left out.

40. To this extent I disagree with A. Yarbro Collins, "Mark and His Readers: The Son of God among Jews," *HTR* 92 (1999), 393-408 (395); eadem, "Mark and His Readers: The Son of God among Greeks and Romans," *HTR* 93 (2000), 85-100 (100). Her comments on Mark's lack of preexistence christology in fact concern the Gospel in general and not just the "Son of God" title.

CHAPTER 14

Some Aspects of the Contemporary Theological Debate

There are of course a number of issues that could be tackled here, but this chapter will be restricted to those aspects which are affected by the foregoing discussion of the Synoptics. Furthermore, since I am not a systematician, the discussion here will — in the interests of caution — be kept to a minimum. One omission, for example, will be of the preexistence of Christ in Barth's theology, not least because there are a dizzying array of views as to what Barth's position actually was.[1] This section will be restricted to four brief critical observations and two more constructive points.

I. Preexistence and Virgin Birth

One issue which has been raised perennially concerns the relation between the preexistence of Christ and his virginal conception. Bultmann puts it starkly: "The Virgin birth is inconsistent with the assertion of his preexistence."[2] Pannenberg gives the following as an explanation:

---

1. W. Pannenberg, *Systematic Theology* (Grand Rapids: Eerdmans, 1994), 2:368 n. 127, 370 n. 136, summarizes Barth's view of preexistence as ideal preexistence in the counsel of God. Contrast P. D. Molnar, *Divine Freedom and the Doctrine of the Immanent Trinity: In Dialogue with Karl Barth and Contemporary Theology* (Edinburgh: Clark, 2002). Kuschel sees the issue as more complex still, arguing that there is a significant shift in Barth's thinking around 1924-25. K.-J. Kuschel, *Born before All Time? The Dispute over Christ's Origin* (London: SCM, 1992 [1990]), 92.

2. R. Bultmann, "New Testament and Mythology," in H. W. Bartsch, ed., *Kerygma and*

> In its content, the legend of Jesus' virgin birth stands in an irreconcilable contradiction to the Christology of the incarnation of the pre-existent Son of God found in Paul and John. For according to this legend, Jesus first *became* God's Son through Mary's conception. . . . Sonship cannot at the same time consist in pre-existence and still have its origin only in the divine procreation of Jesus in Mary.[3]

In fact, however, the two concepts seem to cohere rather well. There is nothing that requires Pannenberg's assumption that the virgin birth is an absolute beginning for Jesus' sonship. One would expect a supernatural being to enter the human realm in a supernatural way; if one begins with the Son's preexistence, then his humanity must have started somewhere.[4] To show how alien an opposition of preexistence to the virgin birth was to the biblical authors, we need only look at Matthew and Luke. If it is right that these Gospels presuppose preexistence, then it is highly unlikely that they regarded it as incompatible with Jesus' virginal conception.[5] The clearest illustration of this is Luke 1.78, which we discussed above in chapter 10. Here, in the description of Christ as the *Anatolē* who visits from on high, we have a strong indication of preexistence. Significantly for the current argument, this statement is made *in the Lukan infancy narrative,* in the *Benedictus.* So a reference to Christ's preexistence is in fact embedded in the account of the virgin birth.

II. Preexistence and Christ's Humanity

Similar questions have been raised, this time predominantly by British theologians, about whether preexistence is potentially destructive of Christ's humanity. To cite a recent example, Macquarrie asserts that if one supposes "that Jesus Christ had prior to his birth a conscious personal pre-existence in 'heaven,' this is not only mythological but is, I believe, destructive of his true human-

Myth, by Rudolf Bultmann and Five Critics (New York: Harper, 1961), 1-44 (11). I have chosen this translation because it is rather more crisp than the alternative in R. Bultmann, *New Testament and Mythology and Other Basic Writings* (Philadelphia: Fortress, 1984), 10, though the point is clear in both.

3. W. Pannenberg, *Jesus: God and Man* (Philadelphia: Westminster, [2]1977), 143.

4. On the first point, see J. G. Machen, *The Virgin Birth of Christ* (London: Clarke, 1958 [1930]), 318; on the latter, see D. Macleod, "The Christology of Wolfhart Pannenberg," *Themelios* 25 (2000), 19-41 (22).

5. A further implication of the foregoing exegesis is that the combination of preexistence and virginal conception was not first achieved by Justin, as is the standard view.

ity."[6] Again, however, this betrays a metaphysic completely alien to the biblical authors. Hebrews is perhaps one of the clearest examples of a work which emphasizes very strongly both Christ's human nature and his preexistence, as Macquarrie readily admits.[7] In fact, this combination was also common to non-Christian Jewish messianic expectation. In *4 Ezra,* for example, the preexistence *and* Davidic descent of the Messiah are presented side-by-side.[8] Michael Stone's point, in his commentary on *4 Ezra,* is relevant here:

> It has been suggested that certain editorial adjustments have been made within this vision, in the verses touching on the Messiah. . . . The basis for these suggestions is supposed "contradictions" in the book's ideas about the Messiah. Pre-existence supposedly contradicts Davidid descent. . . . The supposed anomalies are, in fact, far less serious than might be thought. They arise, basically, because modern critics apply to the book categories of logic and consistency that are too rigid.[9]

Or again, the less well known *Prayer of Joseph* presents Jacob as the incarnation of a preexisting spirit: "I (Jacob-Israel) descended to earth and I had tabernacled among men and was called by the name of Jacob."[10] Again, we have shown how Matthew, Mark, and Luke assume preexistence without regarding it as in any way detrimental to Jesus' historical life. In the Synoptics, preexistence is the presupposition of Jesus' human life rather than potentially destructive of it.

III. Ideal Preexistence?

We saw above in the introduction that R. Hamerton-Kelly has made extensive use of the concept of "ideal preexistence" in his exegesis of the New Testa-

---

6. J. Macquarrie, *Jesus Christ in Modern Thought* (London: SCM, 1990), 57; cf. J. A. T. Robinson, *The Human Face of God* (London: SCM, 1973), 179. Both are influenced in this respect by John Knox's *The Humanity and Divinity of Christ: A Study of Pattern in Christology* (Cambridge: Cambridge University Press, 1967).

7. J. Macquarrie, "The Pre-existence of Jesus Christ," *ExpT* 77 (1965-66), 199-202 (200).

8. On Davidic descent, see *4 Ezra* 12.32, and the very same verse might also imply his preexistence, which is in any case clearer in ch. 13. On the issue, see M. E. Stone, "The Concept of the Messiah in IV Ezra," in J. Neusner, ed., *Religions in Antiquity: Essays in Memory of Erwin Ramsdell Goodenough* (Leiden: Brill, 1968), 295-312, much of which is incorporated into Stone's commentary (see below).

9. M. E. Stone, *Fourth Ezra* (Hermeneia; Minneapolis: Fortress, 1990), 210.

10. *Prayer of Joseph* frag. A 4.

ment. A *real* preexistence of the Son would mean an actual existence in relation to the Father prior to the incarnation; ideal preexistence, on the other hand, means just preexistence *in the mind or plan of God.*[11] Similarly, Macquarrie understands preexistence to mean "that from the beginning Christ the incarnate Word was there in the counsels of God. . . ."[12] The problem here, however, is that this sense of preexistence is far too attenuated. Whether ideal preexistence refers simply to foreknowledge, or — in a stronger sense — to active predestination by God, the problem is that most early Jewish and Christian groups held, in varying degrees, that God foreordained the lives of all people and in some cases the existence of all things as well. As such, for them, the category of ideal preexistence would extend to almost everything, and so becomes meaningless as a christological predication.[13] By contrast, the emphasis on Jesus' action in the "I have come" sayings in Matthew, Mark, and Luke means that this concept of ideal preexistence does not do justice to the presentation of preexistence in the NT. The category of "ideal preexistence" should probably be abandoned in favor simply of foreknowledge and election or predestination.

IV. A Marginal Doctrine?

As has been noted by others, it is clear that Karl-Josef Kuschel's *Born before All Time?* aims to show that preexistence is a marginal feature of the NT.[14] This is apparent particularly in the summary of his NT exegesis. One of the factors which, he maintains, relativizes the traditional doctrine of preexistence is that "of the twenty-seven writings in the New Testament, twenty can speak of Jesus as the Son of God without being drawn to the notion of his real pre-existence."[15] He argues further that the historical Jesus, Mark, and Q say nothing about it, that Paul does not have a preexistence christology, and that Matthew and Luke go a different route altogether in narrating a virginal conception.[16]

11. See, e.g., his use of the Matthean genealogy as evidence. R. G. Hamerton-Kelly, *Pre-Existence, Wisdom, and the Son of Man: A Study of the Idea of Pre-Existence in the New Testament* (SNTSMS 21; Cambridge: Cambridge University Press, 1973), 78.

12. J. Macquarrie, *Christology Revisited* (London: SCM, 1998), 114.

13. Similarly, D. McCready, "'He Came from Heaven': The Pre-existence of Christ Revisited," *JETS* 40 (1997), 419-32 (424).

14. B. Byrne, "Christ's Pre-existence in Pauline Soteriology," *TS* 58 (1997), 308-30 (309).

15. Kuschel, *Born before All Time,* 491.

16. Kuschel, *Born before All Time,* 491.

When it comes to Paul, Kuschel argues that there is preexistence in the pre-Pauline hymn in Philippians 2, but emphasizes that the idea "does not have any independent significance" there.[17] This relativizing is exaggerated further, when Kuschel concludes that Paul does not develop the thought of the hymn further, as he could conceivably have done.[18] However, both of these points bear examination. The first, on the lack of independence of the theme of preexistence, is a red herring. Is there any doctrine in Paul which is independent of all the others? As far as Paul's developing the hymn is concerned, we actually have no idea, really, of the extent to which Paul has modified his source, if indeed it was originally a hymn at all. Similar rhetoric is apparent in the interpretation of the mention of Christ's mediation at creation in 1 Cor. 8.6. Kuschel twice protests that this calls for cautious restraint because Paul does not develop the idea.[19] It is still there, however, and is in fact clearly developed in Colossians 1, Hebrews 1, and John 1. Kuschel's arguments against the consensus view on Paul are clearly not going to get us very far.

Furthermore, if the exegesis of the Synoptics in the previous chapters is correct, then the argument that preexistence is a marginal aspect of NT theology receives a further blow. This lends additional weight to the assessment by Pannenberg that "We certainly do not do justice to the evidence in the primitive Christian tradition if we regard the idea of the preexistence of the Son of God who was manifested in Jesus as a marginal phenomenon. . . ."[20] Rather, as we have seen above, preexistence is in fact the very presupposition of the Gospel narrative.

There is some similarity between Kuschel's assessment of the biblical data and that of Robert Jenson, who warns that "we should be taught by what may seem the inconsequence of biblical reference to Christ's pre-existence."[21] Jenson sees preexistence primarily in two senses, the first of which is the preexistence of the Son in and as Israel: "to the pre-existence of Jesus Christ there belongs among other factors his pre-existence in and as the nation of Israel. For Israel also is the human Son."[22] Second, there is a more mysterious

---

17. Kuschel, *Born before All Time,* 258. Cf. the similar comments in K.-J. Kuschel, "Exegese und Dogmatik — Harmonie oder Konflikt? Die Frage nach einer Präexistenzchristologie bei Paulus als Testfall," in R. Laufen, ed., *Gottes ewiger Sohn. Die Präexistenz Christi* (Paderborn: Schöningh, 1997), 143-61 (155).

18. Kuschel, *Born before All Time,* 298-99, 491-92.

19. Kuschel, *Born before All Time,* 286, 287.

20. Pannenberg, *Systematic Theology,* 2:369.

21. R. W. Jenson, *Systematic Theology,* Volume 1: *The Triune God* (Oxford: Oxford University Press, 1997), 139.

22. R. W. Jenson, "Christ as Culture 1: Christ as Polity," *IJST* 5 (2003), 323-29 (326).

sense in which there is a kind of logical priority to Jesus' divine identity over against his human identity. So Jenson affirms that "the Son's eternal birth from the Father eternally precedes his reality as incarnate . . . ,' although this must not be understood as a temporal, linear precedence.[23] As a result, a key component of the traditional understanding of preexistence is jettisoned: "What, we may want to ask, of the Son before Mary's pregnancy? But if the one Mary bore is the eternal Son, there can be no before."[24] Some of the problems with Jenson's position have been discussed elsewhere, and so here we will merely note two ways in which his exegesis leads him to this wrong conclusion, noted above, of "the inconsequence of biblical reference."[25] The first case is Col. 1.15-20, in which Jenson comments that "When Christ appears in Colossians as mediator and goal of creation, it is as 'the head . . . of the church' that he has this position."[26] This is only half true, however, and has the consequence of eliding the protological dimensions of the passage. Similarly, in the discussion of 1 Corinthians 8, Jenson argues as follows: "Yet even here Paul's purpose is not to enforce the idea of creation itself or to develop it christologically, but to ward off any temptation to take the pagan gods seriously except as occasions of temptation. . . ."[27] Again, what Paul actually says falls victim to Jenson's construal of Paul's overall purpose in the passage as a whole, as if the components of Paul's argument were irrelevant. In this respect, Jenson's argumentation resembles that of Kuschel: preexistence is relativized as a result of accentuating points which in a biblical framework belong with, rather than compete with preexistence.

V. The Will of the Son in the Advent

We turn to another area to which Jenson's account does not really do justice.[28] It has been noted already that one of the most significant passages in the NT which talks of preexistence is Phil. 2.6-11. One of the key aspects of the

---

23. Jenson, *Systematic Theology,* 1:141 n. 85.

24. Jenson, "For Us . . . He Was Made Man," in C. R. Seitz, ed., *Nicene Christianity: The Future for a New Ecumenism* (Grand Rapids: Brazos, 2002), 75-86 (84).

25. The fuller discussion is in Gathercole, "Pre-Existence, and the Freedom of the Son in Creation and Redemption: An Exposition in Dialogue with Robert Jenson," *IJST* 7 (2005), 38-51 (especially 46-50).

26. R. W. Jenson, *Systematic Theology,* Volume 2: *The Works of God* (Oxford: Oxford University Press, 1999), 4.

27. Jenson, *Systematic Theology,* 2:4.

28. Gathercole, "Pre-existence, and the Freedom of the Son," 46-47.

account there is that Christ *acts* to take on human existence: though in the form of God, he *empties himself* to become a servant (v. 7). What is striking, if the exegesis in the foregoing chapters is correct, is that the "I have come" sayings of Jesus imply a very similar sequence. There is little reflection in Matthew, Mark, and Luke on the prior state of the Son in his preexistence: although there is the depiction of Christ standing over the whole history of Israel in Matt. 23.37, this is only mentioned in a single instance. The more numerous "I have come" sayings, on the other hand, repeatedly imply the prior intent and purpose of the Son. Jesus' coming is not merely as a passive envoy, since "I have come" + purpose implies a will of Christ. This is perhaps the most important theological implication of the preexistence christology in the Synoptic Gospels, that they point to the *will* of the Son in his entering the human realm.

This is in contrast to the view of some scholars who merely see an "inactive" preexistence in the Synoptics with the sending of the son in the parable of the wicked tenants being the only hint of preexistence in the first three Gospels. Fuller sums up this "inactive" view in his comment on the christological implications of the parable:

> For the first time, the Son's pre-existence is broached: God "had" yet one, a beloved Son (Mark 12:6) even before he "sent" him. This type of pre-existence is to be distinguished from the type which postulates an activity of the pre-existent One, and his own initiative in the incarnation.[29]

However, the language of the "I have come" + purpose formula places the emphasis on the action of the envoy rather than on the sender.[30] As such, we do have an "active preexistence" in the Son's purposeful advent into the world.[31]

29. R. H. Fuller, *The Foundations of New Testament Christology* (New York: Scribner, 1965), 194. Fuller is followed in this by H. Merklein, "Zur Entstehung der urchristlichen Aussage vom präexistenten Sohn Gottes," in G. Dautzenberg, H. Merklein, and K. Müller, eds., *Zur Geschichte des Urchristentums* (Freiburg: Herder, 1979), 33-62 (61-62), and Talbert, who talks of "an undeveloped concept of an inactive pre-existence of the Son (cf Mk 12:6)" in C. H. Talbert, *What Is a Gospel? The Genre of the Canonical Gospels* (London: SPCK, 1978), 39. Cf. also W. G. Kümmel, *The Theology of the New Testament according to Its Major Witnesses: Jesus-Paul-John* (London: SCM, 1974), 119-20. For Fuller, the idea of preexistence would be comprehensible to the Hellenistic community in which it emerged via the understanding of, e.g., Romulus's preexistence. He appears to have changed his mind on this, however, by the time he wrote "The Conception/Birth of Jesus as a Christological Moment," *JSNT* 1 (1978), 37-52.

30. See the discussion of Bühner's observations on this point in chapter 4 above.

31. This goes at least part of the way to answering whether the preexistence of Christ is as

VI. Preexistence and the Cross

Finally, the purpose of this book is by no means to overemphasize the preexistence of the Son either in the Synoptic Gospels or for dogmatics. The emphasis in Matthew, Mark, and Luke — and indeed throughout the NT — is on the death and resurrection of Jesus and his saving work. The problem arises when theologians use the canonical focus on soteriology as a means of excluding a preexistence christology. This is particularly apparent throughout Kuschel's work.

We have already seen some related instances above. We can cite two specifically on the theme of soteriology. First, Kuschel insists that in the sending motif in Gal. 4.4 preexistence "has no independent significance detached from the event of revelation and salvation."[32] But this is surely a straw-man argument. Has anyone argued that preexistence in these texts *is* detached from revelation and salvation? Again, is any doctrine independent of all the others?

Similarly, we can see the same questionable rhetorical strategy in Kuschel's discussion of Colossians 1 and Hebrews 1:

> Colossians 1.15-20 and Hebrews 1.2f. contain a statement about Christ's *real* pre-existence in terms of mediation at creation. But in these passages the statement about christological pre-existence is not isolated protology, independent speculation; it is grounded in eschatology and has a soteriological aim. So even in the generation after Paul there can be no question of an independent pre-existence christology in the New Testament.

So the statements of preexistence are acknowledged briefly at the outset but immediately relativized by Kuschel's comment that they are not "isolated protology," "independent speculation," or "an independent pre-existence christology." Again, who has argued for an "isolated protology" in these texts or that Colossians and Hebrews do in fact contain "independent speculation"? Kuschel is clearly reacting against something here and is anxious to

---

a personification or is more personal. As Caird points out, "there is all the difference in the world between a pre-existent personification and a pre-existent person." G. B. Caird, *New Testament Theology,* completed and edited by L. D. Hurst (Oxford: Clarendon, 1994), 340. However, it is very difficult to see how a personification could be in view if the Son took the active part in the incarnation, as has been argued above. Nevertheless, this is not to say that the concept of "person" does not raise another set of questions of its own, as scholars such as Frenschkowski have pointed out (M. Frenschkowski, *Offenbarung und Epiphanie* [WUNT; Tübingen: Mohr, 1995], 198).

32. Kuschel, *Born before All Time,* 274, quoting J. Blank with approval.

demote and — in the final analysis — reject the concept of preexistence as a result.[33]

The remedy for this error is not to go to the opposite extreme but to recover the biblical balance. As we have seen in chapter 13 above, the scandal of the cross in the Synoptic Gospels is that it is precisely the heavenly Son of God who is crucified. It is appropriate to conclude by considering that the revelation of Jesus as "the beloved Son" in the transfiguration stands in extraordinary contrast to the fact that it is the same figure who, tried as Son of God (Mark 14.61 par. Matt. 26.63; Luke 22.70) and taunted as such (Matt. 27.40, 43), is crucified and then proclaimed as "Son of God" by the centurion (Mark 15.39 par. Matt. 27.54). The heavenly preexistence of Christ, then, does not diminish the importance of his death, but rather is part of the reason for the scandalous paradox of that death.

33. See the comment on Ephesians and 1 Peter in Kuschel, *Born before All Time,* 362: "Here, as in Pauline christology, the word 'pre-existence' in the strict sense is open to misunderstanding and should be avoided in the future." Part of the problem here is evident from the fact that Kuschel defines preexistence in such a maximal way as including a well-thought-out and defined independent, pretemporal existence, a function of the preexistent Son in God's eternity, agency in creation, and ultimately everything that comes under the dogmatic locus of the "deity of Christ" (Kuschel, "Exegese und Dogmatik," in Laufen, ed., *Gottes ewiger Sohn,* 143). As such, it is hardly surprising that when Kuschel looks for all these in individual passages, he does not find them.

Conclusion

I. Summary

The core of the argument, in Part II, was concerned with contending that the "I have come" sayings of Jesus as we have them in Matthew, Mark and Luke are important evidence for preexistence. This argument was based on:

(a) the logic of the phrase "I have come in order to . . ." *as a summary of Jesus' whole life and ministry,* which suggests a coming from somewhere with a prior intent, a movement "from a to b";

(b) the lack of a Greek idiom or technical usage which would suggest a more likely meaning;

(c) the ample parallels to the "I have come" + purpose formula in the language of angels in Second Temple and rabbinic Judaism; and, finally,

(d) in the sayings in the Gospels, the great cosmic scale the purposes expressed (e.g., "I have come to cast fire on the earth . . . ," Luke 12.49) and the dynamic imagery used to describe Jesus' coming (e.g., "the Son of Man came to seek . . . ," Luke 19.10).

This argument stands in sharp contrast to the standard scholarly view of the Synoptic Gospels as presupposing a restrained christology from below. However, the argument for the "I have come" sayings above actually makes good sense when the evidence of chapters 1 and 2 above is borne in mind. In the first place, preexistence christology was widespread even in early Christianity before 70 CE, one presumes particularly — though not exclusively — under

the influence of Paul and his associates. Second, the Synoptic Gospels (as discussed in chapter 2) show in other ways that their portrayals of Jesus are by no
means merely primitive and "low" in their christologies. This, happily, is being increasingly acknowledged by scholars, as was also noted in the Introduction. So there are good grounds for expecting, or at least not being surprised
by, references to preexistence in Matthew, Mark, and Luke.

In addition to the "I have come" sayings, there are additional, more
scattered indications of the preexistence motif elsewhere in the Synoptic Gospels. First, the statement in Luke 1.78 that "the *Anatolē* will visit from on high
to shine on those in darkness" in fact has certain similarities with the "I have
come" sayings. The advent from heaven is made more explicit ("from on
high"), but the motif of coming with a purpose is very similar.

In one place in the Gospel tradition (discussed in chapter 9) there is a
statement about a continual action of the preexistent Christ — in his desire for
Israel's repentance through the nation's history: "Jerusalem, Jerusalem, who
kills the prophets and stones those sent to her — *how often have I desired to
gather your children . . ."* (Matt. 23.37). Here, then, Jesus is portrayed as one who
has been alive beyond his earthly existence in a supernatural, divine capacity.

Another probable indication of preexistence christology is in Mark
12.35-37 par., in the dispute between Jesus and the scribes over whether the
Messiah is Son of David. There is a good possibility here that the Gospel writers are tapping into the tradition in LXX Psalm 109 — the Psalm quoted in
the controversy — about a preexistent redeemer figure born of God before
the dawn (Ps. 109.3 LXX) who also resembles the immortal Melchizedek (Ps.
109.4 LXX). This may well have been intended by the Evangelists and picked
up by Septuagint-sensitive readers.

More speculative was the argument in chapter 12 about the Son of
Man's association with the preexistent kingdom emphasizing the figure's pre-
historic existence in Matthew's Gospel. Johannes Weiss confidently asserted
that the figure speaking through Psalm 78 ("I will open my mouth in parables") as quoted in Matt. 13.35 was the preexistent Christ, the Son of Man.
While his certainty is probably ill-founded, there may well be something in
the suggestion.

Finally, chapters 13 and 14 emphasized — in dialogue first with NT
scholarship and then with contemporary dogmatics — the motif of the sending of the Son. Here, three aspects of the Gospel narrative come into sharp
tension. In the first case, we have (a) the "sending" theme, which we argued in
chapter 7 should be interpreted along the same lines as the "I have come" sayings and thereby as referring to God's sending *from heaven.* This fits well, in
the narratives of the Synoptic Gospels, with (b) the heavenly identity of the

Son, seen particularly in the transfiguration but also elsewhere (Mark 1.9-11; 13.32 par.). Where these two themes clash, however, is in the fact that (c) God sends his heavenly Son *to his death* (Mark 12.1-12 par.). So preexistence in the Gospels is an important aspect of the characterization of the Son and functions to highlight the inexplicable mystery of Jesus' execution on the cross and its atoning function.

II. The Synoptic Gospels and John

To the extent that this study has found a number of references to preexistence in Matthew, Mark, and Luke, it should be concluded that the ditch often assumed between the Synoptic Gospels and the Fourth Gospel is not as ugly as many think. References to Jesus' coming have much the same sense in all four Gospels, although John does of course make explicit what is only implicit in the other three: it is a coming "down from heaven" "into the world."

The difference in language between the Synoptics and John on this point is far from problematic for the argument here. In fact, one of the reasons why scholars have perhaps failed to recognize preexistence in Matthew, Mark, and Luke is that they have judged the Synoptics against Johannine standards of preexistence. In fact, however, as we saw with the angelic parallels, the angels hardly ever qualify statements about their comings with "down from heaven" or the like. Crucially, *the objection that the Synoptics, if they presupposed preexistence, would look more like John's Gospel is only possible from the perspective of one who has read John's Gospel.* This is a luxury which Matthew, Mark, and Luke almost certainly did not have.

On the other hand, this should not be understood as a simple annihilation of the differences among the Gospels. There is still a great deal in John's Gospel which has not been touched on in the Synoptics. In particular, there is no thought in Matthew, Mark, and Luke of participation in the creation of the world, such as is propounded in John 1.1-3. Similarly, with the possible exception of Matt. 13.35 and the broader portrait of the Son of Man in Matthew's Gospel, there is no indication of a pre-cosmic existence of the Son. Nevertheless, the basic point that all four Gospels share the idea of preexistence is a valid one.

III. The Nature of Preexistence

This very brief comparison with John's Gospel will help to clarify our conclusions about the nature of the Son's preexistence in Matthew, Mark, and Luke.

The most basic point we made above was in connection with the *will* of the Son (chapters 6 and 14): the advent of Jesus is described as something which came about as a result of his purposeful action. This presupposes a prior co-ordination of the Son's will with that of the Father, because of the parallelism between the Father's sending and the Son's coming. As a result, one can talk of a relationship between the Father and the Son before the coming, although it would go beyond the evidence to say much more than that. In addition, the conclusion of our exegesis in chapter 9 is that there is a continual action of the preincarnate Christ throughout Israel's history, as is indicated by the "Je-rusalem, Jerusalem, how often have I longed . . ." saying in Matt. 23.37.

IV. The Emphasis in Matthew, Mark, and Luke

As we have also noted in the course of the various chapters, there is no special thematization of preexistence in the Synoptic Gospels. Preexistence is the presupposition of "I have come" sayings, but the focus is on the actual *pur-poses* of the coming. Luke 1.78, with its poetic statement about the *Anatolē* vis-iting from on high, highlights the theme a little more strongly, but again, this leads straight into the purpose of "shining on those in darkness" (v. 79). To this extent, one can agree with the point made by K.-J. Kuschel, discussed in chapter 14 above, that preexistence is not an object of independent specula-tion. On the other hand, however, this argument cannot be used to margin-alize or exclude preexistence.

In closing, then, we can consider some possible avenues of research which might be prompted by the present study. In the first place, the com-parison between Johannine christology and that of the Synoptics could cer-tainly be explored further in the light of the exegesis above. As has been sug-gested here, there are certainly some significant differences of emphasis, even if some rapprochement between them has been achieved. Second, this could be applied to the broader question of the development of early Chris-tian thought: as is the case with John, the christology of the Synoptics as it is presented above has a little more in common with Paul (for example) than has previously been assumed; again, however, this is not to minimize the dis-tinctive character of the christologies in Paul and elsewhere in the NT. Thirdly, it may also be the case that the present study has implications for historical Jesus study. In addition, perhaps most obviously, the present study has implications for the way in which the christologies of Matthew, Mark, and Luke are construed. The present study has focused on only one aspect of those christologies, but it is an aspect which may well have knock-on effects for the study of other elements in the Synoptic Gospels. Finally, however, it is hoped that the present study will contribute to an appreciation of the importance of the preexistence of Christ in NT theology and in contemporary theological thinking and serve as a reminder of the gospel of the heavenly-yet-crucified Son.

Select Bibliography

I. Primary Sources

Abegg, M., P. Flint, and E. Ulrich, eds. *The Dead Sea Scrolls Bible.* Edinburgh: T&T Clark, 1999.

Aland, B., et al. *The Greek New Testament.* Stuttgart: UBS/Deutsche Bibelgesellschaft, ⁴1993.

Amélineau, E. *Contes et Romans de L'Égypte Chrétienne.* Paris: Leroux, 1888.

Barthélemy, D., J. T. Milik, et al. *Discoveries in the Judaean Desert.* Vols. 1- . Oxford: Clarendon Press, 1955- .

Bertrand, D. A. *La Vie Grecque d'Adam et Ève.* Paris: Maisonneuve, 1987.

Bin Gorion, E., and M. J. Bin Gorion. *Der Born Judas.* Part 2: *Legenden, Märchen und Erzählungen.* Frankfurt: Insel Verlag, 1973.

Bin Gorion, M. J., ed. *Mimeqor Yisrael.* Tel Aviv: Dvir, 1965/66.

Black, M., ed. *Apocalypsis Henochi graece.* A.-M. Denis, ed., *Fragmenta Pseud-epigraphorum quae supersunt Graeca.* PVTG 3; Leiden: Brill, 1970.

Bonnet, M. *Acta Thomae.* Leipzig: Mendelssohn, 1883.

Braude, W. G., ed. *Pesikta Rabbati: Discourses for Feasts, Fasts and Special Sabbaths.* New Haven: Yale University Press, 1968.

———, and I. J. Kapstein, eds. *Pesikta de-Rab Kahana: R. Kahana's Compilation of Discourses for Sabbaths and Festal Days.* Philadelphia: Jewish Publication Society of America, 2002 (1975).

Brock, S. *Testamentum Iobi.* J. C. Picard, *Apocalypsis Baruchi Graece.* PVTG 2; Leiden: Brill, 1967.

Buber, S. *Midrasch Tanchuma: Ein Agadischer Commentar zum Pentateuch von Rabbi Tanchuma ben Rabbi Abba.* Vilna: Romm, 1885.

Chadwick, H. *Origen: Contra Celsum.* Cambridge: Cambridge University Press, 1953.

Charles, R. H. *Apocrypha and Pseudepigrapha of the Old Testament.* Volume 1: *Apocrypha.* Volume 2: *Pseudepigrapha.* Oxford: Clarendon Press, 1913.

Charlesworth, J. H., ed. *The Dead Sea Scrolls.* Volume 1: *The Rule of the Community and Related Documents.* Volume 2: *Damascus Document, War Scroll, and Related Documents.* PTSDSSP; Tübingen/Louisville: Mohr/Westminster John Knox, 1994-95.

———, ed. *The Old Testament Pseudepigrapha.* Volumes 1 and 2. New York: Doubleday, 1983.

Colson, F. H., G. H. Whitaker, R. Marcus, et al., eds. *Philo.* Loeb edition. 10 volumes and 2 supplements. London: William Heinemann; Cambridge: Harvard University Press, 1929-62.

Copenhaver, B. P. *Hermetica: The Greek* Corpus Hermeticum *and the Latin* Asclepius *in a New English Translation, with Notes and Introduction.* Cambridge: Cambridge University Press, 1992.

Danby, H., ed. *The Mishnah.* Oxford: Oxford University Press, 1985 (1933).

Delcor, M. *Le Testament d'Abraham: Suivi de la Traduction des Testaments d'Abraham, d'Isaac et de Jacob d'après les Versions Orientales.* SVTP; Leiden: Brill, 1973.

Díez Macho, A. *Neophyti 1: Targum Palestinense Ms de la Biblioteca Vaticana.* Volume 4: *Números.* Madrid: CSIC, 1974.

———. "Un nuevo Targum a los Profetas." *Estudios Bíblicos* 15 (1956), 287-300.

Etheridge, J. W., ed. *The Targums of Onkelos and Jonathan Ben Uzziel on the Pentateuch with the Fragments of the Jerusalem Targum (from the Chaldee).* New York: Ktav, 1968.

Even-Shmuel, Y. מדרשי גאלה. Jerusalem: Mosad Byalik ʿal yede Masadah, 1953/1954.

Fahr, H., and U. Glemer. *Jordandurchzug und Beschneidung als Zurechtweisung in einem Targum zu Josua 5 (Edition des Ms. T.-S. B 13,12).* Orienta Biblica et Christiana; Glückstadt: Verlag J. J. Augustin, 1991.

Freedman, H., and M. Simon. *Midrash Rabbah.* 5 volumes. London: Soncino Press, 1977.

García Martínez, F., and E. J. C. Tigchelaar, eds. *Dead Sea Scrolls Study Edition.* Volume 1: *1Q1-4Q273.* Volume II: *4Q274-11Q31.* Leiden: Brill, 1997-98.

Gaster, M. *The Exempla of the Rabbis.* New York: Ktav, 1968 (1924).

Ginzberg, L. *The Legends of the Jews.* 7 volumes. Baltimore: Johns Hopkins University Press, 1998 (1913).

———. "Vision of Daniel." In idem, *Geniza Studies in Memory of Dr. Solomon Schechter.* Volume 1: *Midrash and Haggadah*, 313-23. New York: Jewish Theological Seminary of America, 1928.

Gordon, R. P. *The Targum of the Minor Prophets.* The Aramaic Bible 14; Edinburgh: T&T Clark, 1989.

Hammer, R. *Sifre: A Tannaitic Commentary on the Book of Deuteronomy.* Yale Judaica Series XXIV; New Haven/London: Yale University Press, 1986.

Holladay, C. R. *Fragments from Hellenistic Jewish Authors.* Volume 2: *Poets* (Atlanta: Scholars, 1989).

Holmes, M. W., ed. *The Apostolic Fathers: Greek Texts and Translations of Their Writings.* Translated by J. B. Lightfoot and J. R. Harmer. Grand Rapids: Baker, 1992.

Jacobson, H. *A Commentary on Pseudo-Philo's Liber Antiquitatum Biblicarum. With Latin Text and English Translation.* Leiden: Brill, 1996.

Jellinek, A. *Beit ha-Midrash.* 3 vols. Jerusalem: Wahrmann, 1967 (1853).

———. "Das Noah-Buch." In idem, *Beit ha-Midrash,* 3:155-60. Jerusalem: Wahrmann, 1967 (1853).

Klijn, A. F. J. *The Acts of Thomas: Introduction, Text and Commentary.* Second revised edition. NovTSuppS; Leiden: Brill, 2003.

Kuhn, K. H. "A Coptic Jeremiah Apocryphon." *Muséon* 83 (1970), 95-135, 291-350.

Laurence, R. *The Book of Enoch the Prophet, Translated from an Ethiopic MS. in the Bodleian Library.* Oxford, 1821.

Lauterbach, J. Z. *Mekilta de-Rabbi Ishmael.* 3 volumes. Philadelphia: Jewish Publication Society of America, 1976 (1933).

Lichtenberger, H., et al., eds. *Jüdische Schriften aus hellenistisch-römischer Zeit.* Gütersloh: Gütersloher Verlagshaus, 1973-99.

Linforth, I. M. *Solon the Athenian.* Berkeley: University of California Press, 1919.

McNamara, M., and E. G. Clarke. *Targum Neofiti 1: Numbers. Targum Pseudo-Jonathan: Numbers.* Edinburgh: T&T Clark, 1995.

Meyer, M. W., ed. *The Nag Hammadi Library in English.* Leiden: Brill, 1977.

Milik, J. T. *The Books of Enoch: Aramaic Fragments.* Oxford: Clarendon, 1976.

Mingana, A., and R. Harris, eds. "A Jeremiah Apocryphon." In Mingana, *Woodbrooke Studies,* volume 1 (Cambridge: Heffers, 1927), 125-38 (introduction by Harris), 148-49 (preface by Mingana), 149-91 (translation by Mingana), 192-233 (facsimiles).

Neusner, J. *The Mishnah.* New Haven: Yale University Press, 1988.

Picard, J.-C., ed. *Apocalypsis Baruchi Graece.* PVTG 2; Leiden: Brill, 1967.

Rahlfs, A., ed. *Septuaginta: Id est Vetus Testamentum graece iuxta LXX interpretes,* volumes 1 and 2. Stuttgart: Württembergische Bibelanstalt, 1935.

Roberts, A., and J. Donaldson, eds. *The Ante-Nicene Fathers.* Volume 4. Grand Rapids: Eerdmans, 1994.

Schäfer, P., and H.-J. Becker, eds. *Synopse zum Talmud Yerushalmi.* Volume II/5-12. TSAJ 83; Tübingen: Mohr, 2001.

Schmidt, F. *Le Testament Grec d'Abraham: Introduction, Édition Critique des Deux Recensions Grecques, Traduction.* TSAJ; Tübingen: Mohr, 1986.

Schneemelcher, W. *New Testament Apocrypha.* Volume 1: *Gospels and Related Writings.* Louisville: Westminster John Knox, 1991.

Schwemer, A.-M. *Vitae Prophetarum.* TSAJ 49-50; Tübingen: Mohr, 1995-96.

Sharf, A. "Appendix I: The Vision of Daniel." In idem, *Byzantine Jewry from Justinian to the Fourth Crusade,* 201-4. London: Routledge and Kegan Paul, 1971. (Translation.)

Sparks, H. F. D., ed. *The Apocryphal Old Testament.* Oxford: Clarendon Press, 1984.

Sperber, A. *The Bible in Aramaic.* Volume 1: *The Pentateuch according to Targum*

Onkelos. Volume 2: *The Former Prophets according to Targum Jonathan.* Volume 3: *The Latter Prophets according to Targum Jonathan.* Leiden/Boston: Brill, 2004.

Thackeray, H. St. J., R. Marcus, et al., eds. *Josephus.* Loeb edition. 9 volumes. London: Heinemann; Cambridge, Mass.: Harvard University Press, 1926-65.

Townsend, J. T., ed. and trans. *Midrash Tanḥuma, Translated into English with Indices and Brief Notes (S. Buber Recension).* Volume 2: *Exodus and Leviticus.* Hoboken, N.J.: Ktav, 1997.

Tromp, J. *The Assumption of Moses: A Critical Edition with Commentary.* Leiden: Brill, 1993.

VanderKam, J. C. *The Book of Jubilees: A Critical Text.* Corpus Scriptorum Christianorum Orientalium Vol. 510/Scriptores Aethiopici Tomus 87; Louvain: E. Peeters, 1989.

Vermes, G. *The Dead Sea Scrolls in English.* Harmondsworth: Penguin, 1995.

Visotsky, B. L. *Midrash Mishle: A Critical Edition Based on Vatican MS. Ebr. 44, with Variant Readings from All Known Manuscripts and Early Editions, and with an Introduction, References and a Short Commentary.* New York: The Jewish Theological Seminary of America, 1990.

———. *Midrash on Proverbs: Translated from the Hebrew with an Introduction and Annotations.* Yale Judaica Series; New Haven: Yale University Press, 1992.

Weeks, S. D. E., S. J. Gathercole, and L. T. Stuckenbruck, eds. *The Book of Tobit: Texts from the Principal Ancient and Medieval Traditions. With Synopsis, Concordances, and Annotated Texts in Aramaic, Hebrew, Greek, Latin, and Syriac.* Berlin: Walter de Gruyter, 2004.

Wewers, G. A. *Übersetzung des Talmud Yerushalmi.* Volume 2/11: *Hagiga (Festopfer).* Tübingen: Mohr, 1983.

Whiston, W. *The Works of Josephus.* Peabody, Mass.: Hendrickson, 1992.

Wise, M., M. Abegg, E. Cook. *The Dead Sea Scrolls: A New Translation.* London/San Francisco: Harper Collins, 1996.

Yonge, C. D. *The Works of Philo.* Peabody: Hendrickson, 1995.

II. Secondary Literature

Abegg, M. G., and C. A. Evans. "Bibliography of Messianism and the Dead Sea Scrolls" (completed by G. Oegema). In J. H. Charlesworth, H. Lichtenberger, and G. Oegema, eds., *Qumran-Messianism: Studies on the Messianic Expectations in the Dead Sea Scrolls,* 204-14. Tübingen: Mohr, 1998.

Aland, K., ed. *Text und Textwert der Griechischen Handschriften des Neuen Testaments: I. Die Katholischen Briefe.* Volume I: *Das Material.* Berlin: Walter de Gruyter, 1987.

Albright, W. F., and C. Mann. *Matthew.* Anchor; New York: Doubleday, 1971.

Allen, W. C. *A Critical and Exegetical Commentary on the Gospel according to St. Matthew.* ICC; Edinburgh: T&T Clark, 1907.

Allison, D. C. "Matt. 23:39 = Luke 13:35b as a Conditional Prophecy." *JSNT* 18 (1983), 75-84.

―――. *The Testament of Abraham.* CEJL; Berlin: Walter de Gruyter, 2003.

Arens, E. *The HΛΘON-Sayings in the Synoptic Tradition: A Historico-Critical Investigation.* Orbis Biblicus et Orientalis 10; Freiburg: Universitätsverlag Freiburg; Göttingen: Vandenhoeck und Ruprecht, 1976.

Argyle, A. W. "The Evidence for the Belief That Our Lord Himself Claimed to Be Divine." *ExpT* 61 (1950), 228-32.

―――. "Luke xxii.31f." *ExpT* 64 (1952-53), 222.

Ashby, E. "The Coming of the Son of Man." *ExpT* 72 (1960-61), 360-63.

Attridge, H. W. *The Epistle to the Hebrews.* Hermeneia; Minneapolis: Fortress, 1989.

Bacon, B. W. *The Gospel of Mark: Its Composition and Date.* New Haven: Yale University Press, 1925.

Bader, R. *Der Ἀληθὴς Λόγος des Kelsos.* Stuttgart: Kohlhammer, 1940.

Barker, M. *The Great Angel: A Study of Israel's Second God.* London: SPCK, 1992.

Barrett, C. K. *The Holy Spirit and the Gospel Tradition.* London: SPCK, 1966.

Barth, K. *Church Dogmatics.* Volume IV: *The Doctrine of Reconciliation,* Part 2. Edinburgh: T&T Clark, 1958.

Bauckham, R. J. *God Crucified: Monotheism and Christology in the New Testament.* Carlisle: Paternoster, 1998.

―――. *Jude, 2 Peter.* WBC; Waco: Word, 1983.

―――. *Jude and the Relatives of Jesus in the Early Church.* Edinburgh: T&T Clark, 1990.

―――. "The Sonship of the Historical Jesus in Christology." *SJT* 31 (1978), 245-60.

―――. "The Throne of God and the Worship of Jesus." In J. R. Davila, C. C. Newman, and G. S. Lewis, eds., *The Jewish Roots of Christological Monotheism,* 43-69. Leiden: Brill, 1999.

Bauernfeind, O. *Die Worte der Dämonen im Markusevangelium.* BWANT; Stuttgart: W. Kohlhammer, 1927.

Beale, G. K. *Revelation.* NIGTC; Grand Rapids: Eerdmans, 1999.

Beardslee, W. A. "The Wisdom Tradition and the Synoptic Gospels." *JAAR* 35 (1967), 231-40.

Beare, F. W. *The Gospel according to Matthew.* Oxford: Blackwell, 1981.

Beaton, R. *Isaiah's Christ in Matthew's Gospel.* SNTSMS; Cambridge: Cambridge University Press, 2002.

Benoit, P. "The Divinity of Jesus in the Synoptic Gospels." In idem, *Jesus and the Gospel,* 47-70. London: Dartman, Longman and Todd, 1973.

―――. "L'Enfance de Jean-Baptiste selon Luc I." *NTS* 3 (1956-57), 169-94.

―――. "Préexistence et Incarnation." In idem, *Exégèse et Théologie,* 4:11-61. Paris: Cerf, 1982.

Berger, K. *Die Auferstehung des Propheten und die Erhöhung des Menschensohnes: Traditionsgeschichtliche Untersuchungen zur Deutung des Geschickes Jesu in frühchristlichen Texten.* SUNT 13; Göttingen: Vandenhoeck und Ruprecht, 1976.

Best, E. *The Temptation and the Passion: The Markan Soteriology.* SNTSMS; Cambridge: Cambridge University Press, 1965.

Betz, H. D. *The Sermon on the Mount: A Commentary on the Sermon on the Mount, including the Sermon on the Plain (Matthew 5,3–7,27 and Luke 6,20-49).* Hermeneia; Minneapolis: Fortress Press, 1995.

Beyer, H. W. "ἐπισκέπτομαι κτλ." In *TDNT* 2:599-622.

Black, M. "Notes on Three NT Texts." In W. Eltester, ed., *Apophoreta: Festschrift für Ernst Haenchen zu seinem siebzigsten Geburtstag,* 39-45. Berlin: Töpelmann, 1964.

———. "Not Peace but a Sword." In E. Bammel and C. F. D. Moule, eds., *Jesus and the Politics of His Day,* 287-94. Cambridge: Cambridge University Press, 1984.

Blank, J. "Die Sendung des Sohnes: Zur christologischen Bedeutung des Gleichnisses von den bösen Winzern." In J. Gnilka, ed., *Neues Testament und Kirche. FS R. Schnackenburg,* 11-41. Freiburg: Herder, 1974.

Blass, F., and A. Debrunner. *Grammatik des neutestamentlichen Griechisch.* Edited by F. Rehkopf. Göttingen: Vandenhoeck und Ruprecht, [14]1976.

Blomberg, C. "Messiah in the New Testament." In R. S. Hess and M. D. Carroll R., eds., *Israel's Messiah in the Bible and the Dead Sea Scrolls,* 111-41. Grand Rapids: Baker, 2003.

Bock, D. L. *Blasphemy and Exaltation in Judaism and the Final Examination of Jesus.* WUNT; Tübingen: Mohr, 1998.

———. *Jesus according to Scripture: Restoring the Portrait from the Gospels.* Grand Rapids: Baker Book House; Leicester, UK: Apollos, 2002.

———. *Luke.* BECNT; Grand Rapids: Baker, 1996.

Boling, R. G., and G. E. Wright. *Joshua.* Anchor Bible; New York: Doubleday, 1982.

Bolyki, J. "Human Nature and Character as Moving Factors of Plot in the Acts of Thomas." In J. N. Bremmer, ed., *The Apocryphal Acts of Thomas,* 91-100. Leuven: Peeters, 2001.

Boobyer, G. H. "Mark xii.35-37 and the Pre-Existence of Jesus in Mark." *ExpT* 51 (1939-40), 393-94.

Boring, E. "The Christology of Mark: Hermeneutical Issues for Systematic Theology." *Semeia* 30 (1984), 125-51.

———. "Markan Christology: God-Language for Jesus?" *NTS* 45 (1999), 451-71.

Bornkamm, G., G. Barth, and H.-J. Held. *Tradition and Interpretation in Matthew.* London: SCM, 1963.

Borsch, F. H. *The Christian and Gnostic Son of Man.* London: SCM, 1970.

———. *The Son of Man in Myth and History.* London: SCM, 1967.

Botha, F. J. "'Umas [*sic*] in Luke xxii.31." *ExpT* 64 (1952-53), 125.

Bovon, F. *Das Evangelium nach Lukas.* Volume 1: *Lk 1,1–9,50;* Volume 2: *Lk 9,51–14,35;* Volume 3: *Lk 15–19,27.* EKK; Zürich: Benziger, 1989-2001.

———. *Luke 1: A Commentary on the Gospel of Luke 1:1–9:50.* Hermeneia; Minneapolis: Fortress, 2002.

Braumann, G. "Der sinkende Petrus. Matth. 14, 28-31." *TZ* 22 (1966), 403-14.

Breech, J. *The Silence of Jesus: The Authentic Voice of the Historical Man*. Philadelphia: Augsburg, 1987.

Breytenbach, C. "Grundzüge markinischer Gottessohn-Christologie." In C. Breytenbach and H. Paulsen, eds., *Anfänge der Christologie: FS F. Hahn*, 169-84. Göttingen: Vandenhoeck und Ruprecht, 1991.

Broadhead, E. K. *Naming Jesus: Titular Christology in the Gospel of Mark*. JSNTSS; Sheffield: Sheffield Academic Press, 1999.

Brown, R. E. *The Birth of the Messiah: A Commentary on the Infancy Narratives in Matthew and Luke*. London: Geoffrey Chapman, 1977.

Bruce, F. F. *The Book of the Acts*. London: Marshall, Morgan and Scott, 1965.

———. *The Epistle to the Hebrews*. NICNT; Grand Rapids: Eerdmans, 1990.

Büchli, J. *Der Poimandres: Ein paganisiertes Evangelium. Sprachliche und begriffliche Untersuchungen zum 1. Traktat des Corpus Hermeticum*. WUNT II/27; Tübingen: Mohr, 1987.

Buckwalter, H. D. *The Character and Purpose of Luke's Christology*. SNTSMS; Cambridge: Cambridge University Press, 1996.

Budesheim, T. "Paul's *Abschiedsrede* in the Acts of the Apostles." *HTR* 69 (1976), 9-30.

Bühner, J.-A. *Der Gesandte und sein Weg im vierten Evangelium: Die kultur- und religionsgeschichtlichen Grundlagen der johanneischen Sendungschristologie sowie ihre traditionsgeschichtliche Entwicklung*. WUNT 2; Tübingen: Mohr, 1977.

———. "Zur Form, Tradition und Bedeutung der ἦλθον-Sprüche." *Das Institutum Judaicum der Universität Tübingen* (1971-72), 45-68.

Bultmann, R. "Die Bedeutung der neuerschlossenen mandäischen und manichäischen Quellen für das Verständnis des Johannesevangeliums." *ZNW* 24 (1925), 100-146.

———. *Die Geschichte der synoptischen Tradition*. Göttingen: Vandenhoeck und Ruprecht, 1921.

———. *History of the Synoptic Tradition*. Oxford: Blackwell, 1968.

———. "New Testament and Mythology." In H. W. Bartsch, ed., *Kerygma and Myth, by Rudolf Bultmann and Five Critics*, 1-44. New York: Harper, 1961.

———. *New Testament and Mythology and Other Basic Writings*. Philadelphia: Fortress, 1984.

———. "Die religionsgeschichtliche Hintergrund des Prologs zum Johannes-Evangelium." In H. Schmidt, ed., *Eucharisterion: Studien zur Religion und Literatur des Alten und Neuen Testaments. Hermann Gunkel zum 60. Geburtstag*, 2:3-26. FRLANT; Göttingen: Vandenhoeck und Ruprecht, 1923.

Burchard, C. "A Note on 'Ρῆμα in JosAs 17:1f.; Luke 2:15, 17; Acts 10:37." *NovT* 27 (1985), 281-95.

Burkett, D. *The Son of Man Debate*. Cambridge: Cambridge University Press, 1999.

Burkill, T. A. *Mysterious Revelation: An Examination of the Philosophy of St. Mark's Gospel*. Ithaca, N.Y.: Cornell University Press, 1963.

Burnett, F. W. "Appendix V: Ἐξέρχομαι in Matthew." In idem, *Testament of Jesus-*

Sophia: A Redaction-Critical Study of the Eschatological Discourse in Matthew, 428-34. Washington, D.C.: University Press of America, 1979.

————. "Excursus I: The Pre-Existence of Jesus in Matthew." In idem, *Testament of Jesus-Sophia: A Redaction-Critical Study of the Eschatological Discourse in Matthew*, 169-71. Washington, D.C.: University Press of America, 1979.

————. *The Testament of Jesus-Sophia: A Redaction-Critical Study of the Eschatological Discourse in Matthew*. Washington, D.C.: University Press of America, 1979.

Byrne, B. "Christ's Pre-existence in Pauline Soteriology." *TS* 58 (1997), 308-30.

Caird, G. B. *New Testament Theology*. Completed and edited by L. D. Hurst. Oxford: Clarendon Press, 1994.

————. *Saint Luke*. Harmondsworth: Penguin, 1963.

Campbell, D. A. "The Story of Jesus in Romans and Galatians." In B. W. Longenecker, ed., *Narrative Dynamics in Paul: A Critical Assessment*, 97-124. Louisville: Westminster/John Knox, 2002.

Caragounis, C. C. *The Son of Man*. Tübingen: Mohr, 1986.

Carson, D. A. *Matthew*. Grand Rapids: Zondervan, 1995.

Carter, W. "Jesus' 'I have come' Sayings in Matthew's Gospel." *CBQ* 60 (1998), 44-62.

Casey, P. M. *An Aramaic Approach to Q: Sources for the Gospels of Matthew and Luke*. SNTSMS; Cambridge: Cambridge University Press, 2002.

————. "Aramaic Idiom and the Son of Man Problem." *JSNT* 25.1 (2002), 3-32.

————. *From Jewish Prophet to Gentile God: The Origins and Development of New Testament Christology*. Cambridge: James Clarke; Louisville: Westminster John Knox, 1991.

————. "General, Generic and Indefinite: The Use of the Term 'Son of Man' in Aramaic Sources and the Teaching of Jesus." *JSNT* 29 (1987), 21-56.

————. "The Jackals and the Son of Man (Matt. 8.20//Luke 9.58)." *JSNT* 23 (1985), 3-22.

————. "Method in Our Madness, and Madness in Their Methods: Some Approaches to the Son of Man Problem in Recent Scholarship." *JSNT* 42 (1991), 17-43.

————. *Son of Man: The Interpretation and Influence of Daniel 7*. London: SPCK, 1979.

————. "The Use of the Term (א)שׁנ(א) בר in the Aramaic Translations of the Hebrew Bible." *JSNT* 54 (1994), 87-118.

Catchpole, D. R. "The Angelic Son of Man in Luke 12:8." *NovT* 24 (1982), 255-65.

————. "The Poor on Earth and the Son of Man in Heaven: A Reappraisal of Matthew xxv.31-46." *BJRL* 61 (1979), 355-97.

————. "The Son of Man's Search for Faith (Luke xviii 8b)." *NovT* 19 (1977), 81-104.

Cerfaux, L. "Les Sources scripturaires de Mt XI,25-30." In idem, *Recueil L. Cerfaux*, 139-59. Leuven: Leuven University Press, 1985.

Chapman, J. "Dr Harnack on Luke x 22: No Man Knoweth the Son." *JTS* 10 (1908-9), 552-66.

Charlesworth, J. H., ed. *The Messiah: Developments in Earliest Judaism and Christian-*

ity: The First Princeton Symposium on Judaism and Christian Origins. Minneapolis: Fortress, 1992.

―――, H. Lichtenberger, and G. Oegema, eds. *Qumran-Messianism: Studies on the Messianic Expectations in the Dead Sea Scrolls.* Tübingen: Mohr, 1998.

Chilton, B. "(The) Son of (the) Man, and Jesus." In B. Chilton and C. A. Evans, eds., *Authenticating the Words of Jesus,* 259-88. Leiden: Brill, 1999.

Christ, F. *Jesus Sophia: Die Sophia-Christologie bei den Synoptikern.* ATANT 57; Zürich: Zwingli-Verlag, 1970.

Coke, P. T. "The Angels of the Son of Man." *SNTSU* 3 (1978), 91-98.

Collins, J. J. *Apocalypticism in the Dead Sea Scrolls.* London/New York: Routledge, 1997.

―――. *Daniel.* Hermeneia; Minneapolis: Fortress, 1993.

―――. *The Scepter and Star: The Messiahs of the Dead Sea Scrolls and Other Ancient Literature.* New York: Doubleday, 1995.

―――. "The *Son of God* Text from Qumran." In M. C. De Boer, ed., *From Jesus to John: Essays on Jesus and New Testament Christology in Honour of Marinus de Jonge,* 65-82. Sheffield: Sheffield Academic Press, 1993.

Conzelmann, H. *A Commentary on the Acts of the Apostles.* Hermeneia; Minneapolis: Fortress Press, 1987.

―――. *Der erste Brief an die Korinther.* KEK; Göttingen: Vandenhoeck und Ruprecht, [12]1981.

―――. "The Mother of Wisdom." In J. M. Robinson, ed., *The Future of Our Religious Past: Essays in Honour of Rudolf Bultmann,* 234-40. London: SCM, 1971.

Corell, J. "Actos 10,36." *Estudios Franciscanos* 76 (1975), 101-13.

Cotter, W. J. "The Parable of the Children in the Market-Place, Q (Lk) 7:31-35: An Examination of the Parable's Image and Significance." *NovT* 29 (1987), 289-304.

Craddock, F. B. *The Pre-existence of Christ in the New Testament.* Nashville: Abingdon, 1968.

Cranfield, C. E. B. "The Baptism of Our Lord: A Study of St. Mark 1:9-12." *SJT* 9 (1955), 53-63.

―――. *The Gospel according to St Mark.* CGTC; Cambridge: Cambridge University Press, 1959.

Crump, D. "Jesus, the Victorious Scribal Intercessor in Luke's Gospel." *NTS* 38 (1992), 51-65.

Cullmann, O. *Die Christologie des Neuen Testaments.* Tübingen: Mohr, [2]1958.

―――. *The Christology of the New Testament.* Philadelphia: Westminster, 1963.

Davies, P. E. "The Projection of Pre-existence." *Biblical Research* 12 (1967), 28-36.

Davies, W. D. "Appendix IV: Isaiah XLI.2 and the Pre-existent Messiah." In *The Setting of the Sermon on the Mount,* 445. Cambridge: Cambridge University Press, 1963.

―――. "The Jewish Sources of Matthew's Messianism." In J. H. Charlesworth, ed., *The Messiah: Developments in Earliest Judaism and Christianity: The First Princeton Symposium on Judaism and Christian Origins,* 494-511. Minneapolis: Fortress, 1992.

————, and D. C. Allison. *A Critical and Exegetical Commentary on the Gospel according to Saint Matthew*. 3 volumes. ICC; Edinburgh: T&T Clark, 1988-97.

Davila, J. R., G. S. Lewis, and C. C. Newman, eds. *The Jewish Roots of Christological Monotheism*. Leiden: Brill, 1999.

Davis, P. G. "Mark's Christological Paradox." *JSNT* 35 (1989), 3-18.

Davis, S., D. Kendall, and G. O'Collins, eds. *The Incarnation: An Interdisciplinary Symposium on the Incarnation of the Son of God*. Oxford: Oxford University Press, 2002.

Day, J. *King and Messiah in Israel and the Ancient Near East: Proceedings of the Oxford Old Testament Seminar*. JSOTSup 270; Sheffield: JSOT, 1998.

Delling, G. "Βάπτισμα βαπτισθῆναι." *NovT* 2 (1958), 92-115.

Derrett, J. D. M. "Why and How Jesus Walked on the Sea." *NovT* 23 (1981), 330-48.

Deutsch, C. *Hidden Wisdom and the Easy Yoke: Wisdom, Torah and Discipleship in Matthew 11:25-30*. JSNTSS; Sheffield: JSOT Press, 1987.

Dibelius, M. *Die Formgeschichte des Evangeliums*. Tübingen: Mohr, [2]1933.

————. *From Tradition to Gospel*. London: Nicholson and Watson, 1934.

Dietrich, W. *Das Petrusbild der lukanischen Schriften*. BWANT; Stuttgart: Kohlhammer, 1972.

Dömer, M. *Das Heil Gottes: Studien zur Theologie des lukanischen Doppelwerkes, 63-68*. Bonner Biblische Beiträge 51; Cologne/Bonn: Verlag Peter Hanstein, 1978.

Drijvers, H. J. W. "The Acts of Thomas." In W. Schneemelcher, ed., *New Testament Apocrypha*, 2:322-411. Louisville: Westminster John Knox, 1991.

Drury, J. "The Sower, the Vineyard, and the Place of Allegory in the Interpretation of Mark's Parables." *JTS* 24.2 (1973), 367-79.

Dunn, J. D. G. *Christ and the Spirit*. Volume 1: *Christology*. Grand Rapids: Eerdmans, 1998.

————. *Christology in the Making: A New Testament Inquiry into the Origins of the Doctrine of the Incarnation*. Philadelphia: Westminster, 1980/[2]1989.

————. *The Theology of Paul the Apostle*. Edinburgh: T&T Clark, 1998.

Dupont, J. *Les Béatitudes*. 2 volumes. Paris: J. Gabalda, 1969-73.

Earle, R. *The Gospel of Mark*. Grand Rapids: Baker Book House, 1961.

Eckey, W. *Das Lukasevangelium unter Berücksichtigung seiner Parallelen*. Volume II: *11,1–24,53*. Neukirchen-Vluyn: Neukirchener, 2004.

Ellingworth, P. *The Epistle to the Hebrews*. NIGTC; Grand Rapids: Eerdmans, 1993.

Elliott, J. K. "The Conclusion of the Pericope of the Healing of the Leper and Mark i.45." *JTS* 22 (1971), 153-57.

————. "Is ὁ ἐξελθών a Title for Jesus in Mark 1.45?" *JTS* 27 (1976), 402-5.

Ellis, E. E. "Deity Christology in Mark 14:58." In J. B. Green and M. Turner, eds., *Jesus of Nazareth: Lord and Christ. Essays on the Historical Jesus and New Testament Christology*, 192-203. FS I. H. Marshall. Carlisle: Paternoster Press, 1994.

Evans, C. A. "In What Sense 'Blasphemy'? Jesus before Caiaphas in Mark 14:61-64." *SBLSP* 30 (1991), 215-34.

————. *Mark 8:27–16:20*. WBC; Nashville: Thomas Nelson, 2001.

Fascher, E. *Prophētēs: Eine sprach- und religionsgeschichtliche Untersuchung.* Giessen: A. Töpelmann, 1927.

Fee, G. *The First Epistle to the Corinthians.* NICNT; Grand Rapids: Eerdmans, 1987.

Feuillet, A. "La Coupe et le Baptême de la Passion (Mc 10, 35–40)." *RevB* 74 (1967), 356-91.

———. "Jésus et la Sagesse Divine d'après les Évangiles Synoptiques: Le 'logion johannique' et l'Ancien Testament." *RevB* 62 (1955), 161-96.

———. "Témoins oculaires et serviteurs de la Parole (Luc 1.2b)." *NovT* 15 (1973), 241-59.

Firchow, O. "Die Boten der Götter." In idem, ed., *Ägyptologische Studien: FS Hermann Grapow,* 85-92. Berlin: Institut für Orientforschung, 1955.

Fitzmyer, J. A. *The Gospel according to Luke: Introduction, Translation and Notes.* Anchor; New York: Doubleday, 1981.

———. "The New Testament Title 'Son of Man' Philologically Considered." In idem, *A Wandering Aramaean,* 143-60. Atlanta: Scholars, 1979.

Fletcher-Louis, C. H. T. *Luke-Acts: Angels, Christology and Soteriology.* Tübingen: Mohr, 1997.

———. "Wisdom Christology and the Partings of the Ways between Judaism and Christianity." In S. E. Porter and B. W. R. Pearson, eds., *Christian-Jewish Relations through the Centuries,* 52-68. JSNTSS; Sheffield: Sheffield Academic Press, 2000.

Focant, C. "Du fils de l'homme assis (Lc 22,69) au fils de l'homme debout (Ac 7,56)." In J. Verheyden, ed., *The Unity of Luke-Acts,* 563-76. Leuven: Leuven University Press.

Foerster, W. "Lukas 22 31f." *ZNW* 46 (1955), 129-33.

Fokkelman, J. P. *Narrative Art and Poetry in the Books of Samuel: A Full Interpretation Based on Stylistic and Structural Analyses.* Volume II: *The Crossing Fates (I Sam. 13–31 and II Sam. I).* Assen/Dover: Van Gorcum, 1986.

Ford, J. M. "'He That Cometh' and the Divine Name." *JSJ* 1 (1970), 144-47.

Fossum, J. *The Image of the Invisible God: Essays on the Influence of Jewish Mysticism on Early Christology.* Novum Testamentum et Orbis Antiquus 30; Freiburg/Göttingen: Vandenhoeck und Ruprecht, 1995.

———. "Kyrios Jesus as the Angel of the Lord in Jude 5-7." *NTS* 33 (1987), 226-43.

France, R. T. *The Gospel of Mark: A Commentary on the Greek Text.* NIGTC; Grand Rapids: Eerdmans, 2002.

———. "The Worship of Jesus: A Neglected Factor in Christological Debate?" In H. H. Rowdon, ed., *Christ the Lord: Studies Presented to Donald Guthrie,* 17-36. Leicester: Inter-Varsity Press, 1982.

Frenschkowski, M. *Offenbarung und Epiphanie.* WUNT; Tübingen: Mohr, 1995.

Frost, G. "The Word of God in the Synoptic Gospels." *SJT* 16 (1963), 186-94.

Fuller, R. H. "The Conception/Birth of Jesus as a Christological Moment." *JSNT* 1 (1978), 37-52.

———. *A Critical Introduction to the New Testament.* London: Duckworth, 1966.

―――――. *The Foundations of New Testament Christology*. New York: Scribner, 1965.

Garrett, S. R. *The Demise of the Devil: Magic and the Demonic in Luke's Writings*. Minneapolis: Fortress, 1989.

Gathercole, S. J. "The Heavenly ἀνατολή (Lk. 1.78-79)." *JTS* 56.2 (2005) 471-88.

―――――. "Jesus' Eschatological Vision of the Fall of Satan: Luke 10.18 Reconsidered." *ZNW* 94.2 (2003), 143-63.

―――――. "The Justification of Wisdom (Mt. 11.19b/Lk 7.35)." *NTS* 49 (2003), 476-88.

―――――. "On the Alleged Aramaic Idiom behind the Synoptic ἦλθον-sayings." *JTS* 55.1 (2004), 84-91.

―――――. "Pre-existence, and the Freedom of the Son in Creation and Redemption: An Exposition in Dialogue with Robert Jenson." *IJST* 7 (2005), 38-51.

―――――. "The Son of Man in Mark's Gospel." *ExpT* 115 (2004), 366-72.

Gench, F. T. *Wisdom in the Christology of Matthew*. Lanham: University Press of America, 1997.

George, A. "La Venue de Jésus, Cause de Division entre les Hommes." *AsSeign* 51 (1972), 62-71.

Gerhardsson, B. "The Christology of Matthew." In M. A. Powell and D. R. Bauer, eds., *Who Do You Say That I Am? Essays on Christology*, 14-32. Louisville: Westminster John Knox, 1999.

Gerleman, G. *Der Menschensohn*. Leiden: Brill, 1983.

Gibbs, J. M. "The Son of God as the Torah Incarnate in Matthew." In F. L. Cross, ed., *Studia Evangelica* IV, 38-46. Texte und Untersuchungen 102; Berlin: Akademie-Verlag, 1968.

Glasson, T. F. "'Plurality of Divine Persons' and the Quotations in Hebrews I.6ff." *NTS* 12 (1965-66), 270-72.

Glombitza, O. "Die christologische Aussage des Lukas in seiner Gestaltung der drei Nachfolgesorte Lukas IX 57-62." *NovT* 13 (1971), 14-23.

Gnilka, J. *Das Evangelium nach Markus*. Volume 1: *Mk 1–8,26*. Einsiedeln: Benziger Verlag, 1978.

―――――. "Der Hymnus des Zacharias." *BZ* 6 (1962), 215-38.

―――――, ed. *Neues Testament und Kirche: Für Rudolf Schnackenburg*. Freiburg: Herder, 1974.

Goulder, M. "Psalm 8 and the Son of Man." *NTS* 48.1 (2002), 18-29.

Gräßer, E. *Der Brief an die Hebräer*. EKK; Zürich: Benziger, 1990.

Green, J. B. *The Gospel of Luke*. Grand Rapids: Eerdmans, 1997.

Grelot, P. "Étude critique de Luc 10,19." *RSR* 69 (1981), 87-100.

Grimm, W. *Weil Ich Dich Liebe: Die Verkundigung Jesu und Deuterojesaja*. Bern: Herbert Lang, 1976.

Groezinger, K.-E. *Ich bin der Herr, dein Gott! Eine rabbinische Homilie zum Ersten Gebot (PesR 20)*. Frankfurter Judaistische Studien; Frankfurt am Main: Peter Lang, 1976.

Grundmann, W. *Das Evangelium nach Lukas*. THKNT; Berlin: Evangelischer Verlagsanstalt, 1969.

———. *Das Evangelium nach Markus.* THKNT; Berlin: Evangelische Verlagsanstalt, 1968.

———. "Matth. XI.27 und die johanneischen 'Der Vater-Der Sohn'–Stellen." *NTS* 12 (1965), 42-49.

———. "Weisheit im Horizont des Reich Gottes." In R. Schnackenburg, J. Ernst, and J. Wanke, eds., *Die Kirche des Anfangs. FS H. Schürmann,* 175-79. Freiburg, 1978.

Guelich, R. A. *Mark 1–8:26.* WBC; Dallas: Word Books, 1989.

Gundry, R. H. *Mark: A Commentary on His Apology for the Cross.* Grand Rapids: Eerdmans, 1993.

Habermann, J. *Präexistenzaussagen im Neuen Testament.* Europäische Hochschulschriften; Frankfurt am Main: Peter Lang, 1990.

———. "Präexistenzchristologie Aussagen im Johannesevangelium: Annotationes zu einer angeblich 'verwegenen Synthese.'" In R. Laufen, ed., *Gottes ewiger Sohn: Die Präexistenz Christi,* 115-41. Paderborn: Schöningh, 1997.

Haenchen, E. *The Acts of the Apostles: A Commentary.* Oxford: Blackwell, 1971.

———. "Matthäus 23." In J. Lange, ed., *Das Matthäus-Evangelium,* 134-63. Darmstadt: Wissenschaftliche Buchgesellschaft, 1980.

Hagner, D. A. *Matthew 1–13.* WBC; Dallas: Word Books, 1993.

Hamerton-Kelly, R. G. *Pre-Existence, Wisdom, and the Son of Man: A Study of the Idea of Pre-Existence in the New Testament.* SNTSMS 21; Cambridge: Cambridge University Press, 1973.

Hampel, V. *Menschensohn und historischer Jesus: Ein Rätselwort als Schlüssel zum messianischen Selbstverständnis Jesu.* Neukirchen-Vluyn: Neukirchener, 1990.

Hannah, D. D. "The Throne of His Glory: The Divine Throne and Heavenly Mediators in Revelation and the Similitudes of Enoch." *ZNW* 94 (2003), 68-96.

Hanson, A. T. *Jesus Christ in the Old Testament.* London: SCM, 1965.

———. "The Reproach of the Messiah in the Epistle to the Hebrews." In E. A. Livingstone, ed., *Studia Theologica VII. Papers Presented to the Fifth International Congress on Biblical Studies Held at Oxford, 1973,* 231-40. Berlin: Akademie Verlag, 1982.

Hanson, R. P. C. *Allegory and Event.* London: SCM, 1959.

Hare, D. R. A. *The Theme of Jewish Persecution of Christians in the Gospel according to St Matthew.* SNTSMS 6; Cambridge: Cambridge University Press, 1967.

Harnack, A. "'Ich bin gekommen.' Die ausdrücklichen Selbstzeugnisse Jesu über den Zweck seiner Sendung und seines Kommens." *ZTK* 22 (1912), 1-30.

———. *The Sayings of Jesus: The Second Source of St. Matthew and St. Luke.* London: Williams and Norgate, 1908.

Hartman, L. "Into the Name of the Lord Jesus: A Suggestion Concerning the Earliest Meaning of the Phrase." *NTS* 20 (1974), 432-40.

———. *"Into the Name of the Lord Jesus": Baptism in the Early Church.* Edinburgh: T&T Clark, 1997.

Hauck, F. *Das Evangelium des Markus.* THKNT; Leipzig: Scholl, 1931.

Hauck, R. J. *The More Divine Proof: Prophecy and Inspiration in Celsus and Origen.* Atlanta: Scholars, 1989.

Hayward, C. T. R. "Sacrifice and World Order: Some Observations on Ben Sira's Attitude to the Temple Service." In S. W. Sykes, ed., *Sacrifice and Redemption: Durham Essays in Theology,* 22-34. Cambridge: Cambridge University Press, 1991.

Head, P. M. "A Text-Critical Study of Mark 1.1: 'The Beginning of the Gospel of Jesus Christ.'" *NTS* 37 (1991), 621-29.

Heil, J. P. *Jesus Walking on the Sea: Meaning and Gospel Functions of Matt 14:22-33, Mark 6:45-52 and John 6:15b-21.* Rome: Biblical Institute Press, 1981.

Hengel, M. "Christological Titles in Early Christianity." In J. H. Charlesworth, ed., *The Messiah: Developments in Earliest Judaism and Christianity. The First Princeton Symposium on Judaism and Christian Origins,* 425-48. Minneapolis: Fortress, 1992.

―――. "Präexistenz bei Paulus?" In C. Landmesser, H.-J. Eckstein, and H. Lichtenberger, eds., *Jesus Christus als die Mitte der Schrift: Studien zur Hermeneutik des Evangeliums,* 479-518. BZNW 86; Berlin/New York: Walter de Gruyter, 1997.

Herter, H. *De Priapo.* Giessen: A. Töpelmann, 1932.

Hill, D. *The Gospel of Matthew.* London: Oliphants, 1972.

Hofius, O. "Die Allmacht des Sohnes Gottes und das Gebet des Glaubens." *ZTK* 101 (2004), 117-37.

―――. "Christus als Schöpfungsmittler und Erlösungsmittler: Das Bekenntnis 1 Kor 8,6 im Kontext der paulinischen Theologie." In idem, *Paulusstudien II,* 181-201. WUNT; Tübingen: Mohr, 2002.

―――. "Ist Jesus der Messias? Thesen." *JBT* 8 (1993), 103-29.

―――. "Jesu Zuspruch der Sündenvergebung: Exegetische Erwägungen zu Mk 2,5b." In idem, *Neutestamentliche Studien,* 38-56. WUNT 132; Tübingen: Mohr, 2000.

―――. "Vergebungszuspruch und Vollmachtsfrage: Mk 2,1-12 und das Problem priesterlicher Absolution im antiken Judentum." In idem, *Neutestamentliche Studien,* 57-69. WUNT 132; Tübingen: Mohr, 2000.

Hooker, M. D. *A Commentary on the Gospel according to St. Mark.* Black's New Testament Commentary; London: A. and C. Black, 1991.

Horbury, W. *Jewish Messianism and the Cult of Christ.* London: SCM, 1998.

―――. *Messianism among Jews and Christians: Biblical and Historical Studies.* London/New York: Continuum, 2003.

Hornschuh, M. *Studien zur Epistula Apostolorum.* Berlin: Walter de Gruyter, 1965.

Hoskyns, E. C. *The Fourth Gospel.* London: Faber and Faber, 1954.

Hultgård, A. "La Chute de Satan. L'arrière plan iranien d'un logion de Jésus (*Luc* 10,18)." *RHPR* 80 (2000), 69-77.

Hultgren, A. *Jesus and His Adversaries: The Form and Function of the Conflict Stories in the Synoptic Tradition.* Minneapolis: Augsburg, 1979.

Humphrey, H. M. "Jesus as Wisdom in Mark." *Biblical Theology Bulletin* 19 (1989), 48-53.

Hurst, L. D. "The Christology of Hebrews 1 and 2." In L. D. Hurst and N. T. Wright, eds., *The Glory of Christ in the New Testament*, 151-64. Oxford: Clarendon, 1987.

Hurtado, L. W. *Lord Jesus Christ: Devotion to Jesus in Earliest Christianity*. Grand Rapids: Eerdmans, 2003.

———. *One God, One Lord: Early Christian Devotion and Ancient Jewish Monotheism*. Edinburgh: T&T Clark, ²1998.

———. "Pre-Existence." In G. F. Hawthorne, R. P. Martin, and D. G. Reid, eds., *Dictionary of Paul and His Letters*, 743-746. Downers Grove, Ill.: InterVarsity Press, 1993.

———. "Pre-70 CE Jewish Opposition to Christ-Devotion." *JTS* 50 (1999), 35-58.

Iwe, J. C. *Jesus in the Synagogue of Capernaum*. Rome: Gregorian University Press, 1999.

Jacoby, A. "*Anatolē ex hupsous* [Luke 1:78]." *ZNW* 20 (1921), 205-14.

Jastrow, M. *A Dictionary of the Targumim, the Talmud Babli and Yerushalmi, and the Midrashic Literature*. London: Luzac, 1903.

Jenni, E. "'Kommen' im theologischen Sprachgebrauch des Alten Testaments." In H. J. Stoebe, J. J. Stamm, and E. Jenni, eds., *Wort, Gebot, Glaube: Beiträge zur Theologie des Alten Testaments: Walther Eichrodt zum 80. Geburtstag*, 251-61. Zürich: Zwingli, 1970.

Jenson, R. W. "Christ as Culture 1: Christ as Polity." *IJST* 5.3 (2003), 323-29.

———. "For us . . . he was made man." In C. R. Seitz, ed., *Nicene Christianity: The Future for a New Ecumenism*, 75-86. Carlisle: Paternoster; Grand Rapids: Baker (Brazos Imprint), 2002.

———. *Systematic Theology*. 2 volumes. Oxford: Oxford University Press, 1997-99.

Jeremias, J. "Das Lösegeld für viele." In *Abba: Studien zur neutestamentlichen Theologie und Zeitgeschichte*, 216-29. Göttingen: Vandenhoeck und Ruprecht, 1966.

———. "Die älteste Schicht der Menschensohn-Logien." *ZNW* 58 (1967), 159-72.

———. *Jesus' Promise to the Nations*. London: SCM, 1968.

———. *New Testament Theology*. London: SCM Press, 1971.

———. *The Parables of Jesus*. New Testament Library; London: SCM, 1963.

Johnson, L. T. *The Acts of the Apostles*. SacPag 5; Collegeville: Liturgical Press, 1992.

———. *The Gospel of Luke*. SacPag 3; Collegeville: Liturgical Press, 1991.

Johnson, M. D. "Reflections on a Wisdom Approach to Matthew's Christology." *CBQ* 36 (1974), 44-64.

Juel, D. H. "The Messiah in Mark's Christology." In J. H. Charlesworth, ed., *The Messiah: Developments in Earliest Judaism and Christianity. The First Princeton Symposium on Judaism and Christian Origins*, 449-60. Minneapolis: Fortress, 1992.

Jülicher, A. *Die Gleichnisreden Jesu*. Freiburg: Mohr, 1888.

Jüngel, E. *God's Being Is in Becoming*. Translated by John Webster. Edinburgh: T&T Clark, 2001.

Kammler, H.-C. "Die Prädikation Jesu Christi 'als' Gott. (Röm 9,5b)." *ZNW* 94 (2003), 164-80.

Kampling, R. *Israel unter dem Anspruch des Messias: Studien zur Israelthematik im Markusevangelium.* Stuttgarter biblische Beiträge 25; Stuttgart: Katholisches Bibelwerk, 1992.

Käsemann, E. "Die Anfänge christlicher Theologie." In idem, *Exegetische Versuche und Besinnungen,* 82-104. Göttingen: Vandenhoeck und Ruprecht, 1970.

Kazmierski, C. R. "Evangelist and Leper: A Socio-Cultural Study of Mark 1.40-45." *NTS* 38 (1992), 37-50.

Keck, L. E. "Mark 3 7-12 and Mark's Christology." *JBL* 84 (1965), 341-58.

Kee, H. C. "The Transfiguration in Mark: Epiphany or Apocalyptic Vision?" In J. Reumann, ed., *Understanding the Sacred Text. FS M. Enslin,* 135-52. Valley Forge, Pa.: Judson, 1972.

Keener, C. S. *A Commentary on the Gospel of Matthew.* Grand Rapids: Eerdmans, 1999.

Kellett, E. E. "Note on Jude 5." *ExpT* 15 (1903-4), 381.

Kertelge, K. *Die Wunder Jesu im Markusevangelium: Eine redaktionsgeschichtliche Untersuchung.* Munich: Kosel-Verlag, 1970.

Kilpatrick, G. D. "Mark i 45." *JTS* 42 (1941), 67-68.

———. "Mark i 45 and the Meaning of λόγος." *JTS* 40 (1939), 389-90.

Kim, S. *The "Son of Man" as the Son of God.* Tübingen: Mohr, 1983.

Kingsbury, J. D. *Matthew: Structure, Christology, Kingdom.* London: SPCK, 1975.

———. "On Following Jesus: The 'Eager' Scribe and the 'Reluctant' Disciple." *NTS* 34 (1988), 45-59.

———. "The Title 'Son of Man' in Matthew's Gospel." *CBQ* 37 (1975), 193-202.

Klauck, H.-J. *Allegorie und Allegorese in synoptischen Gleichnistexten.* Neutestamentliche Abhandlungen; NS 13; Münster: Aschendorff, 1978.

———. *Vorspiel im Himmel? Erzähltechnik und Theologie im Markusprolog.* BThSt 32; Neukirchen: Neukirchener Verlag, 1997.

Klijn, A. F. J. "Jude 5 to 7." In W. C. Weinreich, ed., *The New Testament Age: Essays in Honor of Bo Reicke,* 1:237-44. Macon, Ga.: Mercer University Press, 1984.

Klostermann, E. *Das Markusevangelium.* HNT; Tübingen: Mohr, ⁵1971.

Knight, J. M. *Disciples of the Beloved One: The Christology, Social Setting and Theological Context of the Ascension of Isaiah.* JSPSupS 18; Sheffield: Sheffield Academic Press, 1996.

———. *2 Peter and Jude.* New Testament Guides; Sheffield: Sheffield Academic Press, 1995.

Knox, J. *Christ the Lord: The Meaning of Jesus in the Early Church.* Chicago/New York: Willett, Clark and Co., 1945.

Knox, J. *The Humanity and Divinity of Christ: A Study of Pattern in Christology.* Cambridge: Cambridge University Press, 1967.

Koester, C. *Hebrews: A New Translation with Introduction and Commentary.* Anchor; New York: Doubleday, 2001.

Kruijf, T. de. *Der Sohn des lebendigen Gottes: Ein Beitrag zur Christologie des Matthäus-Evangeliums.* AnBib; Rome: Pontifical Biblical Institute, 1962.

Kuhn, K. H. "The Testament of Isaac." In H. F. D. Sparks, ed., *The Apocryphal Old Testament,* 423-39. Oxford: Clarendon, 1984.

Kümmel, W. G. *The Theology of the New Testament according to Its Major Witnesses: Jesus-Paul-John.* London: SCM, 1974.

Kupp, D. D. *Matthew's Emmanuel: Divine Presence and God's People in the First Gospel.* SNTSMS; Cambridge: Cambridge University Press, 1996.

Kuschel, K.-J. *Born Before All Time? The Dispute over Christ's Origin.* London: SCM, 1992 (1990).

———. "Exegese und Dogmatik — Harmonie oder Konflikt: Die Frage nach einer Präexistenzchristologie bei Paulus als Testfall." In R. Laufen, ed., *Gottes ewiger Sohn: Die Präexistenz Christi,* 143-61. Paderborn: Schöningh, 1997.

Kwaak, H. van der. "Die Klage über Jerusalem (Matth. xxiii 37-39)." *NovT* 8 (1966), 156-70.

Lagrange, M. *Évangile selon saint Marc.* Études Bibliques; Paris: Victor Lecoffre, 1911.

———. *Évangile selon saint Matthieu.* Études Bibliques; Paris: Victor Lecoffre, 1923.

Lambertz, M. "Sprachliches aus Septuaginta und Neuem Testament: I: Ev. Luc. 1 78b: Ἀνατολὴ ἐξ ὕψους." *Wissenschaftliche Zeitschrift der Universität Leipzig* (1952-53), 79-84.

Landon, C. *A Text-Critical Study of the Epistle of Jude.* JSNTSS; Sheffield: Sheffield Academic Press, 1996.

Lane, W. F. *The Gospel according to Mark.* NICNT; Grand Rapids: Eerdmans, 1974.

Laufen, R. "Der anfanglose Sohn: Eine christologische Problemanzeige." In idem, ed., *Gottes ewiger Sohn: Die Präexistenz Christi,* 9-29. Paderborn: Schöningh, 1997.

———, ed. *Gottes ewiger Sohn: Die Präexistenz Christi.* Paderborn: Schöningh, 1997.

Laughlin, J. C. H. "Capernaum from Jesus' Time and After." *BAR* 19.5 (1993), 54-63, 90.

LaVerdière, E. "Calling down Fire from Heaven." *Emmanuel* 95 (1989), 322-29.

Légasse, S. *L'Évangile de Marc.* Paris: Cerf, 1997.

Lendrum, J. "Into a Far Country." *ExpT* 36 (1924/25), 377-80.

Lichtenstein, E. "Die älteste christliche Glaubensformel." *ZKG* 63 (1950-51), 1-74.

Lindars, B. *New Testament Apologetic: The Doctrinal Significance of the Old Testament Quotations.* London: SCM Press, 1961.

Lindemann, A. "Die Erzählung von Sämann und der Saat und ihre Auslegung als allegorisches Gleichnis." *Wort und Dienst* 21 (1991), 115-31.

Linton, O. "The Parable of the Children's Game: Baptist and Son of Man (Matt. xi.16-19 = Luke vii.31-5): A Synoptic Text-Critical, Structural and Exegetical Investigation." *NTS* 22 (1976), 159-79.

Lips, H. von. *Weisheitliche Traditionen im NT.* WMANT 64; Neukirchen: Neukirchener Verlag, 1990.

Lods, A. "La Chute des Anges: Origine et Portée de Cette Speculation." *RHPR* 7 (1927), 295-315.

Lohmeyer, E. "Die Verklärung Jesu nach dem Markus-Evangelium." *ZNW* 21 (1922), 185-215.

———. *Evangelium des Markus*. KEK; Göttingen: Vandenhoeck und Ruprecht, 1937.

———. *Das Evangelium des Matthäus*. Edited by W. Schmauch. Göttingen: Vandenhoeck und Ruprecht, ^{3}1962.

Löning, K. "Die Füchse, die Vögel, und der Menschensohn (Mt 8,19f.)." In H. Frankemölle and K. Kertelge, eds., *Vom Urchristentum zu Jesus. Für Joachim Gnilka*, 82-102. Freiburg/Basel/Vienna: Herder, 1989.

Lührmann, D. *Das Markusevangelium*. HNT 3; Tübingen: Mohr, 1987.

Luria, S. "Zur Quelle von Mt 8.19." *ZNW* 25 (1926), 282-86.

Luz, U. *Das Evangelium nach Matthäus*: Volume 1. EKK; Neukirchen-Vluyn/Zürich: Neukirchener Verlag, ^{1}1985.

———. *Das Evangelium nach Matthäus*: Volume 4. Zürich: Benziger, 2002.

———. *Matthew 8-20: A Commentary* Hermeneia; Minneapolis: Augsburg, 2001.

———. "The Son of Man in Matthew: Heavenly Judge or Human Christ?" *JSNT* 48 (1992), 3-21.

Machen, J. G. *The Virgin Birth of Christ*. London: James Clarke, 1958 (1930).

Macleod, D. "The Christology of Wolfhart Pannenberg." *Themelios* 25.2 (2000), 19-41.

———. *The Person of Christ*. Contours of Christian Theology; Leicester: Inter-Varsity Press, 1998.

Macquarrie, J. *Christology Revisited*. London: SCM, 1998.

———. *Jesus Christ in Modern Thought*. London: SCM, 1990.

———. "The Pre-existence of Jesus Christ." *ExpT* 77 (1965-66), 199-202.

Madden, P. J. *Jesus' Walking on the Sea: An Investigation of the Origin of the Narrative Account*. Berlin: Walter de Gruyter, 1997.

Maier, F. "Zur Erklärung des Judasbriefes (Jud 5)." *BZ* 2 (1904), 391-97.

Manson, T. W. *The Sayings of Jesus: As Recorded in the Gospels according to St. Matthew and St. Luke*. London: SCM, 1949.

Marcus, J. "Mark — Interpreter of Paul." *NTS* 46.4 (2000), 473-87.

———. *Mark 1–8: A New Translation with Introduction and Commentary*. Anchor; New York: Doubleday, 2000.

———. "Mark 14:61: 'Are You the 'Messiah-Son-of-God?'" *NovT* 31 (1989), 125-41.

———. *The Mystery of the Kingdom of God*. SBLDS; Atlanta: Scholars Press, 1987.

———. "Son of Man as Son of Adam." *RevB* 110.1 (2003), 38-61.

———. *The Way of the Lord: Christological Exegesis of the Old Testament in the Gospel of Mark*. Louisville: Westminster/John Knox, 1992.

Marmorstein, A. "Die Quellen des neuen Jeremia-Apocryphons." *ZNW* 27 (1928), 327-37.

Marshall, I. H. "The Divine Sonship of Jesus." *Interpretation* 21 (1967), 87-103.

———. *The Gospel of Luke: A Commentary on the Greek Text*. NIGTC; Carlisle: Paternoster, 1978.

———. "The Son of Man and the Incarnation." *Ex Auditu* 7 (1991), 29-43.

———. "The Synoptic Son of Man Sayings in Recent Discussion." *NTS* 12 (1966), 326-51.

Marx, A. "La chute de 'Lucifer' (Esaïe 14,12-15; *Luc* 10,18): Préhistoire d'un Mythe." *RHPR* 80 (2000), 171-85.

März, C.-P. "'Feuer auf die Erde zu werfen, bin ich gekommen. . . .'" In F. Refoulé, ed., *À cause de l'Évangile: Études sur les Synoptiques et les Actes. Offertes au P. Jacques Dupont, O.S.B., à l'occasion de son 70ème Anniversaire*, 479-511. Paris: Cerf, 1985.

Matthews, A. J. "Depart from Me; for I Am a Sinful Man, O Lord." *ExpT* 30 (1918-19), 425.

McCready, D. "'He Came from Heaven': The Pre-existence of Christ Revisited." *JETS* 40 (1997), 419-32.

McDermott, J. M. "Jesus and the Son of God Title." *Gregorianum* 62 (1981), 277-317.

Meeks, W. A. Review of Hamerton-Kelly, *Pre-existence, Wisdom, and the Son of Man*, in *JBL* 93 (1974), 617-19.

Merklein, H. "Zur Entstehung der urchristlichen Aussage vom präexistenten Sohn Gottes." In G. Dautzenberg, H. Merklein, and K. Müller, eds., *Zur Geschichte des Urchristentums*, 33-62. Freiburg/Basel/Vienna: Herder, 1979.

Metzger, B. M. *A Textual Commentary on the Greek New Testament*. London: United Bible Societies, 1971.

Meye, R. "Psalm 107 as 'Horizon' for Interpreting the Miracle Stories of Mark 4.35–8.26." In R. A. Guelich, ed., *Unity and Diversity in New Testament Theology: Essays in Honour of George E. Ladd*. Grand Rapids: Eerdmans, 1978.

Michel, H. J. *Die Abschiedsrede des Paulus an die Kirche (Apg. 20,17-38): Motivgeschichte und theologische Bedeutung*. Munich: Kosel-Verlag, 1973.

Michel, O. "Ich komme." *TZ* 24 (1968), 123-24.

Milgrom, J. *Numbers*. JPS Torah Commentary; Philadelphia: Jewish Publication Society, 1990.

Miller, R. J. "The Rejection of the Prophets in Q." *JBL* 107 (1988), 225-40.

Miranda, J. P. *Der Vater, der mich gesandt hat: Religionsgeschichtliche Untersuchungen zu den johanneischen Sendungsformeln, zugleich ein Beitrag zur johanneischen Christologie und Ekklesiologie*. Frankfurt/Bern: Peter Lang, 1972.

Mittmann-Richert, U. *Magnifikat und Benediktus*. WUNT II/90; Tübingen: Mohr, 1996.

Miyoshi, M. *Der Anfang des Reiseberichts, Lk 9,51–10,24: Eine redaktionsgeschichtliche Untersuchung*. AnBib 60; Rome: Pontifical Biblical Institute, 1974.

Mohr, T. A. *Markus- und Johannespassion. Redaktions- und traditionsgeschichtliche Untersuchung der Markinischen und Johanneischen Passionstradition*. ATANT 70; Zürich: Zwingli-Verlag, 1982.

Molnar, P. D. *Divine Freedom and the Doctrine of the Immanent Trinity: In Dialogue with Karl Barth and Contemporary Theology*. Edinburgh: T&T Clark, 2002.

Montefiore, C. G. *The Synoptic Gospels: Edited with an Introduction and a Commentary*. London: Macmillan, ²1927.

Morris, L. *The Gospel according to Matthew.* Pillar New Testament Commentary; Grand Rapids: Eerdmans, 1992.

Motyer, J. A. *The Prophecy of Isaiah.* Leicester: Inter-Varsity Press, 1993.

Moule, C. F. D. *The Origin of Christology.* Cambridge: Cambridge University Press, 1977.

———. "'The Son of Man': Some of the Facts." *NTS* 41 (1995), 277-79.

Moulton, W. F., and A. S. Geden. *Concordance to the Greek New Testament.* Edited by I. H. Marshall. London: T&T Clark, 2002.

Mowery, R. J. "Subtle Differences: The Matthean 'Son of God' References." *NovT* 32 (1990), 193-200.

Mullen, E. T., Jr. *The Divine Council in Canaanite and Early Hebrew Literature.* Chico: Scholars Press, 1980.

Müller, U. B. "Die christologische Absicht des Markusevangeliums und die Verklärungsgeschichte." *ZNW* 64 (1973), 159-93.

Murphy-O'Connor, J. "Christological Anthropology in Phil. 2.6-11." *RevB* 83 (1976), 25-50.

———. "1 Cor. 8.6: Cosmology or Soteriology?" *RevB* 85 (1978), 253-67.

Mussner, F. "Der nicht erkannte Kairos (Mt 11,16-19 = Lk 7,31-35)." *Biblica* 40 (1959), 599-612.

Neirynck, F. "Ac 10,36-43 et l'Évangile." *ETL* 60 (1984), 109-16.

———. "Acts 10,36a τὸν λόγον ὅν." *ETL* 60 (1984), 118-23.

Nineham, D. E. *The Gospel of Saint Mark.* Harmondsworth: Penguin Books, 1969.

Nock, A. D. "Early Gentile Christianity and Its Hellenistic Background." In idem, *Essays on Religion and the Ancient World,* 1:49-133. Oxford: Clarendon, 1972.

———. "A Vision of Mandulis Aion." *HTR* 27 (1934), 53-104.

Nolland, J. *Luke 9:21–18:34.* WBC; Waco: Word, 1993.

———. *Luke 18:35–24:53.* WBC; Waco: Word, 1993.

Norden, E. *Agnostos Theos: Untersuchungen zur Formengeschichte religioser Rede.* Berlin: Teubner, 1913.

O'Neill, J. C. "The Charge of Blasphemy at Jesus' Trial before the Sanhedrin." In E. Bammel, ed., *The Trial of Jesus: Cambridge Studies in Honour of C. F. D. Moule,* 72-77. London: SCM, 1970.

Osburn, C. D. "The Text of Jude 5." *Biblica* 62 (1981), 107-15.

Owen, P., and D. Shepherd. "Speaking Up for Qumran, Dalman and the Son of Man: Was *Bar Enasha* a Common Term for 'Man' in the Time of Jesus?" *JSNT* 81 (2001), 81-122.

Pamment, M. "The Son of Man in the First Gospel." *NTS* 29 (1983), 116-29.

Pannenberg, W. *Jesus: God and Man.* Philadelphia: Westminster, ²1977.

———. *Systematic Theology.* Volume 2. Edinburgh: T&T Clark, 1994.

Pax, E. *Epiphaneia: Ein religionsgeschichtlicher Beitrag zur Biblischen Theologie.* Munich: Karl Zink, 1955.

Payne, P. B. "Jesus' Implicit Claim to Deity in the Parables." *TrinJ* 2 (1981), 3-23.

Perkins, P. "The Gospel of Mark." In *The New Interpreter's Bible*, 8:507-733. Abingdon Press: Nashville, 1995.

Pesch, R. *Die Apostelgeschichte*. 2 vols. EKK; Zürich: Benziger, 1986.

———. *Das Markusevangelium*. 2 vols. HTK; Freiburg: Herder, 1976.

Peterson, D. G. *Hebrews and Perfection: An Examination of the Concept of Perfection in the Epistle to the Hebrews*. SNTSMS; Cambridge: Cambridge University Press, 1982.

Plath, M. "Der neustestamentliche Weheruf über Jerusalem (Luk 13,34-35 = Matth. 23,37-39)." *TSK* 78 (1905), 455-60.

Plummer, A. *An Exegetical Commentary of the Gospel according to S. Matthew*. London: Robert Scott, 1909.

Pregeant, R. "The Wisdom Passages in Matthew's Story." *SBLSP* (1990), 469-93.

Provan, I. W. *1 and 2 Kings*. NIBC; Peabody: Hendrickson, 1995.

Raatschen, J. H. "Empfangen durch den Heiligen Geist: Überlegungen zu Mt 1,18-25." *Theologische Beiträge* 11 (1980), 262-77.

Rawlinson, A. E. J. *The New Testament Doctrine of the Christ*. London: Longmans, 1929.

Reitzenstein, R. *Das mandäische Buch des Herrn der Grösse und die Evangelienüberlieferung*. Sitzungsberichte der Heidelberger Akademie der Wissenschaften; Heidelberg: Carl Winter, 1919.

———. *Poimandres: Studien zur griechisch-ägyptischen und frühchristlichen Literatur*. Leipzig: Teubner, 1904.

Rengstorf, K. H. *Das Evangelium nach Lukas*. NTD; Göttingen: Vandenhoeck und Ruprecht, 1978.

Riesenfeld, H. "The Text of Acts 10.36." In E. Best and R. McL. Wilson, eds., *Text and Interpretation: Studies Presented to Matthew Black*, 191-94. Cambridge: Cambridge University Press, 1979.

Riesner, R. "Präexistenz und Jungfrauengeburt." *Theologische Beiträge* 12 (1981), 177-87.

Ritt, H. "Der 'Seewandel Jesu' (Mk 6, 45-52 par): Literarische und theologische Aspekte." *BZ* 23 (1979), 71-84.

Robbins, V. K. "Foxes, Birds, Burials and Furrows." In B. L. Mack and V. K. Robbins, *Patterns of Persuasion in the Gospels*, 69-84. Sonoma, Calif.: Polebridge Press, 1989.

Roberts, T. A. "Some Comments on Matthew x.34-36 and Luke xii.51-53." *ExpT* 69 (1957-58), 304-6.

Robinson, J. A. T. *The Human Face of God*. London: SCM, 1973.

———. *Jesus and His Coming*. London: SCM, 1957.

———. *Redating the New Testament*. London: SCM, 1976.

Robinson, J. M. "Basic Shifts in German Theology." *Interpretation* 16 (1962), 76-97.

Rolland, P. "Jésus connaissait leurs pensées." *ETL* 62 (1986), 118-21.

Rose, W. H. *Zemah and Zerubbabel: Messianic Expectations in the Early Postexilic Period*. JSOTSup; Sheffield: Sheffield Academic Press, 2000.

Rosenstiel, J. M. "La Chute de l'Ange." *Journée d'Études Coptes* (1982-83), 37-60.

Ross, J. M. "The Rejected Words in Luke 9$^{54\text{-}56}$." *ExpT* 84 (1972-73), 85-88.

Ruck-Schröder, A. *Der Name Gottes und der Name Jesus: Eine neutestamentliche Studie.* WMANT; Neukirchen: Neukirchener Verlag, 1999.

Sabbe, M. "Matthew's Use of Q in Chapter 11." In J. Delobel, ed., *Logia: Les Paroles de Jésus — The Sayings of Jesus. Mémorial Joseph Coppens*, 363-71. BETL LIX; Leuven: Leuven University Press, 1982.

Sabourin, L. "Christ's Pre-existence." *Religious Studies Bulletin* 4.1 (1984), 22-29.

Sahlin, H. "Wie würde ursprunglich die Benennung 'Der Menschensohn' verstanden?" *ST* 37 (1983), 147-79.

Sanders, E. P. *Jesus and Judaism.* London: SCM, 1984.

Schäfer, P. *Rivalität zwischen Engeln und Menschen: Untersuchungen zur rabbinischen Engelvorstellung.* Berlin: Walter de Gruyter, 1975.

Schaper, J. *Eschatology in the Greek Psalter.* WUNT; Tübingen: Mohr, 1995.

Schenke, H.-M., and K. M. Fischer. *Einleitung in die Schriften des Neuen Testaments. II: Die Evangelien und die anderen neutestamentlichen Schriften.* Gütersloh: Mohn, 1978.

Schenke, L. "Gibt es im Markusevangelium eine Präexistenzchristologie?" *ZNW* 91 (2000), 45-71.

———. *Das Markusevangelium.* Urban-Taschenbücher; Stuttgart: Kohlhammer, 1988.

———. *Die Urgemeinde: Geschichtliche und theologische Entwicklung.* Stuttgart: Kohlhammer, 1990.

Schlatter, A. *Erläuterungen zum Neuen Testament: Die Evangelien nach Markus und Lukas.* Stuttgart: Calwer Verlag, 1928.

Schlatter, A. *Der Evangelist Matthäus: Seine Sprache, sein Ziel, seine Selbständigkeit.* Stuttgart: Calwer Verlag, 1948.

———. *Das Evangelium nach Lukas aus seinen Quellen erklärt.* Stuttgart: Calwer, 1931.

———. *Markus: Der Evangelist für die Griechen.* Stuttgart: Calwer, 1984 (1935).

Schimanowski, G. "Die frühjüdischen Voraussetzungen der urchristlichen Präexistenzchristologie." In R. Laufen, ed., *Gottes ewiger Sohn: Die Präexistenz Christi*, 31-55. Paderborn: Schöningh, 1997.

———. *Weisheit und Messias: Die jüdischen Voraussetzungen der urchristlichen Präexistenzchristologie.* Tübingen: Mohr, 1985.

Schmidt, K. L. "Lucifer als gefallene Engelmacht." *TZ* 7 (1951), 161-79.

Schneider, G. *Apostelgeschichte.* 2 vols. Freiburg: Herder, 1980-82.

———. "Das Bildwort von der Lampe." *ZNW* 61 (1970), 183-209.

———. "Christologische Präexistenzaussagen im Neuen Testament." *Communio* 6 (1977), 21-30.

———. "Die Davidssohnfrage." *Biblica* 53 (1973), 65-90.

———. "ἔρχομαι κτλ." In G. Kittel, ed. *TWNT* II, 662-72.

———. "'Der Menschensohn' in der lukanischen Christologie." In idem, *Lukas,*

Theologe der Heilsgeschichte: Aufsätze zum Lukanischen Doppelwerk, 98-113. Bonner biblische Beiträge; Bonn: Peter Hanstein Verlag, 1985.

———. "Präexistenz Christi." In J. Gnilka, ed., *Neues Testament und Kirche: für Rudolf Schnackenburg,* 399-412. Freiburg: Herder, 1974.

Schniewind, J. *Das Evangelium nach Markus.* NTD; Göttingen: Vandenhoeck und Ruprecht, 1956.

Schnutenhaus, F. "Das Kommen und Erschienen Gottes im Alten Testament." *ZAW* 76 (1964), 1-22.

Schottroff, L. *Der Glaubende und die feindliche Welt: Beobachtungen zum gnostischen Dualismus und seiner Bedeutung für Paulus und das Johannesevangelium.* WMANT 37; Neukirchen-Vluyn: Neukirchener, 1970.

Schreiber, J. "Die Christologie des Markusevangeliums." *ZTK* 58 (1961), 154-83.

———. *Die Markuspassion: Eine redaktionsgeschichtliche Untersuchung.* BZNW 68; Berlin: Walter de Gruyter, 1993.

Schürmann, H. *Das Lukasevangelium.* Volume 1: *Kommentar zu Kap. 1,1–9,50.* HTK; Freiburg: Herder, 1969.

Schweitzer, A. *The Quest of the Historical Jesus: First Complete Edition.* London: SCM, 2000.

Schweizer, E. "Aufnahme und Korrektur jüdischer Sophiatheologie im Neuen Testament." In idem, *Neotestamentica: Deutsche und Englische Aufsätze, 1951-1963/ German and English Essays, 1951-1963,* 110-21. Zurich: Zwingli Verlag, 1963.

———. *Das Evangelium nach Markus.* NTD; Göttingen: Vandenhoeck und Ruprecht, 1967.

———. *The Good News according to Mark.* London: SPCK, 1971.

———. *The Good News according to Matthew.* London: SPCK, 1976.

———. *Matthäus und seine Gemeinde.* Stuttgart: Verlag Katholisches Bibelwerk, 1974.

———. *Neotestamentica: Deutsche und Englische Aufsätze, 1951-1963/German and English Essays, 1951-1963.* Zurich: Zwingli Verlag, 1963.

———. "What Do We Mean When We Say 'God Sent His Son . . .'?" In J. T. Carroll et al., eds., *Faith and History: Essays in Honour of Paul W. Meyer,* 298-312. Atlanta: Scholars Press, 1990.

———. "Zur Herkunft der Präexistenzvorstellung bei Paulus." In idem, *Neotestamentica: Deutsche und Englische Aufsätze, 1951-1963/German and English Essays, 1951-1963,* 105-9. Zurich: Zwingli Verlag, 1963.

Segbroeck, F. van. "Le Scandale de l'incroyance: La signification de Mt 13,35." *ETL* 41 (1965), 344-72.

Seper, H. "*Kai ti thelō ei ēdē anēphthē* (Lk 12,49b)." *VD* 36 (1958), 147-53.

Sevenster, J. "Christologie I: Christologie des Urchristentums." In K. Galling et al., eds., *RGG*³ I, cols. 1745-62.

Sharf, A. *Byzantine Jewry from Justinian to the Fourth Crusade.* London: Routledge and Kegan Paul, 1971.

Sievers, J. "*Shekinah* and Matthew 18.20." In A. Finkel and L. Frizzell, eds., *Standing be-*

fore God: Studies on Prayer in Scriptures and in Tradition with Essays in Honor of
John M. Oesterreicher, 171-82. New York: Ktav, 1981.

Sigal, P. "Further Reflections on the 'Begotten' Messiah." *Hebrew Annual Review* 7
(1983), 221-33.

Slater, T. B. "One Like a Son of Man in First-Century CE Judaism." *NTS* 41 (1995), 183-
98.

Smith, M. H. "No Place for a Son of Man." *Forum* 4.4 (1988), 83-107.

Snodgrass, K. *The Parable of the Wicked Tenants.* WUNT 27; Tübingen: Mohr, 1983.

Söding, T. "Gottes Sohn von Anfang an: Zur Präexistenzchristologie bei Paulus und
den Deuteropaulinen." In R. Laufen, ed., *Gottes ewiger Sohn: Die Präexistenz
Christi,* 53-93. Paderborn: Schöningh, 1997.

Spitta, F. "Jesu Weigerung, sich als 'Gut' bezeichnen zu lassen." *ZNW* 9 (1908), 12-20.

———. "Satan als Blitz." *ZNW* 9 (1908), 160-63.

Stanton, G. N. "Salvation Proclaimed: X. Matthew 11:28-30: Comfortable Words?"
ExpT 94 (1982-83), 3-9.

Stauffer, E. *New Testament Theology.* New York: Macmillan, 1955.

———. *Theologie des Neuen Testaments.* Gütersloh: Mohn, ⁴1948.

Steck, O. H. *Israel und das gewaltsame Geschick der Propheten: Untersuchungen zur
Überlieferung des deuteronomistischen Geschichtsbildes im Alten Testament,
Spätjudentum und Urchristentum.* Neukirchen: Neukirchener Verlag, 1967.

Stemberger, G. *Introduction to the Talmud and Midrash: Second Edition Translated and
Edited by Markus Bockmuehl.* Edinburgh: T&T Clark, 1995.

Stettler, H. *Die Christologie der Pastoralbriefe.* WUNT; Tübingen: Mohr, 1998.

Stinespring, W. F. "Testament of Isaac." In J. H. Charlesworth, ed., *The Old Testament
Pseudepigrapha,* 1:903-18. New York: Doubleday, 1983.

Stone, M. E. "The Concept of the Messiah in IV Ezra." In J. Neusner, ed., *Religions in
Antiquity: Essays in Memory of Erwin Ramsdell Goodenough,* 295-312. Leiden:
Brill, 1968.

———. *Fourth Ezra.* Hermeneia; Minneapolis: Fortress, 1990.

Strack, H., and P. Billerbeck. *Kommentar zum Neuen Testament aus Talmud und Midrash.* 7 volumes. Munich: Beck, 1922-56.

Strauss, D. F. "Jesu Weheruf über Jerusalem und die σοφία τοῦ θεοῦ." *Zeitschrift für
die Wissenschaftliche Theologie* 6 (1863), 84-93.

Strecker, G. *Theology of the New Testament.* Louisville: Westminster John Knox, 2000.

Strobel, A. "Textgeschichtliches zum Thomas-Logion 86 (Mt 8,20/Lk 9,58)." *VC* 17
(1963), 211-24.

Stuckenbruck, L. T. *Angel Veneration and Christology: A Study in Early Judaism and in
the Christology of the Apocalypse of John.* WUNT; Tübingen: Mohr, 1995.

Stuhlmacher, P. "Existenzstellvertretung für die Vielen: Mk 10,45 (Mt 20,28)." In idem,
Versöhnung, Gesetz und Gerechtigkeit: Aufsätze zur Biblische Theologie, 27-42.
Göttingen: Vandenhoeck und Ruprecht, 1981.

Suggs, M. J. *Wisdom, Christology and Law in Matthew's Gospel.* Cambridge, Mass.:
Harvard University Press, 1970.

Swete, H. B. *The Gospel according to St. Mark.* London: Macmillan, 1898.

Swetnam, J. "Some Remarks on the Meaning of ὁ δὲ ἐξελθών in Mark 1,45." *Bib* 68 (1987), 245-49.

Sybel, L. von. "Vom Wachsen der Christologie im synoptischen Evangelien." *TSK* 100 (1927-28), 362-401.

Talbert, C. H. *What Is a Gospel? The Genre of the Canonical Gospels.* London: SPCK, 1978.

Tannehill, R. C. *The Sword of His Mouth.* Philadelphia: Fortress, 1975.

Tàrrech, A. Puig, "Lc 10,18: La Visió de la caíguda de Satanàs." *RCataT* 3 (1978), 217-43.

Taylor, V. *The Gospel according to St. Mark.* London: Macmillan, 1952.

Theisohn, J. *Der auserwählte Richter: Untersuchungen zum traditionsgeschichtlichem Ort der Menschensohngestalt der Bilderreden des Äthiopischen Henoch.* Göttingen: Vandenhoeck und Ruprecht, 1975.

Theobald, M. "Gottessohn und Menschensohn: Zur polaren Struktur der Christologie im Markusevangelium." *SNTSU* 13 (1988), 37-79.

Thiselton, A. C. *The First Epistle to the Corinthians.* NIGTC; Grand Rapids: Eerdmans, 2000.

Thornton, C.-J. *Der Zeuge des Zeugen: Lukas als Historiker der Paulusreisen.* WUNT; Tübingen: Mohr, 1991.

Tödt, H. E. *The Son of Man in the Synoptic Tradition.* London: SCM, 1965.

Trakatellis, D. C. *The Pre-Existence of Christ in the Writings of Justin Martyr.* Chico: Scholars, 1976.

Trilling, W. *Das wahre Israel: Studien zur Theologie des Matthäus-Evangeliums.* SANT 10; Munich: Kösel-Verlag, 1964.

Tuckett, C. "The Present Son of Man." *JSNT* 14 (1982), 58-81.

Vanhoye, A. "L'οἰκουμένη dans l'épitre aux Hébreux." *Biblica* 45 (1964), 248-53.

Vermes, G. "Appendix E: The Use of בר נשא/בר נש in Jewish Aramaic." In M. Black, *An Aramaic Approach to the Gospels and Acts,* 310-28. Oxford: Oxford University Press, 1967.

———. *Jesus the Jew.* London: SCM, ²1983.

Verseput, D. *The Rejection of the Humble Messianic King: A Study of the Composition of Matthew 11–12.* Europäische Hochschulschriften: Frankfurt am Main/New York: Peter Lang, 1986.

———. "The Role and Meaning of the 'Son of God' Title in Matthew's Gospel." *NTS* 33 (1987), 532-56.

Vielhauer, P. "Das Benedictus des Zacharias." *ZTK* 49 (1952), 255-72.

Vögtle, A. "Todesankündigungen und Todesverständnis Jesu." In K. Kertelge, ed., *Der Tod Jesu. QD* 74 (1976), 51-113.

Wainwright, A. W. *The Trinity in the New Testament.* London: SPCK, 1969.

Walter, N. "Geschichte und Mythos in urchristlicher Präexistenzchristologie." In H. H. Schmid, ed., *Mythos und Rationalität,* 224-34. Gütersloh: Gütersloher Verlag, 1988.

Warfield, B. B. "Jesus' Mission, according to His Own Testimony." *Princeton Theological Review* 13 (1915), 513-86.

Watson, F. B. "Is There a Story in These Texts?" In B. W. Longenecker, ed., *Narrative Dynamics in Paul: A Critical Assessment,* 231-39. Louisville/London: Westminster/John Knox, 2002.

Weinert, F. D. "Luke, the Temple and Jesus' Saying about Jerusalem's Abandoned House (Luke 13:34-35)." *CBQ* 44 (1982), 68-76.

Weinreich, O. H. "Οὐκ ἄγνωστος Φοῖβος θεός." *Archiv für Religions-wissenschaft* 18 (1915), 34-45.

Weiser, A. *Apostelgeschichte.* 2 vols. Gütersloh: Gütersloher Verlagshaus/Gerd Mohn, 1981.

———. *The Psalms: A Commentary.* London: SCM, 1962.

Weiss, H. F. *Der Brief an die Hebräer.* KEK; Göttingen: Vandenhoeck und Ruprecht, 1991.

Weiss, J. *Die Schriften des Neuen Testaments.* 2 vols. Göttingen: Vandenhoeck und Ruprecht, 1907.

———. *Das Urchristentum.* Göttingen: Vandenhoeck und Ruprecht, 1917.

Wenham, D. *Paul: Follower of Jesus or Founder of Christianity?* Grand Rapids: Eerdmans, 1995.

Wichelhaus, M. "Am ersten Tage der Woche: Mk 1.35-39 und die didaktischen Absichten des Markus-Evangelisten." *NovT* 11 (1969), 45-66.

Wiefel, W. *Das Evangelium nach Lukas.* THKNT; Berlin: Evangelischer Verlagsanstalt, 1988.

Wikgren, A. "Some Problems in Jude 5." In B. L. Daniels and M. J. Suggs, eds., *Studies in the History and Text of the New Testament in Honor of Kenneth Willis Clark,* 147-52. Studies and Documents; Salt Lake City: University of Utah Press, 1967.

Wilckens, U. "Kerygma und Evangelium bei Lukas (zu Act 10 34-43)." *ZNW* 49 (1958), 223-37.

———. "σοφία." In G. Kittel, ed., *TDNT* 7:465-526.

———. *Weisheit und Torheit: Eine exegetisch-religionsgeschichtliche Untersuchung zu 1. Kor. 1 und 2.* Tübingen: Mohr, 1959.

———. "Zu 1Kor 2,1-16." In C. Andresen and G. Klein, eds., *Theologia Crucis — Signum Crucis. FS E. Dinkler,* 501-37. Tübingen: Mohr, 1979.

Wiles, M. "Early Exegesis of the Parables." *SJT* 11 (1958), 287-301.

Williams, C. *I Am He: The Interpretation of 'Anî 'Hû' in Jewish and Early Christian Literature.* Tübingen: Mohr, 1999.

Winandy, J. "Le Logion de l'Ignorance (Mc, XIII,32; Mt., XXIV,36)." *RevB* 75 (1968), 63-79.

Windisch, H. "Die göttliche Weisheit der Juden und die paulinische Christologie." In A. Deissmann, ed., *Neutestamentliche Studien: Georg Heinrici zu seinem 70. Geburtstag,* 220-34. Leipzig: Hinrichs, 1914.

———. "Urchristentum und Hermesmystik." *Theologisch Tijdschrift* 52 (1918), 186-240.

323

Wink, W. *The Human Being*. Minneapolis: Fortress, 2002.

Winter, P. "Mt XI 27 and Lk X 22 from the First to the Fifth Century: Reflections on the Development of the Text." *NovT* 1 (1956), 112-48.

———. "Two Notes on Luke I,II with Regard to the Theory of 'Imitation Hebraisms': (1) ἀνατολὴ ἐξ ὕψους." *Studia Theologica* 7 (1953), 158-64.

Witherington, B. *The Acts of the Apostles: A Socio-Rhetorical Commentary*. Grand Rapids: Eerdmans, 1998.

———. *The Christology of Jesus*. Minneapolis: Fortress, 1990.

———. *Conflict and Community in Corinth: A Socio-Rhetorical Commentary on 1 and 2 Corinthians*. Grand Rapids: Eerdmans, 1995.

———. *The Gospel of Mark: A Socio-Rhetorical Commentary*. Grand Rapids: Eerdmans, 2001.

Wrede, W. *The Messianic Secret*. Cambridge: J. Clarke, 1971.

———. *Das Messiasgeheimnis in den Evangelien: Zugleich ein Beitrag zum Verständnis des Markusevangeliums*. Göttingen: Vandenhoeck und Ruprecht, 1963.

———. "The Task and Methods of 'New Testament Theology.'" In R. Morgan, ed., *The Nature of New Testament Theology: The Contribution of William Wrede and Adolf Schlatter*, 68-116. SBT; London: SCM, 1973.

———. *Vorträge und Studien*. Tübingen: Mohr, 1907.

Wright, N. T. *The Climax of the Covenant: Christ and the Law in Pauline Theology*. Edinburgh: T&T Clark, 1991.

———. *Jesus and the Victory of God*. London: SPCK, 1996.

Yarbro Collins, A. "The Charge of Blasphemy in Mark 14.64." *JSNT* 26 (2004), 379-401.

———. "Mark and His Readers: The Son of God among Greeks and Romans." *HTR* 93 (2000), 85-100.

———. "Mark and His Readers: The Son of God among Jews." *HTR* 92 (1999), 393-408.

———. "Rulers, Divine Men, and Walking on the Water (Mark 6:45-52)." In L. Bormann, K. Del Tredici, and A. Standhartinger, eds., *Religious Propaganda and Missionary Competition in the New Testament World: Essays Honoring Dieter Georgi*, 207-27. Leiden: Brill, 1994.

Zeller, D. "Entrückung zur Ankunft als Menschensohn (Lk 13, 34f.; 11, 29f.)." In F. Refoulé, ed., *À cause de l'Évangile: Études sur les Synoptiques et les Actes. Offertes au P. Jacques Dupont, O.S.B., à l'occasion de son 70ème Anniversaire*, 513-30. Paris: Cerf, 1985.

———. "Die Menschwerdung des Sohnes Gottes im Neuen Testament und die antike Religionsgeschichte." In D. Zeller, ed., *Menschwerdung Gottes — Vergöttlichung von Menschen*, 141-76. NTOA 7; Freiburg/Göttingen, 1988.

Zerwick, M. "Vidi Satanam sicut fulgur de caelo cadentem (Lc 10,17-20)." *VD* 26 (1948), 110-14.

Zimmermann, J. *Messianische Texte aus Qumran: Königliche, priesterliche und prophetische Messiasvorstellungen in den Schriftfunden von Qumran*. WUNT; Tübingen: Mohr, 1998.

Zmijewski, J. *Die Apostelgeschichte.* Regensburg: Pustet, 1994.

————. "Die Sohn-Gottes-Prädikation im Markusevangelium: Zur Frage einer eigenständigen markinischen Titelchristologie." *SNTU* 12 (1987), 5-34.

Zunz, L. *Die gottesdienstlichen Vorträge der Juden, historisch entwickelt: Ein Beitrag zur Alterthumskunde und biblischen Kritik, zur Literatur- und Religionsgeschichte.* Frankfurt: J. Kauffmann, [2]1892.

Index of Authors

Index of Subjects

Adam, 26
Angels, 18, 50, 55, 113-47, 175, 178, 179, 241-42, 267-68, 269
   Angel of the Lord, 164-65
Aramaic background, 17, 93, 99-101, 172, 253

Baptism, 65, 72-73
Blasphemy, 15, 59-61

Capernaum, 156, 182
Christ,
   Action, 56-57, 176, 210-21
   Worship/devotion/reverence, 15, 64, 69-70, 79
   Heavenly identity, 20
   Humanity, 54-55, 285-86
Christology,
   Developmental/Evolutionary, 14
Coming,
   "the coming one" title, 91, 107
   historicity of sayings, 93, 95, 99-101, 108
   as technical vocabulary, 108, 111-12
Creation, 18, 27-28, 33-34, 41

David, 13, 168-69, 180-81, 235, 236-38, 240, 244-45, 248, 251, 256-57, 274-75, 281-82, 294

Demons, 53-54, 123, 134-35, 150-53, 166, 170, 173, 235, 244, 247, 250, 275, 277

Early Catholicism, 26
Earth, 13, 34, 54, 114-15, 161-65, 170, 176, 268, 275
Elijah, 13, 48-49, 54, 114, 137-41, 162, 166, 276
Epiphany, 62, 108-9

Father. *See* God
Fire, 161-63, 170

Gnosticism, Gnostic Redeemer myth, 3, 10, 12, 14, 18, 186, 249, 255
God,
   Divine Identity of Christ, 15, 24-25, 54-77 (esp. 65-68), 79
   Divine function, 58, 61, 62-63, 169
   Divine hierarchy, 72-73, 76
   Divine knowledge, 70-71
   Election, 55-57, 76
   Kingdom of, 154-55, 204, 262-64, 265-66, 279
   Love, 29, 291-92
   Preexistence of, 16 n. 63
   Sending Son, 177-92. *See also* Sending

Index of Ancient Sources

343